World War II

PROBLEMS IN EUROPEAN
CIVILIZATION SERIES

World War II

Roots and Causes

Second Edition

Revised, Edited and with an Introduction by

Keith Eubank

City University of New York, Queens College

D. C. HEATH AND COMPANY

Lexington, Massachusetts   Toronto

Address editorial correspondence to:

D. C. Heath and Company
125 Spring Street
Lexington, MA 02173

Cover: The Bettmann Archive

Published simultaneously in Canada.

Printed in the United States of America.

International Standard Book Number: 0-669-24969-6

Library of Congress Catalog Number: 91-75370

10 9 8 7 6 5 4 3 2 1

Preface

World War II: Roots and Causes, Second Edition, offers the reader a representative selection of works by historians who have written about the causes of the terrible conflict that erupted in Europe over half a century ago.

My aim has been to give the reader a cross section of the debate surrounding the roots and causes of World War II. The debate continues; it is important because there is a riddle in the study of the origins of the war. Why, after emerging from the horrors of 1914–1918, did men and women permit political, economic, and social conditions to deteriorate into a new war that eventually engulfed the world? Why did the peace-keepers fail?

In updating the material that appeared in the First Edition, I was struck by the extent to which recent scholarship necessitates extensive substitutions. Only three of the original selections remain. The new selections draw upon that recent scholarship by examining the role of military intelligence, the influence of Joseph Stalin, the effect of the purges on Soviet foreign policy, the occupation of the Rhineland, and the crisis over Czechoslovakia.

Every effort has been made to reproduce faithfully the writings of the authors selected for this volume. Cuts have been made in order to eliminate material that is not directly relevant to the topic of the war's origins.

My thanks go to the reviewers whose recommendations on the draft of this new edition were most helpful: Holger H. Herwig, University of Calgary; Konrad H. Jarausch, University of North Carolina, Chapel Hill; Charles Jelavich, Indiana University;

J. Kim Munholland, University of Minnesota; and Ted Uldricks, University of North Carolina, Asheville. Finally, I want to thank James Miller of D. C. Heath, whose advice and counsel eased my task.

K. E.

Contents

Chronology of Events   xi

Principal Proper Names   xv

Variety of Opinion   xix

Reference Maps: Europe on the Eve of
                World War II   xxi
                Austria, Czechoslovakia,
                and Poland, 1938–
                1939   xxii

Introduction   1

I A Problem in Interpretation   11

   P. M. H. Bell
      Another Thirty Years War?   11

II The Hitler Enigma   33

    Adolf Hitler
       A Policy for Germany   33

    A. J. P. Taylor
       A Revisionist View   50

    Norman Rich
       The Ideology of Expansion   60

Andreas Hillgruber
Hitler's Program   69

III   Aggression and Appeasement   77
Edward W. Bennett
The First Victory   77
James T. Emmerson
The Rhineland Coup   89
Adolf Hitler
The Four Year Plan   100
The Hossbach Memorandum
A Strategy Conference?   109
Jonathan Wright and Paul Stafford
The Hossbach Memorandum
Evaluated   120
Keith Eubank
Appeasement and Appeasers   129

IV   Czechoslovakia and Munich   137
British Chiefs of Staff
Military Implications of German
Aggression Against
Czechoslovakia   137
Gerhard L. Weinberg
Munich Conference: War
Postponed   154
Williamson Murray
War over Czechoslovakia?   167

V   The Intelligence Muddle   179
Wesley K. Wark
British Military Intelligence   179

Anthony Adamthwaite
French Military Intelligence and the
Coming of War 196

VI The Russian Riddle 213

Robert C. Tucker
Stalin's Foreign Policy 213
Jiri Hochman
The Great Purges and Collective
Security 235

VII The Devil's Bargain 253

German Foreign Ministry
The Nazi-Soviet Pact 253
Dmitri A. Volkogonov
A Soviet Version 256
Gerhard L. Weinberg
The Nazi-Soviet Pact: A Half
Century Later 272

VIII The Holocaust 285

Lucy S. Dawidowicz
World War II and the Holocaust 285

IX The Verdict 303

Donald Cameron Watt
Summing Up 303
Adolf Hitler
A Confession 314

Suggestions for Additional
Reading 320

Chronology of
Events

1914	June 28	Assassination of Archduke Franz Ferdinand precipitates the crisis leading to World War I
1918	November 11	Armistice ends World War I
1919	January 18	Peace Conference meets in Paris
	June 28	Treaty of Versailles signed
1920	January 10	Treaty of Versailles and League of Nations Covenent take effect
1923	November 8–9	Adolf Hitler's Beer Hall Putsch in Munich fails
1924	April 1	Hitler sentenced to five years in prison
	December 20	Hitler released from prison
1925	October 5–16	Locarno Conference
1928	August 27	Briand-Kellogg Peace Pact signed
1930	September 14	Nazi Party wins 107 seats in Reichstag
1931	September 16	Japanese troops attack Manchuria
1932	February 2	Disarmament conference opens in Geneva
	July 31	Nazi Party wins 231 seats in Reichstag
1933	January 30	Hitler appointed chancellor of Germany
	October 14	Germany leaves Disarmament Conference and the League of Nations
1934	January 26	Germany and Poland sign a ten-year nonaggression pact.
	July 25	Austrian Nazis fail in attempted coup
	August 2	Death of President Paul von Hindenburg; Hitler becomes Führer, combining offices of president and chancellor

1935	March 16	Germany repudiates military clauses of the Versailles treaty
	May 2	Franco-Russian Treaty of Mutual Assistance signed
	June 18	Anglo-German Naval Agreement signed
	October 3	Italian troops invade Ethiopia
1936	March 7	Germany denounces Locarno Treaty and German troops occupy the Rhineland
	July 18	Spanish Civil War breaks out
1937	May 28	Neville Chamberlain becomes British prime minister
	November 5	Hossbach Conference
1938	February 4	Hitler becomes minister of war
	February 12	Hitler pressures Austrian Chancellor Kurt von Schuschnigg at Berchtesgaden
	March 11	German troops occupy Austria; *Anschluss* (German annexation of Austria) proclaimed next day
	April 24	Konrad Henlein demands autonomy for the Sudeten Germans
	May 30	Hitler signs directive for Operation Green: Invasion of Czechoslovakia
	September 15	Chamberlain meets Hitler at Berchtesgaden
	September 22–23	Chamberlain and Hitler confer at Godesberg
	September 29	Munich Conference, resulting in agreement on German annexation of Sudetenland
	October 1–10	German troops occupy Sudetenland
1939	March 10	Joseph Stalin's speech to the Eighteenth Party Congress
	March 15	German troops occupy rest of Bohemia and Moravia; Slovakia becomes a German puppet state
	April 28	Hitler denounces nonaggression pact with Poland
	May 22	Germany and Italy sign the Pact of Steel

August 23	Nazi-Soviet nonaggression pact signed
August 29	German ultimatum to Poland
September 1	German troops invade Poland
September 3	Britain and France declare war on Germany

Principal Proper Names

Astakhov, G. A.: Counselor of the Soviet Embassy in Berlin.

Baldwin, Stanley: British Prime Minister, 1935–1937.

Beck, Colonel Jósef: Polish Foreign Minister, 1932–1939.

Beneš, Eduard: President of Czechoslovakia, 1935–1938.

Bismarck, Otto von: German consul in London, 1932–1936.

Blomberg, Marshal Werner von: German Minister of War and commander of the Wehrmacht, 1933–1938

Bonnet, Georges: French Foreign Minister, 1938–1939.

Cadogan, Sir Alexander: Permanent Undersecretary of State for Foreign Affairs, British Foreign Office, 1938–1946.

Chamberlain, Neville: British Prime Minister, 1937–1940.

Churchill, Winston: Member of Parliament; First Lord of the Admiralty, 1939–1940; British Prime Minister, 1940–1945.

Ciano, Count Galeazzo: Italian Foreign Minister, 1936–1943.

Comintern: Communist International.

Cooper, Alfred Duff: British Secretary of State for War, 1935–1937; First Lord of the Admiralty, 1937–1938.

Coulondre, Robert: French Ambassador to the Soviet Union, 1936–1938; to Germany, 1938–1939.

Daladier, Edouard: French Minister of National Defense, 1936–1938; French Premier, 1938–1940.

Dirksen, Herbert von: German Ambassador to the Soviet Union, 1928–1933; to Japan, 1933–1938; to Great Britain, 1938–1939.

Eichmann, Adolf: SS Officer; implemented the Holocaust.

Eden, Anthony: British Foreign Secretary, 1935–1938.

François-Poncet, André: French Ambassador to Germany, 1931–1938.

Goebbels, Joseph: German Minister of Propaganda, 1933–1945.

Goering, Field Marshal Hermann: Commander in Chief of the Luftwaffe, 1935–1945.

Hacha, Emil: President of Czechoslovakia, 1938–1939.

Halifax, (Lord) Edward Third Viscount: British Foreign Secretary, 1937–1940.

Hassell, Ulrich von: German Ambassador to Italy.

Henderson, Neville: British Ambassador to Germany, 1937–1939.

Heydrich, Reinhard: SS Obergruppenführer, Chief of the Nazi Party Security Service (SD) and the Gestapo; implemented the Holocaust.

Hitler, Adolf: German Führer, 1933–1945.

Hoare, Sir Samuel: British Foreign Secretary, 1935; First Lord of the Admiralty, 1936–1937.

Hossbach, Colonel Friedrich: Hitler's Army Adjutant.

Litvinov, Maxim: Soviet Commissar for Foreign Affairs, 1930–1939.

Lloyd George, David: Liberal Member of Parliament, 1890–1945; British Prime Minister, 1916–1922.

MacDonald, J. Ramsay: British Prime Minister, 1931–1935.

Maisky, Ivan: Soviet Ambassador to Great Britain, 1932–1943.

Mussolini, Benito: Italian Prime Minister and dictator, 1922–1943.

Molotov, Vyacheslav M.: Soviet Commissar for Foreign Affairs, 1939–1956.

Nadolny, Rudolf: Head of German delegation to the Disarmament Conference; Ambassador to Great Britain, 1933–1934.

Neurath, Constantin Freiherr von: German Foreign Minister, 1932–1938.

Paul-Boncour, Joseph: French Premier, 1932–1933; French Foreign Minister, 1933–1934.

Phipps, Sir Eric: British Ambassador to Germany, 1933–1937.

Radek, Karl: Soviet politician and journalist; imprisoned in 1937 and later executed.

Raeder, Admiral Eric: Commander in Chief, German navy, 1935–1943.

Ribbentrop, Joachim von: German Foreign Minister, 1938–1945.

Rosenberg, Alfred: Head of the Foreign Policy Office of the Nazi Party.

Schulenberg, Friedrich Werner, Count von der: German Ambassador to the Soviet Union, 1934–1941.

Simon, Sir John: British Foreign Secretary, 1931–1935.

Stalin, Joseph: General Secretary of the Central Committee of the Communist Party, 1922–1953; Soviet Union dictator, late 1920s.

Tukhachevsky, General Michael N.: Chief of the General Staff of the Red Army; executed 1937.

Vansittart, Sir Robert: Permanent Undersecretary in the British Foreign Office, 1930–1938.

Weizsäcker, Ernst von: State Secretary, German Foreign Ministry, 1938–1943.

Wilson, Horace: Chief Industrial Advisor to the British Government and Personal Advisor to Neville Chamberlain.

Zinoviev, Grigori: Soviet Communist Party Leader in the 1920s; executed 1936.

Variety of
Opinion

Hitler was dismayed by the outbreak of war:

> *Hitler probably intended a great war of conquest against Soviet Russia as far as he had any conscious design; it is unlikely that he intended the actual war against Great Britain and France, which broke out in 1939. He was as much dismayed on 3 September 1939 as Bethmann had been on 4 August 1914.*
>
> A. J. P. Taylor

The Western Powers failed to take action:

> *If the Western Powers had recognized the threat earlier and shown greater resolution in resisting Hitler's (and Mussolini's) demands, it is possible that the clash might not have led to war, or at any rate not to a war on the scale on which it had finally to be fought. The longer they hesitated, the higher the price of resistance. . . . Hitler understood their state of mind perfectly and played on it with skill.*
>
> Alan Bullock

Hitler prepared a series of wars:

> *Hitler was preparing for a series of wars each of which Germany would win by launching a quick campaign against an isolated enemy, with victory in each such war helping prepare for the next one by increasing Germany's resources and terrifying others into submission or at least abstention from intervention. Ultimately this sequence would lead to world domination. . . .*
>
> Gerhard L. Weinberg

Incompetence:

> *If we accept, then, incompetence as the basis of human behavior, the performance of those facing Hitler in the late 1930s is perhaps less*

surprising, though no more excusable. Those who molded the response to Hitler acted no more effectively than those responding to the depression or to the wreckage of the First World War. . . . And after all, those who led Britain throughout the 1930s argued that they were particularly competent to manage the ship of state. The results belie their claim.

Williamson Murray

The Jews were responsible:

It is not true that I or anybody else in Germany wanted war in 1939. It was wanted and provoked exclusively by those international statesmen who either were of Jewish origin or worked for Jewish interests. . . . Centuries will pass, but from the ruins of our towns and monuments hatred of those ultimately responsible will always grow anew, those whom we have to thank for all this: international Jewry and its helpers!

Adolf Hitler

EUROPE ON THE EVE
OF WORLD
WAR II

NORWAY
FINLAND
North
Sea
SWEDEN
Leningrad
UNITED
KINGDOM
DENMARK
EST.
EIRE
LATVIA
Moscow
LITH.
Danzig
London
NETH.
Berlin
U. S. S. R.
ATLANTIC
BELG.
GERMANY
Warsaw
OCEAN
Paris
LUX.
Godesberg
POLAND
Nuremberg
FRANCE
Munich
Vienna
SWITZ.
AUSTRIA
HUNGARY
RUMANIA
ITALY
PORTUGAL
YUGOSLAVIA
Black   Sea
Madrid
Rome
BULGARIA
SPAIN
Gibraltar
GREECE
TURKEY
MOROCCO
Mediterranean
FRENCH NORTH
Sea
AFRICA
MALTA
CYPRUS

☐ Rhineland

■ Territorial gains
by Germany, 1938-39

▨ Territorial gains by Italy, 1938-39

▥ Territorial gains by Hungary, 1938-39

■ Territorial gains by Poland, 1938

AUSTRIA, CZECHOSLOVAKIA, AND POLAND, 1938-39

German Anschluss with Austria, March 1938

Sudetenland: Annexed by Germany, October 1938

Southern Slovakia: Annexed by Hungary, October 1938

Těšín: Annexed by Poland, October 1938

Protectorate of Bohemia and Moravia:
Occupied by Germany, March 1939

Slovakia: Nominally independent, March 1939

Subcarpatian Ukraine: Annexed by Hungary, March 1939

Memelland: Annexed by Germany, April 1939

Danzig: Annexed by Germany, September 1939

Polish territory annexed by Germany, September 1939

Polish territory annexed by U.S.S.R., September 1939

Introduction

German armed forces attacked Poland on September 1, 1939. All the efforts and sacrifices made to avoid another European war had failed. The war that erupted that morning would escalate into the second world war of the twentieth century — one of the most terrible wars that humanity has ever suffered. Millions would die fighting, millions would be slaughtered in death camps, and countless other men, women, and children would die from bombings, hunger, and disease. The balance of power would be completely altered before peace came again in 1945. What led to this war?

The readings in this anthology are concerned with the ideas, the events, the plans, and the people involved in the origins of World War II. The selections introduce the reader to some of the problems and issues that have concerned historians about the roots and causes of World War II.

The subject is provocative, because after an earlier world conflict in 1914–1918, no one was able to avoid an even more ghastly war. It seems that one world bloodbath should have made politicians and statesmen wise enough to prevent another conflict from overwhelming the world. Why did they not perceive the threat and take action at once? Why did they wait until the unthinkable became real and the democracies in Europe had to face the very war they had hoped to avoid?

War was finally thrust on Europe by the German invasion of Poland, ordered by Adolf Hitler, chancellor of the Third German Reich. Hitler came to power in Germany, even though he was Austrian-born, by exploiting the crisis created by the Great Depression. Due to this economic catastrophe, Hitler was able to organize his own political movement, National Socialism, and build the largest and strongest political party in Germany. His party gave him the leverage to attain power in January 1933. Once in office, Hitler destroyed all political opposition and at the same time created one of the most authoritarian governments in modern history.

In his rise to power, Hitler also exploited popular dissatisfaction stemming from the German defeat in World War I and the disgrace from the terms imposed on Germany by the victors in the Treaty of Versailles.

Under the treaty terms, Germany lost territory in Europe and all of her colonies. The loss of colonies did little harm, for it relieved the Germans of an unnecessary expense, and the territorial losses in Europe were not great enough to affect radically the nation's industrial potential. Germany, still the largest nation in central Europe, except for Russia, was potentially the strongest. The treaty disarmed Germany, reducing the army to 100,000 officers and men. The air force was disbanded, and the navy was limited in size. However, the general staff, although banned, went underground and with the blessing of the new democratic government of Germany, secretly planned to restore Germany's armed might. Germany was also obliged to pay reparations for damage caused during the First World War. However, Germany suffered only a limited occupation. The treaty was deceptive because its strength was an illusion. Although it was not enforced rigorously, it was harsh enough to provide Hitler with a cause to rally discontented people to the Nazi Party.

Reversing the verdict of 1919 and breaking the bonds imposed on Germany by the Versailles Treaty became Hitler's aim. Once this had been attained, he could rearm Germany and restore her prewar position in European affairs. But Hitler would not stop there, because his ultimate intention was to dominate Europe. It was his drive toward mastery of Europe that finally led to war in September 1939.

As the record shows, World War II cannot be separated from Hitler, his ideas, and his plans. It was he who issued the order for German soldiers to invade Poland and to begin a European war that escalated into a global conflict. His responsibility for issuing this order cannot be denied.

Why did Hitler make this decision? What forces drove him to end the twenty-year peace? What ideas, dreams, and philosophy shaped his decision for war? Was the war a product of a carefully drafted plan, developed over the years by Hitler? Or was it the result of uncontrollable forces that set off a chain reaction culminating in the outbreak of war?

To what degree was the policy of appeasement responsible for causing the war? This policy was respected in the 1920s and 1930s when it was eagerly pursued by British and French politicians. It did not have the notoriety it would acquire after Western powers failed to prevent Hitler's aggression through appeasement policies. Eventually appeasement came to mean outright surrender to the aggressor's demands, but that was never the original meaning. Prior to World War II appeasement referred to a policy of satisfying German complaints about the Treaty of Versailles through negotiations that would lead to détente and a general relaxation of tension in Europe after Germany had been pacified.

Although appeasement may have been among the causes of World War II, there were other forces that brought about the war. The Soviet Union contributed to causing the war through Stalin's aid to the Nazis and ultimately through the nonaggression pact with Germany. Failures in Anglo-French military intelligence estimates helped to cause the war. A major cause was Hitler's determination to achieve a final solution of the Jewish question.

On the other hand, it has been argued that the war was not the result of a mixture of causes. Instead it may have been the second phase of another Thirty Years War. Was it the second round in the battle against Germany's efforts to dominate Europe? This hypothesis is examined by P. M. H. Bell in the first selection of this book. Was Hitler only a symptom of the disruptive impact of World War I on the European nations? Or was he a consequence of the Great Depression?

To understand Hitler, however, it is necessary to examine his ideas, aims, and plans. These are revealed in a selection from his book, *Mein Kampf*, which he dictated in prison after the failure of the Munich Beer Hall Putsch in 1923 wrecked the Nazi Party.

Among historians there have been differences of interpretation over Hitler's intentions. The task of discovering his objectives has been complicated because, except for his speeches and two books, he did not leave quantities of memoranda or letters. Among the explanations of Hitler and his policies, the most controversial is found in A. J. P. Taylor's *Origins of the Second World War*. The book engendered violent criticism when it was published because Taylor seemed to imply that Hitler was really no worse than his contemporaries and that the outbreak of war was not a premeditated effort on Hitler's part. Taylor's book was controversial since it appeared to redeem Hitler while blaming others. According to Taylor, Hitler was not a planner; rather, he was an opportunist taking advantage of opportunities presented to him by others.

In contrast to Taylor, Norman Rich, in a selection from his book *Hitler's War Aims*, found expansionism at the center of Hitler's ideology. The threat to Germany came from the east, and it was there that land would be found at Russia's expense. There would be war; it could not be avoided. But Andreas Hillgruber goes even further in *Germany and the Two World Wars*, seeing in Hitler's plans a dream of world power commencing with the conquest of Europe.

If Hitler were to achieve his plans for conquest, Germany had to restore her military sovereignty by controlling the development and size of the armed forces. The Treaty of Versailles specifically limited German armed forces, but the generals and admirals, with the blessing of the Weimar Republic, carried on a program of secret rearmament. This program was suddenly jeopardized by proposals presented to the Geneva Disarmament Conference in 1933 by Britain and France. Hitler challenged them, at the risk of war, when he ordered the German delegation to leave the conference and withdrew Germany from the League of Nations in October 1933. Edward W. Bennett, in a selection from *German Rearmament and the West, 1932–1933*, looks at a crisis forced on Hitler by the action of other nations. German rearmament had to be protected, and Hitler's success was a major step in the process. Eighteen months later Hitler regained full military sovereignty for Germany by announcing the existence of the German Air Force (Luftwaffe), the resumption of military conscription, and a planned army of thirty-six divisions. Through this action Hitler annulled Part V of the Treaty of Versailles, which limited the German armed forces.

Hitler's next action — the remilitarization of the Rhineland — not only violated another provision of the Treaty of Versailles (as well as the Treaty of Locarno), but it changed the balance of power in Europe. France lost the strategic advantage gained through the Versailles Treaty. In the selection from *The Rhineland Crisis, 7 March 1936*, James T. Emmerson examines the consequences of the coup for Hitler, Britain, and France and the lessons to be learned from the events of March 1936.

One reason for the failure of Britain and France to retaliate against remilitarization of the Rhineland was the British government's determination to practice a policy of appeasement. No prewar policy has been so bitterly denounced as appeasement has; no politicians have been condemned as harshly as those who supported this policy, which seems to have led to war. In a selection from *The Origins of World War II*, Keith Eubank surveys the practice of appeasement in the 1920s and

1930s when it was considered a sensible policy that would benefit the world.

By occupying the Rhineland, Hitler broke the last restriction on German freedom of action. Before he dared risk confrontation with foreign powers over the expansion of the Third Reich, more planning and directives were necessary in regard to rearmament. By the summer of 1936 decisions had to be made concerning the economy and its relation to the military forces. Should they be maintained at a level that the economy could support or should Germany fully arm itself for a lengthy conflict such as that of 1914–1918? The next selection is Hitler's memorandum concerning a Four Year Plan, which he drafted in August 1936. Here he set down the policy for the economy and the armed forces. Hitler wanted the armed forces ready for war within four years when Germany would solve her long-term need for resources through territorial conquest. He rejected stockpiling resources for a war of attrition with the intention of having a series of short lightning wars —*Blitzkrieg.*

Hitler soon discovered that the demands made by the military services on the German economy were overwhelming. Shortages developed that led to quarrels among the leaders of the armed services. The minister of war, General Werner von Blomberg, denounced Hermann Goering, who was in charge of the Four Year Plan, for his greed in allocating raw materials for the Luftwaffe. Likewise Admiral Erich Raeder, commander in chief of the navy, was unhappy with Goering's administration of the plan. To restore harmony, Hitler called a conference of a select group of ministers and military leaders in the Reichs-chancellery on November 5, 1937. There he discussed his goals and specific cases in which military action might be necessary. The only surviving record of this conference, the Hossbach Memorandum, is the next selection. This document has become a source of controversy. It was entered as evidence in the Nuremberg trials to prove that Hitler planned a war of aggression. Yet historians such as A. J. P. Taylor argued that Hitler's remarks in the memorandum amounted to day-dreaming, unrelated to the real world. During the conference, Hitler indicated that he considered Czechoslovakia more dangerous to German security than Austria. But the German armies' first conquest was Austria on March 11, 1938.

The Hossbach Memorandum has been so controversial that an

analysis and interpretation, the next selection, has been developed by Jonathan Wright and Paul Stafford. They assert that Hitler explained his policy to a chosen group of men because they had to carry out his plans for conquest.

When German forces occupied Austria, European capitals knew that Czechoslovakia was endangered. In London and Paris politicians debated future policy with regard to Germany and Czechoslovakia. On March 15, French defense minister Edouard Daladier informed the Permanent Committee on National Defence that France could not send aid to Czechoslovakia.

In London on March 28, a report from the Chiefs of Staff in response to a request from Prime Minister Neville Chamberlain to consider the military implications of a German attack on Czechoslovakia ended any chance of British support to Czechoslovakia. The report, the next selection, became ammunition for Chamberlain to use in his appeasement campaign. Its influence would be felt in the Munich Conference over the fate of Czechoslovakia.

Shortly after annexing Austria, Hitler seized on the issue of self-determination for the Sudeten Germans as a wedge to split apart Czechoslovakia, a state containing a variety of minorities who were all formerly part of the vanished Hapsburg Empire. If the Sudetens were granted their demands, which amounted to autonomy, other minorities would insist on equal treatment. Czechoslovakia would become a collection of weak autonomous states, easy prey for Hitler. The British and the French, fearful of a war in which they believed justice was on the side of the Sudeten Germans, pushed the Czechs to make concessions to the Sudetens. Meanwhile, in Berlin plans had been drafted for a German attack on Czechoslovakia. During the summer of 1938 German armed forces were mobilized.

When negotiations between the Czech government and Sudeten leaders collapsed in September 1938, Neville Chamberlain, seeking an understanding with Hitler and hoping to avoid war, attempted personal negotiations with the Führer. The Sudeten Nazis, who were in collusion with Hitler, insisted that the Sudetenland become a part of the Third Reich. Hitler now had the basis to demand that the Sudetenland be ceded to Germany and immediately occupied by German troops. Although the British and French governments accepted the principle of cession and occupation, their negotiations with Hitler reached an impasse over the timing of the occupation. The impasse was resolved at the Munich Conference of September 29–30, 1938. Gerhard L. Weinberg, in a selection from *The Foreign Policy of Hitler's Germany*, describes the drama of this "summit conference" when four men — Hitler, Benito Mussolini, Chamberlain, and Daladier — settled the fate of Czechoslovakia and the Sudetenland. For believers in appeasement, it was their finest hour. Hitler was furious, as Weinberg shows, because he had been tricked out of his war. He would never let this happen again.

Critics of the Munich settlement condemned Britain and France for failing to call Hitler's bluff and failing to make him fight for Czechoslovakia. Defenders of the Munich Agreement have argued that Britain and France were unprepared for war with Germany. France, for example, had no plans to attack Germany. In a selection from *The Change in the European Balance of Power 1938–1939: The Path to Ruin*, Williamson Murray argues that not only were France and Britain unprepared but so was Germany. He finds that it would have been better in the long run for Britain and France to have gone to war in 1938 than in 1939.

The decision by the British and French governments to avoid war in 1938 was certainly influenced by intelligent estimates that exaggerated the capabilities of the German armed forces. In *The Ultimate Enemy: British Intelligence and Nazi Germany 1933–1939*, the next essay selection, Wesley Wark demonstrates the problems encountered by British intelligence agencies in preparing estimates of the German armed forces. A more realistic appraisal of the strengths and weaknesses of the German war machine would have made British foreign policy more effective.

Anthony Adamthwaite, in a selection from "French Military Intelligence and the Coming of the War 1935–1939," finds that the failure of French intelligence agencies contributed to the paralysis of the general staff and the government.

No area in Europe was more difficult for intelligence estimates than the Soviet Union. Nevertheless, it played a pivotal role in the origins of World War II. Robert Tucker, in the selection from his book, *Stalin in Power: The Revolution from Above, 1928–1941*, examines Soviet foreign policy as directed by Joseph Stalin. According to Tucker, first Stalin helped the Nazis attain power and then he sought to collaborate with Hitler, even if it resulted in a European war.

When Stalin unleashed the purges that terrorized the Soviet people, the effect on Soviet foreign policy was disastrous because military officers were executed for collaborating with the Nazis. In a selection from *The Soviet Union and the Failure of Collective Security, 1934–1939*, Jiri Hochman shows the impact of the purges on Soviet relations with Britain, France, and Germany. Could it not be said that the purges made the Soviet Union impotent in foreign affairs?

In 1939, Soviet influence became vital in the mounting crisis over Poland and Germany. Soon after the Munich Conference, the Germans began to demand concessions from Poland. The German occupation of Czechoslovakia in March 1939 meant that Poland was threatened from three sides. To isolate Poland completely meant an agreement between Germany and the Soviet government. Stalin had always been eager to make a deal with Hitler over eastern Europe. Here was the opportunity the Soviet ruler had longed for. Moreover, Hitler was the suppliant. Stalin laid down the conditions and Hitler accepted them. On August 23, 1939, V. M. Molotov and Joachim von Ribbentrop signed a nonaggression pact containing secret provisions that apportioned spheres of influence to Nazi Germany and the Soviet Union. The text of the pact, the next essay selection, shocked the world; it spelled the doom of Poland.

The British and French governments dispatched military delegations to Moscow in August 1939 to negotiate an agreement with Molotov, who acted for his master. Because the negotiations failed and war broke out, critics have complained that the British and French should have made whatever concessions were demanded in order to achieve an agreement. Russian historians have blamed the British and French for the failed negotiations. The next two selections approach the question of the Nazi-Soviet Pact from two different points of view.

A Soviet historian, D. M. Volkogonov, presents a view of the pact that is critical by Soviet standards, but he still blames the British and the French for failing to form an alliance with Stalin. Volkogonov claims that Stalin had no alternative other than coming to terms with Hitler. Gerhard L. Weinberg, in "The Nazi-Soviet Pacts: A Half Century Later," argues that Stalin was delighted to join in a pact that would lead to war between Nazi Germany and the capitalist western countries. He had at last sealed the deal with Hitler, and World War II could begin.

Along with the war came the Holocaust, the slaughter of the Jewish people by order of Hitler. In a selection from Lucy S. Dawidowicz's

The War Against the Jews, 1933–1945, she argues that in preparing for war Hitler was at the same time preparing the Holocaust. The war and the annihilation of the Jews were interrelated. The Holocaust was not the result of an afterthought on Hitler's part. From the beginning, Hitler had intended a war against the Jews: the Holocaust.

The next selection is in the form of a summation from D. C. Watt's *How the War Came.* In the final analysis it all came down to Germany and Hitler as the root and cause of World War II.

The last document in the anthology is Hitler's speech to his skeptical generals on November 23, 1939, when he boasted about instigating what ultimately became World War II.

Much of the study about the origins of World War II becomes entrapped in "what if" history. If Allied occupation forces had not been withdrawn from their Rhineland bases in the 1920s, perhaps the Nazi Party would not have become so powerful and Hitler would have been kept out of office. If Allied forces had been more forceful in enforcing the disarmament clauses of the Versailles Treaty, German rearmament could have been stopped. If the French, British, and Belgians had somehow invaded the Rhineland in 1936, perhaps Hitler might have been toppled, but then it might have become a European war. If Europe had aided Austria in 1938 or Britain and France had gone to war in support of Czechoslovakia, Hitler might have been stopped. If Stalin had been eager to help the capitalist nations instead of looking to Hitler for an arrangement, the rush to war could have been prevented. But that is not history, only speculation.

German military might displayed in honor of Hitler's birthday, April 20, 1939.
(Wide World Photos)

I A Problem in Interpretation

P. M. H. Bell

Another Thirty Years War?

P. M. H. Bell, reader at the University of Liverpool, explores the broad explanations advanced for the causes of World War II. Was it only a phase of another Thirty Years War in which Europe once again had to battle against a German attempt to dominate the continent? Was there a basic continuity in German policy in the years 1914–1941? Did the instability of Europe after 1919 make a second world war almost inevitable? Bell finds an opposing case. Europe had recovered from the 1914–1918 war only to be wrecked by the Great Depression and its terrible product: Adolf Hitler.

In 1939 and the following years there was a powerful and general sense that men were engaged, not in a second war, but rather in the second phase of a Thirty Years War, another round in a struggle against the

From *The Origins of the Second World War in Europe* by P. M. H. Bell, pp. 14–19, 21–29, 31–38, 1986. Reprinted by permission of Longman Group Ltd.

German domination of Europe. Since 1919 Europe had moved so rapidly through an attempt at reconstruction and stabilization into a time of renewed tension and conflict that it was hard to recognize anything which could properly be called peace. . . . The formidable Marshal Foch, generalissimo of the allied armies in France in 1918, had said of the Treaty of Versailles, 'This is not peace. It is an armistice for twenty years.' Churchill, in the preface to the first volume of his memoirs of the Second World War, wrote: 'I must regard these volumes as a continuation of the story of the First World War which I set out in *The World Crisis.* . . . Together . . . they will cover an account of another Thirty Years War.' General de Gaulle, Eduard Benes, and other notables could be added to the list. In a more straightforward way, any Belgian over the age of twenty-six in 1940, seeing the German Army marching past his doorstep for the second time in his life, could have had little doubt that a nightmarish film had got stuck, and the same events were coming round once more.

In retrospect, such views have continued to carry a good deal of conviction. Europe was indeed wrecked by the First World War. The peace settlement which followed it had grave defects. Germany did try twice in thirty years for the domination of Europe. Taking all this into account, a school of thought has developed which regards the Second World War as the culmination of a disintegration of the European order, begun by the First World War and continued by the abortive peace, which left the Continent in a state of chronic instability. . . . The basic premise of the 'Thirty Years War' thesis lies in the disruptive impact of the First World War, which shook the political, economic, and social systems of Europe to their foundations. The political and psychological damage was probably greater than the physical. It is true that casualties were very heavy: 8.5 million dead among the armed services is a generally accepted estimate, without trying to count the civilian casualties, direct and indirect. Yet, except in France, where the war losses struck a population which was already barely reproducing itself, the blow in purely demographic terms was absorbed and recovered from with less difficulty than was expected. The more lasting damage was to the mind and spirit. . . . By 1918, there was a profound weariness and disillusionment pervading the armies of Europe which was a far cry from the fire and enthusiasm of 1914. The question repeatedly asked in German units by August 1918 was '*Wozu?*' — What's it all for? — and this found its echo everywhere.

The economic disruption caused by the war was also severe. There was material devastation in the areas of heavy fighting, especially in the battle zones of north-east France and Belgium. All over Europe there was unusual wear and tear, arising from the working of industry, agriculture, and transport under heavy pressure and without adequate maintenance. The men and women who did the work, often for long hours and with insufficient food, were also worn out — the European influenza epidemic of 1919 told its tale of exhaustion and lowered resistance. The end of the war saw the breakdown of transport over much of central and eastern Europe, and shortages of both coal and food, caused partly by falling production and partly by problems of distribution. Financial and monetary problems were less immediately obvious than the material destruction, but were more lasting and insidious in their effects. Britain and France were forced to sell substantial quantities of their foreign investments to pay for the war; and other investments (notably French) were lost in the Bolshevik revolution in Russia. The Germans had their investments in enemy countries confiscated, and lost the rest of their foreign holdings at the peace. Britain borrowed heavily from the USA, and France and Italy from the USA and Britain; all ended the war with a new and heavy burden of foreign debt. There was also a great increase in internal government debts, because most war expenditure was met by loans rather than taxation. In many ways the most profound economic problem was that of inflation, the dramatic rise in prices and fall in the value of money which took place all over Europe during the war years. (In Britain, retail prices rather more than doubled between 1914 and 1918; and the position in some other countries was worse.) The confusion caused by this was the more marked after a period of generally stable prices before 1914; and the social effects spread out in all directions, to the benefit of those who could keep pace with or profit from inflation, and to the severe detriment of those who had to live on fixed incomes. In all this, it was the material damage which proved easiest to repair. Even the great scar across France and Flanders, where the battle-line had run for four years, was patched over by 1925–26 with towns and villages rebuilt and land brought back into cultivation. It was the removal of the landmark of a stable currency which had the most lasting effects, psychological as much as material.

The political effects of the war were similarly far-reaching; and again were the more shocking because they came after a long period of comparative stability. In the whole of central and eastern Europe at the end of 1918, no government remained as it had been in 1914; and over large areas there was no effective government at all. The dynasties and empires of the Habsburgs in Austria-Hungary, the Hohenzollerns in Germany, and the Romanovs in Russia had all fallen; and the regimes and states which sought to replace them were struggling to come into being amid sporadic fighting and a fog of uncertainty. Three great autocratic empires had collapsed, and the parliamentary democracies of western Europe, along with the greatest of democratic powers, the USA, were intact and victorious. But if in this sense the democracies had won, the liberalism and individualism of the nineteenth century had clearly lost during the war years. The whole nature of the war meant that state control, state initiative, and state interests, had all had a field day. The individual had been subordinated to the state — in Britain, the greatest symbol of this was the introduction of conscription for the armed forces, for the first time in British history. Paradoxically, this process was accompanied by a revulsion felt by many people against their own state, caused often by disillusionment, in some cases with the war and its pretences, in others with defeat or the inadequate rewards of victory. In either event, men turned away from their own state or form of government and looked elsewhere — often to communism on the one hand or fascism on the other.

By the end of the war, Europe seemed on the verge not only of political chaos but of revolution. In Russia in 1917 there were two revolutions, with the Bolsheviks precariously established in power by the end of the year. There was a revolution of sorts in Germany at the end of 1918. The hope of revolution for some, the fear of it for others, were widespread in Europe, with Bolshevik Russia as a beacon light or a menacing glare according to one's viewpoint. In the event, both hopes and fears proved much exaggerated. The new German republic turned out to be a mild form of social democracy, with large chunks of the old regime firmly embedded within it. Elections in Britain in 1918 and France in 1919 produced substantial right-wing majorities. Yet the revolutionary atmosphere had been real enough; it was not forgotten; and it had its effects later.

On this view, the war shook the foundations of Europe to an extent which was virtually irreparable. When the peacemakers gathered in Paris in 1919, they faced an impossible task; and in the event, it is widely argued, they proceeded to make the situation worse rather than better. The 1919 settlement, and particularly its centre-piece, the Treaty of Versailles with Germany, was criticized at the time and for the next twenty years for its harshness, its economic errors, and its inherent instability.

The accusations of harshness referred both to the terms imposed upon Germany and to the manner of their imposition. Germany lost territory. In the west Alsace and Lorraine were annexed by France (or, as the French said, were restored after wrongful seizure in 1871) and the districts of Eupen and Malmédy went to Belgium. In the east, Germany lost Posnania and parts of East Prussia to Poland; and the port of Danzig became a free city under League of Nations administration, with special rights for Poland. Plebiscites were to be held in various other areas to determine whether or not they should remain part of Germany. These resulted in part of Schleswig going to Denmark; two districts of West and East Prussia (Marienwerder and Allenstein) voting overwhelmingly to stay in Germany, which they were allowed to do; and an inconclusive vote in Upper Silesia which ended in the Council of the League of Nations allotting to Poland rather more than the plebiscite would have allowed, and certainly more than the Germans thought due. The port of Memel was ceded by Germany for transfer to Lithuania. In all, Germany lost about 65,000 square kilometres of territory and nearly 7 million inhabitants. She also lost all her colonies, which were handed over to various of the victorious powers under the cover of League of Nations mandates. All this was not unexpected after a country had lost a long and bitter war; and it compared quite favourably with the treatment meted out by Germany to the defeated Russia in March 1918. But the Germans found it harsh. They resented handing over any territory to the Poles; and they claimed that plebiscites were used arbitrarily, and usually when there was a chance of them going against Germany; they were not used at all in Alsace-Lorraine or in most of the territory lost to Poland. Moreover, when in Austria a series of unofficial plebiscites showed overwhelming majorities in favour of union with Germany, the treaty laid it down firmly that such a union was forbidden. The victorious Allies had claimed loudly that they were fighting for democracy and self-determination, but they applied these great principles selectively, or even cynically. The Germans could thus claim unfair treatment; and after a time their claims found an attentive audience in western Europe.

The harshness was also claimed to lie in the severity of the disarmament provisions imposed upon Germany. The army was limited to 100,000 men, with no tanks or heavy artillery; the navy was to have no warships of over 10,000 tons, and no submarines; there was to be no military or naval aviation. Not least, the German General Staff, the brain and nerve centre of the army, and for long a separate centre of power within the state, was to be dissolved. . . . The ostensible purpose of the disarmament clauses was 'to render possible the initiation of a general limitation of the armaments of all nations'; and when no such limitation followed, the Germans could again claim to have been unfairly treated.

The same was true of two other aspects of the treaty whose impact was more psychological than practical. The first was the clause put at the head of the reparations section of the treaty, by which Germany was compelled to accept 'the responsibility of Germany and her allies for causing all the loss and damage to which the Allied and Associated Governments and their nationals have been subjected as a consequence of the war imposed upon them by the aggression of Germany and her allies.' This was almost universally referred to as the 'war guilt' clause of the treaty; though it does not use the word guilt, and it may be that its drafters did not intend to convey a moral judgement on Germany. Such niceties were of no importance. The clause aroused deep resentment in Germany, where it was thought that equal (or greater) responsibility for the outbreak of war could be found in the actions of other countries. German historians worked hard to undermine the validity of this clause, and their claims found a ready acceptance among 'revisionist' writers in France, Britain, and the USA. Germany's case against the 'war guilt' thesis grew steadily stronger. . . .

To all this was added the claim that the Versailles Treaty was a 'dictated peace.' In one sense, this merely stated the obvious. The whole object of winning the war was to impose upon Germany terms which she would never accept voluntarily. Again, the claim referred more to the methods adopted than to the substance of what happened. At the Paris Peace Conference, the German delegation was simply presented with the Allied terms on a basis of take them or leave them; there was not even a show of negotiation, still less any real chance for Germany to influence the contents of the treaty while it was being prepared. The German complaints about this procedure reached a wide audience and it soon came to be thought (especially in Britain) that terms imposed in this fashion were not morally binding.

The significance of these claims about the harshness of the treaty lay less in their objective fairness (if there be such a standard), or in comparative justice when Versailles is matched against other peace settlements after great wars, but in the widespread and lasting impression which was created. It was natural enough that Germans should resent the fact of defeat, especially when for so much of the war they were sure that they were winning; and it was natural too for this resentment to attach to the peace settlement which registered their defeat. What was less to be expected was the extent to which the same view took hold among the victors. This was especially true of Britain, where it spread rapidly across the whole political spectrum. In France its hold was strongest on the Left — as late as August 1939 some socialist speakers still began their remarks on foreign affairs with a ritual condemnation of the Treaty of Versailles. The stability of the settlement thus came to be undermined by both vanquished and victors alike.

The accusation of harshness was particularly levelled at the reparations section of the treaty; and this may be best considered along with general assertions about the economic errors of the peace settlement. It was not unusual for cash payments, or indemnities, to be imposed upon the losing side in war; and a substantial indemnity was imposed on France as the defeated power at the end of the Franco-Prussian War in 1871. At the end of the First World War the victors renounced the idea of an indemnity, but claimed the right to exact 'compensation for all damage done to the civilian population of the Allied and Associated Powers and to their property.' The treaty itself set no figure for these 'reparations'; but it did establish the headings under which claims could be made, including not only material destruction (under which both France and Belgium had important claims), but also payment of war pensions, an almost unlimited demand which was inserted at the request of Great Britain. The task of producing a figure for reparations, and of deciding how they were to be paid, was delegated to the Reparations Commission, a body established by the victorious allies. In May 1921 this Commission arrived at a figure of 132,000 million gold marks; though at the same time the debt was divided into three sections, represented by A, B, and C class bonds, and the C class bonds were to be held by the Commission until Germany's capacity to pay had been established — which amounted to indefinite postponement of about 80,000 millions, or rather under two-thirds of the total. . . .

Quite apart from its general distorting and complicating effects, the reparations question also brought about a very sharp international crisis, with far-reaching consequences. In 1923 France and Belgium seized upon a German failure to make deliveries of reparations in kind to occupy the industrial area of the Ruhr, with the object (certainly as far as the French were concerned) either of making the Germans pay, or of inflicting serious damage on the German economy — contradictory aims, doubtless, but either of them satisfactory from a French point of view. The occupation of the Ruhr involved the use of force (invasion, the Germans claimed; police action according to the French) and helped to precipitate the catastrophic German hyperinflation of 1923. This inflation had little direct connection with reparations payments themselves, but a great deal to do with the way the German government chose to subsidize industry and to pay the costs of the passive resistance to the occupation by extravagant use of the printing press. Inflation was already running strongly in 1922; in June 1923 the mark stood at 100,000 to the dollar; in November at 4,000 million. A pay-packet was worthless before a worker got home; and anyone with assets tied to the mark (which meant anyone with savings, insurance policies, or a fixed income) saw their value vanish absolutely. The effects of this in terms of individual lives and collective confidence were far-reaching; and they later contributed to the appeal of nazism. The Ruhr occupation and the German hyperinflation were not inevitable consequences of the reparation clauses of Versailles; but as events turned out, they were among the actual results.

Going deeper than claims about the harshness of the peace settlement or its economic errors is the judgement that it was inherently and disastrously unstable. This instability was apparent in a number of ways. The war destroyed the pre-1914 European balance, and the peace could put nothing adequate in its place. A profound shift in the pattern of power occurred while the war was in progress. French losses and weariness were such that France became dependent, even by 1916, on the help of the British Empire; and by 1918 both were dependent on the USA, which alone could provide the economic resources and the fresh troops to defeat Germany. . . .

This bleak outlook stood revealed by the facts of war. What could the aspirations of peace do to soften its outlines? It was plain by as early as 1920 that the answer was, very little. The USA, having done so much to win the war and shape the peace treaties which followed it, withdrew her strength and activity back across the Atlantic — not into 'isolation,' which is altogether too absolute a term, but into an indifference towards the European balance of power which came only too naturally to a people who found the phrase itself distasteful. The British, surveying with a grievous sense of loss the cost in lives of commitment to a Continental war, thought it best to turn back to empire and the more hopeful patterns of former centuries, or to turn away from all power politics into some form of pacifism. Russia stood transformed by revolution, weak in armed or industrial strength, but powerful in menace to ordered bourgeois society.

No country felt this change more than France. In 1914 her position against Germany rested on her long-standing alliance with Russia and her *entente* with Britain. In the crisis of a German invasion, both came to her help, and in 1914 the Russian attack on East Prussia helped to check the German offensive in France. By 1919–20, Russia was gone, powerless and in any case unreliable, and Britain was anxious to diminish her European commitments. It was possible that the newly created League of Nations might be turned into an organization capable of restraining German power; but this was by no means certain. . . .

The peace settlement had been harsh enough to infuriate the Germans, but not so crushing as to render them powerless. Machiavelli once advised: 'If you see your enemy in the water up to his neck, you will do well to push him under; but if he is only in it up to his knees, you will do well to help him to the shore.' The peace treaty did neither

All this has concentrated on France and Germany. But there was another area of instability in Europe: the whole of the eastern half of the Continent was in confusion in 1919, with consequences which persisted for the next twenty years or more. From a British point of view, eastern Europe is a long way off and hard to comprehend. Austen Chamberlain, when Foreign Secretary in 1925, remarked that the Polish Corridor was not worth the bones of a British grenadier; and his half-brother Neville, in a famous broadcast on 27 September 1938, described the crisis in Czechoslovakia as 'a quarrel in a far-away country between people of whom we know nothing.' Yet that quarrel brought Europe to the brink of conflict; and in 1939 British grenadiers (and many others) marched off to a war which arose, at least immediately, from the Polish Corridor. It was an area which had a way of forcing itself upon the attention even of the distant and uncomprehending British.

In 1919, the contrast between western and eastern Europe was striking. In the west, there were some minor territorial changes; but the map remained basically as it had been in 1914. In the east all was transformed. North of the Danube, the whole territory had previously been shared between the three empires of Germany, Austria-Hungary, and Russia. Now in their place there appeared no fewer than eight new or revived states: Finland, Estonia, Latvia, Lithuania, Poland, Czechoslovakia, Hungary, and Austria. To the south, in the Balkans, there was only one new state (Yugoslavia); but most of the others were markedly different in shape, whether larger (Rumania, Greece) or smaller (Bulgaria).

It is certain that the problems created in this wholesale transformation were numerous and profound. It is arguable that they were insoluble, and that they led Europe inexorably towards war. In part, these problems were territorial, in the simple sense that there was scarcely a line on the new map which was not disputed to some degree. But in nearly every case territory was primarily important because it had become a national symbol, or because it involved conflicts of nationality. Nations are troublesome creatures. No one can define them with precision or in such a way as to command general consent; yet if a group of people feel themselves to be a nation there tends to be no limit to what some of them will do to assert their nationality. In eastern Europe, the First World War and the settlement which followed it marked the high-water mark of nationalism and separatism. Nationalist movements flourished both spontaneously and with the encouragement of belligerent states seeking to damage their opponents — Germany, for example, encouraged Polish and Ukrainian nationalism against Russia, and Britain and France supported Czech nationalism against Austria-Hungary. But while nationalist aspirations were aroused, they could not all be satisfied: they conflicted with one another, with the interests of existing states, and with the facts of history, geography, and economics, which made it impossible to draw clear and satisfactory dividing lines between the territory of one nationality and that of another.

The consequence was that eastern Europe produced a welter of conflicting aspirations and claims. Sometimes a nation was left without a state of its own, and so with a restless urge to create one. . . .

In other cases, the problem was different. A nation-state was created, but many people of its particular nationality were separated from it, as was inevitable in the historical scattering of peoples across the map. The numbers involved were large, and the complaints were bitter. In all, it has been estimated that the 1919 settlement left nearly 19 million people as national minorities in nine nation-states, out of a total population of about 98 million. The position of Poland and Czechoslovakia was particularly difficult, with one person in three belonging to a minority nationality — and that counted the Slovaks as being among the majority in Czechoslovakia: the Czechs themselves did not amount to half the total population. . . .

All the new states claimed to be nation-states, with nationality as their only principle of legitimacy. The principle of their governments, at any rate at the start, was democratic. In these circumstances, national minorities were bound to remain minorities. If they were oppressed (and most thought they were) their only hope of release lay in the intervention of a 'big brother' (their own nation-state) over the border; or perhaps in rebellion or war. (It is true that the Covenant of the League of Nations included provisions for the protection of minorities, but these usually remained a dead letter.)

The result was a set of territorial disputes, rooted in questions of nationality, which festered for some twenty years after the settlement of 1919–20, and gave much force to the thesis of a Thirty Years War. One after another they broke out afresh in 1938, 1939, and 1940, precipitating repeated crises and providing at least the circumstances, and arguably the causes, of European war.

The most obvious of these involved the boundary between Germany and Poland, where resentment was particularly concentrated on the issues of Danzig and the Polish Corridor. Danzig was a city and port which had been German (or Prussian) since 1793; it was overwhelmingly German in population; and yet in 1919 it was proclaimed a 'Free City' in order to give Poland access to the sea through a port which was not in German territory. The Polish Corridor, territory formerly German but now providing Poland's access to the Baltic, and cutting East Prussia off from the rest of Germany, contained a substantial German population; and according to some estimates and forms of measurement it was impossible to create such a corridor through territory with a clear Polish majority. The Poles, on the other hand, were disappointed that their own claims to annex Danzig and almost the whole of Upper Silesia, which had at first been accepted by the Peace Conference's Commission on Polish Affairs, had not finally been upheld. More important, they were convinced that their commerce, security, and independence were all bound up with Danzig and the Corridor. . . .

Before 1918 the Duchy of Teschen, with its capital of the same name, was part of the Austro-Hungarian Empire. On the collapse of Habsburg authority, the district, which had a mixed population (according to the last Austrian census, 55 per cent Polish, 27 per cent Czech, and 18 per cent German), was disputed between the two new states of Poland and Czechoslovakia. An eventual award by the Allied powers at the conference of Spa (1920) was favourable to Czechoslovakia, leaving Poland with the actual town of Teschen, but allotting the important suburb of Freistadt, along with the whole of the Karvin coalfield, to the Czechs. Both sides felt aggrieved; and the Teschen dispute was one of the issues which divided Poland and Czechoslovakia in the inter-war period, resurfacing during the Munich crisis of 1938. . . .

But the fact was that almost every frontier drawn in eastern Europe between 1919 and 1921 was unsatisfactory to one state or another, and sometimes to more than one at once. Poland was in particularly difficult straits. Not just Danzig and the Corridor, but the whole of the German-Polish boundary was unacceptable to Germany; while in the east the frontier with Russia laid down by the Treaty of Riga in 1921 was thought in Moscow to be far too favourable to the Poles. It was drawn at the end of a long and swaying struggle, in which Russia finally accepted defeat, and Poland secured territories which contained large numbers of Ukrainians and Byelorussians.

Even those states which did well out of the settlement in eastern Europe were not united in defending it. . . . Relations between Poland and Czechoslovakia were particularly embittered and irritable. The Teschen dispute was only part of the story. The two countries differed sharply in their views of the Soviet Union: the Poles were deeply hostile, on both historical and ideological grounds; while the Czechs were anxious for Soviet friendship, out of historic sympathy, and because they sought support against Germany. Many Poles took the view that the whole state of Czechoslovakia was an artificial creation, and both Poland and Europe would be better off without it — a view which influenced policy in 1938 and early 1939.

To all except those involved, the Polish-Czech feud was obviously suicidal. The whole of the east European settlement only came about because, in freakish circumstances, Russia and Germany had both been defeated within a year, one after the other. These two great powers had long dominated eastern Europe; indeed, they had ruled most of it. As the giants regained their strength, which was as certain as anything can be in human affairs, their dominance would be restored. If this process was to be resisted, its potential victims would have to stand together; which they were in no mind to do. Even if they had, success would not have been assured; and it is here that there lay the final and most important element of instability in the east European settlement. It was founded upon the sand; and as the tides of German and Soviet power rose from the low ebb of 1918–19, the sand would be washed away.

It is clear enough that the European order as it stood before 1914 had disintegrated, and that its replacement rested on unstable foundations. From this premise, it is easy, and to some degree convincing, to argue that the whole rickety edifice was likely to collapse in ruin at any time. It held out the prospect of war in a number of different guises: a war launched by Germany to re-establish her dominance in Europe (eastern or western, or both); a preventive war by France or Poland to forestall such action; or war in eastern Europe over one or more of the many points of conflict in that calamitous region. Why look further for the origins of another war in Europe?

The case appears all the stronger if, as many people believed, there was a fundamental continuity in German policy over the whole period between 1914 and 1941. Many Frenchmen never thought otherwise: if the Germans got another chance, they would try again; the only safe course was to sap their economy, keep them disarmed, and surround them with France's allies. Churchill obviously thought the same when he telegraphed to President Roosevelt during the night of 4/5 August 1941: 'It is twenty-seven years ago today that the Huns began the last war. We must make a good job of it this time. Twice ought to be enough.' More strikingly, in the 1960s a similar view began to gain ground in Germany itself, when the writings of Fritz Fischer emphasized the elements of continuity between the war aims of Germany in the First and Second World Wars. This raises the whole question of whether, or how far, German policy in fact embodied such continuity; of whether the advent of Hitler marked a break with the past and the start of a new era, even if it borrowed something from the old. If the continuity of German policy from one war to the next is accepted, this seems to slot the final piece into place in the thesis of a Thirty Years War. The stable, orderly Europe of 1914, with its roughly equal balance of strength between opposing alliances, had not prevented the dynamism and the expansionism of Germany from breaking loose. It took four years of war, and the powerful advent of the USA, to defeat Germany. If Germany still had the same dynamism, the same will to expand, and was set on the same course, but was faced with a Europe in decay, with no balance of strength, and no Americans to restore the balance — if this was so, surely the die was cast, and another European war was a certainty. Only the details of time and occasion remained to be decided.

It is a powerful thesis, resting on much solid evidence and strong internal logic. Yet, in the debate on the origins of the Second World War in Europe, it is confronted by another thesis, of apparently equal cogency and consistency. . . .

The arguments summarized in the previous [section], if accepted in their entirety, lead to the conclusion that the instability of Europe after 1919 rendered the outbreak of another war almost inevitable. But, however powerful they appear, they have been widely questioned, qualified, or indeed rejected outright. It is impossible to squeeze out of our history the men and events 'between the wars,' as though they were nothing more than the ghostly inhabitants of an extended half-time interval. Not even the most fatalistic observer would claim to trace a wholly predestined line from the situation of 1919 to that of 1939–41, leaving no liberty of choice whatsoever to the statesmen and peoples of the inter-war years. At the very least, it remains to be explained how it was that a war of some sort, inherently probable from 1919 onwards, became the specific conflicts which overtook Europe between 1939 and 1941. But it is possible to take the challenge to the 'Thirty Years War' thesis further than that.

In the late 1920s it appeared to contemporaries in western Europe that peace was at length returning to the troubled Continent. The errors which were by that time widely perceived in the 1919 settlement were thought to be not beyond remedy, and steps were taken to put some of them right, notably by changes in the method and extent of reparations payments, and by admitting Germany to a place in the normal working of European relations. It was also hoped that the instability of the Continent could be remedied, on the one hand by the resurrection of something like the nineteenth-century 'Concert of Europe,' an informal grouping of the great powers to provide a guiding influence in international affairs, and on the other by the development of the League of Nations. In practice these two devices often overlapped, because the great European powers were also the most influential members of the League. Finally, it appeared also that the economic and social disruption left by the war had been overcome: currencies were stabilized, industrial production reached and passed the levels of 1913, threats of revolution diminished, and the new states settled down. It was not outrageously optimistic to think that things were looking up.

The symbol of this change in European affairs was the Treaty of Locarno, and the group of political and economic agreements which preceded and followed it. Austen Chamberlain, the British Foreign Secretary, who played a considerable part in the achievement of the Locarno agreements, said afterwards that they marked 'the real dividing-line between the years of war and the years of peace'; and this verdict commanded widespread agreement at the time. The Treaty of Locarno itself was rather a limited measure to bear this heavy symbolic weight. Signed in London on 1 December 1925, after being initialled at the Swiss resort of Locarno on 16 October, it embodied the acceptance of the Franco-German and Belgian-German frontiers by the three states concerned, with an outside guarantee of those frontiers by Britain and Italy. The same acceptance and guarantee applied to the demilitarized zone in the Rhineland, which was imposed on Germany by the Treaty of Versailles. Under this extremely important provision, Germany was forbidden to maintain troops or construct fortifications in an area which included the whole of the left bank of the Rhine and a zone 50 kilometres wide on the right bank; and in the Locarno Treaty the German government freely accepted this limitation, which it previously regarded as only a part of the *diktat* of Versailles.

Though limited, these terms were important in themselves, as confirming the territorial settlement in western Europe on a freely negotiated basis. They were also important for what they represented. An important gain from the French point of view was the British guarantee of their frontier with Germany, which was something the British had avoided giving ever since 1919, when the proposed Anglo-American guarantee which was intended to accompany the Treaty of Versailles was allowed to lapse. This reassurance to France, which contributed to a sense of security, was the counterpart of the other main theme of this agreement, which was Franco-German reconciliation. Looking to the future, this seemed the crucial aspect of the whole affair. The formal political treaty did not stand alone. It was buttressed by an association, perhaps amounting to friendship, between the French and German Foreign Ministers, Aristide Briand and Gustav Stresemann. . . .

The Treaty of Locarno was accompanied by other agreements. There was a series of arbitration treaties between Germany on the one hand and France, Belgium, Czechoslovakia, and Poland on the other, laying down that certain types of dispute between the signatories should be submitted to outside arbitration. There were also treaties of mutual guarantee between France on the one hand and Poland and Czechoslovakia on the other, which were intended to close, at least partially, the obvious gap left by Locarno, which was that it concerned only western Europe.

Locarno and its accompanying agreements, and the spirit of reconciliation which flourished with them, were only possible because in the previous year a partial settlement of the reparation problem had been reached. In 1923, with the French occupation of the Ruhr to enforce payment upon Germany, this had seemed scarcely feasible — France was firmly embarked on the course of imposing reparations, not negotiating about them. But in October of that year the French government accepted a British proposal to set up a committee of experts to consider the problem. This committee, set up by agreement between the British, French, Belgian, Italian, American, and German governments, was to consider (supposedly from a purely technical standpoint) means of balancing the German budget, stabilizing the German currency, and fixing both an achievable level of reparation payments and means by which they might be made and secured. The chairman of the committee was an American banker, and Director of the US Bureau of the Budget, Charles G. Dawes; and its recommendations, made early in 1924, came to be known as the Dawes Plan. A vital recommendation was for the stabilization of the German currency, at the rate of 20 Reichsmarks to the pound sterling, controlled by the creation of a new bank of issue, independent of the German government and run by a body of which half had to be non-Germans. The committee then went on to deal with reparation payments. It left the total unchanged, but recommended a new scheme of annual payments starting at 1,000 million gold marks in the first year, rising to 2,500 million in the fifth and thereafter. Some variation in the annual payments was provided for in case of sharp movements in the price of gold or severe transfer problems. Payment of reparations was to be ensured by the appropriation of certain indirect taxes and bonds for the state railways for that purpose; and a Reparations Agency, including Allied representatives, was to be set up to control these arrangements. A foreign loan of 800 million marks was to be raised, partly to back the new currency, and partly to help with the payment of the first annual instalment under the new reparations scheme.

The Dawes Plan was accepted by the French government in April 1924, which was a vital first step, because the whole scheme was contingent upon French withdrawal from the Ruhr; and then by an international conference in London in July and August. The loan was raised without difficulty in October, rather more than half in the USA and a quarter in Britain, with the rest in a number of west European countries. Germany then made reparation payments regularly under the terms of the Dawes Plan. In February 1929 a new committee, under the chairmanship of another American banker, Owen D. Young, was set up to work out a definitive settlement of the reparations question. Its report, presented to the governments concerned in June, recommended a reduction of about a quarter in the total of reparations, with a rising scale of annual payments to be completed by 1988 — the first mention of a final date. The Reparations Agency was to be withdrawn, and foreign surveillance of German finances brought to an end. The proposals were accepted by the various governments; and a German payment under the new arrangement was made in May 1930.

These agreements were not in any final sense a settlement of the reparations problem. Paying reparations at all was still unwelcome to Germany; and there was still a strain on the German balance of payments. However, it was shown that in certain circumstances reparations could be paid, and indeed that they were compatible with a general recovery in European commerce and industry. . . . Trade between France and Germany grew rapidly: French imports from Germany increased by 60 per cent between 1926 and 1930, including large quantities of coal, iron and steel, chemical products, and machine tools. French industrial growth in the period was closely linked to German production — at the time, another sign of Franco-German co-operation.

Economic progress was accompanied by the stabilization of the major west European currencies. In Germany, this was a matter of replacement rather than stabilization. In November 1923, at the height of the hyperinflation, a new currency, the Rentenmark, was introduced, based on the security of land and buildings. For a time it circulated alongside the old mark; then in August 1924, with the backing of the Dawes loan, a new Reichsmark was introduced to replace the old currency, at the rate of one new Reichsmark to 1 million millions of the old. This registered the acceptance of the obliteration of all holdings in the old currency; but it was a fresh start, and in the following years prices held steady. . . .

One of the agreements reached at Locarno in 1925 was that Germany should be admitted to the League of Nations and become a permanent member of its Council. This focused attention on another great sign of hope in the 1930s: the apparently firm rooting and strong flowering of the League. Founded in 1919 under the combined impulse of Lord Robert Cecil and President Wilson, the League suffered an early blow when it was rejected by the USA in 1920, and it was viewed with suspicion by most practitioners of the old diplomacy, who saw it, at best, as being no more than a fifth wheel on a carriage. But despite set-backs and doubts, the League began to flourish. . . . The Council of the League, with its permanent membership made up of great powers (Britain, France, Italy, and Japan), acted as a successor to the old Concert of Europe. The Covenant bound all member states to submit disputes to the League before resorting to force, and so held out the opportunity of avoiding war. . . .

With Germany's admission to membership in 1926, the League escaped the stigma of being merely a 'League of victors.' By 1928 every European state except the USSR was a member, and nearly every Foreign Minister attended its sessions. Notably, in the post-Locarno period, Briand, Stresemann, and Austen Chamberlain made a point of meeting at Geneva. In the late 1920s the League was at the height of its prestige, and a beacon of hope in international affairs.

All these achievements of the late 1920s had their flaws, some of which were potentially dangerous. The Locarno agreements contained serious faults and contradictions. Some were immediately apparent, certainly to those whom they affected most nearly. The treaties distinguished between Germany's western frontiers, which were voluntarily accepted by Germany and guaranteed by outside powers, and her eastern borders, which were not. The implication, which was not lost on the Poles, was that some frontiers were more firmly established than others. Other faults were temporarily concealed. By the treaties, Britain publicly guaranteed the Franco-German and Belgian-German frontiers, but she took no steps to ensure that this guarantee could be fulfilled: there was no military commitment nor planning for the defence of any of the territories involved. Most serious of all, the agreements merely disguised a profound difference of approach between France and Germany. It was true that both Briand and Stresemann spoke the language of reconciliation; but each hoped to reconcile the other to something different. Briand wanted to reconcile Germany to the acceptance of the Versailles settlement; Stresemann wanted to reconcile France to its revision. It must be doubted whether so fundamental a contradiction could have been glossed over for long.

It also appeared in retrospect that the economic recovery of Europe was excessively dependent on American loans. . . . The Dawes loan of 1924, which was oversubscribed in New York, was the start of a considerable flow of lending by American investors to Germany (especially to the firms of Krupps and Thyssen, and to German municipalities), and later to other European countries. In the Dawes years (1924–29), German borrowing from abroad always far exceeded her reparation payments. Hence a curious cycle of payments developed: Germany borrowed from the USA; which helped her to pay reparations to France, Britain, and Italy; and in turn these countries made payments on their war debts to the USA. When the source of American loans dried up with the stock market crash in 1929, this cycle was broken at its starting point; and with the calling in of short-term American loans, an important element in the German economic recovery was removed.

The extravagant hopes invested in the League of Nations by Western liberals and socialists, and by aspiring small states, were probably always greater than that organization could be expected to fulfil. It was easy to exaggerate the success over Greece and Bulgaria, and ignore the League's failure to deal with the Polish-Lithuanian conflict over Vilna. The basic problem presented to the League by the absence of the USA and the Soviet Union had not been resolved. There was a dangerous element of euphoria in the atmosphere of Geneva.

All this may be granted. But does it mean that all the hopes which followed the Dawes-Locarno agreements were illusory? Surely not. The case must remain hypothetical; but it is perfectly conceivable that, without the stock market crash in America in 1929, American support for the European financial system would not have been so abruptly removed, and the system might have adjusted itself gradually to a lesser dependence on US loans. It was first the great crash, and then the even greater world depression which it signalled, which cut off the hopes of recovery in their prime. All over Europe, the British Empire, and the USA, the depression had the effect of driving states (or groups of states) in upon themselves, to try to find salvation in some form of self-sufficiency. Similarly, the political contradictions underlying the Locarno agreements were real; but there was a reasonable chance that they could be resolved, as long as Germany moved towards the revision of Versailles with prudence, and with limited objectives. Britain would have accepted such movement readily and France reluctantly; but the result would have been the same. Locarno at least opened the way for Germany to resume her place as a partner in the European Concert; and after that, perhaps, by stages, to her former predominance, without encountering determined — still less armed — opposition.

In this hypothesis, then, it was the great depression which destroyed a situation offering a real chance of evolution towards a stable European peace. The depression wrecked all the gains in terms of economic stabilization, prosperity, and material progress secured since 1924. It provoked over much of Europe a flight towards political extremes which plunged the Continent into ideological strife, and various forms of economic nationalism which generated constant friction. Above all, by destroying German prosperity and rendering 6 million Germans unemployed, it played a crucial part in the rise of Hitler to power. That, in the eyes of many, was the fatal event, the conjuring up of the demon king. In Churchill's words: '. . . into that void after a pause there strode a maniac of ferocious genius, the repository and expression of the most virulent hatreds that have ever corroded the human breast — Corporal Hitler.' It then requires only one link to complete the chain: the depression brought Hitler, and Hitler brought the war. For many, like the French historian Maurice Baumont, the link presents no difficulty: 'the origins of the war of 1939 go back essentially to the insatiable appetites of Adolf Hitler.'

A rival hypothesis to that of a Thirty Years War thus takes shape. Instead of the continuation of the First World War, arising almost inevitably out of the effects of that war and the instability of the peace settlement, there appears the outline of a successful European recovery, cut off in its prime by the great depression and its dreadful consequence, the advent of Hitler. These two broad interpretations have bred many variations, advanced with varying degrees of sharpness, and sometimes venom.

Hitler speaking to the people of Hamburg about the April 10, 1938, plebiscite on the Austrian Anschluss. (Joseph Schorer/Bildarchiv Preussischer Kulturbesitz)

II The Hitler Enigma

Adolf Hitler

A Policy for Germany

After Adolf Hitler failed in his attempt to seize power in the Munich Beer Hall Putsch in November 1923, he was convicted of treason and sentenced to five years in prison. While there, he began dictating *Mein Kampf*, which became a best-seller only after he became chancellor. In this book, part autobiography, ideological tract, and theory of tactics and propaganda, Hitler set forth his ideas on foreign policy, the Jews, and Bolshevik Russia. Who among the few readers could imagine that this Austrian-born failed politician would actually attempt to carry out the ideas in *Mein Kampf*? Who could believe that his call for *Lebensraum* (living space) for the German people would be transformed into a world war?

In 1928, Hitler wrote a second book, which was published posthumously. Hitler's publisher had no wish to lose more money. In 1958,

Professor Gerhard L. Weinberg found the manuscript among the captured German documents.

If under foreign policy we must understand the regulation of a nation's relations with the rest of the world, the manner of this regulation will be determined by certain definite facts. As National Socialists we can, furthermore, establish the following principle concerning the nature of the foreign policy of a folkish state:

The foreign policy of the folkish state must safeguard the existence on this planet of the race embodied in the state, by creating a healthy, viable natural relation between the nation's population and growth on the one hand and the quantity and quality of its soil on the other hand.

As a healthy relation we may regard only that condition which assures the sustenance of a people on its own soil. Every other condition, even if it endures for hundreds, nay, thousands of years, is nevertheless unhealthy and will sooner or later lead to the injury if not annihilation of the people in question.

Only an adequately large space on this earth assures a nation of freedom of existence.

Moreover, the necessary size of the territory to be settled cannot be judged exclusively on the basis of present requirements, not even in fact on the basis of the yield of the soil compared to the population. For, as I explained in the first volume, under 'German Alliance Policy Before the War,' *in addition to its importance as a direct source of a people's food, another significance, that is, a military and political one, must be attributed to the area of a state.* If a nation's sustenance as such is assured by the amount of its soil, the safeguarding of the existing soil itself must also be borne in mind. This lies in the general power-political strength of the state, which in turn to no small extent is determined by geomilitary considerations.

Hence, the German nation can defend its future only as a world power. For more than two thousand years the defense of our people's interests, as we should designate our more or less fortunate activity in the field of foreign affairs, was *world history.* We ourselves were witnesses to this fact: for the gigantic struggle of the nations in the years 1914–1918 was only the struggle of the German people for its existence on the globe, but we designated the type of event itself as a *World War.*

The German people entered this struggle as a *supposed* world power. I say here 'supposed,' for in reality it was none. If the German nation in 1914 had had a different relation between area and population, Germany would really have been a world power, and the War, aside from all other factors, could have been terminated favorably.

Germany today is no world power. Even if our momentary military impotence were overcome, we should no longer have any claim to this title. What can a formation, as miserable in its relation of population to area as the German Reich today, mean on this planet? In an era when the earth is gradually being divided up among states, some of which embrace almost entire continents, we cannot speak of a world power in connection with a formation whose political mother country is limited to the absurd area of five hundred thousand square kilometers.

From the purely territorial point of view, the area of the German Reich vanishes completely as compared with that of the so-called world powers. Let no one cite England as a proof to the contrary, for England in reality is merely the great capital of the British world empire which calls nearly a quarter of the earth's surface its own. In addition, we must regard as giant states, first of all the American Union, then Russia and China. All are spatial formations having in part an area more than ten times greater than the present German Reich. And even France must be counted among these states. Not only that she complements her army to an ever-increasing degree from her enormous empire's reservoir of colored humanity, but racially as well, she is making such great progress in negrification that we can actually speak of an African state arising on European soil. The colonial policy of present-day France cannot be compared with that of Germany in the past. If the development of France in the present style were to be continued for three hundred years, the last remnants of Frankish blood would be submerged in the developing European-African mulatto state. An immense self-contained area of settlement from the Rhine to the Congo, filled with a lower race gradually produced from continuous bastardization.

This distinguishes French colonial policy from the old German one.

The former German colonial policy, like everything we did, was carried out by halves. It neither increased the settlement area of the German Reich, nor did it undertake any attempt — criminal though it would have been — to strengthen the Reich by the use of black blood. The Askaris in German East Africa were a short, hesitant step in this direction. Actually they served only for the defense of the colonies themselves. The idea of bringing black troops into a European battlefield, quite aside from its practical impossibility in the World War, never existed even as a design to be realized under more favorable circumstances, while, on the contrary, it was always regarded and felt by the French as the basic reason for their colonial activity.

Thus, in the world today we see a number of power states, some of which not only far surpass the strength of our German nation in population, but whose area above all is the chief support of their political power. Never has the relation of the German Reich to other existing world states been as unfavorable as at the beginning of our history two thousand years ago and again today. Then we were a young people, rushing headlong into a world of great crumbling state formations, whose last giant, Rome, we ourselves helped to fell. Today we find ourselves in a world of great power states in process of formation, with our own Reich sinking more and more into insignificance.

We must bear this bitter truth coolly and soberly in mind. We must follow and compare the German Reich through the centuries in its relation to other states with regard to population and area. I know that everyone will then come to the dismayed conclusion which I have stated at the beginning of this discussion: *Germany is no longer a world power, regardless whether she is strong or weak from the military point of view.*

We have lost all proportion to the other great states of the earth, and this thanks only to the positively catastrophic leadership of our nation in the field of foreign affairs, thanks to our total failure to be guided by what I should almost call a testamentary aim in foreign policy, and thanks to the loss of any healthy instinct and impulse of self-preservation.

If the National Socialist movement really wants to be consecrated by history with a great mission for our nation, it must be permeated by knowledge and filled with pain at our true situation in this world; boldly and conscious of its goal, it must take up the struggle against the aimlessness and incompetence which have hitherto guided our German nation in the line of foreign affairs. Then, without consideration of 'traditions' and prejudices, it must find the courage to gather our people and their strength for an advance along the road that will lead this people from its present restricted living space to new land and soil, and hence also free it from the danger of vanishing from the earth or of serving others as a slave nation.

The National Socialist movement must strive to eliminate the dis-proportion between our population and our area — viewing this latter as a source of food as well as a basis for power politics — between our historical past and the hopelessness of our present impotence. And in this it must remain aware that we, as guardians of the highest humanity on this earth, are bound by the highest obligation, and the more it strives to bring the German people to racial awareness so that, in addi-tion to breeding dogs, horses, and cats, they will have mercy on their *own* blood, the more it will be able to meet this obligation.

If I characterize German policy up to now as aimless and incompe-tent, the proof of my assertion lies in the actual failure of this policy. If our people had been intellectually inferior or cowardly, the results of its struggle on the earth could not be worse than what we see before us today. Neither must the development of the last decades before the War deceive us on this score; for we cannot measure the strength of an empire by itself, but only by comparison with other states. And just such a comparison furnishes proof that the increase in strength of the other states was not only more even, but also greater in its ultimate effect; that consequently, despite its apparent rise, Germany's road actu-ally diverged more and more from that of the other states and fell far behind; in short, the difference in magnitudes increased to our disfavor. Yes, as time went on, we fell behind more and more even in popula-tion. But since our people is certainly excelled by none on earth in heroism, in fact, all in all has certainly given the most blood of all the nations on earth for the preservation of its existence, the failure can reside only in the *mistaken way* in which it was given.

If we examine the political experiences of our people for more than a thousand years in this connection, passing all the innumerable wars and struggles in review and examining the present end result they cre-ated, we shall be forced to admit that this sea of blood has given rise to only three phenomena which we are justified in claiming as endur-ing fruits of clearly defined actions in the field of foreign and general politics:

1. The colonization of the *Ostmark*, carried out mostly by Bavarians;

2. the acquisition and penetration of the territory east of the Elbe; and

3. the organization by the Hohenzollerns of the Brandenburg-Prussian state as a model and nucleus for crystallization of a new Reich.

An instructive warning for the future!

The first two great successes of our foreign policy have remained the most enduring. Without them our nation today would no longer have any importance at all. They were the first, but unfortunately the only successful attempt to bring the rising population into harmony with the quantity of our soil. And it must be regarded as truly catastrophic that our German historians have never been able to estimate correctly these two achievements which are by far the greatest and most significant for the future, but by contrast have glorified everything conceivable, praised and admired fantastic heroism, innumerable adventurous wars and struggles, instead of finally recognizing how unimportant most of these events have been for the nation's great line of development.

The third great success of our political activity lies in the formation of the Prussian state and the resultant cultivation of a special state idea, as also of the German army's instinct of self-preservation and self-defense, adapted to the modern world and put into organized form. The development of the idea of individual militancy into the duty of national militancy [conscription] has grown out of every state formation and every state conception. The significance of this development cannot be overestimated. Through the discipline of the Prussian army organism, the German people, shot through with hyperindividualism by their racial divisions, won back at least a part of the capacity for organization which they had long since lost. What other peoples still primitively possess in their herd community instinct, we, partially at least, regained artificially for our national community through the process of military training. Hence the elimination of universal conscription — which for dozens of other peoples might be a matter of no importance — is for us fraught with the gravest consequences. Ten German generations without corrective and educational military training, left to the evil effects of their racial and hence philosophical division — and our nation would really have lost the last remnant of an independent existence on this planet. Only through individual men, in the bosom of foreign nations, could the German spirit make its contribution to culture, and its origin would not even be recognized. Cultural fertilizer, until the last remnant of Aryan-Nordic blood in us would be corrupted or extinguished.

It is noteworthy that the significance of these real political successes won by our nation in its struggles, enduring more than a thousand years, were far better understood and appreciated by our adversaries than by ourselves. Even today we still rave about a heroism which robbed our people of millions of its noblest blood-bearers, but in its ultimate result remained totally fruitless.

The distinction between the real political successes of our people and the national blood spent for fruitless aims is of the greatest importance for our conduct in the present and the future.

We National Socialists must never under any circumstances join in the foul[1] hurrah patriotism of our present bourgeois world. In particular it is mortally dangerous to regard the last pre-War developments as binding even in the slightest degree for our own course. From the whole historical development of the nineteenth century, not a single obligation can be derived which was grounded in this period itself. In contrast to the conduct of the representatives of this period, we must again profess the highest aim of the foreign policy, to wit: *to bring the soil into harmony with the population.* Yes, from the past we can only learn that, in setting an objective for our political activity, we must proceed in two directions: *Land and soil as the goal of our foreign policy, and a new philosophically established, uniform foundation as the aim of political activity at home.*

I still wish briefly to take a position on the question as to what extent the demand for soil and territory seems ethically and morally justified. This is necessary, since unfortunately, even in so-called folkish circles, all sorts of unctuous big-mouths step forward, endeavoring to set the rectification of the injustice of 1918 as the aim of the German nation's endeavors in the field of foreign affairs, but at the same time find it necessary to assure the whole world of folkish brotherhood and sympathy.

---

[1] '*übel.*' In preparing the second edition, the frugal copy-reader substitutes '*üblick*,' usual.

I should like to make the following preliminary remarks: *The demand for restoration of the frontiers of 1914 is a political absurdity of such proportions and consequences as to make it seem a crime. Quite aside from the fact that the Reich's frontiers in 1914 were anything but logical. For in reality they were neither complete in the sense of embracing the people of German nationality, nor sensible with regard to geomilitary expediency. They were not the result of a considered political action, but momentary frontiers in a political struggle that was by no means concluded; partly, in fact, they were the results of chance.* With equal right and in many cases with more right, some other sample year of German history could be picked out, and the restoration of the conditions at that time declared to be the aim of an activity in foreign affairs. The above demand is entirely suited to our bourgeois society, which here as elsewhere does not possess a single creative political idea for the future, but lives only in the past, in fact, in the most immediate past; for even their backward gaze does not extend beyond their own times. The law of inertia binds them to a given situation and causes them to resist any change in it, but without ever increasing the activity of this opposition beyond the mere power of perseverance. So it is obvious that the political horizon of these people does not extend beyond the year 1914. By proclaiming the restoration of those borders as the political aim of their activity, they keep mending the crumbling league of our adversaries. Only in this way can it be explained that eight years after a world struggle in which states, some of which had the most heterogeneous desires, took part, the coalition of the victors of those days can still maintain itself in a more or less unbroken form.

All these states were at one time beneficiaries of the German collapse. Fear of our strength caused the greed and envy of the individual great powers among themselves to recede. By grabbing as much of the Reich as they could, they found the best guard against a future uprising. A bad conscience and fear of our people's strength is still the most enduring cement to hold together the various members of this alliance.

And we do not disappoint them. By setting up the restoration of the borders of 1914 as a political program for Germany, our bourgeoisie frighten away every partner who might desire to leave the league of our enemies, since he must inevitably fear to be attacked singly and thereby lose the protection of his individual fellow allies. Each single state feels concerned and threatened by this slogan.

Moreover, it is senseless in two respects:

1. because the instruments of power are lacking to remove it from the vapors of club evenings into reality; and
2. because, if it could actually be realized, the outcome would again be so pitiful that, by God, it would not be worth while to risk the blood of our people for *this*.

For it should scarcely seem questionable to anyone that even the restoration of the frontiers of 1914 could be achieved only by blood. Only childish and naïve minds can lull themselves in the idea that they can bring about a correction of Versailles by wheedling and begging. Quite aside from the fact that such an attempt would presuppose a man of Talleyrand's talents, which we do not possess. One half of our political figures consist of extremely sly, but equally spineless elements which are hostile toward our nation to begin with, while the other is composed of good-natured, harmless, and easy-going softheads. Moreover, the times have changed since the Congress of Vienna: *Today it is not princes and princes' mistresses who haggle and bargain over state borders; it is the inexorable Jew who struggles for his domination over the nations.* No nation can remove this hand from its throat except by the sword. Only the assembled and concentrated might of a national passion rearing up in its strength can defy the international enslavement of peoples. Such a process is and remains a bloody one.

If, however, we harbor the conviction that the German future, regardless what happens, demands the supreme sacrifice, quite aside from all considerations of political expediency as such, we must set up an aim worthy of this sacrifice and fight for it.

The boundaries of the year 1914 mean nothing at all for the German future. Neither did they provide a defense of the past, nor would they contain any strength for the future. Through them the German nation will neither achieve its inner integrity, nor will its sustenance be safeguarded by them, nor do these boundaries, viewed from the military standpoint, seem expedient or even satisfactory, nor finally can they improve the relation in which we at present find ourselves toward the other world powers, or, better expressed, the real world powers. The lag behind England will not be caught up, the magnitude of the Union will not be achieved; not even France would experience a material diminution of her world-political importance.

Only one thing would be certain: even with a favorable outcome, such an attempt to restore the borders of 1914 would lead to a further bleeding of our national body, so much so that there would be no worth-while blood left to stake for the decisions and actions really to secure the nation's future. On the contrary, drunk with such a shallow success, we should renounce any further goals, all the more readily as 'national honor' would be repaired and, for the moment at least, a few doors would have been reopened to commercial development.

As opposed to this, we National Socialists must hold unflinchingly to our aim in foreign policy, namely, *to secure for the German people the land and soil to which they are entitled on this earth.* And this action is the only one which, before God and our German posterity, would make any sacrifice of blood seem justified: before God, since we have been put on this earth with the mission of eternal struggle for our daily bread, beings who receive nothing as a gift, and who owe their position as lords of the earth only to the genius and the courage with which they can conquer and defend it; and before our German posterity in so far as we have shed no citizen's blood out of which a thousand others are not bequeathed to posterity. The soil on which some day German generations of peasants can beget powerful sons will sanction the investment of the sons of today, and will some day acquit the responsible statesmen of blood-guilt and sacrifice of the people, even if they are persecuted by their contemporaries.

And I must sharply attack those folkish pen-pushers who claim to regard such an acquisition of soil as a 'breach of sacred human rights' and attack it as such in their scribblings. One never knows who stands behind these fellows. But one thing is certain, that the confusion they can create is desirable and convenient to our national enemies. By such an attitude they help to weaken and destroy from within our people's will for the only correct way of defending their vital needs. For no people on this earth possesses so much as a square yard of territory on the strength of a higher will or superior right. Just as Germany's frontiers are fortuitous frontiers, momentary frontiers in the current political struggle of any period, so are the boundaries of other nations' living space. And just as the shape of our earth's surface can seem immutable as granite only to the thoughtless soft-head, but in reality only represents at each period an apparent pause in a continuous development, created by the mighty forces of Nature in a process of continuous growth, only to be transformed or destroyed tomorrow by greater forces, likewise the boundaries of living spaces in the life of nations.

State boundaries are made by man and changed by man.

The fact that a nation has succeeded in acquiring an undue amount of soil constitutes no higher obligation that it should be recognized eternally. At most it proves the strength of the conquerors and the weakness of the nations. And in this case, right lies in this strength alone. If the German nation today, penned into an impossible area, faces a lamentable future, this is no more a commandment of Fate than revolt against this state of affairs constitutes an affront to Fate. No more than any higher power has promised another nation more territory than the German nation, or is offended by the fact of this unjust distribution of the soil. Just as our ancestors did not receive the soil on which we live today as a gift from Heaven, but had to fight for it at the risk of their lives, in the future no folkish grace will win soil for us and hence life for our people, but only the might of a victorious sword.

Much as all of us today recognize the necessity of a reckoning with France, it would remain ineffectual in the long run if it represented the whole of our aim in foreign policy. It can and will achieve meaning only if it offers the rear cover for an enlargement of our people's living space in Europe. For it is not in colonial acquisitions that we must see the solution of this problem, but exclusively in the acquisition of a territory for settlement, which will enhance the area of the mother country, and hence not only keep the new settlers in the most intimate community with the land of their origin, but secure for the total area those advantages which lic in its unified magnitude.

The folkish movement must not be the champion of other peoples, but the vanguard fighter of its own. Otherwise it is superfluous and above all has no right to sulk about the past. For in that case it is behaving in exactly the same way. The old German policy was wrongly determined by dynastic considerations, and the future policy must not be directed by cosmopolitan folkish drivel. In particular, we are not constables guarding the well-known 'poor little nations,' but soldiers of our own nation.

But we National Socialists must go further. *The right to possess soil can become a duty if without extension of its soil a great nation seems doomed to destruction.* And most especially when not some little nigger nation or other is involved, but the Germanic mother of life, which has given the present-day world its cultural picture. *Germany will either be a world power or there will be no Germany.* And for world power she needs that magnitude which will give her the position she needs in the present period, and life to her citizens.

And so we National Socialists consciously draw a line beneath the foreign policy tendency of our pre-War period. We take up where we broke off six hundred years ago. We stop the endless German movement to the south and west, and turn our gaze toward the land in the east. At long last we break off the colonial and commercial policy of the pre-War period and shift to the soil policy of the future.

If we speak of soil in Europe today, we can primarily have in mind only *Russia* and her vassal border states.

Here Fate itself deems desirous of giving us a sign. By handing Russia to Bolshevism, it robbed the Russian nation of that intelligentsia which previously brought about and guaranteed its existence as a state. For the organization of a Russian state formation was not the result of the political abilities of the Slavs in Russia, but only a wonderful example of the state-forming efficacity of the German element in an inferior race. Numerous mighty empires on earth have been created in this way. Lower nations led by Germanic organizers and overlords have more than once grown to be mighty state formations and have endured as long as the racial nucleus of the creative state race maintained itself. For centuries Russia drew nourishment from this Germanic nucleus of its upper leading strata. Today it can be regarded as almost totally exterminated and extinguished. It has been replaced by the Jew. Impossible as it is for the Russian by himself to shake off the yoke of the Jew by his own resources, it is equally impossible for the Jew to maintain the mighty empire forever. He himself is no element of organization, but a ferment of decomposition. The Persian[2] empire in the east is ripe for collapse. And the end of Jewish rule in Russia will also be the end of Russia as a state. We have been chosen by Fate as witnesses of a catastrophe which will be the mightiest confirmation of the soundness of the folkish theory.

Our task, the mission of the National Socialist movement, is to bring our own people to such political insight that they will not see their goal for the future in the breath-taking sensation of a new Alexander's

---

[2] Second edition has 'giant' instead of 'Persian.'

conquest, but in the industrious work of the German plow, to which the
sword need only give soil.

It goes without saying that the Jews announce the sharpest resistance to such a policy. Better than anyone else they sense the significance of this action for their own future. This very fact should teach
all really national-minded men the correctness of such a reorientation.
Unfortunately, the opposite is the case. Not only in German-National,
but even in 'folkish' circles, the idea of such an eastern policy is vio-
lently attacked, and, as almost always in such matters, they appeal to
a higher authority.

It just happens to be impossible to overwhelm with a coalition of
cripples a powerful state that is determined to stake, if necessary, its
last drop of blood for its existence. As a folkish man, who appraises the
value of men on a racial basis, I am prevented by mere knowledge of
the racial inferiority of these so-called 'oppressed nations' from linking
the destiny of my own people with theirs.

And today we must take exactly the same position toward Russia.
Present-day Russia, divested of her Germanic upper stratum, is, quite
aside from the private intentions of her new masters, no ally for the
German nation's fight for freedom. *Considered from the purely military*
angle, the relations would be simply catastrophic in case of war between
Germany and Russia and Western Europe, and probably against all
the rest of the world. The struggle would take place, not on Russian,
but on German soil, and Germany would not be able to obtain the
least effective support from Russia. The present German Reich's instruments of power are so lamentable and so useless for a foreign war, that
no defense of our borders against Western Europe, including England,
would be practicable, and particularly the German industrial region
would lie defenselessly exposed to the concentrated aggressive arms of
our foes. There is the additional fact that between Germany and Russia
there lies the Polish state, completely in French hands. In case of a
war between Germany and Russia and Western Europe, Russia would
first have to subdue Poland before the first soldier could be sent to the
western front. Yet it is not so much a question of soldiers as of technical
armament. In this respect, the World War situation would repeat itself,
only much more horribly. Just as German industry was then drained
for our glorious allies, and, technically speaking, Germany had to fight
the war almost single-handed, likewise in this struggle Russia would be

entirely out of the picture as a technical factor. We could oppose practically nothing to the general motorization of the world, which in the next war will manifest itself overwhelmingly and decisively. For not only that Germany herself has remained shamefully backward in this all-important field, but from the little she possesses she would have to sustain Russia, which even today cannot claim possession of a single factory capable of producing a motor vehicle that really runs. Thus, such a war would assume the character of a plain massacre. Germany's youth would be bled even more than the last time, for as always the burden of the fighting would rest only upon us, and the result would be inevitable defeat.

But even supposing that a miracle should occur and that such a struggle did not end with the total annihilation of Germany, the ultimate outcome would only be that the German nation, bled white, would remain as before bounded by great military states and that her real situation would hence have changed in no way.

Let no one argue that in concluding an alliance with Russia we need not immediately think of war, or, if we did, that we could thoroughly prepare for it. *An alliance whose aim does not embrace a plan for war is senseless and worthless.* Alliances are concluded only for struggle. And even if the clash should be never so far away at the moment when the pact is concluded, the prospect of a military involvement is nevertheless its cause. And do not imagine that any power would ever interpret the meaning of such an alliance in any other way. Either a German-Russian coalition would remain on paper, or from the letter of the treaty it would be translated into visible reality — and the rest of the world would be warned. How naïve to suppose that in such a case England and France would wait a decade for the German-Russian alliance to complete its technical preparations. No, the storm would break over Germany with the speed of lightning.

And so the very fact of the conclusion of an alliance with Russia embodies a plan for the next war. Its outcome would be the end of Germany.

On top of this there is the following:

1. *The present rulers of Russia have no idea of honorably entering into an alliance, let alone observing one.*

Never forget that the rulers of present-day Russia are common blood-stained criminals; that they are the scum of humanity which, favored by circumstances, overran a great state in a tragic hour, slaughtered and wiped out thousands of her leading intelligentsia in wild blood lust, and now for almost ten years have been carrying on the most cruel and tyrannical régime of all time. Furthermore, do not forget that these rulers belong to a race which combines, in a rare mixture, bestial cruelty and an inconceivable gift for lying, and which today more than ever is conscious of a mission to impose its bloody oppression on the whole world. Do not forget that the international Jew who completely dominates Russia today regards Germany, not as an ally, but as a state destined to the same fate. *And you do not make pacts with anyone whose sole interest is the destruction of his partner.* Above all, you do not make them with elements to whom no pact would be sacred, since they do not live in this world as representatives of honor and sincerity, but as champions of deceit, lies, theft, plunder, and rapine. If a man believes that he can enter into profitable connections with parasites, he is like a tree trying to conclude for its own profit an agreement with a mistletoe.

2. *The danger to which Russia succumbed is always present for Germany.*

Only a bourgeois simpleton is capable of imagining that Bolshevism has been exorcised. With his superficial thinking he has no idea that this is an instinctive process; that is, the striving of the Jewish people for world domination, a process which is just as natural as the urge of the Anglo-Saxon to seize domination of the earth. And just as the Anglo-Saxon pursues this course in his own way and carries on the fight with his own weapons, likewise the Jew. He goes his way, the way of sneaking in among the nations and boring from within, and he fights with his weapons, with lies and slander, poison and corruption, intensifying the struggle to the point of bloodily exterminating his hated foes. *In Russian Bolshevism we must see the attempt undertaken by the Jews in the twentieth century to achieve world domination.* Just as in other epochs they strove to reach the same goal by other, though inwardly related processes. Their endeavor lies profoundly rooted in their essential nature. No more than another nation renounces of its own accord the pursuit of its impulse for the expansion of its power and way of life, but is compelled by outward circumstances or else succumbs to impotence due to the symptoms of old age, does the Jew break off his road to world dictatorship out of voluntary renunciation, or because he represses his eternal urge. He, too, will either be thrown back in his course by forces lying outside himself, or all his striving for world domination will be ended by his own dying out. But the impotence of nations, their own death from old age, arises from the abandonment of their blood purity. And this is a thing that the Jew preserves better than any other people on earth. And so he advances on his fatal road until another force comes forth to oppose him, and in a mighty struggle hurls the heaven-stormer back to Lucifer.

Germany is today the next great war aim of Bolshevism. It requires all the force of a young missionary idea to raise our people up again, to free them from the snares of this international serpent, and to stop the inner contamination of our blood, in order that the forces of the nation thus set free can be thrown in to safeguard our nationality, and thus can prevent a repetition of the recent catastrophes down to the most distant future. If we pursue this aim, it is sheer lunacy to ally ourselves with a power whose master is the mortal enemy of our future. How can we expect to free our own people from the fetters of this poisonous embrace if we walk right into it? How shall we explain Bolshevism to the German worker as an accursed crime against humanity if we ally ourselves with the organizations of this spawn of hell, thus recognizing it in the larger sense? By what right shall we condemn a member of the broad masses for his sympathy with an outlook if the very leaders of the state choose the representatives of this outlook for allies?

The fight against Jewish world Bolshevization requires a clear attitude toward Soviet Russia. You cannot drive out the Devil with Beelzebub.

If today even folkish circles rave about an alliance with Russia, they should just look around them in Germany and see whose support they find in their efforts. Or have folkish men lately begun to view an activity as beneficial to the German people which is recommended and promoted by the international Marxist press? Since when do folkish men fight with armor held out to them by a Jewish squire?

There is one main charge that could be raised against the old German Reich with regard to its alliance policy: not, however, that it failed to maintain good relations with Russia, but only that it ruined its relations with everyone by continuous shilly-shallying, in the pathological weakness of trying to preserve world peace at any price.

I openly confess that even in the pre-War period I would have thought it sounder if Germany, renouncing her senseless colonial policy and renouncing her merchant marine and war fleet, had concluded an alliance with England against Russia, thus passing from a feeble global policy to a determined European policy of territorial acquisition on the continent.

I have not forgotten the insolent threat which the pan-Slavic Russia of that time dared to address to Germany; I have not forgotten the constant practice mobilizations, whose sole purpose was an affront to Germany; I cannot forget the mood of public opinion in Russia, which outdid itself in hateful outbursts against our people and our Reich; I cannot forget the big Russian newspapers, which were always more enthusiastic about France than about us.

But in spite of all that, before the War there would still have been a second way: we could have propped ourselves on Russia and turned against England.

Today conditions are different. If before the War we could have choked down every possible sentiment and gone with Russia, today it is no longer possible. The hand of the world clock has moved forward since then, and is loudly striking the hour in which the destiny of our nation must be decided in one way or another. The process of consolidation in which the great states of the earth are involved at the moment is for us the last warning signal to stop and search our hearts, to lead our people out of the dream world back to hard reality, and show them the way to the future which alone will lead the old Reich to a new golden age.

If the National Socialist movement frees itself from all illusion with regard to this great and all-important task, and accepts reason as its sole guide, the catastrophe of 1918 can some day become an infinite blessing for the future of our nation. Out of this collapse our nation will arrive at a complete reorientation of its activity in foreign relations, and, furthermore, reinforced within by its new philosophy of life, will also achieve outwardly a final stabilization of its foreign policy. Then at last it will acquire what England possesses and even Russia possessed, and what again and again induced France to make the same decisions, essentially correct from the viewpoint of her own interests, to wit: A *political testament.*

The political testament of the German nation to govern its outward activity for all time should and must be:

Never suffer the rise of two continental powers in Europe. Regard

any attempt to organize a second military power on the German fron-
tiers, even if only in the form of creating a state capable of military
strength, as an attack on Germany, and in it see not only the right,
but also the duty, to employ all means up to armed force to prevent the
rise of such a state, or, if one has already arisen, to smash it again. —
See to it that the strength of our nation is founded, not on colonies, but
on the soil of our European homeland. Never regard the Reich as secure
unless for centuries to come it can give every scion of our people his own
parcel of soil. Never forget that the most sacred right on this earth is a
man's right to have earth to till with his own hands, and the most sacred
sacrifice the blood that a man sheds for this earth.

A. J. P. Taylor

A Revisionist View

The late A. J. P. Taylor, whose books were contentious and lively, was a
fellow of Magdalen College, Oxford, and the curator of the Beaverbrook
Library. His books, including *The Struggle for Mastery in Europe, 1848–*
1918; English History, 1914–1945; and *The Course of German History,*
were provocative and well written and displayed a wide range of knowledge.
The Origins of the Second World War, from which this selection is taken,
was immediately praised and condemned. Taylor's critics argued that he
was apologizing for Hitler. But he replied that he was only attempting to
explain Hitler's success. In this book, as in his other works, Taylor stresses
human blunders as being more important in history than preconceived
plans. He downplays premeditation on the part of Hitler in starting the
war.

Hitler . . . changed most things in Germany. He destroyed political
freedom and the rule of law; he transformed German economics and

From *The Origins of the Second World War,* by A. J. P. Taylor, pp. 68–72, 102–104,
131–136. Reprinted with permission of Atheneum Publishers, an imprint of Macmillan
Publishing Company. Copyright © 1961 by A. J. P. Taylor; copyright renewed.

finance; he quarrelled with the Churches; he abolished the separate states and made Germany for the first time a united country. In one sphere alone he changed nothing. His foreign policy was that of his predecessors, of the professional diplomats at the foreign ministry, and indeed of virtually all Germans. Hitler, too, wanted to free Germany from the restrictions of the peace treaty; to restore a great German army; and then to make Germany the greatest power in Europe from her natural weight. There were occasional differences in emphasis. Perhaps Hitler would have concentrated less on Austria and Czechoslovakia if he had not been born a subject of the Habsburg Monarchy; perhaps his Austrian origin made him less hostile originally to the Poles. But the general pattern was unchanged.

This is not the accepted view. Writers of great authority have seen in Hitler a system-maker, deliberately preparing from the first a great war which would destroy existing civilization and make him master of the world. In my opinion, statesmen are too absorbed by events to follow a preconceived plan. They take one step, and the next follows from it. The systems are created by historians, as happened with Napoleon; and the systems attributed to Hitler are really those of Hugh Trevor-Roper, Elizabeth Wiskemann, and Alan Bullock. There is some ground for these speculations. Hitler was himself an amateur historian, or rather a generalizer on history; and he created systems in his spare time. These systems were daydreams. Chaplin grasped this, with an artist's genuis, when he showed the Great Dictator transforming the world into a toy balloon and kicking it to the ceiling with the point of his toe. Hitler always saw himself, in these daydreams, as master of the world. But the world which he dreamt to master and the way he would do it changed with changing circumstances. *Mein Kampf* was written in 1925, under the impact of the French occupation of the Ruhr. Hitler dreamt then of destroying French supremacy in Europe; and the method was to be alliance with Italy and Great Britain. His *Table Talk* was delivered far in occupied territory, during the campaign against Soviet Russia; and then Hitler dreamt of some fantastic Empire which would rationalize his career of conquest. His final legacy was delivered from the Bunker, when he was on the point of suicide; it is not surprising that he transformed this into a doctrine of universal destruction. Academic ingenuity has discovered in these pronouncements the disciple of Nietzsche, the geopolitician, or the emulator of Attila. I hear in them only the generalizations of a powerful, but uninstructed, intellect;

dogmas which echo the conversation of any Austrian café or German beer-house.

There was one element of system in Hitler's foreign policy, though it was not new. His outlook was "continental," as Stresemann's had been before him. Hitler did not attempt to revive the "World Policy" which Germany had pursued before 1914; he made no plans for a great battle-fleet; he did not parade a grievance over the lost colonies, except as a device for embarrassing the British; he was not even interested in the Middle East — hence his blindness to the great opportunity in 1940 after the defeat of France. One could attribute this outlook to Hitler's Austrian origin, far from the ocean; or believe that he learned it from some geopolitician in Munich. But essentially it reflected the circumstances of the time. Germany had been defeated by the Western Powers in November 1918; and had herself defeated Russia the preceding January. Hitler, like Stresemann, did not challenge the Western settlement. He did not wish to destroy the British Empire, nor even to deprive the French of Alsace and Lorraine. In return, he wanted the Allies to accept the verdict of January 1918; to abandon the artificial undoing of this verdict after November 1918; and to acknowledge that Germany had been victorious in the East. This was not a preposterous program. Many Englishmen, to say nothing of Milner and Smuts, agreed with it even in 1918; many more did so later; and most Frenchmen were coming around to the same outlook. The national states of Eastern Europe enjoyed little popularity; Soviet Russia still less. When Hitler aspired to restore the settlement of Brest-Litovsk, he could pose also as the champion of European civilization against Bolshevism and the Red peril. Maybe his ambitions were genuinely limited to the East; maybe conquest there would have been only the preliminary to conquest in Western Europe or on a world scale. No one can tell. Only events could have given the answer; and by a strange twist of circumstances they never did. Against all expectations, Hitler found himself at war with the Western Powers before he had conquered the East. Nevertheless, Eastern expansion was the primary purpose of his policy, if not the only one. . . .

In principle and doctrine, Hitler was no more wicked and unscrupulous than many other contemporary statesmen. In wicked acts he outdid them all. The policy of Western statesmen also rested ultimately on force — French policy on the army, British policy on sea-power. But these statesmen hoped that it would not be necessary to use this force. Hitler intended to use his force, or would at any rate threaten to use it. If Western morality seemed superior, this was largely because it was the morality of the status quo; Hitler's was the immorality of revision. There was a curious, though only superficial, contradiction in Hitler between aims and methods. His aim was change, the overthrow of the existing European order; his method was patience. Despite his bluster and violent talk, he was a master in the game of waiting. He never made a frontal attack on a prepared position — at least never until his judgment had been corrupted by easy victories. Like Joshua before the walls of Jericho, he preferred to wait until the forces opposing him had been sapped by their own confusions and themselves forced success upon him. He had already applied this method to gain power in Germany. He did not "seize" power. He waited for it to be thrust upon him by the men who had previously tried to keep him out. In January 1933 Papen and Hindenburg were imploring him to become Chancellor; and he graciously consented. So it was to be in foreign affairs. Hitler did not make precise demands. He announced that he was dissatisfied; and then waited for the concessions to pour into his lap, merely holding out his hand for more. Hitler did not know any foreign countries at first hand. He rarely listened to his foreign minister, and never read the reports of his ambassadors. He judged foreign statesmen by intuition. He was convinced that he had taken the measure of all *bourgeois* politicians, German and foreign alike, and that their nerve would crumble before his did. This conviction was near enough to the truth to bring Europe within sight of disaster.

Perhaps this waiting was not at first conscious or deliberate. The greatest masters of statecraft are those who do not know what they are doing. In his first years of power, Hitler did not concern himself much with foreign affairs. He spent most of his time at Berchtesgaden, remote from events, dreaming in his old feckless way. When he turned to practical life, his greatest concern was to keep his own absolute control over the National Socialist party. He watched, and himself promoted, the rivalry between the principle Nazi leaders. Then came the maintenance of Nazi control over the German state and the German people; after that, rearmament and economic expansion. Hitler loved details of machinery — tanks, airplanes, guns. He was fascinated by road building, and even more by architectural schemes. Foreign affairs came at the bottom of the list. In any case, there was little he could do until Germany was rearmed. Events imposed upon him the waiting which

he preferred. He could safely leave foreign policy to the old professionals of the foreign office. After all, their aims were the same as his; they,
too, were concerned to sap the settlement of Versailles. They needed
only an occasional spur to action, the sporadic and daring initiative
which suddenly brought things to a head.

This pattern was soon shown in the discussions over disarmament.
Allied statesmen were under no illusions as to Hitler's intentions. They
were given precise and accurate information by their representatives at
Berlin — information which Sir John Simon found "terrifying." For
that matter they could read the truth in any newspaper, despite the
steady expulsion from Germany of British and American correspon-
dents. There is no greater mistake than to suppose that Hitler did not
give foreign statesmen plenty of warning. On the contrary he gave them
only too much. . . .

The German reoccupation of the Rhineland marked the end of the
devices for security which had been set up after the First World War.
The League of Nations was a shadow; Germany could rearm, free
from all treaty restrictions; the guarantees of Locarno were no more.
Wilsonian idealism and French realism had both failed. Europe returned to the system, or lack of system, which had existed before 1914.
Every sovereign state, great or small, again had to rely on armed
strength, diplomacy, and alliances for its security. The former victors
had no advantage; the defeated, no handicap. "International anarchy"
was restored. Many people, including some historians, believe that this
in itself is enough to explain the Second World War. And so, in a
sense, it is. So long as states admit no restriction of their sovereignty,
wars will occur between them — some wars by design, more by miscalculation. The defect of this explanation is that, since it explains everything, it also explains nothing. If "international anarchy" invariably
caused war, then the states of Europe should never have known peace
since the close of the Middle Ages. In fact there have also been long
periods of peace; and before 1914 international anarchy gave Europe
its longest peace since the end of the Roman Empire.

Wars are much like road accidents. They have a general cause and
particular causes at the same time. Every road accident is caused, in
the last resort, by the invention of the internal combustion engine and
by men's desire to get from one place to another. In this sense, the
"cure" for road accidents is to forbid motorcars. But a motorist, charged

with dangerous driving, would be ill-advised if he pleaded the existence of motorcars as his sole defense. The police and the courts do not weigh profound causes. They seek a specific cause for each accident — error on the part of the driver; excessive speed; drunkenness; faulty brakes; bad road surface. So it is with wars. "International anarchy" makes war possible; it does not make war certain. After 1918 more than one writer made his name by demonstrating the profound causes of the First World War; and, though the demonstrations were often correct, they thus diverted attention from the question why that particular war happened at that particular time. Both enquiries make sense on different levels. They are complementary; they do not exclude each other. The Second World War, too, had profound causes; but it also grew out of specific events, and these events are worth detailed examination.

Men talked more about the profound causes of war before 1939 than they had done previously; and in this way these causes counted for more. It became a commonplace after 1919 that future wars could be avoided only if the League of Nations succeeded. Now the League had failed; and men were quick to say that henceforth war was inevitable. Many even felt that it was wicked to try to prevent war by the old-style instruments of alliances and diplomacy. Men said also that Fascism "inevitably" produced war, and there was no denying this, if one believed the pronouncements of the two Fascist leaders themselves. Hitler and Mussolini glorified war and the warlike virtues. They used the threat of war to promote their aims. But this was not new. Statesmen had always done it. The rhetoric of the dictators was no worse than the "saber-rattling" of the old monarchs; nor, for that matter, than what English public-schoolboys were taught in Victorian days. Yet there had been long periods of peace then despite the fiery talk. Even the Fascist dictators would not have gone to war unless they had seen a chance of winning; and the cause of war was therefore as much the blunders of others as the wickedness of the dictators themselves. Hitler probably intended a great war of conquest against Soviet Russia so far as he had any conscious design; it is unlikely that he intended the actual war against Great Britain and France which broke out in 1939. He was as much dismayed on 3 September 1939 as Bethmann had been on 4 August 1914. Mussolini, despite all his boasting, strove desperately to keep out of war, more desperately even than the despised last leaders of the third French republic; and he went to war only when he thought that it was already won. Germans and Italians applauded their leaders; but war was not popular among them, as it had been in 1914. Then cheering crowds everywhere greeted the outbreak of war. There was intense gloom in Germany during the Czech crisis of 1938; and only helpless resignation the following year when war broke out. The war of 1939, far from being welcome, was less wanted by nearly everybody than almost any war in history. . . .

The watershed between the two world wars extended over precisely two years. Postwar ended when Germany reoccupied the Rhineland on 7 March 1936; prewar began when she annexed Austria on 13 March 1938. From that moment, change and upheaval went on almost without interruption until the representatives of the Powers, victorious in the Second World War, met at Potsdam in July 1945. Who first raised the storm and launched the march of events? The accepted answer is clear: it was Hitler. The moment of his doing so is also accepted: it was on 5 November 1937. We have a record of the statements which he made that day. It is called "the Hossbach memorandum," after the man who made it. This record is supposed to reveal Hitler's plans. Much play was made with it at Nuremberg; and the editors of the *Documents on German Foreign Policy* say that "it provides a summary of German foreign policy in 1937–38." It is therefore worth looking at in detail. Perhaps we shall find in it the explanation of the Second World War; or perhaps we shall find only the source of a legend.

That afternoon Hitler called a conference at the Chancellery. It was attended by Blomberg, the minister of war; Neurath, the foreign minister; Fritsch, commander-in-chief of the army; Raeder, commander-in-chief of the navy; and Goering, commander-in-chief of the air force. Hitler did most of the talking. He began with a general disquisition on Germany's need for *Lebensraum*. He did not specify where this was to be found — probably in Europe, though he also discussed colonial gains. But gains there must be. "Germany had to reckon with two hate-inspired antagonists, Britain and France. . . . Germany's problem could only be solved by means of force and this was never without attendant risk." When and how was there to be this resort to force? Hitler discussed three "cases." The first "case" was "period 1943–1945." After that the situation could only change for the worse; 1943 must be the moment for action. Case 2 was civil war in France; if that happened, "the time for action against the Czechs had come." Case 3 was war between France and Italy. This might well occur in 1938; then "our objective must be to overthrow Czechoslovakia and Austria simultaneously." None of these "cases" came true; clearly therefore they do not provide the blueprint for German policy. Nor did Hitler dwell on them. He went on to demonstrate that Germany would gain her aims without a great war; "force" apparently meant to him the threat of war, not necessarily war itself. The Western Powers would be too hampered and too timid to intervene. "Britain almost certainly, and probably France as well, had written off the Czechs and were reconciled to the fact that this question of Germany would be cleared up in due course." No other Power would intervene. "Poland — with Russia in her rear — will have little inclination to engage in war against a victorious Germany." Russia would be held in check by Japan.

Hitler's exposition was in large part daydreaming, unrelated to what followed in real life. Even if seriously meant, it was not a call to action, at any rate not to the action of a great war; it was a demonstration that a great war would not be necessary. Despite the preliminary talk about 1943–1945, its solid core was the examination of the chances for peaceful triumphs in 1938, when France would be preoccupied elsewhere. Hitler's listeners remained doubtful. The generals insisted that the French army would be superior to the German even if engaged against Italy as well. Neurath doubted whether a Mediterranean conflict between France and Italy were imminent. Hitler waved these doubts aside: "he was convinced of Britain's non-participation, and therefore he did not believe in the probability of belligerent action by France against Germany." There is only one safe conclusion to be drawn from this rambling disquisition: Hitler was gambling on some twist of fortune which would present him with success in foreign affairs, just as a miracle had made him Chancellor in 1933. There was here no concrete plan, no directive for German policy in 1937 and 1938. Or if there were a directive, it was to wait upon events.

Why then did Hitler hold this conference? This question was not asked at Nuremberg; it has not been asked by historians. Yet surely it is an elementary part of historical discipline to ask of a document not only what is in it, but why it came into existence. The conference of 5 November 1937 was a curious gathering. Only Goering was a Nazi. The others were old-style Conservatives who had remained in office to keep Hitler under control; all of them except Raeder were to be dismissed from their posts within three months. Hitler knew that all except Goering were his opponents; and he did not trust Goering much. Why did he reveal his inmost thoughts to men whom he distrusted and whom he was shortly to discharge? This question has an easy answer: he did not reveal his inmost thoughts. There was no crisis in foreign policy to provoke a broad discussion of sweeping decisions. The conference was a maneuver in domestic affairs. Here a storm was brewing. The financial genius of Schacht had made rearmament and full employment possible; but now Schacht was jibbing at further expansion of the armament program. Hitler feared Schacht and could not answer his financial arguments. He knew only that they were wrong: the Nazi regime could not relax its momentum. Hitler aimed to isolate Schacht from the other Conservatives; and he had therefore to win them for a program of increased armaments. His geopolitical exposition had no other purpose. The Hossbach memorandum itself provides evidence of this. Its last paragraph reads: "The second part of the conference was concerned with questions of armament." This, no doubt, was why it had been called.

The participants themselves drew this conclusion. After Hitler had left, Raeder complained that the German navy would be in no strength to face war for years ahead. Blomberg and Goering pulled him into a corner, where they explained that the sole object of the conference was to prod Fritsch into demanding a larger arms program. Neurath made no comment at the time. He is said to have grasped the full import of Hitler's wickedness some days later, and then to have suffered "several severe heart-attacks." These attacks were first revealed in 1945 when Neurath was being tried as a war criminal; he showed no sign of ill-health in 1937 or for years afterwards. Fritsch prepared a memorandum, insisting that the German army must not be exposed to the risk of war against France, and took this to Hitler on 9 November. Hitler replied that there was no real risk and that, in any case, Fritsch would do better to speed up rearmament instead of dabbling in political questions. Despite this rebuke, Hitler's maneuver had succeeded: henceforward Fritsch, Blomberg, and Raeder had no sympathy with Schacht's financial scruples. Otherwise, none of the men who attended the meeting on 5 November gave it another thought until Goering found the record produced against him at Nuremberg as evidence of his war guilt. From that moment it has haunted the corridors of historical research. It is the basis for the view that there is nothing to be discovered about the origins of the Second World War. Hitler, it is claimed, decided on war, and planned it in detail on 5 November 1937. Yet the Hossbach memorandum contains no plans of the kind, and would never have been supposed to do so, unless it had been displayed at Nuremberg. The memorandum tells us, what we knew already, that Hitler (like every other German statesman) intended Germany to become the dominant Power in Europe. It also tells us that he speculated how this might happen. His speculations were mistaken. They bear hardly any relation to the actual outbreak of war in 1939. A racing tipster who only reached Hitler's level of accuracy would not do well for his clients.

The speculations were irrelevant as well as mistaken. Hitler did not make plans — for world conquest or for anything else. He assumed that others would provide opportunities, and that he would seize them. The opportunities which he envisaged on 5 November 1937 were not provided. Others were. We must therefore look elsewhere for the man who provided an opportunity which Hitler could take and who thus gave the first push towards war. Neville Chamberlain is an obvious candidate for this position. From the moment that he became prime minister in May 1937, he was determined to start something. Of course he resolved on action in order to prevent war, not to bring it on; but he did not believe that war could be prevented by doing nothing. He detested Baldwin's sceptical, easy-going policy of drift. He had no faith in the hesitant idealism associated with the League of Nations which Eden half-heartedly put forward. Chamberlain took the lead in pressing for increases in British armaments. At the same time, he resented the waste of money involved, and believed it to be unnecessary. The arms race, he was convinced, sprang from misunderstandings between the Powers, not from deep-seated rivalries or from the sinister design of one Power to dominate the world. He believed, too, that the dissatisfied Powers — and Germany in particular — had legitimate grievances and that these grievances should be met. He accepted, to some extent, the Marxist view, held by many people who were not Marxists, that German discontent had economic causes, such as lack of access to foreign markets. He accepted more fully the "liberal" opinion that Germans were the victims of national injustice; and he had no difficulty in recognizing where this injustice lay. There were six million Germans in Austria, to whom national reunification was still forbidden by the peace treaties of 1919; three million Germans in Czechoslovakia, whose wishes had never been consulted; three hundred and fifty thousand people in Danzig who were notoriously German. It was the universal experience of recent times that national discontent could not be challenged or silenced — Chamberlain himself had had to acknowledge this unwillingly in regard to Ireland and India. It was the general belief, though less sustained by experience, that nations became contented and pacific, once their claims were met.

Here was a program for the pacification of Europe. It was devised by Chamberlain, not thrust upon him by Hitler. These ideas were in the air, shared by almost every Englishman who thought about international affairs. . . .

Norman Rich

The Ideology of Expansion

Norman Rich, professor of history emeritus at Brown University, is a specialist in German history and a former editor of the German Foreign Ministry documents captured at the end of World War II. In contrast to A. J. P. Taylor, Rich argues that planning played a major role in Hitler's aggressions. Rich studies Hitler's program for expansion, the machinery used, the course followed, and the policies pursued in the countries he dominated. Hitler's scheming and plotting, Rich discovered, were affected by the knowledge that time was not on Germany's side.

Not the least of Hitler's crimes against the German people was his exploitation and perversion of some of Germany's most cherished values, notably the German veneration for a broadly conceived (and generally somewhat vague) ideal of humanist culture. Yet it was with undoubted sincerity that Hitler, the frustrated artist, paid homage to the German ideal of *Kultur* and made it the foundation of his entire ideological system. It was his conviction that only through culture was the beauty and dignity of a higher humanity, the only justification for the existence of mankind, to be attained. To clear away the obstructions

From *Hitler's Aims*, vol. I, *Ideology, the Nazi State, and the Course of Expansion*, published by W. W. Norton & Company, 1973, pp. 3–10.

to true culture was the aim of the Nazi revolution; to build on the healthy foundations of the past the goal of the Nazi renaissance.

But if Hitler was sincere about his admiration for culture (however perverse his own conception of culture may have been), there is also no doubt that he self-consciously exploited the cultural ideal to provide his followers with a moral impulse more edifying than a mere drive for political power, and a value to reinforce the emotional qualities of nationalism. In culture Hitler thought he had found a spiritual counterpoise to supernatural religions; and, even more important, an ideal he believed could overtrump the crass materialism of Marxism.

Indeed, the ideal of culture might have been even more effective than that of a classless society in transcending the narrow ideological boundaries of nationalism had not Hitler strait-jacketed his own principle the moment he advanced it. For in a concomitant proposition he maintained that only members of the Aryan race were endowed with the creative ability to produce great culture. The preposterous nature of this claim, instead of rendering the entire Nazi movement ridiculous, actually contributed to its strength, for it made Nazism something more than a political movement; it made the acceptance of National Socialism an act of faith — but a faith open only to Germans. For this reason, although the Nazi faith might concentrate tremendous moral energy in one group of people, the racial bomb would never explode with a chain reaction. By limiting the cultural ideal to the Aryans, Hitler had merely loosed upon the world another German particularist religion.

The assumption that the past and future of human civilization depended exclusively on the Aryans, that therefore they alone among the peoples of the earth deserved to live and prosper — this was the basis on which rested the entire superstructure of Hitler's ideological program, his concept of the role of party and state, his plans for the future of the German people. Race, far from being a mere propagandistic slogan, was the very rock on which the Nazi church was built.

Hitler never appears to have had any doubts about the literal truth of his racial theories, nor did his more fanatic followers. With greater objectivity Alfred Rosenberg, the self-appointed high priest of the Nazi movement, saw the difficulty educated people might have in accepting the racial doctrine, and he attempted to give it intellectual plausibility by calling it a myth — the myth of the twentieth century. But the racial myth, he hastened to add, embodied the essence of truth, and in an excess of analogical zeal he declared that the mysteries of the blood had overwhelmed and supplanted the old sacraments. Rosenberg actually acclaimed the particularist character of National Socialism and rejected universality as the intellectual concept of a decadent society. This can hardly have been Hitler's intention. There can be no doubt that for him the Germanic race, supporting as it did the entire complex of his values, was, from a spiritual standpoint, in itself universal. Herein exactly lay the implication of his ideas. Because the Germans were the only true creators of culture, because they were universal in a cultural sense, if followed that they had the moral right to be universal in a territorial sense as well; in other words, that they had a moral right to world territorial dominion.

Hitler did not dwell at length on the morality of German territorial expansion. After his many years of patriotic brooding on the subject, this was something he by now took for granted. What concerned him most at the time he wrote *Mein Kampf,* and in all his subsequent analyses of the problem, was the desperate immediacy of the Germans' territorial requirements.

As Hitler surveyed the international scene, the position of the Germans seemed grim. Across the Channel lay England, jealous of any potential rival on the Continent and perennial opponent of any effort on the part of the Germans to improve their position. But if England desired no increase in German power, France desired no German power at all. The French attitude toward Germany was founded on the motive of self-preservation. Only through the obliteration of Germany could France maintain its world importance. French policy would always be one of waiting to engage in the final destruction of the Germans.

Great as was the danger from France, however, Hitler believed that the truly vital threat to the existence of the Germans lay in the east, where a vast expanse of territory provided the breeding grounds for an inexhaustible supply of a particularly brutal species of humanity. These lesser breeds, separated from Europe by no natural barriers, had been held at bay over the centuries only by the bravery of the Germans, whose racial qualities had enabled them so far to withstand a numerically superior foe. But the peoples of the east, although inferior racially and lacking creative ability, could and did imitate German technology and organization. With their unlimited numbers, equipped with German-invented weapons and using German military techniques, it was only a question of time before these eastern masses would overrun the insignificant area to which the Germans were restricted. The exigencies of Germanic security could only be met by the possession of more land. Hitler examined the alternatives to territorial expansion and rejected each as he considered it.

The Germans could, Hitler reasoned, follow the French example and restrict the percentage of population increase by a wider use of birth control. But once propagation was limited, the natural struggle for existence which selected those who were most worthy to survive would give way to an effort to keep alive every human being that was born. The number of people would certainly be restricted, but the value of each individual would also be lowered. A people that defied nature in this way would some day be forced to give up its place to a stronger generation. To restrict the natural growth of the German population would mean nothing less than to rob the German people of their future.

Hitler next disposed of the possibility of solving the problem by the intensification of domestic production. Through industry and trade food could be purchased to support a growing population, but the First World War had proven to Hitler that an imported food supply was hardly a source of security to a nation. Real economic security could only be achieved by ensuring a people its daily bread within the sphere of its domestic economy. There was, however, a limit to the possibility of increasing agricultural productivity. In Germany higher living standards had already consumed the increased yield resulting from better farming methods, and the constant use of artificial fertilizers was beginning to burn out the soil. A further growth of German agricultural production, therefore, seemed out of the question.

Hitler was a thoroughgoing Malthusian in his fear of the time when it would no longer be possible to adapt the fertility of the soil to the increasing population. In the distant future, nature would have to solve this problem in her own way, but Hitler believed that in his own era only those nations would be in distress which lacked the will to secure for themselves the soil they required of the world. Should the Germans out of mistaken humanitarianism restrict their own expansion and thereby be forced to limit their population, they would be overwhelmed in the future by the sheer weight of numbers of inferior races who had space to reproduce without limit.

Hitler's decisive argument in favor of territorial expansion, however, was the disastrous effect of territorial deficiency on the German military position. It was not only a question of inadequate manpower. Hitler's study of military history had convinced him that a nation's strategic security was in direct proportion to its territorial dimensions. Military victories over nations restricted to narrow boundaries were always more easily achieved and more complete than over nations inhabiting a large land mass. As Germany was situated at the time Hitler wrote *Mein Kampf*, a coalition of hostile powers could not only defeat Germany. They could destroy it for good.

What was involved here, Hitler said, was not the fate of some insignificant Negro tribe; the German mother of all life was in danger. The threat embraced not simply a people, but world civilization. Greater territory alone could give the Germans adequate security for the present; only more land could guarantee their future. Since the rest of the world could not become German, the Germans would have to spread more widely over the rest of the world. This was not simply a moral right; it was a moral duty.

Hitler next addressed himself to the question of where the most practicable territorial acquisitions could be made at the lowest possible cost. Although a demand for colonies was embodied in the official Nazi party program, Hitler himself was convinced that overseas colonies could meet but few of Germany's requirements. The problem was not one of conquering and exploiting people, but of acquiring agriculturally useful space. The majority of so-called colonial territories were hardly fit for large-scale European settlement. Nor would overseas colonies provide the national security Hitler demanded of an expansionist policy. The Netherlands and Portugal were cases in point, and even Britain was no longer proof to the contrary. In admiring the strength of the British Empire, Hitler said, one was prone to forget its dependence on the Anglo-Saxon world as such. Not Britain's colonial empire but its fortunate linguistic and cultural communion with the United States was the real strength of its position. So for Britain, too, security ultimately resided in the resources of a continental power. Germany, which could not depend on American support, must seek its security elsewhere. Overseas colonies were for Hitler no more than a diplomatic and propagandistic weapon. He definitely rejected them as a solution to German needs. The struggle that would in any case be involved in the acquisition of territory could be carried out most suitably, not in faraway lands across the sea, but in the home continent itself. Through the conquest of contiguous territory the natural reproduction of the race, its bread, and its strategic security would all be assured.

Hitler then specifically named his intended victim. If one wanted land and soil on the European continent, the conquests of real value for the future could be achieved by and large only at Russia's expense. There was no question but that there had to be a final reckoning with France, but the defeat of France would be a hollow victory if German policy were restricted thereto. The elimination of the French threat would have and would retain significance only if it provided the rear cover for an enlargement of the German domain in Eastern Europe. National Socialism, therefore, consciously abandoned the foreign policy of the Second Reich. Germany was to cease its fruitless pursuit of a colonial policy and, above all, its drive to the south and west. The Third Reich intended to resume the Germanic expansionist program where it had stopped six hundred years ago, and to press once again over the routes of the medieval crusading orders into the lands of the east.

Hitler believed that fate itself had given the Germans an advantage at this point. In the surrender of Russia to Bolshevism, the Russian people had been robbed of that intelligentsia which heretofore had produced and guaranteed Russia's stability as a state. The Russian Empire was not an achievement of the Slavs, but rather a wonderful example of the state-building capacity of the Germans as leaders of an inferior race. According to the precepts of Hitler's theology, inferior nations with German organizers had more than once expanded into powerful state structures and endured as long as the nucleus of the constructive race maintained itself. As a result of the Bolshevik Revolution, however, the Germanic governing stratum of Russia had been destroyed and replaced by that ferment of decomposition, the Jews. Russia was ripe for Germany's plucking.

Hitler envisioned a German future based primarily on independent German landowners. The lands which in the past had been profitably Germanized were those which the ancient Germans had acquired by the sword and settled with German peasants. The mission of the National Socialist movement was to give the German nation such political insight as to see its future goal fulfilled, not in the intoxicating impressions of a new Alexandrian campaign, but in the consolidation of military victories by the industrious labor of the German peasant. The

Germans would thereby gain not only national security but social security. A nation in communion with the soil would no longer be subject to the restlessness that besets industrial societies and would automatically be freed from many of the social evils of the industrial age. Industry and trade would be forced out of their unwholesome positions of leadership in the national economy into the framework of a more balanced national life. Cities were to be decentralized and made the servants rather than the focal points of society. A people living close to nature and the real fountains of life, a people divorced from the artificial cultural flowering of city pavements, would form a stable society, rich in its appreciation of the real values of life, a sound foundation for true cultural creativity. Never should Germany feel itself secure until it was able to give each citizen his own bit of earth. To possess his own land and to till his own soil was the most sacred right of man.

Hitler had no intention of repeating the mistakes of the ancient Germans whose conquests of land had included conquests of people. The incorporation of non-Germans had in the past resulted in the cleavage in the soul as well as in the body politic of the nation which had been so disastrous in German history, and which had so long prevented the Germans from assuming their natural position of leadership in the world. To establish a sound foundation for German security, the acquisition of soil would have to be accompanied by the purification, by which Hitler meant the Germanization, of the population. In the many areas where Germanization would be impossible, the indigenous population was to be made useful, or removed. In this way alone could expansion be effected without diluting and thereby defeating the conquerors. It was only necessary to recall the suicidal example of the Spaniards, whose intermarriage with inferior native peoples had resulted in racial degradation and national decay. The British, although largely avoiding the error of intermarriage, were also pursuing a mistaken policy, for ultimately they would find it impossible to hold together an empire of three hundred million with a population of forty-five million.

Neither Spain nor Britain should be the models of German expansion, but the Nordics of North America, who had ruthlessly pushed aside an inferior race to win for themselves soil and territory for the future. To undertake this essential task, sometimes difficult, always cruel — this was Hitler's version of the White Man's Burden.

Hitler warned that the fulfillment of his program would require work and sacrifice on an unprecedented scale. The needs of the German race could only be met by pouring into their fulfillment the undivided devotion and entire energy of the German people. The entire authority of the state, too, would have to be dedicated to this end. All policies would have to be based on the consideration of the future security of the German race. To guarantee this security, and with it the future of world civilization, any and all means were justified. One had to make clear to oneself that this goal could only be achieved through fighting, and quietly to face the passage at arms.

There would be war. The attacker would have to overcome the proprietor. Professors and other intellectuals might talk of peaceful economic conquest, but such folly could emanate only from the wishful thinking of those unacquainted with life. Only naive idealists could believe that through friendly and civilized behavior a people might gather the fruits of its ability and endeavor in peaceful competition. Where had economic interests not clashed as brutally as political interests? There were those who pointed to Britain as an example of the success of peaceful economic penetration, but it was precisely in Britain that this theory was most strikingly refuted. No nation had more savagely prepared its economic conquests with the sword, and none had defended those conquests more ruthlessly.

Although Hitler looked to the east as the land of the German future, he realized that in all probability he would not be allowed a free hand there. The moment Germany was deeply involved in campaigns in the east, France would almost certainly seize the opportunity to fall on Germany's flank. The result would be a two-front war, which would be all the more dangerous because the French, by penetrating German land or air defenses in the Ruhr, could deal a mortal blow to the German war economy. To enable Germany to neutralize or eliminate the French threat, Hitler advocated alliances with Italy and Britain. For this purpose he was prepared to concede Italy hegemony in the Mediterranean and give up all German claims to the South Tyrol, and to abandon or drastically curtail Germany's colonial, naval, and economic rivalry with Britain. Hitler actually concluded an alliance with Italy and, as late as his attack on Russia in 1941, he clung to the hope that the British, recognizing how much to their own advantage was the destruction of Russia and international Bolshevism, might yet be persuaded to concede Germany supremacy on the Continent in return for a German guarantee of the British Empire and other favors.

By the later 1930s, however, Hitler had begun to take into account the possibility that his efforts to woo Britain might fail, and that a major drive to extend German dominion in the east would be opposed by Britain as well as France. In that event the danger to the Ruhr would be even greater and it would be all the more necessary to knock out the threat in the west before launching his drive in the east.

Hitler foresaw the possibility of a near future totally consecrated to the needs of war. During that period the abnormal demands of military necessity might exclude cultural tasks altogether, but the sacrifice would be justified. The cultural opportunities of a nation were almost always linked to its political freedom and independence. After the concentration of all endeavor in military affairs had won the required freedom, there would follow a period of compensation in which the hitherto neglected fountains of culture would flow as never before. Out of the Persian Wars had emerged the Golden Age of Pericles, and out of the tortured era of the Punic Wars the Roman state, too, began to dedicate itself to the service of a higher culture. So it would be with Germany.

The conquest of Russia was to be the first step. What would be required by Germans at a later date would have to be left to subsequent generations. The development of great worldwide national bodies was naturally a slow process. But of one thing Hitler was certain, and he concluded *Mein Kampf* with the thought: "A state which, in the epoch of race poisoning, dedicates itself to the cherishing of its best racial elements, must some day be master of the world."

When the Aryan race should at last have spread over the entire world, one might then think of an era of peace as an ideal. But it would be a peace supported not by the palm branches of tearful pacifists, but founded on the victorious sword of a people of overlords who had put the world into the service of a higher culture.

Andreas Hillgruber

Hitler's Program

Andreas Hillgruber, professor of history at the University of Cologne, finds
that Hitler's foreign policy eventually developed into a firm program that
he sought to fulfill. According to Hillgruber, Hitler's program aimed not
only at German rule over Europe but at world domination. He regards
Hitler not as an opportunist but rather as a ruler operating according to a
definite program.

Hitler's conception of his future foreign policy developed in many
stages between 1919 and 1928 before solidifying into a firm program,
to which he then single-mindedly adhered until his suicide in the Reich
Chancellery on April 30, 1945. What was at once decisive and totally
novel in the formation of his program — and this must be stressed —
was the complete permeation of originally crude Machiavellian objectives by the most radical variety of anti-Semitism. Although he drew
on the theory of the worldwide Jewish conspiracy as propagated in the
"Protocols of the Elders of Zion," widely distributed by White Russian
immigrants in *völkisch* circles in Germany in 1919–1920, there were,
in Hitler's case, crucial psychological factors. The wide-ranging political aims of Hitler's foreign policy were subordinated to a central goal:
the eradication of the Jewish "archenemy."

The full scope and thrust of the foreign policy which Hitler had
already set as his life's mission in the 1920s became clear only some
time after the Second World War with the enrichment of our source
materials, especially through the publication of Hitler's early speeches
and his "Second Book" of 1928. This documentation made it possible
to place the programmatic utterances of *Mein Kampf*, which previously
had appeared fragmentary and unrelated to the actual practice of the
Third Reich (at least in the years of peace) in the context of their origin

From *Germany and Two World Wars* by Andreas Hillgruber, 1981, pp. 49–55. Reprinted
by permission of Harvard University Press.

and elaboration. In time it became clear how systematically Hitler had pursued his aims after the mid-1920s without, however, forfeiting any of his tactical flexibility. It emerged that the sentence printed in bold-face letters in *Mein Kampf,* "Germany will either be a world power or there will be no Germany," was, quite literally, the crux of Hitler's program.

In brief, his aim was this. After gaining power in Germany and consolidating his rule in Central Europe, he would lead the Reich to a position of world power in two main stages. First, he would set up a continental empire that would control all Europe with a solid economic and strategic power base in vast stretches of Eastern Europe. Then, by adding a colonial realm in Africa and by building a strong Atlantic-based navy, he would make Germany one of the four remaining world powers (after forcing out France and Russia), beside the British Empire, the Japanese sphere in East Asia, and (most important to Hitler's mind) the United States. He anticipated for the generation after his death a decisive struggle between the two leading world powers, Germany and America, for a sort of world dominion. For this violent confrontation in the future, a battle of continents, he wanted to create in his own time the necessary geopolitical basis (the "sphere of control") for the anticipated "Germanic Empire of the German Nation." Failing this, as Hitler saw the alternative, Germany would inevitably be condemned to insignificance in world politics.

In his "Second Book," Hitler rated American strength extremely high, albeit assuming that it would reach its apogee only around 1980. He therefore saw the unification of all Europe under his rule as impera-tive, and an alliance between this super-Germany and the British Em-pire as desirable in order to challenge America later. By contrast, he held Russian power in extraordinarily low esteem. He believed that a Germany shaped by racial principles need not fear a potential Russian world power, as they should fear the racially "high-grade" Americans. "These people," he wrote of the Russians at a crucial juncture in his "Second Book,"

> live in a state structure whose value, judged traditionally, would have to be even higher than that of the United States. Despite this, however, it would never occur to anybody to fear Russian world hegemony for this reason. No such inner value is attached to the number of Russian

people that this number could endanger the freedom of the world. At least never [like the United States] in the sense of an economic and political mastery of other parts of the globe, but at most in the sense of an inundation by disease bacilli which at the moment have their breeding ground in Russia.

The conquest of European Russia, the cornerstone of the continental European phase of his program, was thus for Hitler inextricably linked with the extermination of these "bacilli," the Jews. In his conception they had gained dominance over Russia with the Bolshevik Revolution. Russia thereby became the center from which a global danger radiated, particularly threatening to the Aryan race and its German core. To Hitler, Bolshevism meant the consummate rule of Jewry, while democracy — as it had developed in Western Europe and Weimar Germany — represented a preliminary stage of Bolshevism, since the Jews had there won a leading, if not yet a dominant influence. This racist component of Hitler's thought was so closely interwoven with the central political element of his program, the conquest of European Russia, that Russia's defeat and the extermination of the Jews were — in theory as later in practice — inseparable for him. To the aim of expansion per se, however, Hitler gave not racial but political, strategic, economic, and demographic underpinnings.

By what method was he to reach this goal, so fantastic from the standpoint of 1928, but brought so close to realization in the turbulent years from the beginning of 1938 to the end of 1941? To understand Hitler's method one must assume that in the development of his schemes, as later in their execution, he had already come to terms, in a complex manner, with the real and imagined experiences of the First World War. Together with his prewar Vienna period and postwar Munich years, the war provided the politician (and later commander-in-chief) Hitler with his formative experiences. It made him recognize the impossibility of a German victory in a war where Germany was pitted against both the continental power, Russia, and the British Empire, let alone the two Anglo-Saxon sea powers. His memory was alive with the hopelessness of Germany's predicament surrounded by enemies in a Central European bastion — even one somewhat expanded by larger perimeters in east and west — in a world war in which the superior economic and armaments potential of the hostile coalition would ultimately tell. While holding firmly to Ludendorff's expansive principles of the latter phase of the First World War, Hitler linked these to considerations of power politics and geopolitical perspectives and drew his own unique conclusions.

In following a systematic foreign policy whose final prize was to be reached in several stages, the immediate objective had always to be limited to a single direction of expansion. The net gain of these intermediate goals (seen in both military-economic and strategic terms, with an eye to the great war expected in the future) was to bring Germany into such a favorable situation that a repetition of the Reich's predicament in the First World War would be forever excluded. The basic hypothesis of the politically and ideologically decisive phase of this program, Germany's "break out" to the east, was that Germany would defer colonial and overseas ambitions in return for British recognition of German hegemony over continental Europe (including European Russia), with the United States standing aside. With his typical equation of political with territorial interests in all great power politics (which he understood in terms of "spheres of influence"), Hitler was incapable of foreseeing any conflict with British and American interests in this phase of his program for expansion. "England does not want Germany to be a world power; but France wants no power that is named Germany," he had maintained in *Mein Kampf*. "Today, however" — that is, the period of the Weimar Republic in the mid-1920s — "we are not fighting for a world power position." Thus, for this period of struggle "for the survival of the Fatherland" (as also for the following period of German expansion on the continent) he deemed an alliance with Great Britain possible and desirable. Furthermore — and this is crucial to an understanding of Hitler's practice of foreign policy from 1933 to 1941 — the alliance was to take the form of a "grand solution" involving German dominance over the whole of continental Europe.

Hitler's ultimate aspiration in power politics, however, went well beyond this. To his mind, the achievement of German rule over continental Europe would itself provide the basis for a German position of world power. This position would then, in a new phase of imperialist expansion — with a view toward an ultimate war with America — be built by a strong German navy and a large colonial empire in Africa. If possible, this would be accomplished with England's acquiescence and at the expense of France, which was to be defeated before the conquest of the East.

The preliminary stage of the program, the winning of a broader base in Central Europe, was to be reached by gradual expansion of German territory and initially by peaceful means. Here the slogan "struggle against Versailles" and the exploitation of pan-German agitation in German Austria and the Habsburg successor-states provided the best opportunities to conceal the real, far more extensive aims. When these means had been exhausted, further partial objectives would be won through localized wars, using a qualitatively superior army against one enemy at a time. In addition to the political gains, Germany's meager military-economic base would thus be broadened to such an extent that the German-ruled sphere could withstand a new world war even with a comprehensive economic blockade by the sea powers. But until that time Germany's position would be vulnerable and a great, long war was to be avoided at all costs.

Only when all of these steps had been taken would Germany no longer need fear the quantitative arms and economic superiority of the established world powers, including American potential. Germany's military-economic and geographical base area, an armaments program geared to superior quality, not quantity, and Hitler's conception of "lightning war" (*Blitzkrieg*) were all closely related central components of his method. If despite such obviously difficult preconditions all the premises proved valid, Hitler believed that he would succeed in creating an autarkic, blockade-proof, and defensible sphere that would grant Germany real autonomy (and not just formal sovereignty) for all time. In short, he would create a German world power to stand beside the other world powers.

In comparison with the German war goals developed during the First World War, Hitler's aims were radically simplified; moreover, the racial-ideological conclusions drawn in his program, which were directed to a complete transformation of Europe along racial principles, represented something entirely different. True, purely in terms of power politics and territory, the war goals of the latter part of the war were not so different from Nazi expansionist aims. But to Hitler, the prerequisite for the establishment and maintenance of German rule over Europe was the physical extermination of the Russian ruling stratum and its putative basis, the millions of Eastern European Jews. In National Socialist ideology, this prerequisite was grounded in the mythical link between Bolshevist rule and Jewry. It was to be followed by the destruction of all Jews in the rest of continental Europe, subjugated, directly or indirectly, to German control. The diverse territories of the former Russian state were not merely, like the rest of continental Europe, to be brought into close dependence on Germany, but reduced to the level of colonies, to be exploited economically and settled by members of the ruling race. Colonialism, which in the imperialist era had been limited to overseas regions and suggestions of which had marked Germany's eastern policy in 1918 (and to a lesser extent the later Allied intervention in the Soviet Union), was now fully transferred to Europe.

These enormous schemes, and particularly their connection with racist ideology, were, to be sure, the program of a single individual. But in the case of such prominent provisions as the revision of the Versailles Treaty and the creation of a "Greater Germany," they overlapped with the aims of the old German leadership and the fantasies of a large part of the German public that had never assimilated the loss of the war. To this one must add, however, that the essence of Hitler's program "violated all traditions of German foreign policy and forsook all established standards and concepts to such a radical degree that it . . . did not penetrate the consciousness of the German public," despite its continual proclamation in his speeches from 1926 to 1930.

The experiences of the First World War had proved the impossibility of a German victory over a coalition of other great powers that, according to elementary rules of power politics, was almost certain to be formed in response to a German "break-out" to the east or west. Thus, only in an uncommonly narrow ideological perspective was it imaginable to achieve the ultimate objective of Hitler's program by taking on isolated enemies one by one and exploiting current and sometimes serious differences among the other European powers. This was unlikely to occur without the planned "duels" in the form of "lightning wars" provoking premature counter-actions on the part of other states and thus engendering an undesired, unwinnable general war.

Hitler's utterly unrealistic image of Russia can only be called mythical. It was devoid of any comprehension of the actual foundations of the Soviet system. He matched it with a one-sided idealized conception of England, in which only certain elements of British reality — the colonial and maritime traditions — were included. That component of British policy most important in respect to his program — Britain's interest in the continental European balance of power — was ignored.

Any German foreign policy based upon such misconceptions was likely to fail fast unless uncommonly favorable conditions in international relations provided a lengthy period for illusory successes. This was precisely the case in the 1930s as, in contrast to the period before 1914, deep antagonisms between Britain and Russia granted Germany a relatively large space for maneuver.

Hitler and the commanders of the German armed forces exchanging salutes, September 14, 1936. From right to left: Blomberg, Goering, Fritsch, and Raeder. (Bildarchiv Preussischer Kulturbesitz)

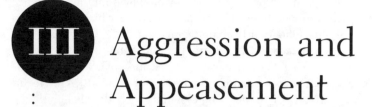

PART

III Aggression and Appeasement

Edward W. Bennett

The First Victory

When Adolf Hitler came to power in January 1933, limited rearmament had gone on secretly during the Weimar Republic, but the armed forces were inadequate for his ambitions. Meanwhile, a disarmament plan proposed at the Geneva Disarmament Conference called for a four-year freeze in armaments while testing disarmament supervision. If supervision proved successful, during the four years, all of the powers would disarm. Approval appeared certain. However, supervised disarmament could uncover German rearmament in violation of the Versailles Treaty. Hitler intended to rearm, not disarm Germany. Consequently he announced Germany's withdrawal from the Geneva Disarmament Conference and the League of Nations. In the following

From *German Rearmament and the West, 1932–1933* by Edward W. Bennett, pp. 475–480, 485, 488–490, 496–498, 502–505. Copyright © 1979 Princeton University Press, reprinted by permission.

selection, Edward W. Bennett focuses on the crisis over withdrawal. Bennett suggests that Hitler's decision to withdraw from the conference was strongly influenced by the Bismarck report, which was sent to Berlin by Prince Otto Von Bismarck, grandson of the Iron Chancellor and the German *chargé d'affaires* in London. The report stated that the British, believing that Germany was weak and isolated, were preparing to reject German demands for samples of weapons. This report strongly angered Hitler. In deciding to withdraw, Hitler challenged the Versailles powers: German national interests would not be subject to international agreements. This was Hitler's first victory in foreign policy. In December 1933, a secret conference of military leaders drafted a plan for a threefold increase in the size of the German army.

Hitler under Compulsion

We are apt to think of Hitler as always the moving force in the European politics of his time. But there is little evidence that he had intended, before receiving Bismarck's report, to withdraw from the Disarmament Conference. After receiving it, he waited for confirmation. On October 6, he approved guidelines for the German delegation that treated British policy as still uncertain. If the British submitted a new plan containing the basic French theses, then the delegation should refuse to negotiate on this and demand a return to the MacDonald plan, or to the original conference objectives of disarmament and equal national security, "intimating" that if this were not done, Germany would withdraw from the conference and the League. Hitler reserved for himself the decision on whether to carry out this threat. On the other hand (the guidelines continued), if the British presented new demands merely in the form of amendments to the MacDonald plan, the delegation should deal with these on their merits, in the light of the existing German position. Probably Hitler would still have preferred negotiations on the old MacDonald basis, under which secret rearmament could have quietly continued. Indeed, even if the report of the new British plan was correct, there was much to be said for staying in the conference and seeking to break down the opposing front, perhaps forcing a decision between the new plan and the MacDonald plan. This was the view that German diplomats tended to take.

But Hitler was afraid that conference debates might expose Germany as seeking rearmament. When he learned of Bismarck's report on the fourth, he emphasized that a conference breakdown over a German rejection of supervision or German rearmament demands "must be absolutely avoided." Again, the October 6 guidelines stated that a situation had to be avoided in which Germany would reject a series of points and possibly withdraw from the conference because her demands for "equal rights to armaments" were refused. In explaining his actions to his cabinet on October 13, he would stress the need to prevent other nations from exploiting the situation propagandistically against Germany. The recently stated German demands for arms, while quite in keeping with the principles of equality of rights and the right to national security, did indeed amount to a proposal for rearmament. If a debate on these demands took place in a general session of the conference, a series of denunciations of Germany would probably be made. No doubt many other nations would side against Germany in Geneva, as had happened in recent League debates on the Jewish-refugee question.

Further, not only were the German proposals vulnerable to attack; other governments might also reveal that Germany was already rearming. Blomberg had pointed out in July that there might be a call in the League Council for investigating Germany. Hitler demonstrated his own awareness of foreign suspicion and his fear of exposure, particularly at this juncture, by now ordering, on October 5, that the SA-Sport (or Ausbildungswesen) schools should drop the planned training in weapons from their courses, which were due to begin in about a week. This step presumably reduced the risks, but the abnormal inductions just carried out by the Reichswehr on October 1 doubtless provided other chances for disclosures. Moreover, Hitler probably learned from Blomberg about the report the Ordnance Office completed on October 7, on the charges of German rearmament appearing in the foreign press. The report showed that there was in fact a foundation for many of the foreign press charges, including that firms were producing unauthorized munitions, that tanks were being built on British patterns, that poison gas had been produced and had been stockpiled in Russia, and that German antitank guns now had real barrels, not wooden ones. The Ordnance Office described the disclosure of German tank production as "very unwelcome," noting that about 150 tanks were being produced.

Reports from Nadolny, now back in Geneva, also pointed up the danger that Germany might soon be placed in the dock. When he spoke with Boncour and Massigli on October 9, Boncour told him that the existing level of German armament had to be established in order to have a point of departure. Nadolny objected that they were there to conclude a new convention, not to check on the execution of the Treaty of Versailles, and Massigli retorted that according to French information, Germany had already rearmed more than the convention would ever permit, and was also violating the Treaty of Locarno (i.e., the demilitarized zone). Nadolny claimed that this was slander. On the next day, Boncour again told Nadolny that the current situation must be established and that the French dossier must be published, although Nadolny managed to divert the discussion to other subjects. . . .

Along with the reporting from Geneva, there now came Hoesch's account of Simon's October 10 statements, which arrived in Berlin on the morning of the eleventh. Now Hitler could scarcely have any illusions about the British viewpoint. And the British support of the French position made the diplomatic situation very hazardous for Germany, as she would stand in isolation. Aside from the risks of a public exposure of German rearmament, Hitler and Blomberg feared that informal negotiations might bring a series of piecemeal concessions, leading to an unsatisfactory final result, as had happened with the four-power pact. Hitler was on the defensive, and he would have to take the initiative if he was to get off of it.

Hitler must have mulled the situation over on the eleventh, and by evening he had apparently reached some tentative decisions. At 8 p.m. on October 11, Neurath sent a telegram to Nadolny advising that Germany would withdraw from the conference if, as Baldwin's speech and Simon's statements to Hoesch suggested, the British proposals for amending the MacDonald plan were incompatible with German equality. This warning, for Nadolny personally, also indicated that any statement on withdrawal would be made by Hitler in Berlin. This message to Nadolny seems to indicate that by this time Hitler had virtually decided on withdrawal, although he still kept open the possibility of changing his mind, if the situation should change.

That same evening, Simon, now in Geneva, repeated to Nadolny what he had told Hoesch, that the British cabinet had made its decision, and Simon added that this was dictated by public feeling against Germany. Nadolny, according to his own report, "pointed out in a very serious way the great responsibility which England took upon herself if she persisted in this attitude," thus "intimating" (as the October 6 instruction had directed) that Germany might leave the conference. But Simon held to his position. The next morning, October 12, presumably after studying the report of this conversation, Hitler ordered Nadolny to come to Berlin for consultation. Apparently Hitler and Neurath considered that Simon had been warned, and that, unless he now backed down, the occasion for withdrawal was almost at hand. Probably Hitler's main reason for recalling Nadolny was to avoid getting drawn into negotiations and unsatisfactory compromises, though Hitler may also have had some interest in hearing Nadolny's account of the Geneva situation so as better to plan his own moves.

Nadolny saw some signs of weakening and division in the opposition alignment, and before and after his return to Berlin on Friday the thirteenth, he tried unsuccessfully to dissuade Hitler from withdrawal. He does seem to have convinced the Chancellor that it would be safe and wise to await a statement by Simon, now scheduled to be made in the Bureau on Saturday morning, October 14. It became clear by the thirteenth that Simon would only sum up the results of the Geneva discussions, rather than replying directly to the German demands, or presenting an Anglo-French-American declaration, and Nadolny suggested that Simon might retract his "discriminatory" position.

Indeed, Hitler could hardly justify a withdrawal action until there had been a public report on the current position of the other powers. But once such a report was given, Hitler had an interest in announcing his withdrawal as rapidly as possible and from outside the conference hall, so as to forestall a session that might turn into a public trial of Germany. As he told his ministers, he wanted to capture world attention in a different manner than before; thus he would try to get away from the issue of rearmament. He would use the occasion to dissolve the Reichstag and the Land parliaments, conduct new Reichstag elections, and hold a plebiscite on his foreign policy. These steps would show the support of the German public for his "peace policy" — and in the process not so incidentally dispose of non-Nazi membership in the Reichstag and eliminate the parliaments of the Länder.

Hitler would also take the initiative by leaving the League as well as the Disarmament Conference. Aside from Hitler's dislike of the whole League of Nations machinery, and his (and Schleicher's) earlier warnings that Germany might leave the League, a departure from the League would show that Germany would not again, as in 1932, resume negotiation in Geneva under the cover of League activity. Germany would also, in effect, be serving notice that she would not cooperate with a League Council investigation or abide by an arbitral decision. In this connection, and because Britain and the United States did not support sanctions, as well as because of Daladier's attitude, Hitler could now at least feel fairly sure that France would not take the ultimate step of preventive action, in which she would find herself quite alone. Certainly, withdrawal from Geneva did not need to imply an end to negotiations — an end to the spinning out of talks while rearmament quietly continued. Instead, withdrawal from the conference could promote the transfer of negotiations to the bilateral format he much preferred, and a break with the League would help to ensure such a transfer. He intended in any case to use a recent (October 8) speech by Daladier as a springboard for further proposals for direct negotiation with France. . . .

The teletyped English text of Simon's speech arrived in Berlin at 11 a.m. . . . Hitler told a noon cabinet meeting that Simon would presumably strike a calmer note, but he added that the basic position remained the same; he therefore proposed to carry out the measures already planned. By this time, Hitler was doubtless set on withdrawal. . . .

Goebbels announced the withdrawal to the Berlin press at 1 p.m., newspapers in Geneva were out with the news by 2 p.m., and Neurath communicated it to Henderson by a telegram received in Geneva by 3 p.m., just after the Bureau meeting. The announcement surprised and disoriented diplomats and newspapermen. The counselor of the British embassy in Berlin telephoned Bülow at his apartment and asked excitedly if he or the ambassador could come over and get some information on the German withdrawal. The German embassies in London and Paris noted that although the newspapers the next day, Sunday, all reported the sensational news, they showed no evidence of governmental guidance. No immediate official response appeared from either capital, not only because of the weekend but also no doubt because both foreign ministers were in Geneva. The disarray in Paris was probably also aggravated by the fact that Hitler, in a radio broadcast on the evening of the fourteenth, made an unexpected and disconcertingly friendly reference to Daladier and to France. Hitler did not, in this case, carefully choose a weekend for his move. The German announcement occurred on Saturday because Simon made his statement that day. But Western disorientation on this occasion must have encouraged Hitler to plan later "Saturday surprises" to take advantage of the weekend holiday custom. . . .

Hitler had shown some hesitation in deciding on withdrawal, and he had mentioned the danger of sanctions to his cabinet on October 13, saying that dealing with this threat was only a matter of keeping cool and remaining true to principles. His remarks convey a forced, zero-hour bravado, and when, in his Saturday night broadcast, he made a public bid for Franco-German friendship and direct negotiation, he probably did this mainly as an extra precaution against a French reaction. Although the odds were favorable, the withdrawal was a gamble, the first serious gamble Hitler had taken in foreign affairs. But by the afternoon of Tuesday, October 17, it was clear that the gamble had succeeded. Then, with the confidence of hindsight, Hitler jubilantly told his ministers that the political situation had developed as was to be anticipated:

> *Threatening steps against Germany had neither taken place nor were they to be expected. Already in the note of reply sent to us by the President of the Disarmament Conference, the internal conflicts between the leading powers in the Disarmament Conference were evident. Germany could now let events take their course. No step by Germany was necessary. Germany was finding herself in the pleasant situation of being able to watch how the conflicts between the other powers turned out.*

. . . Like the British Colonel Nicholson in Pierre Boule's *The Bridge on the River Kwai*, Hitler had outfaced his opponents and established his ascendancy. He knew that he would soon gain a further psychological advantage by winning overwhelming support in a November 12 plebiscite on his foreign policy. The approval of 93.4 percent of the voters was to be obtained in part by coercion and falsification, but the announced vote was to give the impression that most of the German public supported a withdrawal from Geneva. Already, by October 17, the date of Hitler's jubilant cabinet statements, the successful diplomatic coup bore out the correctness of his judgment, as compared with the hesitations of Foreign Ministry officials. The success also strengthened Hitler's hand for dealing with Röhm and the SA, and on this same day, the Führer — probably with reference to his recent cancellation of weapons training in SA-Sport courses —

flatly told the SA leaders that the military training of their following brought a risk of disclosures to the enemy. Röhm reacted with a threat of barring his followers from training within the army, that is, from pilot courses for the projected militia program. But now, with Hitler's prestige involved, Reichenau could retort that Röhm's projected action would make the training of the SA in special courses pointless and the training in the Grenzschutz impossible — implying that the SA would lose its army instructors and indeed any role in national defense.

For that matter, Hitler's success also gave him new stature and independence vis-à-vis the Reichswehr leadership itself. Although Blomberg had apparently encouraged Hitler to withdraw, Hitler made the move in his own way, claiming to reject force, to seek disarmament, and to be ready for negotiations. Some Reichswehr officers would apparently have preferred an open assertion of Germany's right and intention to rearm. Ostensibly to avoid an impression of limitless rearmament — and actually, in all likelihood, to ensure an end to clandestinity and diplomatic hobbles — General Schönheinz had suggested on October 12 an announcement that Germany would rearm to a limited extent, along with a promise to destroy all arms that others might later agree to ban. In May 1934, in deploring proposals for accelerating the clandestine expansion of the army, General Ludwig Beck, then Chief of the Truppenamt, would write: "The failure on October 14 simultaneously to lay the card of rearmament on the table [i.e., alongside that of withdrawal] is least of all, in my opinion, to be made good in this way." The remark suggests that Beck and other officers thought Germany should have frankly and openly claimed its right to rearm in October 1933. But they had to do things Hitler's way now.

As matters stood in November 1933, however, the disunity of the West was all too apparent, and this encouraged great expectations in Berlin. Blomberg happily pointed out to his fellow ministers that the British press was showing sympathy for revision, and he suggested that each ministry should be preparing its demands; the Reichswehr's demand was simple, the removal of Part V. Encouraged also, no doubt, by reports from Joachim von Ribbentrop of his discussions with British leaders, particularly with Baldwin and MacDonald, Hitler's hopes for an Anglo-German understanding seem to have risen. Presumably with his sanction, Admiral Raeder told the British naval attaché on November 29 that neither the navy nor the politicians of Germany wished to build a fleet in competition with England. Raeder also expressed the idea, which he believed to be shared by the "political leadership," that, in view of the parity between the British and American navies, a squadron of German battleships, accompanied by a good Anglo-German understanding, might signify "a political plus for England." On December 5, Hitler himself spoke again with Phipps and, aside from answering some questions on his armament proposal, he stated that Germany must "be in a position to throw her weight into the scales at some future time, and, in this connection, might not Great Britain herself be glad of other alternatives to her present friendships?" He also hinted at an Anglo-German alliance by saying that the standstill he proposed for the "heavily armed" powers only applied to France, Poland, and Czechoslovakia, and that as far as Britain was concerned, "he would even welcome considerable additions to the British fleet and air force." Phipps could say nothing as yet on his government's views on Hitler's armament proposals, much less on the bids for an alliance.

Hitler Proceeds with His Own Plan

Hitler did not confine himself to arms proposals and bids for a British alliance; he now also secretly put the German side of his arms proposal into actual effect. At some date between November 30 and December 9, he approved the abandonment of previous Umbau plans, largely inherited from the Schleicher era, and ordered instead the actual development within four years of a twenty-one-division, 300,000-man peacetime army based on one-year service. This entailed sweeping changes in the peacetime forces and wartime mobilization plans. As far as land forces were concerned, the Reichswehr now dropped the idea — still not generally implemented — of three-month, so-called militia service in the ranks. The army also turned away from the concept of a uniform trebling in the event of mobilization, and instead proposed to mobilize two different grades of troops, thirty-two or thirty-three first-class field divisions and thirty "occupation" or Landwehr divisions: thus there was some reversion to the ideas of General von Seeckt. There would also be cavalry, armor, and other formations. For the time being, the Grenzschutz would be retained, although its future was unclear. Much more certain was the eventual introduction of compulsory service, which the Organization Section of the Truppenamt proposed to initiate on October 1, 1934. General Beck, however, wanted to draw on willing recruits so long as possible; those who didn't want to be soldiers would be placed in the Labor Service, where they would become potential second-class reserves.

The diplomatic situation in early December probably encouraged Hitler's decision to implement his 300,000-man proposal. There was little danger. Poland and Germany had jointly issued, on November 15, a declaration renouncing the use of force. This, the British willingness to negotiate, and Poncet's personal readiness for talks probably convinced Hitler that preventive action could now be entirely ruled out. With his proposals already known to other governments, their implementation, if detected, would show that he was not to be played with. If the execution of the new plan became publicly known, Hitler could still claim that his aims remained modest, and that he had had to go ahead to protect German security.

And there was little to gain by waiting. The British did not respond to Hitler's overtures for an alliance, and on December 8, Phipps passed on the view of his government that 300,000 was too high a figure. But Hitler probably took the British rebuff as a consequence of German weakness, and inferred that the British would only respect him and regard him as a worthwhile ally (bündnisfähig) after German armed power had been substantially increased. He probably concluded, too, that although France would not act against German rearmament, there was no chance of her agreeing to it, at least unless Daladier became Premier again. The Paris government had lately seemed to encourage anti-German press revelations, and on December 5, Boncour sent Poncet a message expressing flat opposition to German rearmament and to any bargaining for a cession of the Saar to Germany; Hitler may well have had a decryption of Boncour's message, from either French or British telegrams, when he was deciding to proceed. In view of the French attitude, Hitler probably now thought it a waste of time to await an agreement before going ahead with the 300,000-man plan. No diplomatic advantages could be gained by pursuing an outdated militia program, designed to maintain a pretense of continued German disarmament. . . .

The Road toward War

Perhaps ironically, just when Hitler was starting to bid for a British alliance, his arms proposals were awakening British leaders to the danger of German rearmament; even though they would continue to seek agreements, they would be unable in future to forget the German threat. Phipps's first report of Hitler's proposals, on October 24, was inaccurate and incomplete, and it seems to have attracted little attention outside the Foreign Office. MacDonald appeared to Hoesch to be unfamiliar with the proposals when they conversed on November 15. But after Neurath's November 6 speech, and especially after Blomberg raised the proposals again with Phipps, on November 20, the British began to study them intensively. On November 23, the ministerial committee on disarmament had a long discussion of the proposed 300,000-man German army. It was pointed out that these proposals in fact meant rearmament, and that (ignoring the cadre element) a German army of that size could mean, with short service, six million trained men in twenty years. This thought, and the general idea that Germany was rearming, seem to have come as new realizations to the ministers. They asked the military experts for an opinion, and the latter soon reported that Hitler's scheme would give Germany a peace establishment of twenty-five to thirty infantry divisions, and enable her to mobilize fifty to sixty divisions in wartime — an estimate rather close to the actual new German plan. The experts also described what they believed to be the current state of German armament, and although this estimate was well below the German reality, it was well above the limits of Part V An appendix to the report called attention to the (legendary) Prussian use of Krümper in the period from 1807 to 1813. But among the findings of the experts, what most impressed the ministers was not the prospective number of infantry divisions, but a calculation that the Germans already had 234 military aircraft and would have at least 400 by the end of 1934. In the interwar period, the threat of aerial attack inspired much the same terror as is now conveyed by the idea of a nuclear holocaust.

This fear of air attack cut more than one way. It meant, on the one hand, that Hitler's dream of an Anglo-German understanding could never succeed, at least as long as he claimed a major air force. His talk of racial brotherhood fell on deaf ears, or repelled, and his offers to forgo naval rivalry no longer touched the heart of British concerns, while the threat of German air power withered any chances of friendship. On the other hand, fear of air attack worked to weaken British land forces and to enhance British isolationism vis-à-vis France.

By the fall of 1933, Neville Chamberlain considered Britain strong enough financially to permit some strengthening of defenses, and in 1934, British ministers debated what should be done. They concerned themselves mainly with the threat of an air attack on England herself, rather than with the growth of the German army. Chamberlain and Sir Warren Fisher favored a stronger defensive air force, but to avoid too heavy a burden on the Treasury, they propounded two ideas: first, that Britain should avoid a naval race by reaching an understanding with Japan, and second, that Britain should renounce any preparations for sending a land expeditionary force to the continent. As Chamberlain saw it, trench warfare after 1914 had only led to a stalemate, and to a reliance on "financial, economic, and psychological attacks." It would be up to the French, presumably, to fight the bloody land battles. The ministers did not explicitly accept the Treasury theses — regard for naval tradition, for the United States, for dominion interests in the Far East, and for Belgium were too strong — and Chamberlain backed down in theory. But in practice, Treasury views prevailed through an assignment of priorities, and in the summer of 1934 the army's request for funds to meet deficiencies was cut in half. When an emergency defense loan was suggested, Chamberlain pointed to the political difficulty of forgoing another reduction in the income tax, and he gave a clear statement of his philosophy that no minister ventured to refute:

> *It was necessary to cut our coat according to the cloth. He regretted that the suggestion of a defence loan had been put forward, as he regarded that as the broad road which led to destruction. No doubt it would be the easiest method of finding the money since it put upon succeeding generations the onus of paying it. He hoped we had not yet come to that stage and would be prepared to pay our own debts in our own generation.*

Chamberlain also noted the lack of public support for an expeditionary force.

There was a gulf between British conditions and German, between Chamberlain's outlook and that of Adolf Hitler. After 1933, the German army, in effect, wrote its own budget as large as it wanted, while Hitler, who gambled on paying all costs by conquest, was to remark (as he recalled in 1942): "No state has ever gone bankrupt for economic reasons — but only as the result of losing a war!" Due to Chamberlain's policy, Britain could still have provided only two divisions in the spring of 1936, and this was a major consideration in the Rhineland crisis of that year. In late 1937, the British government was to decide against any continental role for the British army. Despite a belated reversal of policy, the adoption of conscription in April 1939, and a decision to form fifty-five divisions in September of that year, the neglect of the British army would contribute to the Allied defeat in the spring of 1940, and the expulsion of British forces from the continent. After the defeat and expulsion there would follow in turn Hitler's decision to attack Russia, the eventual Russian counterattack, the land invasion by American, British, and Free French forces, and the present division of Europe.

James T. Emmerson

The Rhineland Coup

Under the terms of articles 42 and 43 of the Treaty of Versailles, the Rhineland (the area between the Rhine River and the Belgian-German border and the German-French border) would be forever devoid of German troops and armaments. On March 7, 1936, acting under Hitler's orders, German troops remilitarized the Rhineland. Before the German soldiers marched in, the French government had decided against sending troops. French reluctance to oppose Hitler over the Rhineland pleased the British government, headed by Stanley Baldwin, who had no wish for Britain to confront Hitler. Attempts to negotiate the crisis collapsed.

The Rhineland crisis had profound and varied effects on Germany, France, and Britain, as James T. Emmerson explains. The Rhineland coup ended one of the last limitations on German sovereignty; it gave Germany a strategic advantage as well as economic and industrial benefits. For Britain and France the events of March 7, 1936, were shocking, yet they evoked a feeling of great relief that there had been no war. Later both

From *The Rhineland Crisis. March 7, 1936. A Study in Multilateral Diplomacy* by James T. Emmerson, pp. 236–248, 1977. Reprinted by permission of Iowa State University Press.

governments were condemned for failing to drive the German troops from the Rhineland.

Looking back over the events of March 1936, it is hard to escape the conclusion that there was only one winner: Germany, or, more specifically, Hitler. He had risked the most and been rewarded in kind. It would be difficult to conceive of a period between 1933 and 1939 when he as Führer and Chancellor enjoyed greater domestic popularity and support than during the months following 7 March. He had successfully restored full sovereignty to the Reich and smashed the last important link in the chains which most Germans believed had been responsible for their problems since 1919. Six months after the coup, ambassador Dodd wrote that 'an overwhelming majority' of Germans would support any venture which Hitler might undertake, 'whether it be one of outright conquest or one cloaked in the guise of expelling an invader.' As Hitler himself explained to Phipps, 'with dictators, nothing succeeds like success.'

It has been suggested that Hitler, because he acted on 7 March against the advice of the generals and diplomats, emerged from his Rhine triumph with a contempt for their advice and for them personally. But the evidence suggests that this was not an immediate effect. Hossbach, for example, has described in detail the cooperation which existed between the top military echelons and the Chancellor throughout 1937. . . .

The change in relationship which occurred as a result of the coup was in the form of increased respect which the diplomats and generals felt towards the Führer and, especially, towards his ability both to size up a situation and to await, rather than force, an opportunity for acting. Nor does it seem probable that the Auswärtiges Amt or Bendlerstrasse suffered any immediate decline in Hitler's estimation as executors of policy. By the same token, however, the Chancellor undoubtedly felt an even greater affinity in matters of policy formation for the advice of Göring, Goebbels and Ribbentrop, all of whom had encouraged him from the outset. He also emerged from the crisis with a much stronger feeling of confidence in his own judgment. These shifts, however, were not so obvious or dramatic as to discourage experienced observers such as Phipps and Vansittart, who had been attempting for nearly three years to strengthen the position of the moderates in the so-called struggle with the radicals for Hitler's ear.

The failure of Britain and France to react forcefully to such a direct threat to their security as the seizure of the demilitarized zone undoubtedly influenced Hitler's attitude towards the limitations of the opposition. The refusal of the Sarraut government to make good on any of its threats helped to convince the Chancellor that France would not risk an attack against Germany without British support. He also assured his generals at the Hossbach conference in November 1937 that the British would not participate in any war in which Germany acted against either the Czechs or the Austrians.

In the event, Hitler's assessment of Britain also proved accurate. But there are at least two reasons why it could not have been based too heavily on his experience during the Rhineland crisis. First was the distinction which the western democracies made between the unilateral repudiation of a treaty and an act of external aggression. Hitler had successfully employed this argument in 1936. But, as *The Times* had stressed on 9 March, the peaceful occupation by German troops of German soil was quite different from an act 'which carries fire and sword into a neighbour's territory.' The Chancellor was also aware that he had acted against articles 42 and 43 [of the Treaty of Versailles] at a moment of acute military weakness for Britain, whose meagre forces were largely occupied in the Mediterranean. Moreover, the British had already begun to rearm, which meant that considerations which worked to neutralize London in 1936 would no longer be so important in his envisaged attack on Czechoslovakia or Austria.

The most important benefits of the remilitarization of the Rhineland for Germany were strategical. The troops at the frontier could not have prevented the French from advancing into Germany, possibly even to the Rhine. But the psychological effect of their presence was real. And, given the state of mind of the French military, this represented a deterrent far beyond their actual strength, as illustrated by defence minister Edouard Daladier's assertion in November 1936 that as much as 80 per cent of the German army was concentrated on the frontiers with France, Belgium and neutral Switzerland. This new situation did not, however, allow Hitler to commit aggression. The Chancellor himself estimated that the army was still at least four or even six years away from being ready for war. The remilitarized Rhineland made it possible for Germany to prepare to commit aggression.

In the first instance, it permitted the eventual construction of fortifications, which, in addition to furnishing protection against attack, allowed the Wehrmacht chiefs to minimize the number of troops required to hold the French front. Not only could offensive strength be thus maximized, but any western attack would be more sudden, since German troops could be concentrated closer to the frontier. Even more significant was the fact that the restoration of military sovereignty in the Rhineland permitted Berlin to organize the Reich's industries for war. As long as the Rhine and Ruhr had remained so vulnerable to French invasion, it had not been possible to take full advantage of their capabilities and resources, which included 80 per cent of Germany's coal production. The action of 7 March enabled Hitler to launch his four-year programme, which was designed to mobilize the German economy for a large-scale war by the autumn of 1940.

Although the remilitarization of the Rhineland was widely regarded in Germany as having been an unmitigated success, the unilateral repudiation of the treaty of Locarno had brought certain disadvantages. These, however, were not those which Hitler or Neurath had anticipated. There had been no imposition of economic sanctions, as the Chancellor had thought possible. Nor had there been any 'automatic and general concentration' against Germany, as the foreign minister had feared. . . . But Berlin had forfeited her guarantees under Locarno from London and Rome, although this had been offset by Britain's desire for friendship and by her determination to exercise restraint on Paris. Furthermore, Mussolini had furnished tangible evidence of his desire to close ranks with Hitler by encouraging Vienna to sign a gentleman's agreement with Berlin on 11 July 1936 and by concluding in October a protocol which provided for Italo-German collaboration on such matters as the western pact negotiations, colonies and commercial policies in the Danube basin.

Perhaps the greatest loss suffered by Germany was to Hitler's credibility. Hassell, for example, believed that the coup had made everyone in Europe unwilling to believe in the sincerity of the Chancellor's assurances. But this judgement was made barely a week after the event, at a moment when distrust and anxiety were still at a high point. It is also difficult to know whether this sentiment brought many fresh converts to the ranks of those who already suspected the Third Reich of sinister intentions. In France it deepened existing fears, but did not do much to eclipse the neo-fascist movement. Nor did it prevent other

European states, including Russia, from entering into trade agreements, or from considering and even urging negotiations with Germany.

In Britain, Eden wrote scathing comments about Hitler's scant regard for international law and stressed that the Chancellor had exploded the myth that his government only repudiated forced treaties. He also warned that Berlin would break any agreement whenever it suited her to do so. But he, like most Britons, had been prepared to begin immediate negotiations in spite of any scepticism they may have felt about the value of German promises. It also appears that the foreign secretary was less affected by the *fait accompli* than by the Chancellor's subsequent refusal to make any gesture to facilitate the early opening of talks.

Eden later argued that Hitler's action had aroused resentment and created watchful foes. But there remained a great reservoir of feeling in Britain that Germany had still not been given her chance. Nor had Hitler been sufficiently exposed to prevent the Labour party in October 1936 from approving a resolution at the annual conference withholding its support from the government's rearmament effort. Nor was Labour MP Sir Stafford Cripps deterred from publicly urging that 'every possible effort should be made to stop recruiting for the armed forces.' Only a clear act of aggression or blatant intimidation could cause a significant hardening against the Third Reich. Once that had happened and people became acutely concerned about Hitler's intentions, the unilateral remilitarization of the Rhineland took on an importance in retrospect which had escaped most members of the British public at the time.

At the official level, however, the Chancellor's coup had a negative and lasting effect. This was manifested, not so much in the diplomatic as in the military sphere. Both Paris and London felt a greater need to press ahead with rearmament as a result of the Rhineland's remilitarization and Hitler's decision of 24 August 1936 to double the army's strength by extending military service from one to two years. The Blum government announced in September its intention to spend £180 million over the next four years on material for the army. This was followed a month later by cabinet approval of a plan to spend a further £50 million on the air force and in December by a decision to build five battleships and ten cruisers by 1943.

In Britain, the rearmament effort which was begun in 1935 had already been increased for 1936 by a further £28.5 million to £158 million. In April and July, supplementary estimates totalling £20 million were announced and in October the Conservative party conference unanimously carried a resolution that one-sided disarmament was more likely to promote war than peace. But, whereas the cabinet minutes from April onwards reveal a greater degree of urgency about the need to hasten rearmament, it was also clear that little more could be done until British industry had overcome a serious shortage of skilled labour and expanded its plant capacity to produce war materials.

The strategical effect on France of a remilitarized Rhineland was more apparent than real in view of the fact that her military leaders had already written off the demilitarized zone, and with it, apparently, any idea of aiding their eastern allies against German aggression. Indeed, many Frenchmen who originally had supported the idea of acquiring Czech and Polish divisions to help contain a weak and disarmed Germany, had by 1936 come to regard these same connexions as capable of embroiling France in a major conflict for a cause as remote to them as Danzig or the Sudeten Germans. . . . After March 1936, with German troops at the frontier, it would not be possible to expect as much of France.

The Rhine coup also forced the government to acknowledge that France not only did not have the army of its policy, but would henceforth be obliged to adopt the policy of its army. Since this was exclusively aimed at the defence of France, the loss of the demilitarized zone was of small importance compared to the effect on French security of Belgium's declaration of neutrality. Nor was any major effort made by the high command after the coup to remedy the organizational deficiency which had made it impossible to detach a force capable of launching an immediate and sustained offensive action. Indeed, the military manual which was rewritten later in 1936 still stressed, as it had in 1921, that modern firepower from prepared positions could withstand any attack almost indefinitely.

The German action of 7 March was heavily felt diplomatically, especially by those who believed that France's prestige and authority had been directly challenged. But, contrary to their predictions, the failure to act against Hitler did not start a gravitation of smaller powers towards Berlin. Most governments already understood the political implications for them of Germany's growing economic and military strength. They also realized that the restoration of full sovereignty to the Reich would give Berlin much greater freedom of action east of the Rhine. But in 1936, most European states were visibly relieved that Paris had not accepted the German challenge.

Although some observers may have detected a serious flaw in French resolve, it was not automatically or generally concluded from her refusal to march alone in defence of articles 42 and 43 that Paris would not fulfil her obligations if Germany attacked Czechoslovakia. Hitler himself was not entirely certain as late as November 1937 that France had written off the Czechs. The Sarraut government had, after all, brought Europe nearer to war than it had been since 1918. It was not so much France's performance during the Rhineland crisis as the internal chaos and industrial strife of 1936 and 1937, coupled with Blum's growing dependence on London, which confirmed to the British foreign office that France would not act as an independent force in east European affairs. Hitler's own assertion at the Hossbach conference that Paris would not march without British support was also based heavily on the domestic turmoil which he believed was capable of causing a civil war at any time.

On the positive side, the French people could be thankful that war had been averted. They also proved more amenable to increased armaments expenditure. The government, for its part, had reason to be satisfied that it had avoided a split with London and had retained Britain's guarantee. Moreover, Paris had laid the foundation, by the terms of the letter of 19 March, for the eventual creation of a defensive bloc which would have committed London to an anti-German alliance.

Her failure to bring this potential commitment to fruition, or indeed to persuade London to join in punishing Hitler, was primarily due to the refusal of His Majesty's Government to take any action which might bring war closer than 1939. Any such move would have had the effect of short-changing the foreign office in its efforts to 'buy time' for the rearmament programme. This consideration was paramount with Vansittart and the central department, as well as those members of the cabinet, such as Duff Cooper, who had already decided that nothing could prevent war, save perhaps Hitler's death or a miscalculation by the Führer which would give Britain and France sufficient time to become so strong that he would not dare to risk aggression. To them, the state of British public opinion was important primarily in so far as it affected the rearmament effort. 'We have heard far too much of this alleged public opinion,' Vansittart wrote in July 1936, 'and it has a paralysing effect.'

To most cabinet ministers, however, the prospect of crossing swords with the electorate was a deterrent to action only slightly less powerful than the so-called 'empty cupboard.' The British people, more than most, had succumbed to the argument that Europe had lived for the past eighteen years in the shadow of the treaty of Versailles. As a result, it was felt, Germany had never been treated on a basis of mutual respect and equality. The coup of 7 March had laid to rest the last important remaining clauses of the peace treaty which had restricted Germany's sovereignty. Never again would the leaders of the Third Reich be able to play so effectively on domestic and world opinion by alluding to the 'Diktat' of 1919. In this respect, the abolition of articles 42 and 43 was both a milestone and a blessing.

But this latest German violation did not evoke from the British people any desire for punishment. On the contrary, such measures were seen as part and parcel of the French policies which many blamed more than Hitler for the lack of stability and security in Europe. Nor did the unilateral repudiation of a freely-negotiated treaty alter the widely-held conviction that the leaders of the Third Reich might respond positively if London and Paris seized the opportunity to join with Berlin in concluding a general settlement which also removed Germany's legitimate grievances. Others agreed with foreign office economic adviser Gladwyn Jebb, who argued that the cancerous symptoms of Nazism would respond 'to the radio-active treatment of increased international trade.' Those who subscribed to these views were not necessarily Nazi apologists. But there still existed in Britain at this time an element of opinion which held that National Socialism was a revolutionary movement whose excesses were a tactic of necessity rather than a strategy of conviction. Now that success had been achieved, the Reich's sovereignty had been restored and Hitler was in firm control, the argument continued, the Führer would pass out of his violent phase and adopt a more conservative and constructive attitude, especially if he were assisted and guided by Great Britain.

Some cabinet members, including Baldwin and Simon, believed that Hitler would respond to the 'personal' touch and were therefore prepared to take him at his word when he declared that the Rhineland coup had brought the period of surprises to an end. Others were less optimistic, though hardly more willing to face the prospect of an early war. Neville Chamberlain, for example, suspected that Berlin was 'merely playing for time until she feels strong enough to make her next spring.' But both groups, along with their counterparts in the foreign office, were convinced that the British public would turn against Germany and wholeheartedly support rearmament only after Hitler had spurned a fair offer or had committed some other act of lawlessness for which no excuse based on discriminatory treatment could possibly be found. There are few indications that this stage had been reached even a year after the coup. At the same time, however, pro-German sentiment was never again as strong in Britain as it had been in March 1936. . . .

The remilitarization of the Rhineland had brought nearer the day of reckoning, if there was to be one, since it was considered axiomatic that Hitler would not commit aggression without first having locked what at that time was most generally regarded as his back door. But the date had been advanced by a minimum. His Majesty's Government had seen to that by refusing to be drawn into sanctions of any sort and by pursuing the effort to bring about western pact negotiations far longer than could be justified by Germany's attitude. This policy carried the risk that Hitler would conclude that his opponents were too spineless to stand up to him. But that was a chance which the cabinet and foreign office were obliged to take at a moment when the country was judged to have 'neither the means nor the heart' to tell Germany that there was a 'definite limit beyond which Britain would not go.'

The fear of setting Britain on a collision course with Germany had militated against the government becoming embroiled over the Rhineland violation. To take any punitive measures or adopt any other unfriendly attitude, it was felt, might destroy one of London's most useful assets in her efforts to gain time, namely, Hitler's interest in friendship with Britain. Nor would the foreign office recommend any action which might establish a precedent that would oblige the government to resort to progressively more effective — and dangerous — measures in the face of subsequent German violations of treaties or frontiers. 'We have got to be cautious, and not be carried away prematurely,' Vansittart warned in March 1936, 'or we may pay for it with our national existence.' This advice was to prevail for nearly three more years.

At least five lessons are clear from the events of March 1936. First, a nation interested in establishing or maintaining its position as a world or regional power must have the military capacity to support and enforce its policies. 'In foreign affairs,' Wigram once wrote, 'nothing is important but one's armed strength.' The dilemma and frustration created by the absence of such strength was revealed by Eden during the Abyssinian affair when he declared to the House of Commons that 'you cannot close the Canal with paper boats.' Equally important, a nation's armaments must be capable of performing the tasks which might be required by its leaders' foreign policy. Even more fundamental, potential enemies must not be allowed to gain any sizeable military advantage, either in terms of existing forces or, especially, in their capacity to produce war material. As long as a nation maintains its military forces and industries so that they can withstand the strain of rapid expansion and contraction, there need be no agonizing four-year lag, such as the British endured, during which the British foreign office was obliged to weigh virtually every diplomatic move on the basis of whether it would gain or lose time for rearmament.

The second point is that governments in democracies cannot afford to allow public opinion to get out of touch with the realities of the world. In the Rhineland crisis, the British government was not handicapped by public attitudes because the nation's armaments deficiencies reduced the alternatives to acquiescence. But even if the government had felt sufficiently equipped to join France in punitive measures, it is unlikely that the Baldwin cabinet could have effected any immediate reversal of the attitudes which had been developing for nearly eighteen years towards Versailles, Germany and disarmament. Uneducated opinion cannot easily or rapidly be changed unless the people can see the reasons clearly for themselves, as occurred after the Hoare-Laval agreement was made public.

The reactions to the remilitarization of the Rhineland also reinforce the validity of the observation that democracies will normally support military measures against what they regard as an internal affair of another country, even if it involves a breach of international treaty. Such action only becomes feasible if people are convinced that their own security or interests are directly or ultimately threatened. The absence of any concentrated or sustained effort to persuade the British people of the potential menace of Nazi Germany was probably the major shortcoming of the Baldwin government.

Another lesson is the importance of a sound economy in the conduct of foreign affairs. A country which cannot withstand the strain of a run on its currency or economic privation can ill afford to risk incurring international wrath. Britain discovered this during the Suez crisis in 1956 when the United States withdrew its support for the pound. Some twenty years earlier, the French did not even take the chance, partly for fear of precipitating a financial crisis which might have forced a devaluation — a decision which Paris was forced to make anyway, some six months later, as a result of internal weakness.

Finally, it is clear from the reactions to the events of 7 March that allies, both real and prospective, can dilute, as well as strengthen, the resolve of a nation. Most government leaders at this time accepted the view of their foreign-policy advisers, who, like Vansittart, regarded the German menace as a five- or even ten-year problem, which could and probably would become acute before they would be prepared to resist forcefully the realization of Nazi ambitions. Since France alone possessed neither the means nor the desire in 1936 to defeat Hitler decisively, the French government was obliged to discard any measures which could alienate her British ally and weaken the front against Germany. For their part, members of His Majesty's Government had concluded already that victory against the Third Reich would depend to a large measure on the material, financial and possibly even military support of the United States. This chain of ultimate dependence which stretched across the Channel and the Atlantic contributed to the decision to avoid a confrontation at this time.

As a result of all these factors, Hitler won in a walkover. Whether it was worth a *fait accompli* is less certain. In spite of German assertions to the contrary, the Rhine régime would almost certainly have been negotiated out of existence within another year or two. Moreover, the successful conclusion of such negotiations with London and Paris would have raised Hitler's political stature to statesmanlike levels. It would also have made it even more difficult for his opponents to arouse their publics to the threat which was being created, not only by Germany's growing military strength, but also by a system of education and indoctrination which glorified war and demanded total obedience to the Führer.

The abolition of articles 42 and 43 brought to a close the era of Versailles. What would happen next was still not altogether clear. But there could be no doubt that, with the disappearance of the demilitarized Rhineland, Europe had lost her last guarantee against German aggression.

Adolf Hitler

The Four Year Plan

As the German people cheered the Rhineland occupation, Germany entered a crisis of guns or butter. How to pay for the importation of foodstuffs made necessary by a failure in agricultural policy? Where to find the foreign exchange to pay for scarce raw materials needed in the rearming of Germany? Hitler refused to curtail the rearmament program in order to pay for food. Sometime in August 1936 he prepared a memorandum that contained his ideas on the crisis and his policy directive for a four year plan for Germany.

Through his four year plan Hitler aimed at an economy geared to a series of short, limited wars. Germany would fight these wars with first-line strength. Reserves would be limited. Hitler rejected stockpiling resources for a long, drawn-out struggle. Under the four year plan Germany would rely on domestic production in order to conserve foreign exchange for essential imports vital to armaments production. Hitler's time limit of four years was only a device to accelerate the armaments program, because he intended to launch a series of short wars very soon.

The Political Situation

Politics are the conduct and the course of the historical struggle for life of the peoples. The aim of these struggles is the assertion of existence. Even the idealistic ideological struggles [*Weltanschauungskämpfe*] have their ultimate cause and are most deeply motivated by nationally [*volklich*] determined purposes and aims of life.

Germany

Germany will, as always, have to be regarded as the focal point of the Western world in face of the Bolshevist attacks. I do not regard this as

From *Documents on German Foreign Policy*, series C, vol. V, published by the United States Government Printing Office, 1966, pp. 853–862.

an agreeable mission but rather as a handicap and encumbrance upon our national life regrettably resulting from our position in Europe. We cannot, however, escape this destiny.

Our political situation results from the following:

Europe has at present only two States which can be regarded as standing firm in the face of Bolshevism: Germany and Italy. The other countries are either disintegrated through their democratic form of life, infected by Marxism, and thus likely themselves to collapse in the foreseeable future, or ruled by authoritarian Governments whose sole strength lies in their military means of power; this means, however, that, being obliged to secure the existence of their leadership in face of their own peoples by means of the armed hand of the Executive, they are unable to direct this armed hand outwards for the preservation of their States. All these countries would be incapable of ever conducting a war against Soviet Russia with any prospects of success. In any case, apart from Germany and Italy, only Japan can be regarded as a Power standing firm in the face of the world peril.

It is not the aim of this memorandum to prophesy the time when the untenable situation in Europe will become an open crisis. I only want, in these lines, to set down my conviction that this crisis cannot and will not fail to arrive and that it is Germany's duty to secure her own existence by every means in the face of this catastrophe, and to protect herself against it, and that from this compulsion there arises a series of conclusions relating to the most important tasks that our people have ever been set. *For a victory of Bolshevism over Germany would not lead to a Versailles Treaty but to the final destruction, indeed to the annihilation of the German people.*

The extent of such a catastrophe cannot be foreseen. How, indeed, would the whole of densely populated Western Europe (including Germany), after a collapse into Bolshevism, live through probably the most gruesome catastrophe for the peoples which has been visited upon mankind since the downfall of the States of antiquity. *In face of the necessity of defence against this danger, all other considerations must recede into the background as being completely irrelevant.*

Germany's Defensive Capacity

Germany's defensive capacity is based upon several factors. I would give pride of place to the intrinsic value of the German people *per se.*

A German people with an impeccable political leadership, a firm ideology and a thorough military organization certainly constitutes the most valuable factor of resistance which the world of today can possess. Political leadership is ensured by the National Socialist Party; ideological solidarity has, since the victory of National Socialism, been introduced to a degree that had never previously been attained. It must be constantly deepened and hardened on the basis of this concept. This is the aim of the National Socialist education of our people.

Military development [*Auswertung*] is to be effected through the new Army. *The extent and pace of the military development of our resources cannot be made too large or too rapid!* Is is a capital error to think that there can be any argument on these points or any comparison with other vital necessities. However much the general pattern of life of a people ought to be a balanced one, it is nonetheless imperative that at particular times certain disturbances of the balance, to the detriment of other, less vital, tasks, must be adopted. *If we do not succeed in developing the German Wehrmacht within the shortest possible time into the first Army in the world, in training, in the raising of units, in armaments, and, above all, in spiritual education as well, Germany will be lost!* The principle applies here that the omissions of peace-time months cannot be made good in centuries.

Germany's Economic Position

Just as the political movement among our people knows only one goal — to make good the claim to life of our people and Reich, that is to say to secure all the spiritual and other prerequisites for the self-assertion of our people — so too the economy has but this one purpose. The people do not live for the economy or for economic leaders or economic or financial theories; on the contrary, finance and economy, economic leaders and theories must all exclusively serve this struggle for self-assertion in which our people are engaged.

Germany's economic position is, however, in the briefest outline, as follows:

1) We are overpopulated and cannot feed ourselves from our own resources.

2) When our nation has 6 or 7 million unemployed, the food situation improves because these people are deficient in purchasing power. It naturally makes a difference whether 6 million people

have 40 Marks a month to spend or 100 Marks. It should not be overlooked that a third of all who earn their living is involved, that is to say that, taken as a proportion of the total population, through the National Socialist economic policy about 20 million people have been afforded an increase in their former standard of living of, on an average, from at most 50 Marks a month to at least 100–120 Marks. This means an increased and understandable run on the foodstuffs market.

3) But if this rise in employment fails to take place, then a higher percentage of the people must gradually be deducted from the body of our nation, as having become valueless through undernourishment. It is, therefore, in spite of our difficult food situation, the highest commandment of our economic policy to see to it that, by incorporating all Germans into the economic process, the precondition for normal consumption is created.

4) In so far as this consumption applies to articles of general use, it is possible to satisfy it to a *large* extent by increasing production. In so far as this consumption falls upon the foodstuffs market, it is not possible to satisfy it from the domestic German economy. For, although numerous branches of production can be increased without more ado, the yield of our agricultural production can undergo no further substantial increase. It is equally impossible for us at present to manufacture artificially certain raw materials which we lack in Germany, or to find other substitutes for them.

5) It is, however, wholly pointless to keep on noting these facts, i.e., stating that we lack foodstuffs or raw materials; what is decisive is to take those measures which can bring about a *final* solution for the *future* and a *temporary* easing for the *transitional period*.

6) The final solution lies in extending the living space of our people and/or the sources of its raw materials and foodstuffs. It is the task of the political leadership one day to solve this problem.

7) The temporary easing can only be brought about within the framework of our present economy. In this connexion, the following is to be noted:

a) Since the German people will be increasingly dependent on imports for their food and must likewise, whatever happens, import a proportion at least of certain raw materials from abroad, all means must be employed to make these imports possible.

b) An increase in our own exports is theoretically possible, but in practice hardly likely. Germany does not export to a political or economic vacuum but to areas for which competition is unprecedentedly severe. Our exports, compared with the general international economic decline, have sunk not only *not more* but in fact *less* than those of other peoples and States. But since imports of food have, on the whole, hardly dropped at all, but if anything are rising, an adjustment must be found in some other way.

c) It is, however, impossible to use foreign exchange allocated for raw materials to import foodstuffs without inflicting a heavy and perhaps even fatal blow on the rest of the German economy. *But above all it is utterly impossible to do this at the expense of national rearmament.* I must at this point most sharply reject the view that, by restricting national rearmament, i.e., the manufacture of arms and ammunition, we could bring about an "enrichment" in raw materials which might then benefit Germany in the event of war. Such a view is based on a complete misconception — not to use a harsher expression — of the tasks and military requirements with which we are faced. For even a successful saving of raw materials by reducing, for instance, the production of munitions would merely mean that we should stockpile these raw materials in time of peace so as to manufacture them only in the event of war; that is to say, we should be depriving ourselves, during the most critical months, of munitions, in exchange for raw copper, lead or possibly iron. But in such a case it would nonetheless be better for the nation to enter the war without one kilogram of stocks of copper but with full munition depots, rather than with empty depots but so-called "enriched" stocks of raw materials.

War makes possible the mobilization of even the last supplies of metal. For it then becomes not an *economic problem* but solely a *question of will.* And the National Socialist State leadership would possess the will, and also the resolution and the toughness, to solve these problems in the event of war. But it is much more important to prepare for war in time of peace! In addition, however, the following must be stated:

There can be no building up of a reserve of *raw materials* for the event of war, just as there can be no building up of foreign exchange reserves. The attempt is sometimes made today so to represent matters as though Germany went to war in 1914 with well-prepared stocks of raw materials. This is a lie. It is not possible for any State to assemble beforehand the quantities of raw materials necessary for war if the war lasts longer than, say, a year. If any nation was really in a position to assemble the quantities of raw materials needed for a year, then its political, economic and military leaders would deserve to be hanged. For they would in fact be setting aside the available copper and iron in preparation for the conduct of a war, instead of manufacturing shells for that war. But Germany went into the World War without any reserves. What was available at that time in Germany in the way of apparent peace-time reserves was abundantly counterbalanced and rendered valueless by the miserable war-stocks of ammunition. *Moreover, the quantities of raw materials that are needed for a war are so large that there has* NEVER *in the history of the world been a real stockpiling for a duration of any length!* And as regards preparations in the form of piling up foreign exchange, it is quite clear that:

1) War is capable of devaluing foreign exchange at any time, unless it is held in gold, and
2) There is not the least guarantee that gold itself can be converted in time of war into raw materials. During the World War Germany still possessed very large assets in foreign exchange in a great many countries. It was not, however, possible for our cunning economic policy-makers to bring to Germany, in exchange for them, fuel, rubber, copper or tin in any sufficient quantity. To assert the contrary is ridiculous nonsense. For this reason and for the reason that we must safeguard the feeding of our people, therefore, the following task presents itself as imperative:

It is not sufficient merely to draw up, from time to time, raw material or foreign exchange balances, or to talk about the preparation of a war economy in time of peace; on the contrary, it is essential to ensure peace-time food supplies and above all those means for the conduct of a war which it is possible to make sure of by human energy and activity. And I therefore draw up the following programme for a final solution of our vital needs:

I. Like the military and political rearmament and mobilization of our people, there must also be an economic one, and this must be effected in the same tempo, with the same determination, and, if need be, with the same ruthlessness as well.

In future the interests of individual gentlemen can no longer be allowed to play any part in these matters. There is only one interest and that is the interest of the nation, and only one single view, which is that Germany must be brought politically and economically into a state of self-sufficiency.

II. For this purpose, in every sphere where it is possible to satisfy our needs through German production, foreign exchange must be saved in order that it can be applied to those requirements which can under no circumstances be supplied *except* by imports.

III. Accordingly, German fuel production must now be stepped up with the utmost speed and be brought to final completion within 18 months. This task must be attacked and carried out with the same determination as the waging of a war; for on its solution depends the conduct of the future war and not on the laying in of stocks of petroleum.

IV. It is equally urgent that the mass production of synthetic rubber should be organized and secured. The contention that the processes are perhaps not yet fully determined and similar excuses must cease from now on. It is not a matter of discussing whether we want to wait any longer, for that would be losing time, and the hour of peril would take us all unaware. Above all it is not the task of State economic institutions to rack their brains over production methods. This has nothing to do with the Ministry of Economics. Either we possess today a private industry, in which case it is its task to rack its brains over production methods, or we believe that the determination of production methods is the task of the State, in which case we no longer need private industry.

V. The question of the cost of these raw materials is also quite irrelevant, since it is in any case better for us to produce in Germany dearer tyres which we can use, than for us to sell [*sic — verkaufen*] theoretically cheap tyres for which, however, the Ministry of Economics can allocate no foreign exchange and which, consequently, cannot be produced for lack of raw materials and consequently cannot be used at all. If we are in any case compelled to build up a large-scale domestic economy on the lines of autarky — which we are — for lamenting and harping on our foreign exchange plight will in any case not solve the problem — then the price of raw materials individually considered no longer plays a decisive part.

It is further necessary to increase the German production of iron to the utmost. The objection that we are not in a position to produce from the German iron ore, with a 26 per cent content, as cheap a pig-iron as from the 45 per cent Swedish ores, etc., is irrelevant because we are not in fact faced with the question of what we would *rather* do but only of what we *can* do. The objection, moreover, that in that event all the German blast furnaces would have to be converted is equally irrelevant; and, what is more, this is no concern of the Ministry of Economics. It is for the Ministry of Economics simply to set the national economic tasks, and it is for private industry to carry them out. But should private industry believe that it is not able to do this, then the National Socialist State will succeed in carrying out this task on its own. In any case, for a thousand years Germany had no foreign iron ores. Even before the war, more German iron ores were being processed than during the period of our worst decline. *Nevertheless, if we still have the possibility of importing cheap ores, well and good. But the future of the national economy and, above all, of the conduct of war, must not be dependent on this.*

It is further necessary to prohibit forthwith the distillation of alcohol from potatoes. Fuel must be obtained from the ground and not from potatoes. Instead, it is our duty to use any arable land that may become available, either for human or animal foodstuffs or for the cultivation of fibrous products.

It is further necessary for us to make our supplies of *industrial* fats independent of imports as rapidly as possible and to meet them from our coal. This task has been solved chemically and is actually crying out to be done. The German economy will either grasp the new economic tasks or else it will prove itself quite incompetent to survive in this modern age when a Soviet State is setting up a gigantic plan. *But in that case it will not be Germany who will go under, but, at most, a few industrialists.*

It is further necessary to increase Germany's output of other ores, *regardless of cost*, and in particular to increase the production of light metals to the utmost in order thereby to produce a substitute for certain other metals.

It is, finally, necessary for rearmament too to make use even now whenever possible of those materials which must and will replace high-grade metals in time of war. *It is better to consider and solve these problems in time of peace than to wait for the next war, and only then, in the midst of a multitude of tasks, to try to undertake these economic researches and methodical testings too.*

In short: I consider it necessary that now, with iron determination, 100 per cent self-sufficiency should be attained in all those spheres where it is feasible, and not only should the national requirements in these most important raw materials be made independent of other countries but that we should also thus save the foreign exchange which in peacetime we require for our imports of foodstuffs. *Here I would emphasize that in these tasks I see the only true economic mobilization and not in the throttling of armament industries in peacetime in order to save and stockpile raw materials for war. . . .*

Nearly four precious years have now gone by. There is no doubt that by now we could have been completely independent of foreign countries in the sphere of fuel supplies, rubber supplies, and partly also iron ore supplies. Just as we are now producing 700,000 or 800,000 tons of petroleum, we could be producing 3 million tons. Just as we are today manufacturing a few thousand tons of rubber, we could already be producing 70,000 or 80,000 tons per annum. Just as we have stepped up the production of iron ore from 2½ million tons to 7 million tons, so we could be processing 20 or 25 million tons of German iron ore, and if necessary even 30 million. There has been time enough in four years to discover what we cannot do. It is now necessary to state what we can do.

I thus set the following task:

I. The German army must be operational [*einsatzfähig*] within four years.
II. The German economy must be fit for war [*kriegsfähig*] within four years.

A Strategy Conference?

Studies of Hitler's foreign policy at one time or another refer to a conference that Hitler called in the Reich Chancellery on November 7, 1937, spurred by a quarrel over raw materials. Other armed services accused Hermann Goering, Luftwaffe commander and director of the Four Year Plan, of taking more than his fair share. Hitler used the conference to discuss some of his ideas about future German policy. He called it "his last will and testament." Was he considering possible courses of action or was he explaining the strategy he intended to follow in the future? Was he daydreaming, as A. J. P. Taylor alleged? Three of those present for the conference — Neurath, Blomberg, and Fritsch — voiced criticisms of Hitler's ideas, and were soon dismissed. The only record of this meeting was composed some days later by Hitler's military adjutant, Colonel Friedrich Hossbach.

Memorandum

Berlin, November 10, 1937.

Minutes of the Conference in the Reich Chancellery, Berlin, November 5, 1937, from 4:15 to 8:30 p.m.

Present: The Führer and Chancellor
Field Marshal von Blomberg, War Minister
Colonel General Baron von Fritsch, Commander in Chief, Army
Admiral Dr. h. c. Raeder, Commander in Chief, Navy
Colonel General Göring, Commander in Chief, *Luftwaffe*
Baron von Neurath, Foreign Minister
Colonel Hossbach

Reprinted from *Documents on German Foreign Policy, 1918–1945*, series D, vol. I, published by the United States Government Printing Office, 1949, pp. 29–39.

The Führer began by stating that the subject of the present conference was of such importance that its discussion would, in other countries, certainly be a matter for a full Cabinet meeting, but he — the Führer — had rejected the idea of making it a subject of discussion before the wider circle of the Reich Cabinet just because of the importance of the matter. His exposition to follow was the fruit of thorough deliberation and the experiences of his 4½ years of power. He wished to explain to the gentlemen present his basic ideas concerning the opportunities for the development of our position in the field of foreign affairs and its requirements, and he asked, in the interests of a long-term German policy, that his exposition be regarded, in the event of his death, as his last will and testament.

The Führer then continued:

The aim of German policy was to make secure and to preserve the racial community [*Volksmasse*] and to enlarge it. It was therefore a question of space.

The German racial community comprised over 85 million people and, because of their number and the narrow limits of habitable space in Europe, constituted a tightly packed racial core such as was not to be met in any other country and such as implied the right to a greater living space than in the case of other peoples. If, territorially speaking, there existed no political result corresponding to this German racial core, that was a consequence of centuries of historical development, and in the continuance of these political conditions lay the greatest danger to the preservation of the German race at its present peak. To arrest the decline of Germanism [*Deutschtum*] in Austria and Czechoslovakia was as little possible as to maintain the present level in Germany itself. Instead of increase, sterility was setting in, and in its train disorders of a social character must arise in course of time, since political and ideological ideas remain effective only so long as they furnish the basis for the realization of the essential vital demands of a people. Germany's future was therefore wholly conditional upon the solving of the need for space, and such a solution could be sought, of course, only for a foreseeable period of about one to three generations.

Before turning to the question of solving the need for space, it had to be considered whether a solution holding promise for the future was to be reached by means of autarchy or by means of an increased participation in world economy.

Autarchy

Achievement only possible under strict National Socialist leadership of the State, which is assumed; accepting its achievement as possible, the following could be stated as results:

A. In the field of raw materials only limited, not total, autarchy.
   1. In regard to coal, so far as it could be considered as a source of raw materials, autarchy was possible.
   2. But even as regards ores, the position was much more difficult. Iron requirements can be met from home resources and similarly with light metals, but with other raw materials — copper, tin — this was not the case.
   3. Synthetic textile requirements can be met from home resources to the limit of timber supplies. A permanent solution impossible.
   4. Edible fats — possible.
B. In the field of food the question of autarchy was to be answered by a flat "No."

   With the general rise in the standard of living compared with that of 30 to 40 years ago, there has gone hand in hand an increased demand and an increased home consumption even on the part of the producers, the farmers. The fruits of the increased agricultural production had all gone to meet the increased demand, and so did not represent an absolute production increase. A further increase in production by making greater demands on the soil, which already, in consequence of the use of artificial fertilizers, was showing signs of exhaustion, was hardly possible, and it was therefore certain that even with the maximum increase in production, participation in world trade was unavoidable. The not inconsiderable expenditure of foreign exchange to insure food supplies by imports, even when harvests were good, grew to catastrophic proportions with bad harvests. The possibility of a disaster grew in proportion to the increase in population, in which, too, the excess of births of 560,000 annually produced, as a consequence, an even further increase in bread consumption, since a child was a greater bread consumer than an adult.
   It was not possible over the long run, in a continent enjoying a practically common standard of living, to meet the food supply difficulties by lowering that standard and by rationalization. Since, with the

solving of the unemployment problem, the maximum consumption level had been reached, some minor modifications in our home agricultural production might still, no doubt, be possible, but no fundamental alteration was possible in our basic food position. Thus autarchy was untenable in regard both to food and to the economy as a whole.

Participation in World Economy

To this there were limitations which we were unable to remove. The establishment of Germany's position on a secure and sound foundation was obstructed by market fluctuations, and commercial treaties afforded no guarantee for actual execution. In particular it had to be remembered that since the World War, those very countries which had formerly been food exporters had become industrialized. We were living in an age of economic empires in which the primitive urge to colonization was again manifesting itself; in the cases of Japan and Italy economic motives underlay the urge for expansion, and with Germany, too, economic need would supply the stimulus. For countries outside the great economic empires, opportunities for economic expansion were severely impeded.

The boom in world economy caused by the economic effects of rearmament could never form the basis of a sound economy over a long period, and the latter was obstructed above all also by the economic disturbances resulting from Bolshevism. There was a pronounced military weakness in those states which depended for their existence on foreign trade. As our foreign trade was carried on over the sea routes dominated by Britain, it was more a question of security of transport than one of foreign exchange, which revealed, in time of war, the full weakness of our food situation. The only remedy, and one which might appear to us as visionary, lay in the acquisition of greater living space — a quest which has at all times been the origin of the formation of states and of the migration of peoples. That this quest met with no interest at Geneva or among the satiated nations was understandable. If, then, we accept the security of our food situation as the principal question, the space necessary to insure it can only be sought in Europe, not, as in the liberal capitalist view, in the exploitation of colonies. It is not a matter of acquiring population but of gaining space for agricultural use. Moreover, areas producing raw materials can be more usefully sought in Europe in immediate proximity to the Reich, than overseas; the solution thus obtained must suffice for one or two generations. Whatever else might prove necessary later must be left to succeeding generations to deal with. The development of great world political constellations progressed but slowly after all, and the German people with its strong racial core would find the most favorable prerequisites for such achievement in the heart of the continent of Europe. The history of all ages — the Roman Empire and the British Empire — had proved that expansion could only be carried out by breaking down resistance and taking risks; setbacks were inevitable. There had never in former times been spaces without a master, and there were none today; the attacker always comes up against a possessor.

The question for Germany ran: where could she achieve the greatest gain at the lowest cost.

German policy had to reckon with two hate-inspired antagonists, Britain and France, to whom a German colossus in the center of Europe was a thorn in the flesh, and both countries were opposed to any further strengthening of Germany's position either in Europe or overseas; in support of this opposition they were able to count on the agreement of all their political parties. Both countries saw in the establishment of German military bases overseas a threat to their own communications, a safeguarding of German commerce, and, as a consequence, a strengthening of Germany's position in Europe.

Because of opposition of the Dominions, Britain could not cede any of her colonial possessions to us. After England's loss of prestige through the passing of Abyssinia into Italian possession, the return of East Africa was not to be expected. British concessions could at best be expressed in an offer to satisfy our colonial demands by the appropriation of colonies which were not British possessions — e.g., Angola. French concessions would probably take a similar line.

Serious discussion of the question of the return of colonies to us could only be considered at a moment when Britain was in difficulties and the German Reich armed and strong. The Führer did not share the view that the Empire was unshakable. Opposition to the Empire was to be found less in the countries conquered than among her competitors. The British Empire and the Roman Empire could not be compared in respect of permanence; the latter was not confronted by any powerful political rival of a serious order after the Punic Wars. It was only the disintegrating effect of Christianity, and the symptoms of age which appear in every country, which caused ancient Rome to succumb to the onslaught of the Germans.

Beside the British Empire there existed today a number of states stronger than she. The British motherland was able to protect her colonial possessions not by her own power, but only in alliance with other states. How, for instance, could Britain alone defend Canada against attack by America, or her Far Eastern interests against attack by Japan!

The emphasis on the British Crown as the symbol of the unity of the Empire was already an admission that, in the long run, the Empire could not maintain its position by power politics. Significant indications of this were:

a. The struggle of Ireland for independence.
b. The constitutional struggles in India, where Britain's half measures had given to the Indians the opportunity of using later on as a weapon against Britain, the nonfulfillment of her promises regarding a constitution.
c. The weakening by Japan of Britain's position in the Far East.
d. The rivalry in the Mediterranean with Italy who — under the spell of her history, driven by necessity and led by a genius — was expanding her power position, and thus was inevitably coming more and more into conflict with British interests. The outcome of the Abyssinian War was a loss of prestige for Britain which Italy was striving to increase by stirring up trouble in the Mohammedan world.

To sum up, it could be stated that, with 45 million Britons, in spite of its theoretical soundness, the position of the Empire could not in the long run be maintained by power politics. The ratio of the population of the Empire to that of the motherland of 9 : 1, was a warning to us not, in our territorial expansion, to allow the foundation constituted by the numerical strength of our own people to become too weak.

France's position was more favorable than that of Britain. The French Empire was better placed territorially; the inhabitants of her colonial possessions represented a supplement to her military strength. But France was going to be confronted with internal political difficulties. In a nation's life about 10 percent of its span is taken up by parliamentary forms of government and about 90 percent by authoritarian forms. Today, nonetheless, Britain, France, Russia, and the smaller states adjoining them, must be included as factors [*Machtfaktoren*] in our political calculations.

Germany's problem could only be solved by means of force and this was never without attendant risk. The campaigns of Frederick the Great for Silesia and Bismarck's wars against Austria and France had involved unheard-of risk, and the swiftness of the Prussian action in 1870 had kept Austria from entering the war. If one accepts as the basis of the following exposition the resort to force with its attendant risks, then there remain still to be answered the questions "when" and "how." In this matter there were three cases [*Fälle*] to be dealt with:

Case 1: Period 1943–1945

After this date only a change for the worse, from our point of view, could be expected.

The equipment of the army, navy, and *Luftwaffe*, as well as the formation of the officer corps, was nearly completed. Equipment and armament were modern; in further delay there lay the danger of their obsolescence. In particular, the secrecy of "special weapons" could not be preserved forever. The recruiting of reserves was limited to current age groups; further drafts from older untrained age groups were no longer available.

Our relative strength would decrease in relation to the rearmament which would by then have been carried out by the rest of the world. If we did not act by 1943–1945, any year could, in consequence of a lack of reserves, produce the food crisis, to cope with which the necessary foreign exchange was not available, and this must be regarded as a "waning point of the regime." Besides, the world was expecting our attack and was increasing its counter-measures from year to year. It was while the rest of the world was still preparing its defenses [*sich abriegele*] that we were obliged to take the offensive.

Nobody knew today what the situation would be in the years 1943–1945. One thing only was certain, that we could not wait longer.

On the one hand there was the great *Wehrmacht*, and the necessity of maintaining it at its present level, the aging of the movement and of its leaders; and on the other, the prospect of a lowering of the standard of living and of a limitation of the birth rate, which left no choice but to act. If the Führer was still living, it was his unalterable resolve to solve Germany's problem of space at the latest by 1943–1945. The necessity for action before 1943–1945 would arise in cases 2 and 3.

Case 2

If internal strife in France should develop into such a domestic crisis as to absorb the French Army completely and render it incapable of use for war against Germany, then the time for action against the Czechs had come.

Case 3

If France is so embroiled by a war with another state that she cannot "proceed" against Germany.

For the improvement of our politico-military position our first objective, in the event of our being embroiled in war, must be to overthrow Czechoslovakia and Austria simultaneously in order to remove the threat to our flank in any possible operation against the West. In a conflict with France it was hardly to be regarded as likely that the Czechs would declare war on us on the very same day as France. The desire to join in the war would, however, increase among the Czechs in proportion to any weakening on our part and then her participation could clearly take the form of an attack toward Silesia, toward the north or toward the west.

If the Czechs were overthrown and a common German-Hungarian frontier achieved, a neutral attitude on the part of Poland could be the more certainly counted on in the event of a Franco-German conflict. Our agreements with Poland only retained their force as long as Germany's strength remained unshaken. In the event of German setbacks a Polish action against East Prussia, and possibly against Pomerania and Silesia as well, had to be reckoned with.

On the assumption of a development of the situation leading to action on our part as planned, in the years 1943–1945, the attitude of France, Britain, Italy, Poland, and Russia could probably be estimated as follows:

Actually, the Führer believed that almost certainly Britain, and probably France as well, had already tacitly written off the Czechs and were reconciled to the fact that this question would be cleared up in due course by Germany. Difficulties connected with the Empire, and the prospect of being once more entangled in a protracted European War, were decisive considerations for Britain against participation in a war against Germany. Britain's attitude would certainly not be without influence on that of France. An attack by France without British support, and with the prospect of the offensive being brought to a standstill on our western fortifications, was hardly probable. Nor was a French march through Belgium and Holland without British support to be expected; this also was a course not to be contemplated by us in the event of a conflict with France, because it would certainly entail the hostility of Britain. It would of course be necessary to maintain a strong defense [*eine Abriegelung*] on our western frontier during the prosecution of our attack on the Czechs and Austria. And in this connection it had to be remembered that the defense measures of the Czechs were growing in strength from year to year, and that the actual worth of the Austrian Army also was increasing in the course of time. Even though the populations concerned, especially of Czechoslovakia, were not sparse, the annexation of Czechoslovakia and Austria would mean an acquisition of foodstuffs for 5 to 6 million people, on the assumption that the compulsory emigration of 2 million people from Czechoslovakia and 1 million people from Austria was practicable. The incorporation of these two States with Germany meant, from the politico-military point of view, a substantial advantage because it would mean shorter and better frontiers, the freeing of forces for other purposes, and the possibility of creating new units up to a level of about twelve divisions, that is, one new division per million inhabitants.

Italy was not expected to object to the elimination of the Czechs, but it was impossible at the moment to estimate what her attitude on the Austrian question would be; that depended essentially upon whether the Duce were still alive.

The degree of surprise and the swiftness of our action were decisive factors for Poland's attitude. Poland — with Russia at her rear — will have little inclination to engage in war against a victorious Germany.

Military intervention by Russia must be countered by the swiftness of our operations; however, whether such an intervention was a practical contingency at all was, in view of Japan's attitude, more than doubtful.

Should case 2 arise — the crippling of France by civil war — the situation thus created by the elimination of the most dangerous opponent must be seized upon *whenever it occurs* for the blow against the Czechs.

The Führer saw case 3 coming definitely nearer; it might emerge from the present tensions in the Mediterranean, and he was resolved to take advantage of it whenever it happened, even as early as 1938.

In the light of past experience, the Führer did not see any early end to the hostilities in Spain. If one considered the length of time which Franco's offensives had taken up till now, it was fully possible that the war would continue another 3 years. On the other hand, a 100 percent victory for Franco was not desirable either, from the German point of view; rather were we interested in a continuance of the war and in the keeping up of the tension in the Mediterranean. Franco in undisputed possession of the Spanish Peninsula precluded the possibility of any further intervention on the part of the Italians or of their continued occupation of the Balearic Islands. As our interest lay more in the prolongation of the war in Spain, it must be the immediate aim of our policy to strengthen Italy's rear with a view to her remaining in the Balearics. But the permanent establishment of the Italians on the Balearics would be intolerable both to France and Britain, and might lead to a war of France and England against Italy — a war in which Spain, should she be entirely in the hands of the Whites, might make her appearance on the side of Italy's enemies. The probability of Italy's defeat in such a war was slight, for the road from Germany was open for the supplementing of her raw materials. The Führer pictured the military strategy for Italy thus: on her western frontier with France she would remain on the defensive, and carry on the war against France from Libya against the French North African colonial possessions.

As a landing by Franco-British troops on the coast of Italy could be discounted, and a French offensive over the Alps against northern Italy would be very difficult and would probably come to a halt before the strong Italian fortifications, the crucial point [*Schwerpunkt*] of the operations lay in North Africa. The threat to French lines of communication by the Italian Fleet would to a great extent cripple the transportation of forces from North Africa to France, so that France would have only home forces at her disposal on the frontiers with Italy and Germany.

If Germany made use of this war to settle the Czech and Austrian questions, it was to be assumed that Britain — herself at war with Italy

— would decide not to act against Germany. Without British support, a warlike action by France against Germany was not to be expected.

The time for our attack on the Czechs and Austria must be made dependent on the course of the Anglo-French-Italian war and would not necessarily coincide with the commencement of military operations by these three States. Nor had the Führer in mind military agreements with Italy, but wanted, while retaining his own independence of action, to exploit this favorable situation, which would not occur again, to begin and carry through the campaign against the Czechs. This descent upon the Czechs would have to be carried out with "lightning speed."

In appraising the situation Field Marshal von Blomberg and Colonel General von Fritsch repeatedly emphasized the necessity that Britain and France must not appear in the role of our enemies, and stated that the French Army would not be so committed by the war with Italy that France could not at the same time enter the field with forces superior to ours on our western frontier. General von Fritsch estimated the probable French forces available for use on the Alpine frontier at approximately twenty divisions, so that a strong French superiority would still remain on the western frontier, with the role, according to the German view, of invading the Rhineland. In this matter, moreover, the advanced state of French defense preparations [*Mobilmachung*] must be taken into particular account, and it must be remembered apart from the insignificant value of our present fortifications — on which Field Marshal von Blomberg laid special emphasis — that the four motorized divisions intended for the West were still more or less incapable of movement. In regard to our offensive toward the southeast, Field Marshal von Blomberg drew particular attention to the strength of the Czech fortifications, which had acquired by now a structure like a Maginot Line and which would gravely hamper our attack.

General von Fritsch mentioned that this was the very purpose of a study which he had ordered made this winter, namely, to examine the possibility of conducting operations against the Czechs with special reference to overcoming the Czech fortification system; the General further expressed his opinion that under existing circumstances he must give up his plan to go abroad on his leave, which was due to begin on November 10. The Führer dismissed this idea on the ground that the possibility of a conflict need not yet be regarded as so imminent. To the Foreign Minister's objection that an Anglo-French-Italian conflict was not yet within such a measurable distance as the Führer seemed to assume, the Führer put the summer of 1938 as the date which seemed to him possible for this. In reply to considerations offered by Field Marshal von Blomberg and General von Fritsch regarding the attitude of Britain and France, the Führer repeated his previous statements that he was convinced of Britain's nonparticipation, and therefore he did not believe in the probability of belligerent action by France against Germany. Should the Mediterranean conflict under discussion lead to a general mobilization in Europe, then we must immediately begin action against the Czechs. On the other hand, should the powers not engaged in the war declare themselves disinterested, then Germany would have to adopt a similar attitude to this for the time being.

Colonel General Göring thought that, in view of the Führer's statement, we should consider liquidating our military undertakings in Spain. The Führer agrees to this with the limitation that he thinks he should reserve a decision for a proper moment.

The second part of the conference was concerned with concrete questions of armament.

Hossbach

Certified Correct:
Colonel (General Staff)

Jonathan Wright and Paul Stafford

The Hossbach Memorandum Evaluated

A. J. P. Taylor questioned the importance of the Hossbach Memorandum, and some historians have questioned its authenticity.

After a lengthy examination of the origin of the memorandum, Jonathan Wright and Paul Stafford are convinced that it was authentic. Moreover, although the conference was originally called because of problems with rearmament, they find that it had great bearing on Hitler's foreign

From "Hitler, Britain and the Hossbach Memorandum," in *Milit geschichtliche Mitteilungen*, vol. 42 (1987), pp. 82, 84–86, 106–108. Reprinted by permission of Milit geschichtliche Mitteilungen.

policy. Hitler was neither daydreaming nor ranting. He was attempting to explain his future plans to those who would have to carry them out.

We consider the arguments that PS-386 was forged by the Allies extremely unconvincing. Of more importance for understanding the memorandum is the question of Hossbach's motive in making it. Hossbach was present at the meeting on 5 November 1937 in his capacity as the senior adjutant to the Armed Forces on Hitler's staff. He had been appointed to the position in August 1934 and held it until the crisis of January 1938 when he was dismissed for informing the Commander-in-Chief of the Army, General von Fritsch, of the accusation of homosexuality against him. Hossbach's loyalties were to the professional army and in particular to Fritsch and the Chief of the General Staff, General Beck, whom he greatly admired. Hossbach explains that his famous memorandum was not intended as a formal minute but was an unsolicited attempt to record as completely as possible Hitler's lengthy statement with which the meeting began. Hossbach used notes he made in his diary during the meeting as the basis for his record which he wrote up subsequently and dated 10 November. He twice gave it to Hitler to read through but Hitler refused. Hossbach mentions that he made only a brief record of the discussion that followed Hitler's statement and he made no attempt to record the details of the second part of the meeting which was concerned with rearmament questions.

Why was Hossbach so concerned to record Hitler's statement on 5 November? The obvious reason was the importance of what Hitler himself described as his "testamentarische Hinterlassenschaft." It is natural to assume that Hossbach also wanted a record to show General Beck, who was not present at the meeting. Given Hossbach's closeness to Beck, he would have been conversant with Beck's critical attitudes and, in particular, Beck's anxiety that German military action in Central Europe would set off a general war, which Germany was bound to lose. On these grounds Beck had already, in May 1937, criticized a contingency plan for military intervention in Austria in the event of an attempt to restore the Habsburg dynasty. Beck was bound to be acutely interested in the ideas Hitler expressed on 5 November for German expansion and in particular for military action against Austria and

Czechoslovakia. Hossbach's record of the statement did indeed have a profound effect on Beck: he described it as "niederschmetternd" and drew up a detailed critique of Hitler's arguments, dated 12 November.

That Hossbach's record served, and may well have been intended to serve, a tactical purpose in preparing the ground for a refutation of Hitler's argument in no way detracts from its value as a record. That its existence was known to opposition groups in Switzerland is equally no reason to doubt its accuracy. On the contrary, the tactical purpose makes it clearer why Hossbach thought it so important to record Hitler's statement correctly. . . .

Hitler's Statement on 5 November

If we accept that Hitler's statement of foreign policy goals on 5 November deserves to be taken seriously, two questions arise: why did he make it then to that audience and how should one interpret the different parts of his argument? On the first question, the simplest answer has much to recommend it. During 1937 Hitler began to think seriously about how Germany, having re-established its territorial integrity with the re-occupation of the Rhineland in 1936, could go on to the offensive and fulfil the dream of expansion. In that year he had already developed a number of arguments to close party colleagues which he put together in his address on 5 November and revealed for the first time to a group which was not composed of the party faithful (except for Göring) but his service chiefs and Foreign Minister. These were the people whose co-operation he needed to carry out his plans. On this interpretation the address on 5 November was what it appeared to be, an attempt to educate his senior advisers in what lay ahead. This attempt misfired. Blomberg, Fritsch and Neurath were unconvinced and Hossbach records that Hitler's expression showed that he knew he had failed to persuade them. Hitler took no further action immediately, refusing even to read Hossbach's account of the meeting. New military plans were drawn up and endorsed by Hitler but they made allowance for the Generals' reservations. On 4 February 1938, however, Hitler replaced Neurath with Ribbentrop and took the opportunity of the Blomberg scandal to rid himself of Fritsch as well. Having dispensed with the main opposition of 5 November he resumed the search for expansion against Czechoslovakia (Austria falling to the Reich sooner than Hitler had expected and in a way he had not planned).

Let us turn now to the question of the interpretation of Hitler's statement as recorded by Hossbach. It falls into three parts: an introduction where Hitler advanced the case for the acquisition of living space by force in terms familiar from *Mein Kampf* and the *Second Book*, with some added detail on Germany's current raw materials and food shortages; a second section where he commented on British (and French) opposition to German expansion; and a final section where he discussed various "scenarios" for a German attack on Czechoslovakia. Against accepting the text as a guide to Hitler's intentions, it has been objected that no mention is made of Russia, the goal of expansion in *Mein Kampf*. This can easily be answered, however. Hitler was discussing the first phase of expansion, a phase which his audience found quite alarming enough for him not to elaborate further phases. Even so his words implied further phases: the destruction of Czechoslovakia and Austria were described as "our first goal" to secure Germany's flank for possible operations in the West. It was also clear on Hitler's figures that his goal of living space for one or two generations could not be satisfied by the incorporation of Austria and Czechoslovakia since he said Germany had an annual population surplus of 560,000 and Austria and Czechoslovakia would provide food for only 5–6 million people (and that assuming the compulsory emigration of 3 millions from these territories). Hitler's lack of emphasis on the *threat* from the Soviet Union is surprising in comparison with the Memorandum on the tasks of the Four Year Plan but Stalin's purge of his generals in the Summer of 1937 may have made this argument seem less convincing. It has also been objected that Hitler's apparent confidence that, for instance, France would not come to the aid of Czechoslovakia and that the Czech defenses could be overrun was assumed for rhetorical effect and should not be taken seriously — but as Hitler argued, no expansion was without risk and his major thesis was for German expansion in 1943–45 when its rearmament would be complete.

Hitler's remarks about Britain raise more interesting questions. His argument is as follows. In deciding where it could expand with greatest gain at least cost, Germany had to reckon with two "hate inspired" [countries], Britain and France, for whom "a strong German colossus in the center of Europe would be a thorn in the flesh. Both states were opposed to any further strengthening of Germany's position whether in Europe or overseas." Britain, he continued, could not give up any part of its colonial territories to Germany because of the opposition of the

Dominions and after its loss of prestige by the Italian conquest of Abyssinia, it would not be willing to return the former German territory in East Africa either. The most that Britain would consider would be satisfying Germany's colonial wishes with territories such as Angola which were not British. France would follow the same policy.

However, Hitler then added that this would not always be the case. Serious discussion of the return of German colonies would only happen when Britain faced a crisis and Germany was strong and armed: "The Führer did not share the view that the Empire was unshakable." Britain was not the only global power as Rome had been after the Punic wars. On the contrary, it could only defend its colonies by a policy of alliance. How could Britain, for example, defend Canada against the United States or its East Asian interests against Japan? The emphasis put on the Crown as the symbol of the cohesion of the Empire was already an admission that its basis in power could not be maintained in the long term. Hitler instanced Ireland's striving for independence, the constitutional conflicts in India, the weakening of England's position in East Asia by Japan and the conflict with the dynamic power of Italy in the Mediterranean. He concluded that despite its apparent strength the Empire could not be maintained, since the motherland constituted only one ninth of the total Imperial population. Later, in discussing possible German action in 1943–45 against Czechoslovakia, Hitler said he thought it highly probable that Britain (and, he expected, France as well) had already written off Czechoslovakia and accepted that this question would one day be settled by Germany. The difficulties of the Empire and the prospect of being caught up again in a long European war would prevent British intervention and this would deter France.

This lengthy and curious argument raises obvious questions. One can understand the importance for Hitler of being able to demonstrate that Britain and France would not intervene in a continental war against Germany, but why did he feel it necessary to argue emphatically first that Britain and France were opposed to any further strengthening of Germany either in Europe or overseas? This view was in marked contrast to Hitler's professed strategy in the 1920's, to combine a German guarantee of the British Empire with British acquiescence in German continental expansion East. It also appeared to be contradicted by the British Government's willingness to discuss peaceful revision of the Versailles Treaty in Germany's favour.

Again, the simplest answers appear to be correct. First, Hitler believed what he said. He had come to the conclusion both that Britain's ostensible willingness to appease Germany with concessions was a sham intended only to separate Germany from Italy and also that despite its deep-rooted hostility to Germany, Britain was too weak to fight. Second, he had to convince his audience of these views because they did not believe them. They were attracted rather by the idea of a negotiated settlement with Britain and believed equally that Britain was an insuperable global power. To get them to accept his goal of the conquest of living space by force, Hitler had to convince them that they were wrong on both counts. There may have been an additional reason at the forefront of his mind for arguing like this on 5 November 1937. Hitler had agreed on 3 November to meet a British Cabinet Minister, Lord Halifax, a meeting requested by the British Government and put to Hitler by Neurath and Göring. The visit was expected to take place in the near future and Halifax was also to meet Neurath, Göring and Blomberg. There was therefore an immediate incentive for Hitler to make his views about Britain clear to his senior advisers, particularly as they disagreed with him.

There are convincing reasons to explain Hitler's progressive disillusionment with Britain. His original concept of an agreement to share the world had been rebuffed by Britain. The British concept of a general settlement ran exactly counter to Hitler's. Hitler wanted a free hand in Eastern Europe in return for a guarantee of the Empire. Britain wanted a German guarantee of the *limits* of German ambitions in Eastern Europe, broadly in accord with the principle of self-determination, in return for British agreement to limited revision following this principle and possibly some colonial concessions. The second major development which affected Hitler's view of Britain was the Abyssinian conflict. Originally Hitler had hoped that this would lead Britain to accept German expansion but instead it showed only Britain's inability to restrain Italy without British policy becoming any more favourable to Germany. Italy by contrast emerged with credit in Hitler's eyes by its successful defiance of Britain.

Conclusion

Setting Hitler's statement in the context of the views held by his audience, as well as those of Schacht and Ribbentrop, shows the full importance of what he said. The themes he addressed, living space, autarchy, the tactics of expansion, Britain's attitude to negotiations, Britain's capacity to intervene in a European war, the way to exploit Italy's involvement in the Mediterranean, the future changes in the balance of force as other powers rearmed and the timetable for expansion which this indicated, were the themes which most concerned his audience. Hitler's views differed from theirs and also from Ribbentrop's. They dreaded Britain's intervention in a European war and therefore continued to believe in the need for understanding with Britain. Hitler dismissed both the chance of understanding with Britain and the danger of British intervention. This enabled him to answer the vital question of how German expansion could succeed, a question to which the professional diplomats and military leadership had no real answer since they knew that Britain was not likely to agree to the kind of European settlement Germany wanted quickly, if at all, and they also accepted that in time the Empire and its allies (including the United States) would be too strong for Germany. Göring was more optimistic at this stage about reaching agreement with Britain but also saw no viable alternative. Even Ribbentrop believed it would be necessary to establish a German bloc superior to the British Empire before a conflict could be risked. Hitler brushed aside their fears and hopes and supplied his own answer: early expansion by force with lightning speed while Italy and, if possible, France and Britain were involved in the Mediterranean, and in any case before Germany's enemies were ready. The reasons which led Hitler to this conclusion and to the decision to face his audience with it on 5 November were many and varied. But the key was his sense that a crucial opportunity for expansion lay within Germany's grasp. If Germany were to seize the opportunity, however, then rearmament had to be completed on time. At this point Hitler's ideas and the occasion of the meeting on 5 November came together, for the serious deficiencies in the rearmament programme (which prompted the meeting) had to be put right, if Hitler's plans were to be realized.

A further assumption, partly hidden, may also have been important. For Hitler, Czechoslovakia and Austria were simply the first stage: they would constitute the foundation from which the racial wars for continental and perhaps even world hegemony would be launched. For his audience on 5 November, on the other hand, with the partial exception of Göring, Austria and Czechoslovakia were themselves the crucial goal. Hitler did not dwell on this difference in his statement, but its existence may have made him even more hostile to negotiations. If Chamberlain were to succeed in convincing the German people of Britain's support for their legitimate aspirations, based on self-determination, and distinguishing them from Hitler's quest for living space, popular support for Hitler's war would be much harder to achieve.

Other considerations re-enforced Hitler's desire for action: concern about living standards, public opinion and his health. In November, he also finally decided to grasp the nettle of Schacht's resignation because Schacht would not submit to the economic preparations for war which Hitler had authorized Göring to carry out. This made it natural for Hitler to use the 5 November meeting, which arose directly from disputes over the rearmament programme, to clarify his disagreement with Schacht and ensure that he retained the support of his other professional advisers.

For all these reasons, Hitler decided to confront them with a solemn statement, which was prepared in advance and took over two hours to deliver, a statement he described as "the fruit of thorough deliberation and experiences of his $4\frac{1}{2}$ years of power" containing "his basic ideas concerning the opportunities for the development of our position in the field of foreign affairs," and he asked that it should be considered as his testament in the event of his death. He may have hoped to win them over, not only by the force of his oratory and the fact that he claimed to have an answer to the problem of German expansion, where they had none, but also through the warning example of Schacht.

His audience was unconvinced and tried in various ways to dissuade him. The Generals prepared new military plans which turned Hitler's assumption that a general European war could be avoided into a condition, thus they hoped postponing action perhaps indefinitely. Neurath tried unsuccessfully to persuade Hitler that what he wanted could be achieved peacefully in time. Göring intensified his pressure on Austria, perhaps to show Hitler that peaceful gains were still possible with British acquiescence and despite Italian objections. Only Raeder accepted the logic of what Hitler said as far as the navy was concerned, and planned as fast as he was able for the capacity to deter Britain from war, or if the worst should happen, for war with Britain.

The objections of his audience did not change Hitler's mind

though he did not contradict them directly, apart from his interview with Neurath in January. Instead, and characteristically, the Führer waited for a crisis to enable him to impose his solution. The chance came at the end of January 1938 with the revelations about Blomberg's wife. This was it seems a genuine blow to Hitler who had probably assumed that he could always bend the pliable Blomberg to his will in the last resort. But the conspiracy against Fritsch, Hitler's assumption of command in place of Blomberg, the replacement of Neurath by Ribbentrop, were all signals of a radical course which was confirmed by his renewed commitment to crush Czechoslovakia in 1938. He was not deflected even when he was forced to accept that he had underestimated Britain's willingness to go to war, which required a fresh analysis of how British military power could be excluded from the continent. The 5 November meeting was not the final expression of Hitler's tactics, but he never wavered on the principles — that Germany must expand and take the best chance of expanding without general war. Nor was the 5 November meeting the only occasion on which Hitler expressed views of this kind, as Goebbels' diary shows. Indeed the consistency of the views he expressed to Goebbels and through the mouthpiece of Dietrich with parts of Hossbach's record is striking. The significance of the 5 November meeting is that on this occasion he tried to impose his views on his most senior advisers and was met with scepticism rather than the uncritical adulation to which he was accustomed from party audiences. Hossbach's record was itself a product of this scepticism. It remains a crucial dividing line in the history of the Führer state.

Keith Eubank

Appeasement and Appeasers

Those politicians who practiced appeasement of Hitler have been assigned much of the responsibility for the outbreak of war in 1939. But appeasement as a policy did not originate simply in response to Hitler's aggression, argues Keith Eubank in this selection. It had a history. In the 1930s appeasement was considered sensible and in agreement with public opinion. After all, what was the alternative?

Since 1945, the word "appeasement" has become a derogatory term to be hurled at any statesman willing to negotiate with an opponent. However, at one time, it was a term applied to a policy that was not only publicly approved, but also praised. Originally "appeasement" did not mean surrendering to a bully's demands nor did it mean that nations must surrender their vital national interests in order to avoid war. Instead "appeasement" meant a reduction of international tensions between states through the removal of the causes of friction. It also meant concessions to disgruntled nations in the hope that the concessions would alleviate their grievances and lessen their tendency to take aggressive action. It was hoped that after the aggrieved nations had been pacified through appeasement, an era of confidence, peace, and prosperity would emerge. Moreover, appeasement would permit a reduction in armaments and consequently lower taxes.

While appeasement has most often been associated with Neville Chamberlain, he did not actually originate the policy, but inherited it from his predecessors. It was not a policy created suddenly in the 1930s to buy off Hitler and Mussolini. It had originated in the minds of Englishmen who believed that World War I need never have come and

From *The Origins of World War II*, 2nd ed. by Keith Eubank, pp. 69–75. Copyright © 1990 by Harlan Davidson, Inc. Used by permission.

that the outbreak of the war was entirely accidental. These Englishmen believed that both Britain and Germany shared responsibility for the outbreak of the war — an idea nurtured by revisionist historians who argued that the Treaty of Versailles was unjust and should be revised.

But appeasement also stemmed from a lack of faith in the British cause in World War I and from a firm resolve to prevent another European catastrophe. Englishmen who looked with favor on the German educational system, on German industrial development, and on German social legislation were inclined to back appeasement. There was no one man or group of men who can be considered responsible for appeasement. Rather, a combination of forces — the horrors of the trenches, the disillusionment over the Treaty of Versailles, and the reluctance to burden Germany with total responsibility for the war — generated and fostered the policy.

Their guilt feelings over the Treaty of Versailles inclined the appeasers to take a soft line whenever Germany complained about the severity of the treaty restrictions. In the early 1920s, French insistence on complete fulfillment of the Versailles treaty alarmed the appeasers, who feared that France would force Germany to take up arms again. Consequently, they argued that war could be prevented only by non-fulfillment of the treaty terms.

British opposition to the French occupation of the Ruhr in 1923–1924 had the effect of preventing the enforcement of the Treaty of Versailles. At the same time, it rescued Germany from being torn apart by the separatist movements that had begun to develop. When French troops withdrew from the Rhineland, the appeasers, as well as the Germans, had won a great victory; if France could not enforce the treaty, then it would never be enforced, and without enforcement, revision of the treaty — the appeasers' goal — would be easier.

J. Ramsay MacDonald, who became Prime Minister in 1924, helped clear up the difficulty that resulted from the Ruhr occupation by pushing the Dawes Plan through to completion. Under his leadership, a conference in London in the summer of 1924 brought Frenchmen and Germans together to consider the reparations problem. The nations who met at the London Conference agreed to end the Ruhr occupation and to assist German recovery with a loan — but they refused to help France and Belgium, both of whom had suffered heavier damage than had Germany. With these concessions granted, Germany agreed to pay the reparations at a reduced rate. Because

Britain and its allies treated the former enemy as an equal, appeasement became more firmly established.

Stanley Baldwin, who later in 1924 succeeded MacDonald as Prime Minister, was well-acquainted with the habits of the British electorate, but he paid as little attention as possible to foreign affairs, preferring to postpone unpopular decisions on the chance that they would solve themselves. Truly ignorant of foreign affairs and socially uneasy with foreigners, he could neither comprehend nor deal with the impending conflict in Europe, and so resolved on peace at any price. He was well aware of the German breaches in the Treaty of Versailles, but he unhesitatingly accepted the Locarno Pact. It did seem at the time that the final solution to Europe's postwar problems had been reached at Locarno. Many of the appeasers envisioned the treaty as creating a new spirit that would bring peace to Europe. Because Germany had freely participated in a conference and had willingly signed an agreement, the appeasers were convinced that they had replaced the ineffective Treaty of Versailles with an agreement that could be maintained.

When Hitler came to power, the arguments in favor of appeasement increased. Whatever faults the new Germany might possess, the appeasers believed that it could not have been as great a threat as the threat of Communist Russia. They believed that German rearmament should be accepted and changes must be made in the Treaty of Versailles.

By 1937, when Neville Chamberlain became Prime Minister, appeasement had become entrenched as British foreign policy. He was not a naive man as many would want to paint him, but actually a seasoned politician. Son of the famous Joseph Chamberlain, Neville had trained for a career in business. He understood contracts, accounts, and production schedules better than the intricacies of European diplomacy. He was conscientious but lacking in imagination; and his brusque and obstinate manner did not gain him popularity. Convinced that the techniques of business would succeed in international diplomacy, Chamberlain approached Hitler and Mussolini as he would a fellow businessman, offering them deals that would be mutually advantageous.

Distrustful of career men in the Foreign Office, he relied too much on his narrow background and on men whose grasp of European affairs was minimal. Men such as Hoare, Simon, Halifax, and Wilson were poor choices for advisors. Both Hoare and Simon had been failures at formulating foreign policy, and Halifax's ignorance of European affairs had made him ill-prepared to be Foreign Secretary. The last member of the quartet, Sir Horace Wilson, was a very capable civil servant, an expert in labor disputes with the title of "Chief Industrial Adviser to the Government," but in foreign affairs he was strictly an amateur. Given an office in No. 10 Downing Street, he acted unofficially for Chamberlain, often presenting his views in behind-the-scenes meetings with German officials.

Chamberlain would not listen to Eden, the Foreign Secretary he had inherited from the Baldwin cabinet. The Prime Minister believed that diplomats wasted time in red tape, and that he must handle his own foreign policy in order to avoid this problem. When he took office, he had resolved to end the policy of drift and inaction that had typified the Baldwin administration; and to do this, he believed he had to act quickly and independently on policy matters. It was to be expected that he would clash with Eden, who preferred more traditional ways of dealing with the fascist powers.

The difficulties between Chamberlain and Eden came into the open over a proposal made by Franklin Roosevelt in January 1938, that the diplomatic corps in Washington meet to consider an agreement on the basic principles of international conduct. This agreement would include decisions on the reduction of armaments, methods of promoting economic security, and measures for protecting neutrals in wartime. Chamberlain objected strenuously to this plan; he was certain that it would not only fail but also ruin all his efforts at appeasement. Without informing Eden of his move, Chamberlain requested Roosevelt to postpone putting his plan into effect. Eden, who thought he saw excellent possibilities in the Roosevelt proposal, had no success in convincing Chamberlain to change his mind. Although he has generally been condemned for rejecting the President's impractical scheme, Chamberlain, because of Roosevelt's previous unwillingness to commit the United States to any international responsibility, had some justification in believing the efforts would come to naught. The only important result of Roosevelt's proposal was to strain the relations between Chamberlain and Eden to the breaking point.

The breaking point came almost immediately — on the question of Ethiopia. In hopes of separating Mussolini from Hitler, Chamberlain wanted immediate discussions over recognition of the Italian conquest of Ethiopia. Eden preferred to negotiate on a *quid pro quo* basis: Mussolini could withdraw his troops from Spain, and then Britain would recognize the conquest of Ethiopia. When Chamberlain rejected Eden's recommendation entirely, the Foreign Secretary resigned on February 20, 1938.

Edward, third Viscount Halifax, who followed Eden as Foreign Secretary, was much more to Chamberlain's liking. A country gentleman, a former Viceroy of India, and a High-Church Anglican with deep spiritual convictions, Halifax was completely unsuspecting when confronted with men such as Hitler and Mussolini. He had never bothered to read *Mein Kampf*, and he believed that the men who had warned against Hitler were exaggerating. But this was the man whom Chamberlain wanted as Foreign Secretary — a faithful servant of the King who would not object to whatever brand of appeasement Chamberlain wanted to practice.

Before he took office, and despite the protests of Eden, Halifax was sent on his first errand for Chamberlain. In November 1937, Halifax accepted an invitation from Hermann Goering to attend the Sporting Exhibition in Berlin. On November 17, the English country gentleman met with Hitler at Berchtesgaden; but he almost wrecked the meeting at the outset by mistaking Hitler for a footman, stopping short of handing the dictator his hat. Halifax was in agreement with Hitler on the inequity of the Treaty of Versailles, but he wanted the potentially dangerous questions arising from the treaty — Danzig, Austria, Czechoslovakia — handled in a peaceful way. He promised that the British government would not "block reasonable settlements . . . reached with the free assent and goodwill of those primarily concerned." This was just short of an invitation for Hitler to do whatever he wanted in Central Europe. Hitler had already — in the Reichschancellery meeting — announced plans for expansion; but now, thanks to Halifax (and Chamberlain), he had the means for taking the territory he wanted. If he could make his moves appear to be in accordance with the wishes of the people in the territories occupied, he would have British consent.

The policy that resulted in this invitation to Hitler had developed considerably since Versailles. In retrospect, appeasement had so managed to root itself into British foreign policy as to make it extremely difficult — if not impossible — for Chamberlain to have taken any other approach. Under Lloyd George, with his attempts to make Wilson lighten the Treaty of Versailles, appeasement became the keystone of British foreign policy. All of Lloyd George's successors followed his example: Andrew Bonar Law denounced the French occupation of the Ruhr in 1923; MacDonald, in his first administration, got the French out of the Ruhr, and in his second administration, preached disarmament of Britain and its allies as a means of satisfying German complaints about military inequities; and Baldwin aided the growth of appeasement by making the Anglo-German Naval Agreement the crowning diplomatic achievement of his third government.

By the time Chamberlain came to office in 1937, appeasement would no longer satisfy Hitler (whom Chamberlain regarded as a German politician with strong feelings about the Versailles treaty and the suffering German people). Nevertheless, Chamberlain prescribed a more vigorous form of appeasement than had his predecessors, pushing for intensive discussions and, if necessary, face-to-face negotiations between heads of state. Appeasement to Chamberlain did not mean surrendering to Hitler's demands, however, but it meant finding ways of satisfying those demands by wise concessions that would avoid further dangers to peace. Chamberlain honestly believed that world peace could be guaranteed by economic prosperity, by ending existing economic difficulties; and he believed that these troubles could be solved by reducing military expenditures and by balancing national budgets. Germany, he believed, would become more peacefully inclined if southeastern Europe were opened to German economic exploitation, thereby ridding the country of the need for a massive army and providing the German economy with a market. This fact has often been minimized in evaluating the years before the war. For Chamberlain practiced appeasement, not out of cowardice or fear, but out of a positive belief that appeasement would open the way to peace for all.

Chamberlain did not deliberately appease Hitler in order to turn his aggressive activities away from the West and toward the Soviet Union — Chamberlain was not as cunning as that. True, he distrusted the Russians, but he feared that another world war would devastate Europe and leave Communists in control. To Chamberlain as well as the other appeasers, the greatest evil of all — the evil to be avoided at all costs — was war. One world war was sufficient to make the appeasers fearful of what the outcome of such a major conflict might be.

The appeasers did ignore one important fact: a policy of appeasement could end only with Germany restored to its former strength. Given the German population, industry, educational system, and —

above all — geographical position, appeasement had to result in German domination of Central Europe and perhaps in an attempt to dominate all of the Continent as well. The appeasers' sins were the sins of all of the post-1919 generation, who read Keynes, regretted the Treaty of Versailles, sorrowed for Germany, and admired Mussolini for running trains on time. They took too optimistic a view of the Germans, always conceding the benefit of the doubt in hopes of bringing peace. Through improved Anglo-German relations, they sought to avoid direct conflict. Although they would later be reviled for their actions, the appeasers did perform a vital task; their efforts for peace proved without a doubt that Hitler could not be trusted and eventually convinced Britain that war was necessary and just.

Neville Chamberlain, upon his return to Britain on September 30, 1938, holds up the agreement he signed with Hitler on Anglo-German relations. (The Granger Collection)

Czechoslovakia and Munich

British Chiefs of Staff

Military Implications of German Aggression Against Czechoslovakia

The German occupation of Austria in March 1938 forced the British government to turn its attention to Czechoslovakia, where a potential military confrontation between Germany and Czechoslovakia over the Sudeten German minority question threatened to escalate into a general European war.

Prime Minister Neville Chamberlain asked the British Chiefs of Staff to examine the strategic situation for Britain if Germany attempted to impose a forcible solution of the Czechoslovak problem. Chamberlain assumed that if it came to war, Britain would have the help of only France and Czechoslovakia. The Chiefs of Staff found that nothing Britain and her probable allies could do would stop Germany from overrunning Czechoslovakia. However, the chiefs were silent on the consequences of a policy of inaction in the Czechoslovak question. Later the Chiefs of Staff report would provide Chamberlain with the ammunition he needed to use against those who argued in favor of Britain's supporting Czechoslovakia.

Part II: Factors and Possible Courses of Action . . .

Section 1. Comparison of Strengths

GREAT BRITAIN

Navy

5.   Our naval superiority will be sufficiently pronounced to ensure control against Germany's naval forces, except in the Baltic.

Our projected measures for the protection of merchant shipping from attack by aircraft are, however, far from complete; and Rosyth naval base, which is essential for war with Germany, is still at a year's notice. The anti-aircraft measures for defence of naval bases and fuel storage in the United Kingdom are quite inadequate.

Army

6.   *The Field Force* — The maximum field force that Great Britain could despatch at present to the Continent is one corps of two regular divisions with corps, L. of C., and base troops. This force could commence embarkation within 14 days, but it would be seriously deficient of modern equipment. . . .

Air Force

7.   Our Air Force is now in the throes of expansion, while the present approved programme is still over a year short of the date originally scheduled for completion. Thirty fighter squadrons (420 aircraft) are in existence, but of these only 27 will be mobilisable. Of the 27 squadrons, 20 will be armed with obsolete or obsolescent aircraft which are slower than the majority of German bombers. The reserves of aircraft behind the 27 mobilisable fighter squadrons will be 1½ weeks.

8.   The total first-line strength of our air striking force on the 1st

April, 1938, will be 67 squadrons (804 aircraft), but of these, only 35 squadrons (420 aircraft) will be mobilisable; 25 of these 35 squadrons would be capable of attacking objectives in Germany from bases in Great Britain. Most of them, however, could not penetrate far into Germany unless they were based or refuelled on the Continent, and our existing plans are made on the assumption that 20 squadrons would ultimately be based in France. We have as yet undertaken virtually none of the conversations with the French that will be essential before these squadrons can be despatched to and operated from France. Ten of the 35 squadrons are armed with an obsolete light-bomber type of aircraft, which is of short range and would be of little use against modern fighters. The reserves of modern aircraft behind the 35 mobilisable bomber squadrons will be 2 to 3 weeks, according to type. In addition to the above, we should be able to mobilise on the 1st April, 126 General Reconnaissance aircraft, which would mainly be employed on trade protection, 84 army co-operation aircraft, for duty with the field force, and there would be approximately 200 aircraft of the fleet air arm employed on duties with the fleet.

9.   There are still many serious deficiencies in equipment, armament, fuel reserves, personnel and organisation. The net result of these deficiencies, taking into account the lack of reserves, which means that the squadrons could not operate for more than a few weeks, is that the air force cannot at the present time be said to be in any way fit to undertake operations on a major war scale. Nor is the war production potential of the aircraft industry capable of replacing wastage for many months after the outbreak of war. . . .

12.   *Radio Directional Finding* — The radio direction-finding system will be limited to 4 stations which would only be of value in detecting attacks approaching London from the east and south and for tracking aircraft flying north or south down the Channel.

13.   *Air Raid Precautions* — Our air raid precaution organisation is only just emerging from the embryonic stage, and there is no centralised control and co-ordination. Air raid shelters for the civil population are at present practically non-existent, and the fire-fighting requirements to meet the effect of heavy bombing raids have not yet been organised. The provision of gas masks, however, has reached satisfactory dimensions. In general, therefore, we cannot ignore the fact that our Air Raid Precautions Organisation has not yet reached a stage when

air attacks could be faced with any confidence, although much valuable preparatory work has been done.

FRANCE

Navy

14.   The addition of the French naval strength to that of the British, will still further increase our naval superiority, but French assistance will not make good the deficiencies referred to in paragraph 5 above.

Army

15.   Although France can mobilise 53 divisions it would be at the expense of industry and agriculture, and she could not hope to keep this number of divisions in the field. Given the raw materials France should be able to maintain 30 to 40 divisions, but at present her armament industry is seriously disorganised. There is grave doubt whether the output of gun ammunition is adequate and there are reports of considerable deficiencies in reserve stocks. The French field artillery is greatly outranged by the German. The French frontier fortifications would prove of great value in defence. A.A. guns and searchlights exist for the defence of important points.

Air Force

16.   The French metropolitan Air Force consists of 297 fighter aircraft and 456 bombers, though it is possible that not all of these are mobilisable on the same basis as our own; approximately half are comparatively short-range. France has in addition some 248 army and general purpose aircraft, some of which could assist in a counter-offensive. The state of the French aircraft industry is deplorable, and for some months of a war output would be less than 100 military aircraft per month. Further, the geographical position of the majority of her factories makes her aircraft industry particularly vulnerable to air attack. Her reserves mainly consist of obsolescent types and it is extremely doubtful whether she could maintain her first-line strength for any length of time in a major war. There are, moreover, indications that the fighting value of the French Air Force at the present time is not of a high standard, partly on account of the relatively poor performance of French aircraft judged by modern first-line standards. . . .

Army

18.   The Czechoslovakian army in peace consists of 17 infantry and 4 cavalry divisions, with adequate reserves well-equipped; the morale is good. Out of a population of 14½ million, 3¼ million are Sudeten Deutsch. It is estimated that they represent 10 per cent. of the armed forces, but the army is officered by Czechs. There are field defences on the Bohemian frontier, but these have now been turned by the incorporation of Ostmark (Austria) in the Reich. There are no effective fortifications on the Czechoslovakian frontier facing Ostmark with the exception of a fortified bridgehead at Bratislava.

Air Force

19.   The first-line air strength is approximately 400 aircraft, composed of 64 bombers, 156 fighters and 180 reconnaissance aircraft. The main role of the Czechoslovakian air force is to co-operate with the army. Her aerodromes may be organised so as to accommodate air reinforcements from the U.S.S.R.

Industrial

20.   In a war of the nature we are considering the vital munition centres at Pilsen and Prague, which are situated close to Czechoslovakia's Western frontier with Germany, would almost certainly fall into enemy hands in the early stages of hostilities. In these circumstances Czechoslovakia could not maintain her full strength in the field for any length of time, and there would be no means of replacing wastage in her air forces unless aircraft were supplied by the U.S.S.R.

Czechoslovakia would cease to be, as heretofore, an important supplier of armaments to Yugoslavia and Roumania. She is dependent upon supplies from or through Yugoslavia for a large proportion of her raw materials and upon Roumania for her oil. It is important to note that absorption of Austria into the Reich has given Germany mastery over Czechoslovakia's main lines of railway, road and river communications, which formerly ran through Austria, with her partners of the Little *Entente* and with the outside world. At present about 75 per cent. by weight of Czechoslovakia's trade passes over German territory, and it would be possible for the German Government by abuse of tolls and tariffs on the Danube and the railways to force Czechoslovakia into submission by economic pressure alone, without resort to hostilities. This process would be facilitated if Germany secured the co-operation and control of Hungary. . . .

GERMANY

Navy

32.   Germany possesses a small modern navy which should ensure her control of the Baltic, and the three ships of the "Deutschland" class represent a serious potential danger to our trade routes. Her submarine fleet numbers 36, of which only 12 are large.

Army

33.   In considering the army strength of Germany we must take account of the old Federal Army of Austria. The German strength by the end of March will be:

36 active infantry divisions (including 6 motorised).

3 active armoured divisions.

18 reserve divisions (mobilised at $Z + 1$ or $Z + 2$ days).

24 Landwehr divisions, armed on a lower scale than the active and reserve divisions.

The old Federal Army of Austria consisted of approximately 9 divisions of a lower fighting value than the Germans, and so with the 81 German divisions, the total of the land force of the new German Reich would amount to 90 divisions. The Landwehr divisions are suitable for garrison duties only and the Ex-Austrian divisions have a comparative low degree of training. There would be, therefore, the 57 active and reserve divisions available for field operations. Given raw materials, it should be possible to maintain about 70 divisions (including Ex-Austrian) in the field after the first three months of war.

Air Forces

34.   It is estimated that Germany will have by the end of March a first-line strength in aircraft as follows:

Bombers	1,300 ⎫	
Dive bombers	270 ⎬ 1,570	

Fighters	540
Army co-operation	270
Coast defence	210
Reconnaissance	270
	2,860

The reserves maintained are 100 per cent. and the power of future production of engines and frames is great. The aircraft industry is organised to maintain a wastage rate of 50 per cent. per month after the second month of war.

In addition she can now count on some 100 aircraft from Ostmark, of which about 80 are heavy bombers of Italian design.

Section 2. Possible Courses of Action of the Powers Concerting with Great Britain

. . .36.   We must assume in such a review that any German action in Czechoslovakia will be assisted by disturbances among the Sudeten Deutsch, engineered from Berlin, and that Germany will invade Western Czechoslovakia and be consolidated there before any allied action could prevent her. Czechoslovakia, owing to her peculiar shape, has a frontier of 2,500 miles, and the German attack could be launched from three sides. An attack from the North-west would be met by the field defences constructed along that mountainous frontier. The frontier with Ostmark is close and hilly except immediately east of Vienna, which is open. The availability of Ostmark for the passage of German troops enables the existing Czechoslovak field defences to be turned, and the situation would probably be that after the opening phase of the war Germany would have absorbed Bohemia and the Czechoslovak army would have fallen back to defend the Moravian quadrilateral in which there are no existent field defences. The use of the munition factories in the Prague–Pilsen area would be lost to Czechoslovakia and to those allied Powers, Roumania and Yugoslavia, which hitherto have depended mainly upon them for their source of armament stores. . . .

GREAT BRITAIN AND FRANCE

Naval Action

38.   In a war in which France and ourselves were opposed by Germany alone our sea power would be adequate to secure our trade

routes, although our preparedness to combat air attack is incomplete, and in the absence of war experience we are unable to assess the degree of embarrassment such attack or threat of attack might produce, particularly on neutral shipping on the short sea routes. We should also be able to undertake offensive operations against sea-borne trade and naval objectives. By this means we should commence to apply economic pressure against Germany, but it would not become effective for a long time, especially as her frontiers with Poland and Italy would remain open, and Germany would control the Baltic.

Unless therefore Germany considered that the intervention of Great Britain would necessarily involve her in a long war she might be inclined to disregard the threat of economic pressure resulting from the exercise of combined French and British sea power.

Land Action

39.   Neither Great Britain nor France could render any direct assistance to Czechoslovakia, and the only method of rendering even indirect assistance would be by staging offensive operations into Germany. The French would be unlikely to cross the Rhine between Switzerland and Strasbourg and get involved in the difficult country of the Black Forest. If they attacked towards the middle Rhine through the Palatinate and the Eifel, they would encounter strong German field defences which are known to exist. The French have based their military doctrine on defence, and it seems unlikely that a nation which always acts on a basis of logical thinking and hates last-hour improvisation would leave their fortified zone to undertake a big-scale offensive against prepared positions in enemy country.

40.   Although even the small British field force of one corps might stiffen the French defence against German aggression, our field force is wholly lacking in equipment for offensive operations. Without tanks and without any modern guns it would not add to the French power to carry out a successful invasion of Germany.

French and British Air Action

41.   The action which British and French air forces could take with a view to assisting Czechoslovakia is affected by several considerations. French aircraft might be able to render direct assistance to Czechoslovakia by flying across Ostmark and participating in the attack of immediate military objectives on the Czechoslovakian front. They would,

however, have to traverse some 170 miles of hostile territory before reaching their objectives, and in view of the rapidity with which the Germans are likely to advance, there would be great difficulty in co-ordinating their action to suit the Czechoslovak plan, and it is very doubtful if they would make the attempt.

42. British air forces could only participate in such action if they refuelled *en route* in France and the intensity of their attack would be greatly reduced owing to the distance of their bases from their objectives.

43. An indirect method of assistance might be to attack vulnerable points in Germany. But this would be open to the objection that France and Britain would be extremely averse to taking the initiative in bombing targets which were less military in nature than those which Germany had already attacked. Germany might in the first instance employ her own bombing force in support of her land operations against Czechoslovakia.

44. In any event, the British offensive effort would be on a low scale and particularly until we had been able to establish our air striking force on the Continent. But actually we should be more likely to be concerned not with how we should use our air striking force to assist Czechoslovakia, but how best we can employ it to reduce the scale of the German air attack upon Great Britain.

45. At the best we cannot anticipate that the Franco-British air attack would have a great deterrent effect partly for the reasons we have developed above, partly because of the strength and efficiency of the German active and passive defences, and partly because the combined bomb lift of this air striking force would only amount to some 575 tons, as compared with the 1,825 tons with which we credit Germany.

This great disparity in air striking power is due in part to the fact that at the present time a high proportion of our bomber squadrons are equipped either with obsolete types, or with modern types with a bomb load considerably lower than that of the Germans. Re-equipment is now taking place at an ever-increasing rate and the situation will be considerably improved during the summer months. . . .

Conclusion

51. This review of the possible courses of action open to the Powers which might concert with Great Britain leads to the conclusion that no military pressure we can exert by sea or land or in the air can

prevent Germany either from invading and overrunning Bohemia or inflicting a decisive defeat on the Czechoslovakian Army. If politically it is deemed necessary to restore Czechoslovakia's lost integrity, this aim will entail war with Germany, and her defeat may mean a prolonged struggle. In short, we can do nothing to prevent the dog getting the bone, and we have no means of making him give it up, except by killing him by a slow process of attrition and starvation.

Section 3.   Review of Possible German Action

52.   Having seized Bohemia and thus brought Great Britain and France in against her, Germany would have to devote her main military effort to defeating her two most powerful opponents. As far as Germany is concerned, therefore, the military situation would have changed from that of a limited adventure into a world war.

German Security Measures

53.   Before embarking on war with Great Britain and France, Germany would have taken certain security measures which are briefly summarised as follows:

54.   At sea Germany could do little or nothing to protect her trade, except in the Baltic.

55.   On land she would probably feel obliged to keep certain forces upon her frontiers. The strengths she would consider necessary would be considerably affected by her own knowledge of the political feeling within the respective neighbouring countries, but on the assumptions given to us, she might feel obliged to employ a considerable proportion of her available divisions upon security duties distributed on the various frontiers. We must, however, assume that some of these divisions would be Landwehr divisions, and she would still have an adequate force available for active operations, including operations against Czechoslovakia.

56.   Against air attack her A.A. defences are already in a high state of efficiency and far more powerful than any others in Europe, while her air raid precautions are also in an advanced state of readiness. Most of her 540 fighters would probably be disposed to face the threat of air attack from France and Great Britain upon Western Germany, but the great number of aerodromes which Germany possesses confers great flexibility upon her air forces and her fighters could concentrate at short notice in any area where they were required.

Weaknesses in Germany's Position

57.   The weak point in Germany's defensive position is that she cannot face the prospect of a long war with confidence. Although she is known to have built up reserves both as regards armament stores and raw materials, there would come a point, as in the War of 1914–18, when the gradual cutting off of essential commodities from outside Europe would have a cumulative effect of reducing her war effort. Her food position must continue for some time to cause anxiety. While in a short war these factors might have little or no effect, in a long war they might become serious. The assertion, however, of German supremacy in Central and East Europe would, as in the Great War, alleviate the economic situation to a considerable extent.

German Courses of Action

58.   Having decided that her immediate object had now become to defeat France and Great Britain, Germany would have to decide how best to employ her forces for this purpose.

Against France she could concentrate both land and air forces in a united effort, and if she was aware of the low state of the French reserves and the weak condition of her industry, she might consider that by making an attack *brusquer* on France with large military and air forces, using surprise before France could mobilise, she could break down the latter's resistance before we could render her material assistance and thus force her to conclude a separate peace. It seems, however, unlikely that with the number of divisions at present available and taking into account the state of their equipment that Germany would be able to break through the French frontier defences.

59.   The Maginot line is an enigma, and Germany might hesitate to attack it unless she had devised some special method. To be held on the Maginot line would be very serious for her. Further, if she thus attempted to defeat France in detail first she would leave us a breathing space to muster our resources and adopt war measures which would materially increase our powers of resistance. There can be no doubt that it is our world resources and the effect of our exercise of sea-power in a long war which Germany fears most. Moreover, if she could succeed in defeating us she would have no doubt of her ability subsequently to subdue France. If, therefore, Germany considered there was a chance that by a ruthless exercise of her air power against us, com-

bined with naval attack on our sea-borne trade, she could obtain an early decision over Great Britain, she might well embark upon this course of action. In this connection it will be remembered that it was for somewhat similar reasons that Germany concentrated her main efforts against the British army and nation in 1918.

We propose, therefore, to review briefly the situation which might arise if Germany decided to attempt the knock-out blow while our defensive preparations are in their present state.

Air Attack on Great Britain

60.   When we previously considered this question in Paper No. C.O.S. 549, with respect to a possible conflict with Germany in 1939, we recorded our opinion as follows:

> . . . *If Germany decides to direct her initial air attacks against this country, with the object of trying to knock us out of the war as rapidly as possible, those attacks are likely to be quite ruthless. She will select the objectives and use the projectiles which she considers most likely to achieve her object without regard to ethical considerations.*
>
> *The two most apparent means by which she might hope to achieve her ends are—*
>
> (a)   *By trying so to disorganise the receipt and distribution of food supplies as to produce conditions of starvation in the United Kingdom which would force our Government to discontinue the war.*
>
> (b)   *By trying to create such moral and material destruction in the large centres of population that the people of this country would be so demoralised, and the material damage would be such, as to force our Government to discontinue the war.*
>
> *The destruction of our industry is a form of attack which in some circumstances would be effective, but it seems unlikely that Germany would select this as the means of producing the most rapid results. The destruction of our Naval forces by an overwhelming surprise attack has been suggested as another decisive form of attack, but the mobility, armour and armament of our ships make it unlikely that the Germans would select this form of attack as a primary objective. On the other hand, if the Germans did decide to engage our Fleet with theirs it is likely that they will temporarily divert a proportion of their Metropolitan air forces in an attempt to off-set their naval disparity.*
>
> *Aiming, as she inevitably must, at a rapid decision, Germany would, therefore, be likely to select and concentrate upon either food supply or moral and material destruction as a means of trying to*

achieve her end and to concentrate her attacks only upon those objectives calculated to further her selected plan.

Events which have not yet happened, and conditions which have not yet arisen, would probably govern Germany's decision as to her action in a war in 1939. It is, however, our aim to foresee the broad alternatives open to her, and hence to deduce the action on her part for which we must be prepared.

Germany would not initiate a war unless her responsible statesmen believed she would win. Her prospects of victory would certainly be greatest during the first few months of war. We are, therefore, convinced that Germany would plan to gain her victory rapidly. Her first attacks would be designed as knock-out blows, and we must anticipate that they would be reinforced by every measure of secret preparation which might effect a surprise.

From the foregoing paragraphs it is clear that in war against us the concentration, from the first day of war, of the whole of the German air offensive ruthlessly against Great Britain would be possible. It would be the most promising way of trying to block this country out, and, if adopted, would be carried out thoroughly.

61.   These remarks were related to the situation in April 1939, and were based upon the assumption that by that date the various defence programmes which had been approved would have reached completion. It also took into account the effects to be expected from a scale of attack which might amount to a sustained rate of 400 tons per day and a very much heavier rate in the first day or two.

In point of fact, the scale of attack which Germany could direct upon us in April this year (1938) is unlikely to be less than 400 tons per day, but, so far from our defence preparations being similarly advanced, they are, in fact, very far from complete.

The danger to this country must, therefore, be considered as correspondingly greater than we thought it would be when we recorded the above opinion.

62.   The crux of the situation, in our view, is whether this would be a knock-out blow. The Germans in their present state could not keep it up indefinitely, and it seems unlikely that they would take on a ruthless attack on London or other centres of population (with all the results that might follow, including the intervention of U.S.A., if it were not a rapid success) unless they were satisfied themselves that they had a reasonable chance of success.

63. The outcome of unrestricted air attack on this country by Germany is impossible to forecast with any accuracy. All we can say is that we are not in a position to prevent them dropping bombs in this country on the scale suggested above, which we think they might be able to sustain for not less than two months. . . .

65. The first preoccupation of all the allies will be to ensure their own security. While the alliance between Great Britain and France would result in close co-operation, the co-operation of those allies in South-East Europe would be weakened by their anxiety as to the security of their territory, due to suspicions of their neighbours whether allied or neutral. It would be impossible for many months for Great Britain to send a field force to the Continent sufficient to undertake offensive operations, and it is extremely unlikely that France would be in a position to stage an effective offensive against Germany. We have also deduced that land forces from Yugoslavia, Roumania and Hungary are likely to have little effect either by invading Ostmark or in preventing a decisive German victory over the Czechoslovak army. The land forces of Turkey and Greece could exert no influence whatever on the situation.

66. We have already shown that the threat to Germany from the air forces of Czechoslovakia and her allies in South-East Europe would be almost negligible. The issue would resolve itself into a struggle between Germany on the one hand and Great Britain and France on the other.

We estimate that on her side Germany would have available some 1,570 Bombers and 540 Fighters under single control against a combined French and British force of 876 Bombers and 675 Fighters. At the present time the German bombers are mostly superior in range and striking power to those of France and Great Britain, though as we have already pointed out, this disparity will be progressively reduced to a material degree during the course of the present year.

67. The German Air Force would have the advantage of unified control, on interior lines, as against a wide territorial dispersion and the difficulties of co-ordinated command on the side of the allies. Their well-organised air raid precautions might well cause them to accept the threat of allied air attack with relative equanimity, while they realised they had much more vital targets, notably London, on which to direct their own air counter-offensive. It is unlikely that at any time in the near future the air pressure which the Allies could impose upon Ger-

many would be on a scale which the Germans could not keep within manageable proportions, or in any way comparable to that which they could inflict upon the Allies.

68.   The direct air assistance that Great Britain and France could give to Czechoslovakia would be limited by the consideration of range and having to fly over enemy territory. Germany would, in this area only have to consider the relatively insignificant air strength of the Little *Entente* Powers.

69.   Possibly the most important military implication which might arise, as the result of action by His Majesty's Government on the lines which have been suggested, is that such action might lead to this country being subjected to the full weight of German air attack at a time when our air rearmament is in a critical stage and our defensive measures generally are incomplete.

70.   The military effort of the allies in South-Eastern Europe will be dependent on the reserves which they possess on the outbreak of war, since the armament industry of Czechoslovakia will be denied to them. Moreover, Germany's war potential will be increased by the possession of this additional source of warlike stores.

71.   There is, however, no doubt that if this country were to concert with France and the Central European Powers an undertaking to resist by force any attempt by Germany to impose a forceful solution on the Czechoslovakian problem, such an undertaking might have a psychological effect upon Germany. On the other hand one of the advantages enjoyed by the totalitarian State is that the populace can be induced to believe only that which [is] vouchsafed to them by Government propaganda.

72.   A pronouncement by Great Britain that she would fight for the maintenance of Czechoslovakian integrity would change the issue for Germany from a *coup* executed with overwhelming force to the possibility of a long war, in which they might reckon that the staying power of the British Empire might eventually prevail. This consideration would be bound to have a deterrent effect on Germany's decision unless she considered that public opinion in Great Britain was not unanimously behind the Government and that she had, in the present inadequate state of our defences, of which she must be fully aware, a good chance of dealing a knock-out blow on Great Britain, in which case our undertaking would lose almost all its deterrent value. . . .

Part VII.   Summary and Conclusions

87.   We conclude that no pressure that we and our possible allies can bring to bear, either by sea, on land or in the air, could prevent Germany from invading and over-running Bohemia and from inflicting a decisive defeat on the Czechoslovakian Army. We should then be faced with the necessity of undertaking a war against Germany for the purpose of restoring Czechoslovakia's lost integrity and this object would only be achieved by the defeat of Germany and as the outcome of a prolonged struggle. In the world situation to-day it seems to us that if such a struggle were to take place it is more than probable that both Italy and Japan would seize the opportunity to further their own ends, and that in consequence the problem we have to envisage is not that of a limited European war only, but of a world war.

On this situation we reported as follows some four months ago:

> *Without overlooking the assistance which we should hope to obtain from France and possibly other allies, we cannot foresee the time when our defence forces will be strong enough to safeguard our territory, trade and vital interests against Germany, Italy and Japan simultaneously.*
> *(C.I.D. Paper 1366-B, para. 42.)*

88.   In general there is no doubt that the potential hostility of the British Empire is a matter which any country, Germany not excluded, must take into most serious account. We have, however, shown that the only pressure this country can exert on Germany is economic pressure, which takes a very considerable time to take effect. In the circumstances under review it appears to us that from the German point of view the effect of this would be largely discounted by the fact that Germany would not be envisaging a long war, and that she would hope to bring about a situation in which Italy and Japan were hostile to us.

In these circumstances we do not consider that the potential threat of the pressure of sea power exercised by this country would necessarily deter Germany from the action under consideration.

89.   The alliance with Yugoslavia, Roumania, Hungary, Turkey and Greece would be of limited assistance to Great Britain and France, and they might ultimately constitute an additional embarrassing commitment by virtue of our moral obligation to assist them against German invasion. In addition Yugoslavia and Roumania obtain the greater part of their warlike supplies from Czechoslovakia, which source would

certainly be denied to them in the circumstances under consideration. The main advantage would be an economic one, but only so long as their frontiers remained closed to Germany. On the other hand, Germany would regard our action as proof that we intended to intervene in an affair which she herself regards as chiefly a domestic matter. We should undoubtedly become the main butt for her indignation and her military policy would immediately be oriented against us before all other countries.

90. The deterrent effect of Great Britain and France opposing German aspirations in Central Europe would depend on the degree of Germany's expectation that she could obtain a knock-out blow against this country by the ruthless use of the German air-striking force.

91. An incidental but very important corollary to a decision by His Majesty's Government to guarantee Czechoslovakia against Germany, or a marshalling of the Powers against Germany, might be the denunciation by Germany of the 35 per cent. Naval Agreement, the financial implications of which would be of extreme seriousness to us.

92. We feel bound to point out the possibility that our association with allies, many of whom are of doubtful military value, against Germany might precipitate a definite military alliance between Germany, Italy and Japan, in place of the somewhat indefinite understanding that appears to exist.

93. This alliance would find us in the present year at a stage of rearmament when we are not yet ready for war. On the naval side we are unfavourably placed with regard to comparative naval strength in capital ships, and our A/A rearmament measures are far from complete. The army has still a long way to go in the process of re-organisation and re-equipment. In the air, the expansion and re-equipment of the Air Force still falls far short of the stage at which it will be adequate for the protection of this country; while the incomplete state of our passive defence arrangements and of our A.A. defences, both at home and throughout the Empire, are well known.

(Signed)   C. L. NEWALL.
GORT.
W. M. JAMES (*D.C.N.S.*).

2 Whitehall Gardens, S.W. 1
March 28, 1938.

Gerhard L. Weinberg

Munich Conference: War Postponed

By September 1938 Hitler had created a crisis over the Sudeten Germans in Czechoslovakia, who demanded that the Sudetenland be returned to the Third Reich. (The Sudetenland had never been a part of Germany.) Hitler was determined to use the crisis to precipitate war.

Fearing that the Sudeten crisis might escalate into a general European war, Neville Chamberlain conferred with Hitler at Berchtesgaden on September 15, 1938. There they agreed on a peaceful cession of the Sudeten area to Germany. Later Chamberlain worked out a deal with the French over the ceding of the Sudetenland to Germany and forced the Czechoslovak government to accept it. Chamberlain met with Hitler at Godesberg on September 22, but their meeting ended in an impasse, which in turn led to the Munich Conference on September 29–30, 1938.

Gerhard L. Weinberg, William Rand Kenan, Jr., Professor of History at the University of North Carolina, Chapel Hill, argues that the Munich Conference was by no means an overwhelming victory for Hitler, as some historians have insisted. Hitler reluctantly decided to postpone war with Czechoslovakia in favor of the Munich Conference. In the future, however, he would not be cheated out of going to war.

When Chamberlain met Hitler again at Bad Godesberg on 22 September, he reviewed recent developments, explained that he had secured approval for territorial transfer, and proceeded to elucidate some suggestions and conditions under which such territorial cessions might be worked out. Presumably to retain some leeway in the negotiations, he suggested that the figure of 65 percent German population provide the basis for a commission to draw the new border rather than the 75 percent Lord Runciman had originally recommended or the bare ma-

From *The Foreign Policy of Hitler's Germany: Starting World War II, 1937–1939*, 1980 by Gerhard L. Weinberg, pp. 446–464. Reprinted by permission of University of Chicago Press.

jority that was provided by the Anglo-French plan. He also explained to Hitler the idea of new guarantees for Czechoslovakia to replace its current security system.

Hitler's response was based on the strategy he had developed after the Berchtesgaden meeting. He professed — perhaps genuine — astonishment at what Chamberlain had managed to do, but he used the conditions he himself had created in the meantime to justify rejection of a settlement on the basis of his prior demands. The activities of the Free Corps provided the pretext for asserting that things were so bad inside Czechoslovakia that he had to move in right away, there could and would be no discussion about properties, commissions, refugees, and such. Huge stretches would be occupied forthwith, and plebiscites — presumably on the recent Austrian model — would be held in them after German occupation, with several additional areas subject to plebiscites as well. In regard to the German-Czechoslovak nonagression pact Chamberlain had suggested, nothing like that was feasible even after Germany's territorial demands had been met until after the Polish and Hungarian demands Hitler had been stimulating had also been accommodated.

The new demands were obviously designed to prevent the peaceful agreement toward which Chamberlain was pushing. . . . He was obviously shocked and upset. Rather than simply break off talks and return to England, he did get into some discussion of the new German ultimatum. Under the impression of Chamberlain's firmness and the news of the Czechoslovak mobilization — which arrived during the later stages of the Bad Godesberg talks after Britain and France had withdrawn their objections to such a step as a result of learning Hitler's newest demands — the Führer changed the timetable for the occupation by a few days and some other minor modifications were also made, but the substantive situation remained unchanged. Dictation was to replace negotiation, and Czechoslovakia was to be punished rather than rewarded for agreeing to the cession of the Sudeten areas.

Chamberlain merely agreed to pass on to the Czechoslovak government the new German demands. As he returned to England disappointed at what certainly looked like the failure of his efforts, he appears to have clutched at the minor concessions that Hitler had made during the Bad Godesberg talks as a possible route to further concessions leading to an agreement after all. Only in this way can one understand the slow but continuous hardening of his attitude after Godesberg. In his first meeting with ministers right after returning and in the following cabinet meeting, the prime minister inclined to the view that some way might be found to work on the basis of the new terms, though his own words show him doubtful about that, while many in the cabinet were convinced it was impossible. It was in this regard that there was an advantage in the prime minister and foreign secretary not having both participated in the sessions in Germany; the prime minister remembered the discussion *after* Hitler's original rejection, while the foreign secretary was naturally most impressed by the outcome of the Godesberg meeting as a whole. That was unacceptable, and he so explained his view at the cabinet meeting on 25 September. Chamberlain fell in with this judgment and so did the whole cabinet with those most dubious about firmness and those equally dubious about concessions for once in agreement.

If the hardening of public opinion in England contributed to this view, so did the similar process in France which was reflected in the attitude of the French ministers, who again came to London to confer with their British counterparts. The English ministers put them through a difficult few hours as they inquired about the military measures which the French proposed to back up their proclaimed support of Czechoslovakia, but after reading these tough exchanges one can also see that they represent the canvassing of last doubts before firm resolution is arrived at. The Czechoslovak government would not be urged to accept the new terms; and in the hope of deterring Hitler from taking the plunge, Sir Horace Wilson would be sent first to suggest a supervised territorial transfer, but also to warn Hitler that if Germany marched, France would honor her alliance and England would fight on her side.

One of the advocates of a firm line, Duff Cooper, who had not participated in the talks with the French or the informal meeting of ministers, commented in his diary about Chamberlain's statement at the subsequent cabinet meeting that England would fight with France that "the Prime Minister made this announcement casually and I could hardly believe my ears." Chamberlain was not the fist-pounding type, but his quiet shift from doubt to resolution was therefore all the more convincing to his colleagues and to the French. They now set about getting ready for war in earnest. The French were beginning to mobilize their army, and Great Britain announced the mobilization of the fleet at the very time on 27 September when Sir Horace was in Germany. The British warned the Dominions that war was practically certain. Whatever the grimness of the predictions made by French and British military leaders, the political leaders in both countries were ready — reluctantly ready, but ready nevertheless — to go to war if Czechoslovakia as expected rejected the new German demands and Germany attacked. The repeated statements of the Russian government asserting loyalty to their treaty commitments and the agreement reached at the Anglo-French meeting in London formed the basis of the British public statement on the evening of the 26th that France, Britain, and the Soviet Union would all be involved in a war initiated by Germany. . . .

On 27 September Hitler received the news of the British public announcement of the likelihood of general war and, in a second meeting with Wilson, the warning in formal terms that Britain and France would stand by Czechoslovakia. The day before he had been so set on his plan for attacking Czechoslovakia that he had almost walked out on Sir Horace in the middle of their first conversation and had been only with difficulty recalled to the fact that as host he really had to hear out his visitor. Having worked himself into a frenzy for the speech he was to deliver that night, Hitler was not about to engage in diplomatic niceties. The speech itself must be read in terms of Hitler's own purposes. Having decided to order mobilization at 2:00 p.m. on 28 September and to attack on the 30th, Hitler now wanted to isolate Czechoslovakia from potential allies and to rally the German public for war, limited if possible, worldwide if necessary. The violent and even hysterial attacks on Beneš covered the latter point; the insistence that Germany did not want any Czechs and that this was Germany's last territorial demand was to assist with the former. The warning that on instructions from London Sir Horace gave Hitler on the 27th produced an unpleasant scene but still did not shake the German leader out of his decision to move. The fact that on the 27th and after the second meeting with Wilson Hitler decided to write an answer to the letter from Chamberlain the reading of which he had almost walked out on the day before can be seen either as the first sign of a shift away from his determination to go to war or, more likely, as a maneuver designed to try to split Britain and France from Czechoslovakia in war.

A development of the 27th that would contribute to Hitler's change of mind on the following day was the reception accorded by the Berlin crowds to a military demonstration on the late afternoon of that day. Motorized units moved through the capital at Hitler's orders, but this grim sign of the imminence of war produced just the opposite reaction from the one Hitler expected after his rousing speech of the night before and the crescendo of press and radio propaganda. The viewing public was anything but enthusiastic, and the propaganda minister himself would remind Hitler of the public's attitude on the following day. All the same, throughout the 27th of September, in spite of the disappointing public response, the warning of Sir Horace Wilson, and the renewed refusal of Hungary to join immediately in war on Czechoslovakia, Hitler was still resolute in his determination to go to war. His comments late that evening to von Ribbentrop and von Weizsäcker of whom the former favored and the latter opposed military action, that he would now destroy Czechoslovakia by war cannot be dismissed as bluff — there was surely no point in bluffing his own immediate advisers of whom one would continue to argue for war after Hitler had changed his mind and the other had argued against it and continued to do so.

On 28 September Hitler did change his mind. The events of the preceding day now had some new elements added to them. In the morning the news of the mobilization of the British fleet reached Berlin. Such signs of the reality of an imminent world war went along with reports on Chamberlain's speech of the preceding evening, which had on the one hand talked of war as an immediately imminent contingency but on the other hand pointed out how minor the *ostensible* issue was: a short time difference in carrying out a territorial cession already agreed to. Combined with the evident lack of enthusiasm in Germany and the concurrence of Göring and Goebbels with the arguments of the generals this appears to have given Hitler some pause. The British government had been putting forward some new compromise ideas to bridge the gap between the Berchtesgaden and Godesberg terms, and the French were even more inventive in trying to get some immediate concessions that would satisfy Hitler without quite accepting the Godesberg demands. In the late morning of the 28th the French ambassador saw Hitler for the first time in several weeks and presented these ideas to him. A message from Mussolini, appealing to Hitler to postpone the mobilization scheduled for that afternoon, interrupted the meeting with François-Poncet; and soon after the resumed meeting was concluded, Mussolini urged on Hitler Chamberlain's idea of a conference to work out the details of territorial cession instead of resorting to war. This sign that Mussolini himself really preferred peace and would not go to war alongside Germany appears to have been the final factor tipping Hitler in the direction of peace. How had this development come about? . . .

While Hitler was generally reassuring the public in the first years after 1933, he planned and hoped for war and fashioned his preparations and policies accordingly. Mussolini tended to do the reverse: he was always speaking publicly and privately about the virtues of war and the need to fight Britain and France, but his plans and policies were geared to postponing such heroics, quite possibly to the Greek calends. When the reality — as opposed to the theoretical possibility — of the immediate outbreak of world war stared Italy in the face after Godesberg, Mussolini was not willing to fight for Germany's aims in Czechoslovakia, especially at a time when Italy had given a hostage to fate in Spain that would surely be an early casualty of any wider war. He was still reluctant to make this point clear to the Germans, perhaps because he was worried about being thought cowardly, perhaps because he still could not believe that the "decadent democracies" would take the plunge. On the contrary, when the Prince of Hessen was sent to Mussolini after the Godesberg meeting to enlighten the Duce about the stalemate in the negotiations, the imminence of war, and Germany's willingness to risk a general war, Mussolini expressed doubt that Britain and France would move but promised that Italy would come into the war as soon as England did. Ciano's comment that this statement urged Germany neither toward war nor away from it is surely inaccurate; Hitler could only take it as encouragement. That such assurances of support would, at the critical moment a few days later, be followed by urgent telephoned requests first to postpone mobilization, and second to agree to a conference must have been read as a last-minute reversal by Hitler, who had every reason to think up to this moment that he had Mussolini at his side. . . .

The British, like the French, government had been casting about for a way out of what indeed would look like a ridiculous situation if one took Hitler's ostensible demands for his real aims. A world war in which many millions would surely lose their lives was to start over the timetable for implementing a previously agreed plan of territorial transfer; it was under these circumstances that the British Dominions were doing their best to get London to change its position of supporting Czechoslovak rejection of the Godesberg terms. It was, on the other hand, precisely the fixed determination to go to war if Germany moved militarily that made both Chamberlain and Daladier hopeful that a negotiated settlement could still be worked out, but the poor state of Franco-Italian relations made it impossible for the French to appeal to Mussolini. Chamberlain therefore asked Mussolini to intervene with Hitler, something the Italian dictator did immediately, first to obtain a twenty-four-hour postponement of mobilization and then to secure agreement to a conference at Munich in which Mussolini himself promised to participate. Ciano was in favor of a peaceful solution and Mussolini also appears to have fallen in with Chamberlain's request quickly and willingly. . . . We cannot know the reason for Mussolini's action with certainty, but it is difficult to avoid the conclusion that in 1938 — as in 1939 — his realism triumphed over his preferences, but on both occasions his pride restrained him from counsels of prudence until the very last moment. One must look at this procedure from Hitler's point of view to understand the impact of what had to look to him like a last-minute Italian change of heart.

Although we do not possess a record of the Prince of Hessen's report to Hitler on the results of his conference with Mussolini and Ciano on 25 September, it can surely be assumed that having been sent by Hitler on this urgent trip, the prince reported to the Führer on 26 or 27 September. Furthermore, on the 27th the Italians themselves suggested that the Germans and Italians coordinate their political strategy for war by having Ciano and von Ribbentrop meet immediately, to which the Germans added the idea of military consultations, so that Keitel, Pariani, and Valle were added to a gathering that was, ironically enough, scheduled for Munich at noon on the 29th. Certainly the exchanges concerning this meeting left Hitler, through the evening of 27 September, with the impression of an Italy ready to move.

It is with this background of a renewed belief by Hitler that if it did come to a general war, Italy would be at his side — and what this meant for the policies of Yugoslavia and Hungary as well — that the impact of Mussolini's requests to postpone mobilization and to agree to a conference must be considered. In the face of dubious generals, warning diplomats, hesitant allies, and a gloomy public, Hitler changed his policy. He would not risk a general war for what he really wanted, the destruction of Czechoslovakia, but would settle for what he had said he wanted and what everyone now assured, promised, even guaranteed he would get. In a way, he was trapped by his own propaganda strategy, and the attempt to escape the route of peaceful settlement by the policies he had followed after the Berchtesgaden meeting had failed. The determination of the Western Powers to fight if he went after his real aims and their eagerness to accommodate the ostensible ones had created a situation in which Hitler decided not to fight. He would afterwards regret his retreat, as we shall see, and he would even pretend to others and perhaps persuade himself that he had simply bullied concessions out of others; but he had also made concessions himself. He would not test the warnings against military action by Germany, at least not in 1938.

Hitler's acceptance of the conference idea in reality ended the danger of war because, whatever the details of the settlement, there could be no doubt that the Czechoslovak government would have to accept the terms agreed to by Britain, France, Germany, and Italy; and the differences between the various schemes then under discussion for the transfer of the Sudeten areas were not sufficient to cause any serious difficulty in arriving at an agreement. Now that Hitler had reversed himself on the issue of war, he was no longer interested, as he had been after Berchtesgaden, in using the Polish and Magyar minorities as obstacles to a settlement, and it was left to Mussolini to put in a word for them.

Hitler and Mussolini met beforehand, and Hitler discoursed at some length on the need for a general war against Britain and France at an appropriate time when the two of them were still alive, a message which in this context was surely Hitler's way of answering whatever arguments had led Mussolini to change his mind and of inoculating him against a repetition the next time. Mussolini already had a set of demands for the Munich conference, limited to the German areas, which he presented as his own although it had been drafted by Göring, von Neurath, and von Weizsäcker and transmitted to Rome via Attolico. After several hours of discussion, in which the British prime minister brought forward the largest number of objections and reservations on details, agreement was reached on a series of texts that provided for cession of territory in stages, an international commission to arrange the implementation and related details, the dropping of all plebiscite projects and special areas, a time limit for settlement of Polish and Hungarian territorial claims (with a new four-power conference if the time expired without agreement), and British and French guarantees of Czechoslovakia against unprovoked aggression immediately, to be followed later by German and Italian guarantees when the Polish and

Hungarian border issues had been settled. All this was done without the participation of any Czechoslovak representative; the Prague government could accept or take the consequences.

War had been averted to the universal relief of vast numbers. The very way in which the crisis had built up into a deadlock from which a new world war appeared to be the most likely issue had brought the memory of 1914, and of what followed, vividly to the minds of people for whom that war was the greatest horror of their lives. The signs of this were numerous. The extraordinary scene in the House of Commons when Chamberlain was handed Hitler's invitation to Munich in the middle of his speech on 28 September and the members and gallery alike stood and cheered; the telegram from Roosevelt as Chamberlain departed for Munich: "Good Man"; the crowds of Germans cheering Chamberlain and Daladier in obvious contrast to the glum crowds that had watched the military demonstration in Berlin; the euphoric crowd that greeted the shame-faced Daladier on his return to Paris; all show a burst of feeling of relief that war had been averted. Having in resignation steeled themselves to do for Czechoslovakia in 1938 what no one even suggested thinking about thirty years later, the population in England and France reacted to the situation in a way that is surely easy to understand.

For the German people, the peaceful settlement also meant something they could not know at the time. The plan of some of those opposed to the regime to overthrow Hitler had been geared to his willingness to risk a world war to get his way, and the peaceful settlement of the Sudeten question thus removed the basis for the intended action. The plot was called off at the last moment, and whether or not it would have succeeded, most of those involved were not to pull themselves together again for another attempt for a long time. By his last-minute change of policy, Hitler averted an internal crisis; by their willingness to work out a peaceful settlement with Hitler — which was what made Hitler's change of policy possible — the Western Powers removed the basis on which Hitler's internal opponents planned to try to take action.

For Czechoslovakia, agreement first to the Anglo-French plan after Berchtesgaden and submission later to the imposition of the Munich agreement meant the loss of the Sudeten areas, soon followed by the loss of land to Poland and Hungary, under the most humiliating circumstances. These circumstances, combined with the shame and regret they inspired in the Western Powers, led the latter to resent and turn away from those they had treated rather shabbily — a not uncommon reaction — and to refuse to make any real effort to assist Czechoslovakia in its desperate attempt under new leaders and new policies to work out a new life for its people within the new boundaries. The international political repercussions of this, surely the most avoidable, failure of Britain and France will be reviewed in their diplomatic context; but the immediate repercussion for the Czechs and Slovaks was to make the adjustment for them even more difficult than it would have been under the best of circumstances; and eventually it left them completely at the mercy of the Germans. This last, however, would, for some time at least, have been their fate in any case. Barring a successful revolt inside Germany — and this writer at least remains skeptical of the success of what some would have tried but to little avail — there was no serious doubt that Czechoslovakia would have been overrun in the initial German onslaught, as Poland would be in the following year, and that liberation would come only at the end of a long and bitter war. Beneš's recognition of this fact was a major element in his agreement to the territorial cessions. Another factor had been the certainty that at the end of such a war — in which Czechoslovakia would surely suffer much — the Sudeten areas would be lost anyway. The Western Powers had repeatedly made this point clear; there could not in any future peace settlement be a return to the borders of 1919, with the prospect of still another war against Germany to maintain that border later. At the height of the crisis, even as they agreed with the Czechoslovak government's rejection of the Godesberg terms, the British urged Prague to accept an alternative procedure for implementing the agreed territorial cession on the basis that if Germany invaded and a general war ensued, "there is no possibility that at the end of that conflict, whatever the result, Czechoslovakia could be restored to her frontiers of today."

Had there been no agreement for the cession of the land with over three million Germans to Germany, an agreement which the German government itself later tore up to reveal its real ambitions, there would certainly not have been the subsequent agreement of the Allies that Czechoslovakia should receive back the territory she had yielded along with permission to expel the Germans who had lived there for centuries. It was, after all, the Germans who had proclaimed to the world that they could not live in the same country with Czechs. By a tragic irony, it was by giving up the Sudeten areas to a Germany governed by Hitler that Czechoslovakia came to be in a position to reclaim them permanently and with universal agreement. The Soviet Union, the one major power to denounce the Munich agreement, would be the one to insist in 1945 that Czechoslovakia yield to her that portion of the country now adjacent to herself in which the population could be claimed to have a greater affinity to that on the Soviet side of the border — precisely the basis of the Munich settlement.

The British and French governments were immensely relieved by the avoidance of war. There was a sense of the need to remedy some of the military weaknesses that had contributed to their reluctance to fight and their doubts about the outcome of war. But there was also, at least for a short time, a sense of hope that with this great crisis resolved, there could be a new beginning in Europe. Although these hopes would soon be dashed, the policies of Britain and France in the months after Munich were certainly influenced by the view that, war having been averted when it had appeared unavoidable, it should surely be possible to arrive at peaceful solutions of other issues. This expectation was symbolized by the Anglo-German declaration that Chamberlain and Hitler signed right after the Munich agreement and the Franco-German declaration issued when von Ribbentrop visited Paris in December 1938; and it should not be surprising that Neville Chamberlain, who had so personally and dramatically identified himself with the peaceful resolution of the Czechoslovak crisis, should long remain the most persistently and stubbornly optimistic of the participants.

The Soviet Union was offended by its exclusion from the Munich conference and could draw comfort from its ability to denounce the weakness of others in not standing up to the dictators under circumstances where its own risks had been minimal. The question of what to do in the new situation created by the Munich agreement was an open one, and there is considerable evidence that in the weeks after Munich the subject was reviewed from a variety of angles in Moscow. It was assumed that Germany would continue on her aggressive course, but Soviet concern continued to be focused primarily on domestic affairs. The international situation would be watched with care, but the most recent developments reinforced the tendency to concentrate on internal problems. . . .

In the United States, the initial sense of relief would give way to a sense of unease and disapproval even greater than among the opponents of Munich in Britain and France. Not having faced the danger of war themselves, it was much easier for Americans to be indignant about concessions made to Germany. For Americans perhaps more than any others Munich came to be a symbol of surrender to pressure, of capitulation before threats. The idea that it was Hitler who had backed down was and remained inconceivable to American observers then and subsequently. Instead, the supposed lesson of Munich was that firmness at the risk of war was the only reasonable policy in the face of a threatening situation; a view which came to be known as a domino theory of international relations where one concession necessarily led to another and the fall of one barrier necessarily promoted the fall of the next.

For Hitler himself, and hence for the Germany he continued to direct, the Munich agreement was a flawed triumph. It was a triumph in the sense that Germany had got, or rather would get in the next few days, what she claimed she wanted, and would get it under circumstances that conspicuously accentuated the leading role of Germany in Europe. The flaw, of course, was that Hitler had been trapped into settling for what he had publicly claimed rather than what he really wanted and had persistently told his associates he would get. He had had to abandon his plan for a war to destroy Czechoslovakia; and the very fact that his diplomatic triumph was so great could easily lead him to even greater annoyance over having refrained from war, because it suggested that perhaps he had been right after all in insisting that Britain and France would not come to Czechoslovakia's aid. In fact, many National Socialists so maintained afterwards, and those in Germany who had warned of a general war were discredited for their warnings, when in reality the accuracy of their predictions had never been put to the test when Hitler himself had dropped his plan to attack. Because of this shift of the facts — with the warners weakened and discredited because of their concern over a general war when it was Hitler who had at the last moment balked at running the risk against which they had cautioned him — Hitler was able to gain an even greater ascendancy over the country's military structure. Since none of the warners among the military or the diplomatic advisers ever mustered the nerve to point out that their predictions had *not* been tested, Hitler could successfully project onto them his own weakness of resolve.

The many recorded expressions of Hitler's dissatisfaction with the Munich agreement not only reflect his regret over having abandoned his original intentions but also reveal an attitude that helped shape his subsequent policies. . . . Above all, he resented Chamberlain's success in maneuvering him into a peaceful solution.

The insistence that he would under no circumstances be cheated out of a war against Poland in 1939 cannot be understood in any way other than as a determination not to repeat the 1938 experience. The only thing he would then worry about, as he told his generals, was that at the last minute some "Schweinehund," some S.O.B., would come along with a compromise to prevent war; there can be no doubt that it was the British prime minister that he had in mind. Hitler would never again make what he came to think of as his greatest mistake: specifying demands that could be propagandistically justified at home and abroad, but which he thereby risked having granted. In 1939 von Ribbentrop would be personally and strictly instructed by Hitler not to let the German demands on Poland out of his hands; they were written to be used to justify a war, and under no circumstances was anyone to have a chance to accede to them. To the last days of his life Hitler regretted his change of plan in 1938. Musing in his Berlin bunker in February 1945 about the causes of his failure, he would regret that the Western Powers had made it so difficult for him to begin war as early as 1938. "We ought to have gone to war in 1938. . . . September 1938 would have been the most favorable date."

In view of the intention of the French in 1938 to follow essentially the same military strategy that they adhered to in 1939, namely, to do next to nothing, it is possible to argue that even given Hitler's erroneous assumption that a war in 1938 would have been an isolated one, his assessment of the military consequences of postponement was correct. A German offensive in the west in 1939 rather than 1940 would hardly have found the French stronger, and it would have met an England without the radar screen and fighter planes so important in the Battle of Britain. Germany, of course, also became militarily stronger in the interval; there is here still another of the many ironies of the time: Germany's use on a considerable scale of Czechoslovak tanks during World War II.

The subject of the military balance of 1938 versus 1939 can be argued indefinitely; the political side is, however, clear-cut. In 1938 whatever might be said about Hitler's prior actions, the question of whether or not they warranted a world war with all its costs and horrors on the basis of belief — however well founded — concerning his future actions was open to much debate. And in a long war, any democracy would find that debate a very difficult one indeed. After Hitler's deliberate destruction of the Munich agreement, however, the picture changed. Assessments of Hitler's intentions in international affairs were now based on solid and sobering experience. As Churchill expressed it during the war when speaking of Chamberlain in the House of Commons after the latter's death in 1940: "Herr Hitler protests with frantic words and gestures that he has only desired peace. What do these ravings and outpourings count before the silence of Neville Chamberlain's tomb? Long and hard, hazardous years lie before us, but at least we entered upon them united and with clean hearts."

Williamson Murray

War over Czechoslovakia?

Defenders of the Munich Agreement claimed that it was better for France and Britain to avoid war in 1938 because German forces were so strong and the Anglo-French troops would have been defeated.

Williamson Murray, associate professor of history at Ohio State University, attacks the defenders of the Munich Agreement. He argues that it would have been better for Britain and France to have gone to war in 1938 over Czechoslovakia than in 1939 over Poland. His views are in contrast to those of the British Chiefs of Staff expressed in CAB 53/37/01476.

The possible outcome of a war over Czechoslovakia in 1938 has intrigued historians since Munich, particularly those interested in either condemning or justifying Chamberlain's diplomatic and strategic policies. Unfortunately, most students of Munich have regarded the 1938 military situation as a peripheral issue. Few have studied the strategic

From Williamson Murray, *The Change in the Balance of Power, 1938–1939: The Path to Ruin*, pp. 217, 222–223, 245–247, 250–253, 261–263. Copyright © 1984 by Princeton University Press. Reprinted by permission.

situation objectively; most have been content to look for factors supporting a particular point of view and to overlook other contradictory elements. As a result, arguments about the military situation have centered on two issues. Those condemning Munich as a strategic disaster point to Germany's lack of ground strength, and her weakness in the west. They suggest that war in 1938 would have led to the relatively swift collapse of Nazi Germany. On the other hand, some argue that Britain's air defenses were desperately weak and that as a result Chamberlain saved Britain at Munich from defeat at the hands of the Luftwaffe. The problem is, however, far more complex than either view suggests. . . .

In nearly every respect, the Wehrmacht was not ready in 1938. It did not possess an armored force capable of winning decisive victories. It could not fight simultaneously in the east and the west. Germany possessed neither trained reserves nor the industrial capacity to put substantial reserve forces in the field. Industry would have faced considerable difficulty in meeting wartime demands for fuel, ammunition, and weapons just for the regular army. Thus, it is hard to see exactly what major military operations the Germans could have mounted after the conquest of Bohemia.

On the other hand the Anschluss and the looming crisis over the Sudeten borderlands came before the Czechs were ready. They had made progress in correcting deficiencies in the regular army, but work on fortifications had advanced haltingly. In some areas the Czechs had nearly completed the defensive system, but in other districts work had hardly begun. In April 1938 the British military attaché reported that, if the Czechs completed their fortification program, their resistance would surprise not only their enemies, "but all those whose judgment of their capacity for defense was based on a glance at the map." . . . Even along the old Austrian border some fortification work had begun. The attaché disclosed that although these defenses except near Bratislava could not hold the Germans for "more than quite a temporary period, a matter of a day or two," they were strong enough to "prevent anything in the nature of a clear run through and to force the enemy to give battle seriously."

The strongest fortifications lay opposite Silesia, where barely one hundred miles separated Austria from German Silesia. A successful German offensive across this narrow neck would slice Czechoslovakia in half. Because of the Anschluss the Germans could now launch a two-pronged assault to split the Czech state. A German strategic study, written after Munich, reported that Czech fortifications along the Silesian frontier represented a solid system of mutually supporting strong points. In view of mountainous terrain along the Saxon frontier, Czech fortifications were limited, and the system on the Bavarian frontier consisted of a mixture of field works and strong points with the valleys heavily fortified. An additional line of field fortifications stood before Prague. Finally, the fortification work opposite Austria was the weakest in the Czech system. . . .

The Air Situation

One of the most persistent myths in postwar historical literature has been that Chamberlain saved Britain at Munich from defeat at the hands of the Luftwaffe and won time for the RAF [Royal Air Force] to win the "Battle of Britain." Supposedly the year's grace allowed the RAF to equip fighter squadrons with Hurricanes and Spitfires and to extend the radar network to cover the whole of the British Isles. The key question that such commentators do not address is whether Germany could actually have launched a "strategic" bombing offensive in 1938. To answer this question one must establish the actual balance of air power in 1938 by comparing the RAF and the Luftwaffe, and discuss in detail Luftwaffe training and support services as well as strategic and tactical planning.

There are striking similarities in the development of the British and German air forces in the late thirties. Both air staffs had to grapple with rapid expansion, a new generation of aircraft, crew training, supply and maintenance — all on a scale far exceeding anything previously experienced. These problems were so great as to make the respective air forces barely fit for combat for much of the late 1930s. . . . Neither air arm was prepared for the war that would come. The RAF saw a future war as a rapier-like surgical operation carried out by opposing air forces on populations hundreds of miles distant. For the Luftwaffe, air war involved more interservice cooperation, but it also believed in a short war with "strategic" bombing playing a major role.

The reality in the Second World War was, of course, quite different. Air war resembled the strategy of the First World War, although attrition was in terms of aircraft, bombs, crews, training programs, fuel supplies, and munitions production. Month after month, year after year, crews climbed into aircraft to fly over a darkened continent. Success was measured in drops of percentage points in bomber losses rather than yards gained. As one commentator has pointed out: "Despite the visions of its protagonists of prewar days, the air war during the Second World War . . . was attrition war. It did not supplant the operations of conventional forces; it complemented them. Victory went to the air forces with the greatest depth, the greatest balance, the greatest flexibility in employment. The result was an air strategy completely unforeseen by air commanders." Neither air force was ready to fight anything resembling such a war in the late 1930s, when the skills, tactical training, and required depth were not yet at hand.

After the Second World War certain leading air marshals argued that Munich saved Britain from destruction. Sholto Douglas claimed that "without any reservations . . . we followed the only course that we could in the circumstances of the time." Slessor, chief of coastal command during the war, writes, "the question has been discussed whether we also over-estimated the dangers of an attack on England; I can only record my own feelings of profound relief that we were not called upon to answer that question in September 1938." If one considers only the British point of view there is some justification for such claims, but considering actual Luftwaffe capabilities, such a position cannot be defended.

Admittedly the Royal Air Force was not ready for war in September 1938. Its rearmament program had made little progress. Reequipment of fighter squadrons was only beginning, and Bomber Command had no modern aircraft in production. Considerable delay would occur before the great four-engined bombers that ravaged Germany came off assembly lines. . . . When Bomber Command mobilized in September, only ten out of forty-two squadrons possessed what at the time passed for heavy bombers. Reserve aircraft numbered only 10 percent of front-line aircraft, and barely 200 out of 2,500 pilots were fully "operationally ready." Many aircraft had no turrets, and parts were in such short supply that Bomber Command had to cannibalize some squadrons to provide spares. By peacetime standards less than 50 percent of the force was combat-ready.

Fighter Command was in scarcely better shape. Instead of the fifty squadrons considered the minimum for Britain's air defense, twenty-nine existed. Only five of those possessed Hurricanes and none Spitfires. The Hurricanes could not operate at high altitudes because their guns did not have required warmers. The remaining squadrons possessed obsolete Gladiators, Furys, Gauntlets, and Demons. As of October 1, British first-line strength was 1,606 machines with only 412 aircraft in reserve. British estimates for France were 1,454 first-line aircraft with 730 in reserve; and for Germany 3,200 first-line with 2,400 in reserve. In fact the Germans had 3,307 aircraft, including transports, but almost no aircraft in reserve. The British anti-aircraft situation was even less encouraging. . . .

Surprisingly, the situation in Germany did not differ substantially from that in Britain. For most of 1938 the Luftwaffe was involved in exchanging first generation aircraft for those with which it would fight World War II. Fighter squadrons received Bf 109s for their biplane Arado Ar 68s, but by fall 1938 there were no more than 500 Bf 109s in regular fighter squadrons. Furthermore, transition to Bf 109s led to a high accident rate in newly converted squadrons. The two bombers in production, the Do 17 and He 111, were twin-engined aircraft that possessed neither the range nor bomb-carrying capacity to act as real "strategic" bombers, and their defensive armament was insignificant. He 111s carried a bomb load of 500 kilograms, and although London was within their range, they could barely reach industrial regions in the midlands from bases in western Germany. The Do 17 had an even shorter range. Early production models could barely reach London with a 500-kilogram bomb load. Moreover, bombing attacks launched from Germany would not have had fighter escort, for even when based on Pas de Calais in 1940, Bf 109s hardly had sufficient range to stay with the bombers over London. The Ju 88, supposedly a significant advance in bomber construction, would not begin initial production until April 1939 and would not reach full production until 1940. In August 1938 most ground attack squadrons still possessed Hs 123s that carried four 50-kilogram bombs and He 45s that carried eighteen to twenty-four 10-kilogram bombs. In view of raw-material scarcities, German industry would have found it difficult to maintain its rate of aircraft production if war had broken out over Czechoslovakia. On the other hand, once production restraints imposed by the Chamberlain government disappeared because of war, British production would have risen much faster than was actually the case in late 1938 and early 1939.

In numbers, the Luftwaffe mustered just over 3,000 aircraft at the end of September. These consisted of 1,128 bombers, none of which were Ju 88s, 773 fighters, 513 reconnaissance aircraft, 226 dive bombers, 195 ground attack aircraft, 164 naval support aircraft, and 308 transports. In May 1940 shortly before the invasion of France Luftwaffe strength was in excess of 5,000: 666 reconnaissance aircraft, 1,736 fighters, 1,758 bombers, 417 dive bombers, 49 ground attack aircraft, 241 coastal aircraft, and 531 transport aircraft. Differences in strength and quality were striking.

Introduction of a new generation of aircraft brought with it problems in aircrew training, maintenance, and supply. The high accident rate during the summer of 1938 resulted from aircrew training in models that were more sophisticated than anything pilots had up to then handled. The Bf 109 with its narrow undercarriage presented fighter pilots with an especially difficult transition problem. Table 1 on crew training status indicates the Luftwaffe's lack of readiness in 1938 to fight any sort of air war, much less a "strategic" air campaign. The Third Air Force reported that two factors contributed to the large number of partly operational crews: bomber crews that were not fully operational lacked required training in instrument flying, and Stuka crews did not possess fully trained radio operators and gunners.

TABLE 1	German Aircrew State of Readiness, August 1938		
		Crew Training Status:	
Type of Aircraft	*Authorized Number of Crews*	*Fully Operational*	*Partly Operational*
Strat Recon	228	84	57
Tac Recon	297	183	128
Fighter	938	537	364
Bomber	1,409	378	411
Dive Bomber	300	80	123
Ground Attack	195	89	11
Transport	117	10	17
Coastal and Navy	230	71	23
Total	3,714	1,432	1,145

SOURCE: Air Ministry, *The Rise and Fall of the German Air Force, 1933–1945*, Air Ministry Pamphlet No. 248 (London, 1948), pp. 19–20.

The Luftwaffe's "in commission" rate for the period August 1 to December 8 [see Table 2] indicates the extent of supply and maintenance problems. There was a significant improvement in September percentages, but this resulted from a deliberate reduction of flying and training time as *Fall Grün* approached. The Third Air Force admitted that it had brought its "in commission" rate up to a high level by carefully planned measures, but that losses, as well as the heavy demands of combat operations, would have quickly lowered these rates. Additionally, its units did not possess adequate reserves of spare parts to support even normal flying. By December 1938 "in commission" rates had fallen considerably. Although it is hard to estimate how much strain the Luftwaffe could have sustained before combat effectiveness suffered, August "in commission" rates could not have given German commanders encouragement. As already mentioned, the high September percentages do not indicate that the Luftwaffe had solved its maintenance problems. The chief of supply services warned that the Luftwaffe was in an impossible situation in late 1938: "[t]he consequence of these circumstances was: a) a constant and, for first line aircraft, complete lack of reserves both as accident replacements and for mobilization; b) a weakening of the aircraft inventory in the training schools in favor of regular units; c) a lack of necessary reserve engines, supplies for the timely equipment of airfields, supply services, and depots both for peacetime needs as well as for mobilization."

In September 1938 the Luftwaffe faced a complicated strategic situation beyond its capabilities. Contrary to what many pro-appeasement historians and contemporary RAF officers have supposed, the Luftwaffe's first strategic task was to support the destruction of

TABLE 2	Luftwaffe "In Commission" Rates (in Percentages)						
	1 Aug	15 Aug	5 Sep	12 Sep	19 Sep	26 Sep	8 Oct	8 Dec
Bombers	49	58	76	84	89	90	90	78
Fighters	70	78	89	88	93	95	90	78
Overall	57	64	79	83	90	94	92	79

SOURCE: Air Historical Branch, Air Ministry, Vol. VII, Translations: Luftwaffe Strength and Serviceability Statistics, G 302694/AR/9/51/50.

Czechoslovakia. Other tasks, such as the disruption of French mobilization, the protection of North Sea trade, and the bombing of Britain were strictly peripheral to the central mission. In fact, the Second Air Force admitted in September that it was completely unprepared to launch air operations against the British Isles. Even the French in their less panicky moments recognized that the Germans had deployed their bombers to the east. On September 26, Gamelin conceded that most German bombers were on airfields in the vicinity of Czechoslovakia. German planning for both *Fall Rot* and *Fall Grün* deployed the mass of the Luftwaffe against Czechoslovakia. Only after a decisive air and land attack had destroyed Czechoslovakia would the Luftwaffe shift to the west. Air operations and the losses suffered in attacking the Czechs would have seriously affected the Luftwaffe's capacity to launch attacks against Britain later in the year. Moreover, German planning for *Fall Grün* indicates that the Germans expected serious French air attacks against targets in western Germany. Luftwaffe planners especially feared that the French air force would hinder deployment of German forces along the Westwall, thus facilitating a successful French offensive against the Rhineland.

Expecting a major war against Britain well in the future and committed to supporting the attack on Czechoslovakia, the Luftwaffe was unprepared to launch bombing attacks against the British Isles and had only just begun to plan for such an eventuality. In August 1938 one member of Second Air Force staff — which had responsibility for operations over the North Sea and against the British Isles — characterized his command's capability as no more than the capacity to inflict pinpricks. The Second Air Force emphasized that the Wehrmacht would have to seize Belgium and Holland before the Luftwaffe could hope to inflict serious damage on Britain. Any offensive operation to capture the Low Countries would have required extensive Luftwaffe support. . . . As the Luftwaffe discovered after the beginning of the war, it could not undertake air operations against Britain until completion of the land campaign in the west. It did not possess the resources for both, and the ground situation ranked first in German priorities. . . .

In September 1938 the Luftwaffe found itself facing a series of problems that severely restricted its effectiveness against the British Isles. In order to frame weather predictions, the German weather service depended on, 1) reports from England, Iceland, Norway, and Greenland, 2) ship reports from the Atlantic, and 3) reports from France,

Spain, and Portugal. At the end of September the Luftwaffe discovered, much to its consternation, that no alternative sources were available.

Once the above reporting stations were lost, the Germans could not forecast weather over England and would have had difficulty in making long-range continental predictions. Even with well-trained aircrews, the Luftwaffe did not yet have the capacity to bomb accurately in bad weather. The future Field Marshal Albert Kesselrings admitted in 1939 that his excellent all-weather aircraft would still not enable his aircrews to hit targets effectively in bad weather. Moreover, in 1938 the Luftwaffe did not possess the radio technology necessary for long-distance navigation and bombing, and navigation equipment in Germany was designed to aid aircraft operating over the North Sea rather than over England.

Considering that air war has proven itself to be the most scientific, precise form of war man has waged, the technical, as well as the operational, inadequacies of the Luftwaffe in 1938 define its weaknesses. In nearly every respect it was unprepared to launch a "strategic" bombing offensive and so could not have significantly damaged Britain's war effort in spite of weaknesses in British air defenses. In addition, the Luftwaffe would have had difficulty just in fulfilling its operational commitments to support ground forces operating against Czechoslovakia and the west.

Conclusion: War in 1938

The striking feature of the 1938 military situation was the relative unpreparedness of *all* the European nations to fight even a limited, much less a major, war. For the Germans the problem was compounded not only by their military unpreparedness, but by their economic vulnerability. Thus, German strategy had to be predicated on winning a war quickly, or at least if that were not possible, on the conquest of an economic and strategic base from which a long war could be prosecuted. For the Germans, the central question was not whether their army could conquer Czechoslovakia. There was no doubt about that and in retrospect it seems likely that the Wehrmacht could have completed the task in one to two months. Such a campaign, however, because of the nature of the terrain, the equipment of the Czech army, Czech fortifications, and the general state of unpreparedness of the German armored force, would have involved significantly higher casualties than the campaign against Poland in 1939. Moreover, such a campaign would have destroyed most of the Czech stocks of armaments that the Germans found so useful the following spring and might well have led to the destruction of the Czech armament industry.

But the conquest of Czechoslovakia would have had only a small impact on the strategic situation of a Germany involved in a world war. The inclusion of Czechoslovakia within the German economic orbit would have done little to alleviate shortages of raw materials. The central problem for the Nazi regime after the conquest of Czechoslovakia would have been, what next? Germany would have embarked on a world war with an unprepared military and an almost desperate economic situation. She might well have had the Italians as allies, which would have added to her economic and military burdens without bringing any corresponding advantages. The Axis economic area would have been limited to Germany, Italy, Hungary, a damaged Czechoslovakia, perhaps Yugoslavia, and the vulnerable ore trade with Sweden. Military operations against Rumania to conquer vital oil would have met a Soviet response and probably would have led to the destruction of the wells and refineries as had occurred in the First World War. . . .

We have pointed out that France possessed overwhelming superiority on Germany's western frontier, but that the French appeared unwilling and unable to take advantage of their superiority should war break out. Nevertheless, if the French were unwilling to attack Germany's western frontier, the Germans were in no position to win a strategic victory in the west. This does not mean that after the conquest of Czechoslovakia Gemany would not have tried. As in 1940 the Germans would have had no other choice but to attack through Belgium and Holland in order to acquire the resources necessary for further prosecution of the war. But it is hard to see how the Germans could have gained the stunning strategic victories of 1940. There were few paratroopers for missions such as seizing Belgian and Dutch forts and bridges. The armored force certainly could not have undertaken the offensive that the Germans launched so successfully through the Ardennes in 1940. Moreover, in view of the shortage of fuel and munitions as well as its internal weaknesses, the Luftwaffe could not have intervened as decisively in a land campaign as it did in 1940. Thus, although the Germans might have won tactical victories in the west in 1938 or early 1939, it is most likely that they could have won a strategic victory and knocked France out of the war. The Germans might also have gained peripheral victories, such as the conquest of Denmark, in order to stave off economic collapse, but each military operation the Germans could launch during this period would have had the counterproductive result of using up scarce resources without supplying compensatory long-range gains for the war economy.

As a result, the war would have turned, as had the First World War, and as the Second World War would, on the economic strength and staying power of the opposing sides. In terms of numbers of divisions, economic resources, industrial capacity, and naval forces, Germany would have faced overwhelming Allied superiority in 1938 whether she faced only Britain and France, or an enlarged coalition that included Russia and perhaps Poland. Even so, the war against Germany would not have been easy, nor would it have been quickly won. But the results would have been inevitable and would have led to the eventual collapse of the Nazi regime at considerably less cost than the war that broke out the following September.

A Stuka dive-bombing Warsaw, September 1939. (Robert Hunt Library, England)

V The Intelligence Muddle

Wesley K. Wark

British Military Intelligence

The British government feared war with Germany in 1938 because of the military intelligence assessment of the German armed forces. Wesley K. Wark, assistant professor of history, University of Toronto, focuses on the phases in British intelligence forecasts and their effect on policy. British intelligence assessments of the German war machine evolved over the years. They were not produced quickly, nor were they clear and accurate. Instead, as they developed, they passed through phases: secrecy, honeymoon, blindness, and war scares that ended in the outbreak of war in 1939. The variations in intelligence assessment made it difficult to make the long-range predictions necessary for strategic planning, foreign policy, and defense.

Reprinted from Wesley K. Wark, *The Ultimate Enemy: British Intelligence and Nazi Germany, 1933–1939*, pp. 225–240. Copyright © 1985 by Cornell University. Used by permission of the publisher, Cornell University Press.

The outbreak of war in September 1939, following the German attack on Poland, offered grim proof of the validity of the original forecast set down by the DRC [Defence Requirements Committee] in 1934 — that Germany would be Britain's ultimate potential enemy and that military preparations might make war possible within five years. Yet in the five years after the first DRC report, that forecast had been heavily overshadowed by the subsequent evolution of an intelligence picture of Nazi Germany. No single intelligence authority, looking back on its record, could claim credit for much foresight. Instead, a solitary and private tribute was paid to the man who had been most consistent in the role of anti-German Cassandra — Sir Robert Vansittart. On Sunday, March 26, 1939, Sir Alexander Cadogan, his successor as permanent undersecretary in the Foreign Office, wrote in his diary, "I must say it is turning out — at present — as Van predicted and as I never believed it would."

The dread of war was still present in 1939, and war was still being painted in those apocalyptic hues that were a feature of interwar literature. George Orwell gave one such portrait in a book composed just after the Munich crisis, *Coming Up for Air*. Orwell's protagonist, George Bowling, cannot escape an obsessive vision of the coming war, the destruction that aerial bombing would cause, and the arrival of fascism (a distinctive Orwellian touch), which the outbreak of war would hasten. Thus, Bowling muses:

> *War is coming. 1941 they say. And there'll be plenty of broken crockery and little houses ripped open like packing cases and the guts of the chartered accountant's clerk plastered over the piano that he's buying on the never-never. It's all going to happen. All the things that you've got at the back of your mind, the things that you tell yourself are just a nightmare and only happen in foreign countries. The bombs, the food queues, the rubber truncheons, the barbed wire, the coloured shirts, the slogans, the enormous faces, the machine guns squirted out of bedroom windows.*

Not all of Orwell-Bowling's nightmare came to pass, though the bombs were to rain on London before 1941.

What did come to pass was a startling change in outlook in Whitehall and among the people of Britain that helped to modulate the fear of war. One aspect of this change was a reappraisal of German military power, beginning with the experience of the Munich crisis and climaxing with the events of February–March 1939. The COS [Chiefs of Staff] 1939 strategic appreciation gave fullest expression to the military's more confident reading of the balance of power. The cabinet showed itself prepared to envisage war, if only as a last resort, by dealing out guaranties to Poland, Romania, and Greece.

The costs of embracing a conviction about the inevitability of an Anglo-German conflict were heavy. The public and the intelligence authorities alike had to put aside contemplation of the terror of a modern, mechanized war. The public, however, being less knowledgeable about the perils of the global balance of power and about Britain's postwar decline in strength, was more free to be moved on the tide of an emotional and moral reaction against Hitler's Germany. Intelligence officers, on the other hand, had to struggle against the inhibiting effects of a previous spate of pessimistic reports. A psychological adjustment was necessary and was found in the search for a German Achilles' heel — whether it was economic exhaustion, problems of internal morale, or unreadiness for a long war. The comments of the air staff member of the JPC [Joint Planning Sub-Committee] Group Captain J. C. Slessor, in the winter of 1938, illustrate this motive well. At one stage in the drafting of the 1939 strategic appreciation, Slessor minuted to his colleagues: "Does it not still present rather too gloomy a picture? There is a considerable amount of evidence available from current literature and intelligence sources to show that Germany's belt is already about as tight as she can bear, and that in making such stupendous efforts to achieve an initial advantage in military strength, she has used up all her hidden resources. Everything she has is in the shop window, and this is not really at all a satisfactory basis on which to commence a war."

The new image of German military power that emerged marked the final stage in a complex process of prewar intelligence assessment. In retrospect, four distinct phases in the British intelligence effort against Nazi Germany can be identified and labeled: the period of secrecy (1933–35); the honeymoon (1935–36); blindness (1936–38); and war scares and war (1938–39). Four such phases have already been identified in the previous chapters dealing with air and army intelligence. It is now possible to extend this same chronology to cover the overall development of a British intelligence picture of the German war machine, taking account of the variant analyses offered by the Admiralty and the IIC [Industrial Intelligence Center], as well as the way in which the JPC and COS strategic appreciations provided a synthesis of the intelligence material. Each phase reveals service intelligence directorates, the IIC, and the COS engaged in elaborating or rebuilding their own images of German power. Each phase was characterized by certain problems with the supply, analysis, and dissemination of intelligence. One common feature was the impact of a cycle of alternating optimism and pessimism on the measurement of German threat.

The work of the intelligence authorities in the first phase, the period of secrecy (1933–35), was determined, more than anything else, by the difficulty of making long-range predictions on the basis of scanty information. The degree of secrecy imposed by the Third Reich on defense programs greatly hindered the efforts of the official intelligence system. Service attachés in Berlin were allowed to see little; official contacts proved reticent; and the press was, of course, controlled by the government. The SIS [Secret Intelligence Service] was in no position to take up the slack. Signals intelligence was almost nonexistent, with only army traffic being monitored; and the secret-agent network was badly run down and short of expertise on technical military matters.

It made little difference that intelligence collection was proving difficult; the demand increased. Press reports, emigré publications, and debates in the House of Commons, particularly those featuring clashes between Winston Churchill and government spokesmen on the growth of the German air force, brought intelligence into a new prominence and increased the pressures on supply. Behind the scenes, cabinet committees insisted upon better information. Occasionally, the wording of documents even suggested that intelligence itself would be a significant weapon in Britain's peacetime arsenal. The third DRC report noted, "The best that we can do is strengthen our Intelligence system and our own war potential (output capacity), so as to be able to increase our forces correspondingly in the case of a German increase."

Another kind of pressure placed on the intelligence system stemmed from demands made by the joint planners. What the planners found they needed in order to compose their strategic appreciations was an assessment of probable German force levels in 1939. Sufficient data was simply not available, however; nor could it have been acquired even in the best of all possible intelligence worlds. German military planning was still in a state of considerable flux, and new generations of weapons would soon appear to increase the difficulties of accurate prediction of future military power.

Instead of approaching the task of long-range prediction with due caution and a degree of self-criticism, the response of the service intelligence directorates and, to some extent, the IIC as well was blithely to substitute general hypotheses for hard facts. These hypotheses were built up from analogies with British practice (mirror images), from preconceptions about the nature of German military and industrial life (above all the notion of Teutonic efficiency), and from received propaganda (the Admiralty's Baltic myth being a case in point).

What resulted from this combination of insufficient information and substituted hypotheses was an early image of future German military might that had many optimistic features. The general expectation was that the German armed forces would be rearmed well above Versailles treaty levels but only to a strength sufficient to satisfy the demands of national security. Thus no aggressive intent was assumed from the evidence of Versailles infractions. The German army, it was supposed, was being increased to enable it to deal with any single Central or Eastern European foe but would not be great enough to prevail in a two-front war. The air force program was assumed to be based on the achievement of parity with the French. Naval rearmament was presumed to be directed toward the assertion of control in the Baltic against the lesser fleets of the Scandinavian powers and the U.S.S.R. The IIC, a dissenting voice amidst the general optimism, did not set such obvious limits to the expansion of German strength in the industrial sphere but reported that Germany would soon become a "formidable military factor" in Europe.

Coupled with the overall assumption that Germany's rearmament goals were limited in conception and defensive in orientation was the notion that the pace of rearmament would be governed by the dictates of efficiency. In British eyes this meant that German rearmament would proceed at a moderate pace to maintain high standards of professionalism and the best possible utilization of weapons systems. This conservative outlook on rearmament, which showed little understanding of the Nazi dynamic, was perhaps the most flagrant contribution to what proved to be a set of grievous underestimates of future German military strength.

The most coherent expression of the British intelligence image of

Nazi Germany in the phase of secrecy came with the long-overdue production of the JPC's draft strategic appreciation in October 1935. In a 1939 conflict between Britain (joined by her Locarno allies France and Belgium) and Germany, the military balance was expected to show comfortable margins of superiority for the Allies in all three dimensions of warfare — air, land, and sea. In other respects, the period of secrecy was brought to a close earlier, in March 1935, when Hitler made propaganda capital from a series of menacing exposures of the official existence and strength of a refurbished German army and air force. Although the figures given out by Hitler were higher than those upon which British Intelligence had been working, no immediate shake-up in the image of German power occurred.

The ensuing period of the honeymoon (1935–36) was shorter in duration but involved little real change in overall assessments. The label *honeymoon* is appropriate in two senses. For one thing, as the German rearmament effort emerged from secrecy, much effort was spent on the British side in the pursuit of arms limitation agreements with the Germans as a substitute for the failure of the Geneva conference. With the exception of the Anglo-German Naval Agreement [AGNA], regarded as a model by few outside the circle of the Admiralty, these pursuits were sterile. Yet hopes persisted. *Honeymoon* serves also as a description of the brief relationship that grew up between the British armed forces and their German opposite numbers. No longer cloaked in secrecy, further German rearmament was ostensibly a matter of public record. Service attachés were allowed opportunities to visit military bases, maneuvers, and armament factories, although the itineraries were always carefully controlled. Officer exchanges were arranged, a German air attaché arrived in London, and the German military attaché began to enjoy a friendly relationship with the MI3 [Military Intelligence, German Division] staff. Naturally, the volume of overt intelligence increased considerably. Its interpretation was still governed by the set of hypotheses generated during the phase of secrecy, depicting a conservative pace in rearmament. The assertions of various German officials, from the führer downward, signaling the limits on rearmament, fitted easily into the already established image of German military power. The War Office, for example, remained wedded to the belief that the regular German army would not exceed the thirty-six-division strength laid down for it by Hitler in his March 1935 pronouncement. The Admiralty accepted German denials of any intent to exceed the 35 percent limit allowed for by the AGNA. The Air Ministry clung to the belief that the Luftwaffe goal was parity with France.

IIC analysis continued to fit uneasily into the overall intelligence image. The center remained true to its primary assumption that the German economy was in the process of being transformed for war purposes. At the same time, the IIC needed to assimilate new information on German production and raw materials difficulties. The explanation it offered for such problems during 1935–36 was that German industry was concentrating its resources on plant expansion. Therefore, fluctuations in output were only to be expected. The third DRC report took note of the potential industrial superiority of Nazi Germany; otherwise, the IIC's consistent warnings caused but little alarm. Without a significant change in service intelligence outlooks, capabilities could not be used to reflect on intentions.

Yet another feature of the honeymoon was the more strident calls made by some service departments for an alternative foreign policy towards Germany. Both the Admiralty and the War Office developed visions of a limited liability policy that would rule out an Anglo-German clash so long as Hitler did not directly threaten Britain or the status quo in the West. These visions, when incautiously circulated, landed both departments in difficulties with the Foreign Office. The one service that did not make any effort to formulate an alternative policy was the Air Ministry. Although there was little love lost between the Air Ministry and the Foreign Office, the air staff could scarcely have formulated any alternative without some cost to itself. It could not stress the German danger more strongly than the Foreign Office for fear that the government might react by accelerating aerial rearmament at an unwise pace. On the other hand, it could not press too strongly for armaments pacts with Germany for fear that an agreement would lead to the abolition of the RAF's bomber force. The Air Ministry case apart, it was one index of the profound change that came over intelligence assessments in the autumn of 1936, that the War Office's dabbling in foreign policy ceased while the Admiralty's efforts grew more defensive.

The change which brought the honeymoon phase to a rather abrupt end was the result of an accumulating weight of evidence that could no longer be made to fit with the old hypothesis of a rearmed but benevolent Nazi Germany. In the autumn of 1936, intelligence authorities in both the War Office and Air Ministry were forced to concede that German rearmament might be theoretically unlimited and practically constrained only by industrial factors. The threat of German military hegemony on the continent for the first time loomed large.

War Office files for September–October 1936, a restricted circulation CID [Committee of Imperial Defence] paper on the Luftwaffe presented in October, and the JPC's strategic appreciation of the same month provide the key documents for a study of the radical shift in outlook that was underway. The reporting contained in these documents was ominous, no more so than in the case of the joint planners' paper. Their assessment, with its portrayal of a dangerous balance of power on land and the possibility of German aerial superiority being employed in a terrible knockout blow against London, marked the beginning of a period in which pessimism was the dominant theme in intelligence analysis.

Just as the IIC became more closely integrated into the study of German military preparations, the Admiralty drew apart. Closer integration of the IIC was a direct result of the concept that limits to German rearmament might have to be discovered in the field of economics. The self-enforced isolation of the Admiralty derived from the fact that so long as the AGNA remained intact, the Admiralty could not conceive of a direct German threat to Great Britain. Yet it was the perceived threat from the air, rather than the lack of threat from the sea, that commanded attention.

The third phase in the evolution of the British image of Nazi Germany, that labeled blindness, lasted from the autumn of 1936 to the autumn of 1938. Within this period a number of major crises occurred — the outbreak of the Spanish Civil War, the *Anschluss*, and the Munich crisis. For the first time, units of the German armed forces ranged beyond the 1919 borders of the Reich. The Four-Year Plan was launched, its provisions for economic autarky seeming to confirm the IIC's long-held conviction that the Third Reich was intent on gearing its industries for total war. British appeasement policy, under a new prime minister, Neville Chamberlain, reached its high point. Undeniably, this policy was influenced by the pessimism that flowed from intelligence circles. The near and medium-term military balance was presumed to be perilous, a perception that was instrumental in convincing the cabinet to avoid the dangers of any attempt at deterrence, above all during the Munich crisis. An Anglo-German confrontation was thereby postponed, yet the German armed forces of September 1938, in terms of war readiness and overall mobilized strength, were a much inferior foe compared to the military machine that performed so impressively in the campaigns of 1940. The label *blindness* seems appropriate to the way in which the intelligence authorities failed to provide a balanced reading of German strengths and weaknesses under the impact of cumulative worst-case assessments.

Also characteristic of this period were the unique difficulties being experienced with the supply of information. An earlier phase of intelligence work, 1933–35, had suffered from outright shortages of information, but during 1937 and 1938, the problem was less quantity than quality of information. With the new appreciation of the German menace, a greater premium was placed on information bearing on the German armed forces' operational capabilities, on technological matters, and on Hitler's mind (and intentions). The last topic was never even assayed by the service intelligence directorates or by the IIC but was left to the Foreign Office and the SIS. Within their own field, the services found themselves in a state of some confusion over the precise striking power and likely strategic doctrine of the German air force and army. During this period the work of the German section of the Air Ministry and the SIS came under review, and both were found unsatisfactory.

The overall result of the phase of blindness and its accompanying message of pessimism can be seen in the series of military appreciations drawn up by the joint planners and the COS during 1937–38. Government leaders became so thoroughly accustomed to the gloomy content of COS reporting that they began to take it for granted and to treat consultation with their senior military advisers as something of a formality. Such was the fate of military advice from the period immediately after the *Anschluss* until late in the Munich crisis. Not only was military advice all too familiar to the cabinet, but in any case the services had little positive guidance to offer. Their *leitmotif* was Britain's unreadiness and the folly of a war over Czechoslovakia. When compelled to speculate on the possibilities of deterrence, they phrased their answer in terms designed to give the government little taste for adventure.

The final phase in the British intelligence portrayal of Nazi Germany occurred during 1938–39, the phase of war scares and war. The chief characteristics of this period were threefold: a sustained crisis atmosphere, which proved extremely wearing on the intelligence staffs; a flood of rumors about German military moves, whose reliability the intelligence staffs had difficulty in determining; and a further shift in the overall assessment of German military power. A belated sense of military confidence, mixed in with exhaustion and a desire to make a stand, provided the backdrop to the Polish guaranty and helped sustain the government in its attempts to deter Hitler from war in the spring and summer of 1939. War Office and Air Ministry officials, both attachés abroad and London-based staff, provided the lead in what was the last and arguably most radical prewar shift from pessimism to optimism.

The new optimism was different from the old. Whereas in 1933–35 intelligence staffs were thinking in terms of a future in which a rearmed Germany would coexist with the other European powers in peace, their counterparts in 1939 were talking about surviving a knock-out blow and going on to crush Nazi Germany at length with an economic stranglehold, an aerial offensive, and perhaps, once resistance was low, a land campaign. Since the eastern front was meant to function as a deterrent to German aggression, intelligence staffs spent some time attempting to find out whether the deterrent was working. But there remains no sign in the surviving records that much faith was invested in the search. Service intelligence directorates had, in any case, too little prior experience with this sort of question to come up with any answers.

Despite the early forecasts and the effort spent on drawing up strategic appreciations, the fact was that the prospect of Britain's being drawn into a European war by 1939 was not treated as real until the year arrived. The military in Britain were not prophets of the inevitability of conflict. Admirable as such an outlook was in theory, it had its cost in the delays in rearmament and in the diplomatic defeats suffered by Britain throughout the decade. There can be no doubt that Britain suffered through a classic intelligence failure stemming, not from an inability to identify one's enemy, but from an inability to understand the real nature of the threat that enemy posed. Variations on such a failure can be seen at work in each of the four phases through which intelligence progressed. The question of how to weigh the degree of overall failure depends on an understanding of the impact of intelligence on policy, and on the contribution made by an unwritten intelligence doctrine.

Even at the time, the British intelligence system was charged with failing to understand that a conflict with Nazi Germany was looming. One British spokesman was badgered by an American audience in the winter of 1938–39 on this very point. Bruce Lockhart, a man with a colorful past in intelligence, recalled being addressed by persistent questions as to why the British were so badly informed. While attempting to reassure his American audience that this was not the case, Lockhart had had flung back at him the rejoinder: "Will you explain why for six years your country did nothing to avert a danger which . . . was obvious to the rest of the world?" Although Lockhart, as a beleaguered visitor to the United States on behalf of the British Council, was in no position to answer this charge, it does raise the issue of the connection between intelligence assessments and policy. . . .

One notable feature is the relationship between the large shifts in the image of German power from 1933 to 1939 and the nature of defense and foreign policy choices. In the early phases of intelligence reporting there was a general lack of conviction about the danger of an Anglo-German conflict. These years, the first three of the Nazi era, witnessed the attempt to frame security pacts and arms limitation agreements with the dictator referred to by one ambassador as "that damnably dynamic man." British rearmament programs lacked urgency and were based on underestimates of future German strength. When the prospect of conflict came to seem less fantastic, as it did after 1936, military advisers used their supply of pessimistic intelligence images to urge that conflict be avoided or at least delayed. Neville Chamberlain, acting on this message and on his own innermost convictions, gave the firmest direction a British cabinet had yet seen to a policy of appeasement in Berlin and Rome. The ill-fated Munich settlement was one result. Acceleration of British rearmament programs occurred from 1936, but valuable time had been lost. Grave troubles arose in virtually every sphere of the British rearmament effort — supply, production, and finances. The German armed forces quickly achieved and held on to a quantitative lead, especially in the air. Yet the course of the Anglo-German arms race came to be seen in a new light after Munich. The intelligence available in 1939 and the uses made of it to paint a more optimistic picture of the balance of power helped confirm the government in a strategic outlook it had already begun to embrace. This new outlook, itself an outcome of the disappointing (for the British) course of events since Munich that climaxed following the German occupation of Prague in March 1939, was the occasion for the achievement of a new synthesis between intelligence and government policy. The government moved to adopt a new foreign policy stance of greater resistance toward Hitler, finding a military rationale in the eastern front and the new intelligence-inspired mood of strategic confidence.

What emerges from this pattern is the mutual support that operated between intelligence assessments and appeasement policy. Despite the gravity of the shifts in the military and economic image of German power, these were accommodated by changes of emphasis in appeasement. At no stage during the 1930s were there any fundamental contradictions between intelligence reporting and the foreign policy of the government. In fact, the intelligence picture tended, if anything, to provide the strongest possible support for the government's efforts to maintain pacific relations with the Third Reich. This was true of the earliest phases of intelligence reporting, which provided a picture of relatively limited German rearmament. And it was especially true of the phase after 1936, when new information brought an exaggeration of the German military threat and pessimism about the survival of Great Britain in a future war. Yet if the major impact of intelligence reporting was habitually to confirm the government in its conduct of foreign policy, this in itself raises questions, for appeasement ultimately failed.

The success of British foreign policy with regard to Nazi Germany during the 1930s can be seen to have depended on two interlocking conditions — that Hitler be induced to accept negotiated settlements to problems in Europe and that British rearmament present a sufficiently threatening face to serve as an ultimate sanction. Neither condition came to pass. It is difficult to resist the conclusion that appeasement policy was, sooner or later, doomed to failure, given the incompatibility of outlook between Great Britain and the Third Reich. But intelligence reporting helped bring on this doom. The contribution of intelligence, in this sense, was strikingly negative.

One of the major flaws of the intelligence picture, as has been pointed out earlier, was the inability to reach a realistic assessment of the balance of strengths and weaknesses in the German military machine. Prior to 1936, the full military potential of Nazi Germany was underrated. This assessment deprived the government of any impetus to convert the British economy to intensive rearmament (in any case a difficult decision) and provided no motive for an examination of the long-term possibilities of peace. In the years between 1936 and the Munich crisis, still following the phases of intelligence reporting, exaggeration of the immediate capability of the German armed forces to fight a decisive land and air war led the government to acquiesce in the exercise of German *force majeure* against Czechoslovakia. Once again, the military intelligence contribution to policy was negative. It served to eliminate serious consideration of alternatives to appeasement of the kind advocated outside the cabinet by Sir Robert Vansittart and inside (though more tentatively) by ministers such as Duff Cooper and Oliver Stanley. Above all, any effort at deterrence was ruled out by the bleak picture of the military balance. By the time the British intelligence system began to adjust its assessments of Nazi Germany to incorporate a more balanced vision of German strengths and deficiencies, it was very late in the day. Having provided the government with the strategic rationale for an effort at deterrence in 1939, the intelligence authorities could then give no indication of whether the deterrence was actually working.

The largely negative contribution made by intelligence to the formulation of policy leads naturally to the question of what effect a different set of military assessments might have had. It is not the purpose of this study to suggest that the history of appeasement policy depended upon misperceptions generated by the official intelligence system alone, but one speculation is irresistible. Had the military confidence of February–March 1939 somehow manifested itself a year earlier (and why not, given the subterranean dimensions of that change of front towards Hitler), events might well have taken a different turn. The data on German deficiencies was at hand and waiting for a more optimistic interpretation in September 1938. The reality was that after March 1939 a British effort at deterrence lacked all conviction in the capitals that mattered — Berlin and Moscow. The only alternative to appeasement was war, not a disastrous war for the British, but very nearly so. The intelligence services of the government, to summarize the negative nature of their contribution to policy, simply failed to be sufficiently thought-provoking, failed to provide challenges to a narrowly conceived and increasingly dogmatic appeasement policy, and were instrumental in delaying the exercise of deterrence until it was too late to be effective.

One curious feature of this period was the evident inability of leading politicians to understand the nature of the intelligence contribution. Even politicians with extensive experience of intelligence, such as Sir Samuel Hoare and Sir Winston Churchill, misunderstood the links between intelligence and policy. Hoare, in his memoirs at least, was completely dismissive of the quality of intelligence supplied to the government and argued that even the purest, high-level information from inside the Third Reich would not have altered appeasement policy at all. He failed to see that it was also intelligence, and not just the convictions of the Chamberlain-led cabinet in which he served, that was fueling appeasement policy. Churchill, a senior but obstreperous back-bench MP, had a very different outlook. It was his conviction that the government was ignoring uncomfortable information from its intelligence services. But if there was any candidate for Churchill's hidden "hand which intervenes and filters down or withholds intelligence from Ministers," it was to be found in the process of analysis within the intelligence community itself, especially in the early years of the 1930s.

That intelligence would have the kind of negative impact it did was partly due to the mechanism by which specialized assessments were fitted into an overall image of German power. Individual departmental failures of perception and the lack of coordination in the system meant that, even once the dynamism of German rearmament was recognized, there would be too little agreement on the precise nature of the strategic threat posed by Germany and, here as well, too few opportunities for appraising German strengths against weaknesses. Worst-case analysis, which came to prevail after 1936, not only inflated particular threats but resulted in a cumulative escalation of the overall menace. The costs of such an analysis became apparent in retrospect. It could easily lead to pessimism and yet only once was the method questioned. The credit goes to Sir Maurice Hankey, who rejected it as a basis for the making of strategic appreciations during the DCOS [Deputy Chiefs of Staff] 1936 meetings. However, the worst-case approach was not moderated until 1939 and then only because it grew too uncomfortable.

Identification of the worst-case approach naturally leads to the question of what other tools the intelligence authorities used during the 1930s. No intelligence doctrine was ever codified but certain nascent elements can be isolated. Most were less obtrusive than the worst-case approach but perhaps no less fundamental. One element was the assumption that intelligence analysis described a rational world in which decisions were taken on the basis of careful calculation of risks and rewards. It is difficult to fault the intelligence authorities for making this assumption, but it grew harder to sustain once perception of Hitler as a leader capable of "mad-dog" acts took hold. Allied to the tendency to see the world as rational and to expect the worst were two other elements of doctrine. The British effort in intelligence during the 1930s revealed a tendency to place greater faith in quantitative measures of power than in qualitative distinctions. For much of the decade German power was seen as an arithmetical sum of the number of divisions, the number of aircraft, and the number of warships she possessed, as well as the quantities coming off the production lines. Such features as the quality of equipment, standards of training, and armed forces morale were much more difficult to assess and tended to be left out of the picture. Thinking about German power in purely quantitative terms encouraged optimism in the early phase of reporting, when levels of German rearmament were low, and later stimulated the exaggeration of German capabilities, when the pace of German rearmament grew alarming.

The reliance on quantitative estimates should not be taken to mean that once a certain level of force was achieved it was expected that war would ensue. A. J. P. Taylor is wrong to suggest that an assumption existed that, "once Germany had rearmed, war would more or less follow of itself." What is striking is almost the reverse assumption. Service departments persisted until at least 1936 and, in the case of the Admiralty, until later in imagining a peaceful future for Europe. Numerical reporting of German power did not lend itself to the assessment of German intentions, and the overt intelligence authorities seem to have deliberately eschewed making such linkages.

Yet a bridge did exist between the measurement of German capabilities and intentions, though not in quite the form imagined by Taylor. It was the product, instead, of the characterization given to the Nazi totalitarian state by the intelligence authorities. The totalitarian state was assumed to combine efficiency with the ruthless exercise of power toward well-defined goals. The advantage such attributes gave a state engaged in rearming impressed both politicians and military men alike. Stanley Baldwin was quoted as saying that "dictatorships always enjoy a two year lead over democracies." Air Marshal Sir Douglas Evill was more specific. Following a visit of inspection to the Luftwaffe in early 1937, he wrote that the work of building up an air force in Germany "is proceeding with entire freedom from all those factors political, financial, bureaucratic and social, to which we in this country have become accustomed." Nothing could have been further from the truth, but Evill's remark illustrates not only the frustrations generated by difficulties with British rearmament but also the belief that in the German system commands could be hammered much more readily into results.

This study has not attempted to investigate the social or intellectual biases of individual intelligence officers or of intelligence personnel as a class. However, the rather widespread tendency to ascribe advantages to the totalitarian state for rearmament purposes suggests a weakening faith in the democratic system. Such loss of faith might well be attributed to the sense of isolation from society experienced by a generation of service personnel following the disasters of World War I. Whatever the nature of the speculation, this built-in exaggeration of the purposefulness of the totalitarian state was a recognizable part of the intelligence doctrine. The totalitarian, and Nazi, state was almost synonymous with efficiency.

One final element might be identified as a misplaced pragmatism. During the 1930s little faith was placed in long-range intelligence forecasts, and they were often badly done. Vansittart believed that such pragmatism had the effect of undermining the value of intelligence prediction and saw it at work in the mind of Stanley Baldwin: "He [Stanley Baldwin] did not believe in foreboding, which is also un-British. 'The man who says he can see far ahead is a charlatan,' he said, but how far is far, since we *must* see ahead to be safe. . . . Yet I wondered how he could be so equable, if he was sure that 'the bomber will always get through.' " A. L. Rowse thought he saw the same dangerous outlook in the minds of an entire generation. He wrote, in *All Souls and Appeasement:* "In this story we see the decadence of British empiricism, empiricism carried beyond all rhyme or reason. . . . The practical way of looking at things, not looking too far . . . not rocking the boat, and other clichés that do duty for thinking ahead, may serve well enough in ordinary, normal times. . . . [It] will certainly not serve in times of revolution, perpetual stress and conflict, war, the reshaping of the world. This conventional British way of looking at things was simply not equal to the times, and it caught these men out badly." Rowse's statement might stand as an epithet to the failure of understanding, by no means unique, displayed by the intelligence authorities concerning the dynamism and nature of the Nazi state.

These elements of an uncodified and only loosely defined intelligence doctrine can be seen to have held the seeds of misperception and ultimate exaggeration when used against the target of the Nazi state in the 1930s. Yet it would be wrong to end this study on an entirely critical or deterministic note. Within the wider context of a study of European military elites in the interwar period, D. C. Watt enumerated the kinds of questions that must be asked about their performance. Among these was the question, "How good were their intelligence-gathering machines?" This study has suggested that the British intelligence effort featured a mixture of major failures and sometimes remarkable successes. The most consistent work was done in the more traditional forms of intelligence — the gathering of order-of-battle data and the monitoring of current German strength. In many respects this kind of intelligence provided the essential basis for the more complex long-range assessments of German power. British successes in the area of current estimates and order-of-battle intelligence may be attributed to one of two conditions: either to a long study of a selected German problem, for example, of secret rearmament prior to 1933; or to the development of an adequate range of sources on a specific topic, as illustrated by the air staff's ability to accurately estimate the first-line strength of the Luftwaffe in March 1935, or the War Office's ability to monitor German army deployments during the Munich crisis. The difficulty that the British experienced was in interpreting the quantitative data to arrive at some indication of the capabilities and future power of the German military. The intelligence authorities were simply too hard-pressed by the kinds of reporting required of them. Demands for estimates of the current strength of a branch of the German armed forces were jumbled together with calls for long-range predictions. Intelligence agencies lacked chances to reflect on the pattern of growth that lay behind the rapid increases in the strength of the German military. As a result the potential of their relative success in monitoring German strength levels went unexploited.

The major intelligence failures came in the overestimation of German striking power and in the poor quality of early long-range predictions. Some degree of failure in the construction of an image of German power was inevitable, and it was prevented from being disastrous, in the British case, by the survival of the original DRC forecast. That survival depended, in turn, on the speed with which the service intelligence directorates adjusted their convictions. Within the space of two years (1934–36), the Air Ministry and the War Office together progressed from a facile optimism about the future German threat to a real appreciation of danger. The IIC consistently ground out its quantitative studies illustrating the formidable progress of the German armaments industries. Finally, the year 1939 witnessed what can only be described as a remarkable recovery of confidence and a fresh reappraisal of military facts. Although this last prewar swing into optimism was perhaps unrealistic, it did at least help save the country from a repetition of a Munich in what would have been far less propitious circumstances.

On the first day of war, the chief of the air staff and his senior planner went so far as to seek out the secretary of state for air in the House of Commons to urge against any scuttling away from the guaranty to Poland. The most concise statement of the new outlook was that expressed by the DMO & I, [Director of Military Operations and Intelligence] General Pownall, "But that the [German] regime must go I am convinced." This conviction might be regarded, late as it was, as the most insightful achievement of the British intelligence system in the 1930s.

Anthony Adamthwaite

French Military Intelligence and the Coming of War

Anthony Adamthwaite, professor of history at the University of Loughborough, examines the claim that French military intelligence was accurate

From Anthony Adamthwaite, "French Military Intelligence and the Coming of War 1935–1939," in *Intelligence and International Relations 1900–1945*, published by the University of Exeter, pp. 191–204. Reprinted by permission of the author.

and without blame for the failure of French foreign policy during the years 1935–1939. However, he shows how its inaccuracy, underestimation of friend and foe, inefficiency, and incompetence left the French government crippled, unable to take decisive action. At the same time, the intelligence failure also contributed to massive collapse of the French government's will to oppose Hitler.

Assessing the influence of intelligence on French policymaking on the eve of the Second World War is an intelligence operation in itself. Sources are a fundamental obstacle. Many secret papers were lost or destroyed during the war, others remain closed. There is no official history of French intelligence. The history of intelligence work has not attracted the same attention in France as in Britain and the United States. The memoirs of former intelligence chiefs require careful handling because they are apologias, written to exculpate themselves from any blame for the defeat of 1940. The aim of this study is to test the claim that Intelligence was blameless and gave accurate and timely notice of external threats. The focus is on the army's intelligence service, the *Deuxième Bureau*, in particular its perceptions of Germany and the Soviet Union.

How was intelligence organised? The *Deuxième Bureau* has been dubbed 'a sort of dirty tricks department,' synonymous with intelligence. In fact six independent intelligence organs flourished. The army, navy and air force operated separate services and from 1937 the ministry of colonies had its own intelligence apparatus. In addition the *Sûreté nationale* and Paris prefecture of police supervised home intelligence and counter-intelligence in metropolitan France. Unlike the British Foreign Office, the French foreign ministry had no special responsibility for any of these agencies nor did it have a service of its own. It did however maintain a *cabinet noir* for the interception of diplomatic communications. Of the six services the most important and best known was the intelligence division of the army general staff. It had two sections, the *Service de Renseignements* (SR), and the *Deuxième Bureau*. The *Service de Renseignements* gathered intelligence which the *Deuxième Bureau* evaluated and forwarded to the general staff.

How accurate and reliable was the evaluation of the German menace? The claim that the general staff and government always received full and ample warning of Germany's designs does not stand up to close scrutiny. The *Deuxième Bureau* reported on the evolution of Germany's strategic and tactical doctrine, especially the revolutionary role of tanks and aircraft, but its criteria were the defensive assumptions of the general staff. For example a 1938 study on the use of tanks and aircraft in Spain concluded: 'in general terms we are finding nothing which would cause us to renounce the basic ideas which we have held up to now.' An early 1939 report suggested that in the light of the Spanish Civil War German officers were wondering whether tanks were really worth their cost.

As for German army strength, fear impelled French leaders to exaggerate it. In April 1935 General Maurice Gamelin, chief of the general staff, spoke of a German army of 32 divisions, perhaps doubling itself by the end of the year, reinforced by 50 divisions of frontier troops, culminating in a programme of 120 divisions. Against which the French metropolitan army had only 31 divisions. Gamelin took it for granted that in a long war — the only kind he envisaged — Germany had the advantage. Where he got his figures is not known but *Deuxième Bureau* estimates were different. In March 1936, on the eve of the Rhineland reoccupation, French army intelligence put German strength at 29 divisions (a figure confirmed by recent German studies). This force, it was stressed, had a crippling weakness in the severe shortage of trained officers. Accordingly, the *Deuxième Bureau* discounted the huge paramilitary formations in Germany because they could not be effectively mobilised without officers.

Two years later the *Deuxième Bureau* made two serious overestimates — the strength of the Siegfried Line and the number of German divisions available for immediate mobilisation. Colonel Maurice-Henri Gauché, head of the *Deuxième Bureau* from 1935–40, stated that the Siegfried Line in September 1938, although unfinished, could be utilised and constituted a formidable barrier. On 27 September, two days before Munich Gauché advised the general staff that Germany could mobilise 120 divisions and was ready for 'general war.' In official discussions with ministers Gamelin exploited this overestimate of German fortifications. Officially he cited it as a reason for not fighting for France's ally, Czechoslovakia; privately he admitted that 'another year or even more would be necessary to make the Siegfried Line really formidable.'

From arms to the man. How accurately did French intelligence predict Hitler's coups? The reintroduction of conscription on 16 March 1935 came well in advance of the *Deuxième Bureau* forecast of October 1935. From late 1935 the likelihood of a Rhineland remilitarisation in 1936 was publicly debated but the timing of the event on 7 March 1936 surprised the French government. In February the *Deuxième Bureau* had warned that parliamentary ratification of the Franco-Soviet pact on 27 February would provide a pretext for reoccupation but no date was given. Similarly, from late 1937 an *Anschluss* was widely predicted for 1938. At the beginning of March 1938 a coup was reported imminent: 'the operation will be sudden and all will be settled within a few hours.' Again, however, no date. Did imminent mean in a few days or a few weeks? For Czechoslovakia in 1938 and Poland in 1939 dates for German aggression were forthcoming — in both crises prediction was relatively easy since gradual German mobilisation could not be concealed. By contrast, without access to Hitler's entourage, accurate prediction of the Rhineland and *Anschluss* was extremely difficult, if not impossible.

A key event in Hitler's decision making was the secret conference of 5 November 1937 when he informed advisers of his resolve to annex Austria and Czechoslovakia at the first favourable opportunity. Paul Paillole, an officer of the *Service de Renseignements* in the 1930s, claims that France's master spy, Hans-Thilo Schmidt, supplied full particulars of the conference. Thus French intelligence scored a major triumph. Alas, the claim is not convincing. According to Paillole, on 6 November 1937 Schmidt reported through an intermediary to the French embassy in Berlin. The ambassador André François-Poncet alerted Paris by telegram and sent a full account by courier. Deeply troubled, Colonel Louis Rivet, chief of the *Service de Renseignements* from 1934–44, saw war minister Edouard Daladier on 12 November and Schmidt's revelations provoked a meeting of the top-level defence policy committee, *Comité Permanent de la Défense Nationale*, on 8 December 1937. So much for Paillole's story. François-Poncet did indeed wire Paris on 6 November that a secret conference had taken place the previous day but his brief telegram (immediately decoded by the Germans) said: 'it is difficult to know what was the subject of this conference' — if it concerned problems of raw materials and iron and steel allocation — 'it is surprising . . . that so many senior officers were called to the chancellery.' This message gives the lie to Paillole's claim that the ambassador had seen a full report of the conference. The other pieces of evidence cited by Paillole are also unconvincing. Rivet's diary, quoted by Paillole, confirms the interview of 12 November but states 'the minister hardly alluded to H. E.'s information' ('H. E.' was the codename for Schmidt). It hardly seems consistent, therefore, in the light of Daladier's reaction on 12 November that he should have summoned a meeting of the *Comité Permanent* for 8 December. The minutes of that meeting make it plain that the reason for its convocation was not central Europe but the government's preoccupation with the Mediterranean.

The problem in Paris was not so much knowing one's enemy as knowing oneself. Until April 1939 there was no will to stop Hitler by force. Well before the Rhineland coup the general staff had decided to do nothing. Gamelin, although accurately informed by the *Deuxième Bureau* of German strength in the Rhineland, gave his political masters vastly inflated estimates. Two years later the month long build-up of tension over Austria allowed the Government ample opportunity to decide its policy. But France had no government on 12 March and no one wanted to fight for Austria. Likewise in the Czech crisis the *Deuxième Bureau* from 8 April alerted the general staff that Germany was preparing an attack and on 25 August gave the operation date as 25 September. It was 'quite exceptional for an intelligence officer to be able to predict with such confidence and without qualification,' Gauché boasted. But all the intelligence in the world could not save Czechoslovakia without the will to fight. And Gauché admitted 'Of course, there will not be a European war since we are not going to fight.'

The *Deuxième Bureau's* performance in the Munich to Prague winter is very difficult to assess because the available evidence is scanty and open to different interpretations. Three points call for comment. Firstly, an allegation needs to be refuted. There is no evidence that in December 1938 and January 1939 the *Deuxième Bureau* deliberately fed British Intelligence secret false information about an imminent German attack in the west. Secondly, perceptions both of Hitler's intentions and state of military preparedness changed considerably within a few months. Thirdly, the claim that from 6 March Paris knew of Hitler's plan to occupy Prague needs substantial qualification. On the first point, no evidence has been produced to corroborate the disinformation accusation. In January 1939 German opposition groups were responsible for feeding alarmist reports to London. British fears about supposed German plans for an attack on Holland and London conflicted with the French view that 'the more probable point of danger was Rumania.' Initially, Paris viewed the Ukraine as Hitler's number one target. French intelligence had no knowledge of Hitler's 21 October 1938 directive for the destruction of the remainder of Czechoslovakia. On 19 December the *Deuxième Bureau* forwarded to the general staff the reported opinions of one of Hitler's familiars. Germany's targets in order of priority were Poland, Rumania and the USSR. Poland would be destabilised by encouraging a separatist movement in the Polish Ukraine and then Germany would demand the Polish Corridor and Upper Silesia. Thereafter Germany might turn to the west against France or continue eastwards at the expense of the Soviet Union. But how much time did France have before Hitler might attack? On this crucial point the oracle was silent and the *Deuxième Bureau* disagreed with its main Berlin source, the French military attaché, General Didelet. On 12 December Didelet argued that Hitler would not be ready for general war until 1942 and would not risk a conflict with France before that date. In the interim Germany might expand in one of three directions — Poland, Rumania or the Soviet Ukraine. Didelet's opinion of German preparedness contradicted Gauché's own view expressed in September 1938 that Germany was ready for 'general war.' Was the French general staff and government misled by Didelet? For some weeks his views may have prevailed in Paris. Gauché states in his memoirs that Didelet's analysis was not accepted and the attaché was cautioned for being too categorical. Unfortunately no date is given for the admonition. Gamelin writing to Daladier on 19 December 1938 commended the attaché's report. By 10 January Didelet had decided that Rumania was most menaced and he repeated his opinion that in the west 'Germany will not be ready militarily, economically or psychologically to run the risk of world war in 1939.' What of Czechoslovakia? The ambassador in Berlin, Robert

Coulondre, successor to François-Poncet, has been praised because, unlike his military attaché, he alerted Paris to Czechoslovakia. While it is true that from late January Coulondre believed Czechoslovakia was next on Hitler's list, his main anxiety was to preserve the Franco-German Declaration of 6 December 1938. Indeed neither the Berlin embassy nor Paris showed any great concern for Czechoslovakia.

This indifference to the fate of central Europe was confirmed by the failure to exploit information received on 6 March from the *Deuxième Bureau's* prime secret source MAD that Hitler planned to seize Prague on 15 March. The memoirs cite this advance information to support the argument that the general staff and government were always fully alerted to German coups. In fact no effort seems to have been made to utilise the 6 March scoop. One obvious reason for inaction was that French intelligence shared the general view that Czechoslovakia was a lost cause. It is also likely that the value of 6 March source was not recognised until the coup took place. A 9 March *Deuxième Bureau* report to the general staff said nothing of 6 March information and concluded that no imminent threat existed. . . . Yet Paris had confirmation of its 6 March source from Czech intelligence. General Moravec, head of Czech intelligence, heard on 3 March from his master spy A-54 of Hitler's designs. In vain he tried to alert the French. At a meeting of the *Conseil supérieur de la Guerre* on 13 March Gamelin did not refer to the secret information. He thought that a crisis might still be avoided. That evening he even denied that there had been 'any form of German mobilisation.' On 15 March Hitler occupied Prague. . . .

In their apologias intelligence chiefs skated over post-Prague alarms and excursions because the confused intelligence signals of March–April 1939 belied the thesis of an omniscient *Deuxième Bureau*. Paradoxically it was in this period when intelligence was worst informed that it probably exercised most influence on ministers. By stressing the imminence of war intelligence appreciations injected a new firmness and decisiveness into French policy. On 16 March the prime minister and war minister Daladier was advised that Prague 'can be the start of a very serious crisis in the near future menacing France directly.' Joint German-Italian action, he was told, might develop 'in a very short time . . . April is the leit-motiv in most of the information received.' The most likely option was German action against Holland, together with Italian operations from Libya. On 23 March Hitler occupied Memel. More alarms and confusion followed. From MAD, the secret source who had predicted 15 March for the Prague coup, came the warning 'The Danzig affair will be settled on 1 April or 2nd at the latest . . . Germany intends to reorganise the Rumanian army and make it a vassal force.' But MAD's own informant considered 'that there will be no war for a year at least.' On the morning of 9 April Gauché forwarded first-class information 'from an excellent source whose sincerity cannot be doubted.' War was 'inevitable and very near; the delay will not last beyond 20 April.' The conflict would begin with a massive air attack on Paris and London accompanied by the seizure of Rumanian oil fields. Gauché believed that 'unity of views' had now been established between the three dictators, Hitler, Mussolini and Franco. That afternoon ministers and service chiefs decided on immediate and far reaching measures, including mobilisation of the fleet and putting the air force on alert. After Prague, Memel and Albania French leaders believed the worst.

Perhaps the greatest single shortcoming of French intelligence was the underestimate of the Soviet alliance and the failure to secure information on German-Soviet relations in the summer of 1939. Conjecture and prejudice prevailed. No sustained attempt was made to reach a balanced appraisal of Soviet military power. The 1935 Franco-Soviet pact, like the 1924 Franco-Czech alliance, had not been cemented by a military accord. Perceptions both of Soviet intentions and preparedness were almost completely pessimistic in the years 1936–9. Before and after the Franco-Soviet pact the *Deuxième Bureau* expressed sharp disapproval: 'We shall without a doubt bring to this alliance more than we shall receive with such an uncertain partner, who could lead us into an adventuristic undertaking and then abandon us.' Needless to say, army intelligence counselled against a military alliance. What most concerned the *Deuxième Bureau* in 1935–36 were the political consequences of the pact. Germany might use the threat of encirclement as a pretext for action and Poland, it was argued, was the preferred ally: 'The Polish alliance . . . must take precedence over the Russian alliance from the political point of view.' In particular the *Deuxième Bureau* apprehended British disapproval. France's security, it was pointed out, depended on the entente and 'in the event of conflict English support outweighs in power, in certainty, and in constancy that which the USSR can give us.' But these were political judgements which were outside the *Bureau's* competence. . . .

The role of political prejudice in shaping military assessments of the Soviet Union is exemplified by the Loizeau and Schweisguth missions of 1935 and 1936. Within a year two separate French general staff missions visited the Soviet Union and reached contradictory conclusions. Impressed by Soviet strength General Loizeau urged further contacts. Paris, he counselled, should not wait too long before responding to Soviet advances for 'the USSR will certainly not accept an equivocal or dilatory attitude.' General Colson, deputy chief of the general staff, blocked Loizeau's report and ensured that neither Gamelin nor the war minister saw it. The Rhineland coup did not soften *Deuxième Bureau* attitudes. Rapprochements with Poland, Czechoslovakia and Italy were recommended but Moscow was anathema — 'its help can only be limited, late and uncertain.' In September 1936 General Schweisguth attended Red Army manoeuvres and advised against any military alliance. Moscow was castigated because it seemed 'to be seeking ever greater cooperation . . . in order to force France into a confrontation with Germany.' Thus the USSR would 'become the arbiter in an exhausted Europe.' So set was the *Deuxième Bureau* on keeping Stalin at arm's length that it disregarded one of its principal sources of information, the French embassy in Moscow. Both the ambassador, Robert Coulondre, and his military attaché, Colonel Palasse, tried to break down the barriers of mistrust and ignorance. Three major reasons — ideological mistrust, the Soviet purges, fears of alienating Poland, Rumania and Britain — combined to ensure the failure of Franco-Soviet military talks in 1937. By autumn 1938 army intelligence believed that 'militarily' the Soviet Union was 'entirely impotent'.

The lengthy and frustrating Moscow negotiations of April–August 1939 allowed Hitler and Stalin ample time to reach agreement. Arguably the course of events would have been different had French leaders been briefed on the progress of German-Soviet talks. Despite two warnings (7 and 22 May) from the French embassy in Berlin, French intelligence failed to discover what was afoot. On 10 May the *Deuxième Bureau* speculated briefly on the dismissal of foreign minister Litvinov. The possibility that his removal meant Stalin wanted to conclude a secret pact with Hitler was rejected — 'such a reversal of Soviet policy' seemed 'difficult to reconcile' with a newly-negotiated Soviet-Turkish accord. By 24 May the possibility was taken seriously. A weekly armed forces and foreign ministry liaison meeting minuted the urgency of reaching agreement with Moscow since Soviet-German contacts had been signalled. A month later the *Deuxième Bureau* had reached the conclusion that 'German diplomacy is actively engaged in sabotaging the Moscow negotiations and even in preparing a German-Soviet entente which could be very rapidly negotiated.' By the end of May therefore French intelligence clearly recognised the danger of a German-Soviet pact but no systematic effort appears to have been made to monitor the progress of Moscow-Berlin exchanges. Thus on 5 July prime minister and war minister Daladier admitted that he 'had no specific information' about German-Soviet negotiations but 'feared that they might be most serious.' When news reached Paris that a Nazi-Soviet pact was to be signed, Daladier reminded the American ambassador, William Bullitt, that 'at least six times since last January' the envoy 'had warned him that most serious negotiations were under way.' Daladier 'told all the French government services to attempt to verify' Bullitt's warnings 'but had been reassured that there were no negotiations other than the commercial negotiations in progress between Germany and the Soviet Union.' Thanks to the German diplomat in Moscow, Johnnie von Herwarth, the United States was well informed on the German-Soviet contacts. But Washington kept Paris in the dark and von Herwarth did not confide in his French or British colleagues.

The Nazi-Soviet pact of 23 August rendered war inevitable. The Soviet Union's benevolent neutrality freed Hitler from the danger of a two front war. Poland could be attacked in safety. The threat of imminent war concentrated the minds of French leaders wonderfully. Their public voice was much more determined than in 1938. Intelligence contributed significantly to this firmness. During the summer patient, methodical investigation revealed the full picture of German mobilisation against Poland. There was no doubting Hitler's intent. On 19 August Gauché confidently predicted that Germany would be ready to attack by the end of the month — 'It was not humanly possible to get closer to the truth.' But the truth was now too close. Desperately ministers and officials clutched at reports of flagging German morale and indecision in high places. In the last week of August hopes of German bluff flickered into life. On 31 August Mussolini proposed a conference. Convinced that Germany and Italy were waging a war of nerves senior foreign ministry officials utilised Italian intercepts to convince an irresolute Daladier that the proposal was a snare and delusion. Firmness, they counselled, was the only answer to Axis manoeuvres.

Most of the reports on Germany came from ambassador Coulondre in Berlin. From 27 August the embassy signalled public discontent, divided leadership, military unreadiness, a hesitant Hitler. The messages culminated on 30 August with a private letter to Daladier:

> *the attack on Poland was fixed for the night of 25–26 August . . .*
> *I have learnt from a reliable source that for the past five days Hitler*
> *has been hesitating. Irresolution has gripped the heart of the Nazi*
> *Party. Reports indicate a growing discontent among the people . . .*

Read out to a bitterly divided Cabinet on 31 August, Coulondre's letter reinforced Daladier and like-minded colleagues in their opposition to Mussolini's conference proposal. The advice was the more telling because before the Cabinet met Daladier had been shown a foreign ministry memorandum which argued from Italian intercepts that Italy was playing Germany's game. The conference proposal was a trap.

How reliable was the government's information on Germany and Italy? On Germany, Coulondre's reporting was largely wishful thinking, derived from consular reports, Berlin diplomatic gossip and personal impressions. . . . But Paul Stehlin, assistant air attaché, disagreed with the ambassador and complained at not being consulted about the letter to Daladier. However Coulondre was not alone in his views. Reports from other sources reaching both the *Deuxième Bureau* and Quai d'Orsay told a similar story. As for the Italian intercepts shown to Daladier on 31 August, Dr Paul Stafford argues that they were fabricated by Quai d'Orsay officials, fearful lest the wobbling prime minister might join his foreign minister Georges Bonnet in supporting Mussolini's conference proposal. The suggestion is unconvincing. Although it would not have been difficult for the foreign ministry's *cabinet noir* to concoct the intercepts (Italian diplomatic ciphers had been read since 1938), it is most improbable that cautious leading functionaries like Alexis Léger, secretary general, and Emile Charvériat, political director, would risk both careers and a first-class political scandal in such a reckless ploy. . . .

How successful was French intelligence in cryptography and the discovery of enemy secrets? The great pre-war scoop was the recruitment in 1931 of a master spy, Hans-Thilo Schmidt, codenamed Asche or HE, employed first in the German army cipher section and later in the *Forschungsamt*, Göring's intelligence communications agency. From Schmidt the *Service de Renseignements* secured operating instructions and keys for the German military Enigma cipher machine. Between 1931 and 1939 Schmidt supplied not only further Enigma material but top-secret political and military information. Sadly, Schmidt was much less of a success story for French intelligence than he should have been. Possession of the Enigma documents should have given France a strong lead in breaking German codes. Unluckily the potential advantage was lost to the Poles.

Exaggerated and misleading claims have been made for France's contribution to the breaking of Enigma. By July 1939, it was asserted, France, with allied help, had succeeded both in replicating and reading Enigma. In point of fact the French role, although vital to the Enigma solution, brought no tangible benefit to French intelligence in the approach to war. Before 1939 France did not attempt to replicate or read Enigma. In November 1931 Gustave Bertrand, head of the cryptography section of the *Service de Renseignements*, handed the enigma material received from Schmidt to the cipher section of the general staff. He was told that Enigma could not be broken. Since British Intelligence was lukewarm Bertrand approached France's Polish ally. Polish Intelligence which had been working on Enigma since the late 1920s welcomed French help. The resulting Polish success in breaking Enigma — by 1933 they had rebuilt it and were reading intercepts — was the fruit of French intelligence work and Polish mathematical and technological skills. The French contribution was indispensable. However the Poles kept their success to themselves and Paris-Warsaw co-operation was one way traffic only. The French continued to feed Enigma keys received from Schmidt without getting anything in return. At a French-British-Polish intelligence conference in Paris in early January 1939 the Poles still kept quiet about their achievement, although recent German modifications to Enigma were making decipherment increasingly difficult. The final wartime breakthrough was a joint Anglo-Franco-Polish effort. The first results came in France in December 1939 but it was not until March 1940 that Enigma began to yield secrets in any quantity.

Given will and resources there was no reason why from 1931

France should not have exploited the Enigma material and achieved as much, if not more, than Poland. Unhappily, instead of stealing a march on friends and foes, France found herself outflanked in the intelligence battle. The consequences for her diplomacy were most grievous. The crumbs of comfort — on the eve of war the codes of 12 countries, including Italy, were being read — were nullified by two disasters. In April 1939 the *Service de Renseignements* discovered that for some time Rome had been reading French diplomatic and naval codes and delivering them to Berlin. The Quai d'Orsay insisted that its Rome diplomats were above suspicion. Only after several months of enquiry was the source of the leak identified — the French embassy safe in Rome, like the British, was being regularly burgled. But by far the most serious blow was Schmidt's revelation in April 1938 that Germany was intercepting Paris-Prague and Prague-London traffic. In addition Germany was reading the codes of fourteen French posts. French diplomacy lost its credibility. The fact that Paris was speaking with two voices in the Czech crisis — publicly promising support for Prague while privately pressurising the Czechs to carry conciliation to the limit — was fully known to Hitler. Rivet warned Daladier personally of the eavesdropping but to no effect. Nor were Berlin and Rome the only eavesdroppers. Captain André Beaufre, a member of France's military mission to Moscow in 1939, believed that telegrams from the French military attaché in Warsaw on 19 August, analysing the breakdown of Anglo-French efforts to persuade the Poles to offer transit to Soviet forces, were read in Moscow and helped to confirm Stalin in his decision to ally with Hitler. Amid so many broken codes it would have been small consolation for the French to have known that after 1935 their secrets were safe at least from the British.

'Never in her history would France enter a war in such initial unfavourable conditions,' Gauché warned the general staff on 1 September 1939. The *Deuxième Bureau* and *Service de Renseignements* must share some responsibility for France's plight. Although German designs against the Rhineland, Austria, Czechoslovakia and Poland were foreseen, German military strength in 1938 was seriously overestimated, Soviet strength underestimated. Blinkered by the prevailing defensive outlook military intelligence did not see the full implications of German innovations in armour and air power. Alerting government to the possibility of a German-Soviet rapprochement, as both diplomats and *Deuxième Bureau* did from October 1938, was one thing, supplying hard information on its realisation was another. On the nitty-gritty of German-Soviet negotiations in 1939 intelligence drew a blank. The record on codebreaking and signals intelligence was especially poor. The failure to break Enigma unaided and the extensive compromising of French codes seriously disadvantaged foreign policy-making.

The explanation of these failures is part administrative, part political and psychological. Intelligence laboured under severe constraints. There was no machinery for the co-ordination and centralisation of intelligence. France lacked an economic intelligence section comparable to the Industrial Intelligence Centre in Britain. Intelligence work was handicapped by the rivalries between the general staff, foreign ministry and interior ministry. The general staff and Quai d'Orsay were deeply suspicious of each other. Grudging co-operation in the First World War ended in 1922 when prime minister and foreign minister Raymond Poincaré stopped the distribution of foreign ministry decrypts to the war ministry. In 1935 the *Service de Renseignements* complained that although they delivered diplomatic decrypts to the Quai d'Orsay they got nothing back. Army intelligence was something of a Cinderella, starved of resources. The *Service de Renseignements* budget for 1938 was the same in real terms as in 1918. There was no money for a printing press and outside contractors had to be used for the printing of secret documents. Pay and conditions were poor. A regular visitor to *Deuxième Bureau* headquarters recalled 'a few bare wooden huts . . . trestle tables, hard wooden chairs.' His visits were welcomed as the signal for 'a slap-up lunch on the expense account.' Within the general staff *Deuxième Bureau* service was not highly regarded; able and ambitious officers avoided it. Inadequate resources and even a certain amateurishness were additional handicaps. Neither the *Service de Renseignements* nor the general staff cipher section had the expertise to tackle Enigma. . . ,

Once gathered and analysed, intelligence had to be put into the hands of the decision makers. Almost nothing is known as to how frequently or infrequently ministers and service chiefs discussed intelligence. What is certain is that neither Gauché nor Rivet of army intelligence had the regular access to policymakers that Quex Sinclair of SIS enjoyed in Britain. The confusion engendered by a weak and unstable executive did not make for effective use of intelligence appreciations. In theory the Cabinet provided co-ordination of political and military leadership but the ephemeral administrations of the period had neither the time nor energy to do justice to the issues. When in 1936 the foreign ministry wanted to know what the army would do about a Rhineland remilitarisation its only means of finding out was a lengthy formal correspondence. Below the Cabinet the top defence policy body was the *Comité permanent de la défense nationale* but it met infrequently — 13 times in three years. Briefly in 1936–37 Léon Blum, Popular Front prime minister, chaired weekly meetings with Gamelin and intelligence chiefs. From 30 March 1938 a weekly interministerial liaison committee of deputy chiefs of staff and senior diplomats met at the Quai d'Orsay but minutes show no trace of intelligence papers. The *Deuxième Bureau* had a daily liaison arrangement with the foreign ministry. In addition the general staff had a liaison officer attached to the Quai d'Orsay. But complaints about inadequate liaison and consultation suggest that at critical moments intelligence analyses may never have reached policymakers. Even Gamelin in 1938–39 had difficulty in getting access to Daladier. . . .

The decisive failure was political and psychological. 'Damned if we do, damned if we don't' describes the dilemma of French decision makers. To fight made war certain and defeat likely; not to fight invited demoralisation, decline and probable collapse. This quandary eroded the will to resist Germany. Filtered through the defensive assumptions of Gauché and the general staff the impact of intelligence was deadened before it reached ministers. Those representatives who challenged the received wisdom on the Soviet Union, Czechoslovakia and Italy — Palasse in Moscow, General Faucher in Prague, General Parisot in Rome — were cold-shouldered. Assessments of German military might had a paralysing effect on military and political leaders already convinced of French inferiority. In an official climate of pessimism, procrastination and vacillation the pursuit of intelligence became an end in itself, intelligence for intelligence's sake. The exercise of intellectual rigour and painstaking analysis offered escape from impending doom. All unfolded like a classical French tragedy — issues and information were discussed and dissected from all angles but action shunned. Internal upheaval undermined intelligence work. Anxiety about the ideological enemy within distracted attention from the enemy without. At a meeting with war minister Daladier on 12 November 1937 to discuss the latest secret intelligence from Schmidt, Rivet was dismayed to find that Daladier hardly mentioned Schmidt and was interested only in German intelligence activities in France and the presence of Spanish Nationalists and Republicans. Moreover the domestic turmoil bred indifference, scepticism and distrust of intelligence. Everyone eavesdropped on each other, secrets were bandied about, spies were everywhere. Even the lorry drivers who dropped off mailbags at *Deuxième Bureau* headquarters would shout: '*Voilà pour les espions.*'

Stalin dictating to a military aide. (Philp Collection, Hoover Institution Archives)

The Russian Riddle

Robert C. Tucker

Stalin's Foreign Policy

In the face of a growing threat from Nazi Germany, many people unhappy with appeasement looked to Soviet Russia as a power willing to oppose nazism and fascism. In the Soviet Union foreign policy was ultimately decided by Joseph Stalin. Robert C. Tucker, professor of politics emeritus at Princeton University, evaluates Stalin's foreign policy. Tucker explains that not only had Stalin been willing to help Hitler come to power in Germany, but as soon as Hitler had attained power, Stalin tried to cooperate with him. Even when he realized that Hitler was bent on war, Stalin sought to promote war, believing that the Soviet Union could profit from a war between Hitler and the western nations. Moreover, Stalin sought an agreement with Hitler in which the Soviet Union would remain neutral in European war in return for a substantial reward from Hitler. As Tucker indicates, all of the people who saw in Stalin a bulwark against nazism would eventually be deceived.

From *Stalin in Power: The Revolution from Above, 1928–1941*, published by W.W. Norton & Company, pp. 228–237, 254–257, 259–260, 341–350.

The Weimar republic went down under the assault of the Great Depression and the Nazi movement, helped along by various political factors: the feebleness of the center forces, the absence of alert and vigorous political leadership on the part of those in authority, and, not least, the tactics pursued by the German Communists on orders from Moscow — from Stalin.

Unemployment in Germany rose steadily from over one million in late 1929 to over six million in 1931–32, the latter number amounting to something like a third of the wage-earning population. Masses of Germans grew responsive to the would-be savior leadership of Adolf Hitler and his National Socialist party, and by the summer of 1932, the Nazis held about a third of the seats in the Reichstag. The stage was now set for the combined propaganda blitz and high-level political maneuvering that brought Hitler to the chancellorship on 30 January 1933. The ensuing "legal revolution" witnessed a wave of Nazi terror, the Reichstag fire of 28 February followed by the Enabling Act ("Law for Removal of the Distress of People and Reich"), and the overthrow of the constitutional order. By the summer of 1933, the Nazi dictatorship was firmly established.

With their mass worker and trade union constituencies, their combined total of close to 40 percent of the Reichstag seats in November 1932 (representing about seven million Social Democratic votes and nearly six million Communist ones), the two parties of the German Left were together a potentially powerful force for preservation of the constitutional order. Whether they could have prevented the Nazi victory by resolutely working in tandem and with other antifascist elements to this end is an unanswerable question. What is certain is that the absence of such cooperation, indeed the strife between the two parties during that critical time, facilitated the downfall of the constitutional order. Not all Communists were blind to the catastrophic character of this strife. As early as September 1930 Trotsky raised his voice from Prinkipo exile to urge the German Communist party (the KPD) to work with the SPD [Social Democratic Party] in a united front against fascism. He accurately forewarned that a Nazi victory would mean the crushing of the German working class and an inevitable war against the USSR. Many German Communists took a similar view.

But Stalin had different ideas. By forcing upon the KPD a policy of uncompromising belligerence against Social Democracy ("social-fascism"), he abetted the Nazi victory. A Comintern Executive

Committee directive to the German Communists in February 1930 demanded "merciless exposure" of Social Democracy. Under Comintern direction, the German Communist leader Heinz Neumann in the summer of 1930 drafted a new KPD "Program of National and Social Liberation," which promised to annul the Versailles treaty and the Young Plan and denounced the SPD as the treasonable party of Versailles. Competition with the Nazis for the mantle of German nationalism went along with a certain amount of collaboration. In the summer of 1931, for instance, the Communists, on orders from Moscow, joined in a Nazi- and rightist-organized plebiscite against the SPD state government in Prussia.

The leaning toward a united antifascist front with the SPD was not entirely confined to the Communist rank-and-file; there were signs of it among the party leaders too. Ernst Thaelmann rebelled at first against the instruction to participate in the anti-SPD Prussian plebiscite. Then he, Hermann Remmele, and Heinz Neumann "were called to Moscow to learn at first hand that this instruction had been issued to the Communist International by Stalin personally." Another former German Communist, who worked in the Comintern offices in Moscow in 1932 and survived a lengthy later incarceration in Soviet concentration camps, recalls that ". . . as early as 1932 there existed in the leadership of the KPD as well as in the Comintern machine a marked readiness to set up a 'united front' with the Social Democrats which would have prevented the victory of National Socialism. But their timid proposals were not adopted. The influence of Stalin — who held fast to his line, while any criticism of it was instantly branded as 'antiparty heresy,' if not as 'provocation by agents of international capitalism' — was decisive."

The SPD leadership, concerned over its ties with the Catholic and center parties, also held back from collaboration with the Communists. By the autumn of 1932, however, the depth of the crisis made the urgency of collaboration clear. An SPD leader, Friedrich Stampfer, obtained an interview with the Soviet envoy in Berlin, Lev Khinchuk, himself a former Russian Menshevik. "Would it be possible to expect the cooperation of Communism in the struggle against National Socialism?" Stampfer asked Khinchuk. Several interviews followed between Stampfer and Soviet Embassy attaché Vinogradov, who finally broke off the exchanges by saying: "Moscow is convinced that the road to Soviet Germany leads through Hitler."

Stalin's decisive personal role in the KPD policies that abetted the Nazi revolution is beyond doubt. Insofar as the possibility existed of heading off this event by encouraging a united front of the German Left and other anti-Nazi forces, he was chiefly responsible for its failure to materialize. To some his decision has seemed an act of monumental political ineptitude stemming from failure to grasp the revolutionary nature of National Socialism or a belief that its victory — as was said in Communist circles at that time — would be short-lived and pave the way to power for German Communism. Such interpretations are unconvincing. The then current version about a short-lived Nazi victory bears earmarks of a convenient rationalization put out by Stalin's headquarters. However inadequate his understanding of Hitler and the Nazi movement may have been in 1930–33, Stalin knew enough about the staying powers of Italian fascism, not to mention Russian Bolshevism, to beware of assuming that the Nazis could not create a stable single-party system and extirpate resistance with ruthless terror. We must take into account that Stalin, for all his doctrinaire cast of mind, was reasonably well informed and given to acting with a carefully thought-out rationale. Although complex, the rationale in this instance is not hard to reconstruct.

First, elemental caution dictated that the German Communists be restrained from any attempt at a seizure of power, no matter how revolutionary the German situation. In the comparable circumstances of 1923, Stalin had argued in a letter to Zinoviev that the German Communists should be restrained on the grounds that their position was not so favorable as the Bolsheviks' in 1917 in Russia and that "if power in Germany were, so to speak, to fall to the street and the Communists picked it up, it would end in failure and collapse." He had ample reason to take the same view in 1932. Even if a coup should initially succeed, the German Communists could not possibly hold out on their own against combined internal and external counterrevolutionary forces. The Soviet Union for its part was in no position to come to their aid or to risk any international complications that might result in early war. Separated from Germany by hostile Poland, preoccupied with its *piatiletka*, stricken by famine, it would be condemned to stand by helplessly and ignominiously while German Communism was being overthrown and destroyed.

For different reasons, Stalin could not look with favor on a KPD bloc with the SPD and other amenable elements to prevent the fall of the Weimar system. Even this policy entailed some small risk of international anti-Soviet complications that had to be avoided at all cost. And supposing the policy succeeded and the Nazis were stopped from taking power, what then? The SPD politicians were inveterate *Westlers*, indeed the chief German force for a Western orientation in foreign policy. As probably the dominant partner in the anti-Nazi coalition, their foreign-policy orientation would be influential. No prospect could have been less pleasing to Stalin.

The only serious remaining possibility was the path that Stalin took. Accepting and even indirectly abetting the Nazi takeover was a course that offered promise along with dangers to the USSR (but in what direction were there no dangers?) and the certainty that German Communism would be repressed. Despite their shrill ideological anti-Bolshevism and anti-Slav racism (along with anti-Semitism, which would not grieve Stalin), the Nazis were no *Westlers*. Their movement was stridently nationalistic, revanchist, illiberal, antidemocratic, anti-pacifist, and anti-Versailles. They were plainly a bellicose force. Their accession to power might, then, be a harbinger of great tension, if not a new war, between Germany and the West. We have direct testimony that this was what Stalin thought. In a conversation with Heinz Neumann at the end of 1931 he said, "Don't you believe, Neumann, that if the Nationalists seize power in Germany they will be so completely preoccupied with the West that we'll be able to build up socialism in peace?"

Stalin's line of thought and action — or inaction — at this critical juncture was consistent with his war-and-revolution scenario. By accepting if not actively facilitating the Nazi takeover, he was guiding events in the direction he had long wanted them to take — toward a war between opposed imperialist countries in Europe. This was not, as he knew, an early prospect, for it would be a matter of years before the Nazis could rearm Germany for war. But an early outbreak of war was not something for which Russia was prepared either. What the Nazi victory portended was the end of passivity in German foreign policy. A liberal democratic Weimar Germany perpetually poised between *Ostpolitik* and *Westpolitik*, wavering between the Russian connection and the Western alignment into which she was regularly being drawn by anti-Soviet politicians in America, Britain, France, and Germany herself, would never go to war against the West for German interests. A Nazi Germany might. There was of course the alternate possibility that it would march against Russia. But Stalin apparently reckoned that he could contain this threat by the devices of diplomacy.

As the Nazi takeover drew near, Moscow signaled its readiness for it, indeed its cautious hopefulness. In July 1932 the counselor of the German Embassy in Moscow, Gustav Hilger, had a talk with Doletsky, the head of the Soviet news agency TASS. Along with Soviet worries, Doletsky communicated to Hilger "his conviction that healthy political common sense would win out in a National Socialist government; even the Nazis would be sensible and continue a policy toward Russia that, in his opinion, was consonant with the long-range interests of Germany." "His" conviction was unquestionably the view that Doletsky had been commissioned to convey informally. He assured Higler that the Soviet press had been ordered to give no appearance of interfering in Germany's crisis and even to avoid criticizing German policy. His only fear was that Hitler's accession might be followed by a disturbed transition period before normal relations could be reestablished. "The general impression in the German Embassy," adds Hilger in his recollections, "was that the Soviet government would have liked to establish contact with the National Socialists for the purpose of preventing such temporary difficulties."

A former German Communist writes that a saying was current in antifascist German circles at that time, "Without Stalin, no Hitler," and that Zinoviev said to him in early 1933: "Apart from the German Social Democrats, Stalin bears the main responsibility to history for Hitler's victory." Be that as it may, Stalin played a part in helping the Nazis to take power.

Using terror to solidify their power, the Nazis seized on the pretext of the Reichstag fire to hound members of the KPD into exile, concentration camps, or underground. Initially, their relations with Moscow were clouded by a series of ugly incidents in which Nazi toughs invaded the premises of Soviet offices in Berlin. The new authorities hastened, however, to assure the Soviet government that their anti-Communist internal policies had nothing to do with their foreign policy.

Some men in Moscow were apprehensive about the Nazi takeover and inclined to respond in a stiffer way than Stalin wanted. Two top commanders, M. N. Tukhachevsky and Yan Gamarnik, are reported to have proposed right after Hitler's accession that Red Army–*Reichswehr* relations be broken off, and to have been overruled by Stalin. They and others who shared their outlook were not in most cases anti-German or opposed to the German orientation. Ordzhonikidze, for example, was appreciatively aware of the contribution that the 5,000 or more German engineers working in the Soviet Union had made to the *piatiletka*. Tukhachevsky and his fellow officers prized the Red Army's connection with the *Reichswehr*. But the rise of the ferociously anti-Communist German radical right to power seemed to jeopardize the long-standing friendly links between the two outcasts of Versailles and show the need for new directions in foreign policy.

A leading figure who reasoned in this fashion was Foreign Commissar Maxim Litvinov. An old Bolshevik of wide foreign experience, who had spent ten pre-revolutionary years in England and returned to Russia in 1918 with an English wife, he was less attached to the German orientation than many other Soviet politicians. Since he was also a Jew, Litvinov could not but harbor extreme antipathy for a force like German National Socialism. Earlier, as the ties with Germany loosened in the prelude to Hitler's taking of power, he had responded to a French initiative for better relations by negotiating the Franco-Soviet nonaggression pact of 1931. Similar accords followed with the border states of Poland, Finland, Latvia, and Estonia. These moves unquestionably had Stalin's approval, and no significant realignment of policy was involved. Still, in the new atmosphere following January 1933, Litvinov and others were bound to be attracted to the idea of a new diplomacy of cooperation with those European states that had cause to fear Hitler's Germany. Stalin, however, had other ideas, and Hitler gave him some encouragement.

On 23 March 1933, the *Fuehrer* declared the Reich ready to cultivate friendly and mutually profitable relations with the Soviet Union. "It is above all the government of the National Revolution who feel themselves in a position to adopt such a positive policy with regard to Soviet Russia," he said further. "The fight against Communism in Germany is our internal affair in which we will never permit interference from outside. Our political relations with other Powers to whom we are bound by common interests will not be affected thereby." In early May, Hitler's government took the symbolic step of ratifying the protocol — signed in 1931 but left unratified by the Brüning and von Papen governments — on an extension of the 1926 Treaty of Berlin. More important, he received Khinchuk a few days before this and made reference to common interests of Germany and Soviet Russia. He said that they were both economic and political because the two countries had the same difficulties and the same enemies. The two countries could complement one another and render mutual services. Stalin must have read this with keen interest.

Moscow's public posture was wary. Its chief commentator on German affairs was Radek, who also served as a behind-the-scenes foreign-policy adviser to Stalin. In articles printed in *Bol'shevik* and *Pravda* in May–June 1933, Radek construed Hitler's conciliatory gestures as a means of gaining time and as a concession to German industrialists concerned to keep Soviet orders during the economic crisis. He also said that Alfred Rosenberg, whom he called "the inspirer of German fascism's foreign policy," had paid an unofficial visit to London to sound out British diehards on a possible deal against the Soviet Union. German fascism was combining its reassurances to Moscow with efforts to build an anti-Soviet coalition.

Stalin did not intend to stand idly by in face of the machinations Radek was describing. He knew that no attack could possibly be imminent at that early stage and was aware of holding strong cards of his own. Hitler had already indicated in his talk with Khinchuk that one common interest, hence potential basis of cooperation, between his Germany and Stalin's Russia were their respective revisionist claims upon different portions of Poland. If Hitler, moreover, were disposed to pursue his revisionist aims in the West by means of war, Stalin was in a position to guarantee him against the specter inherited from 1914–1918 — a two-front war. There was also reason to believe that Hitler's policies might be influenced by those very Reichswehr, nationalist, and capitalist circles that had been proponents of the Eastern orientation all along. One of them, General Hans von Seeckt, had argued in a recently published pamphlet that it was useless for Germany to try and drive a wedge between Britain and France and that she needed Russia's friendship for attainment of her revisionist aims. Radek approvingly quoted the pamphlet at length in one of his articles, clearly implying that the general was talking sense. . . .

Sedately, with no show of anxiety or alarm, Stalin signaled his interest in doing business with Berlin. Having reciprocated Hitler's action in ratifying the protocol on extension of the 1926 treaty, the Soviet government published an *Izvestia* editorial on 5 May 1933, which reaffirmed the Rapallo tradition, pointed out that past unfriendly German politics toward the USSR had only weakened Germany, proclaimed Soviet desire for peace and good economic relations with that country, and concluded that the now extended treaty "will have the significance given it by concrete actions of the parties that concluded it."

Not long afterward Stalin began to communicate with Berlin via special channels, bypassing the Foreign Commissariat. In the summer of 1933 his old friend Abel Yenukidze, whose official post was secretary of the Central Executive Committee of Soviets, took a vacation in Germany. In August, after returning, he arranged an outing at his country house for Ambassador Dirksen and the minister-counselor of the German Embassy, Twardowski. . . .

Yenukidze (described in Dirksen's memoirs as "a fair-haired, blue-eyed, kindly Georgian with definite pro-German leanings") suggested to Dirksen that the National-Socialist reconstruction of the German state could have positive consequences for German-Soviet relations by giving the German government the degree of freedom of action in foreign affairs long enjoyed by the Soviet government. He thought that a German "state political line" was little by little emerging as the "state" elements in the Nazi movement separated from the "agitational" ones. In both Germany and the USSR, however, there were many who put political goals of the party in first place, and these people must be checked by "state-political thinking." Dirksen and Twardowski voiced the view that a *modus vivendi* could be worked out between the Soviet Union and the new German regime. . . .

By then — October 1933 — Stalin was taking a further step in his secret diplomacy vis-à-vis Berlin. He opened a communication channel through an individual whom Twardowski, in telegrams to Berlin, called "our Soviet friend." This go-between is believed by a knowledgeable source to have been Radek. Evgeni Gnedin, who served in the Narkomindel during the 1930s, also reports, from personal knowledge, that Radek around this time was placed in charge of a small foreign-policy section attached to Stalin's secretariat. He would order various studies by foreign-affairs specialists and carry out special assignments for Stalin, with whom he was in direct contact. . . .

"Our Soviet friend" arranged for a meeting to take place in Moscow, but behind Litvinov's back, between Dirksen and a man Stalin knew he could trust — Molotov. Dirksen, then on leave in Germany, was expecting to return to Moscow for a brief farewell visit whose precise timing was not yet decided. His successor in the Moscow ambassadorship was to be Rudolf Nadolny, a strong *Ostler*. Litvinov was to leave Moscow shortly for Washington and talks with President Roosevelt on U.S. recognition of the USSR. Molotov was scheduled to pay a visit to Ankara.

On 24 October Twardowski sent an urgent wire to Berlin for Dirksen. "Our friend" had brought about a conversation the day before. He considered the atmosphere toward Germany "so improved" that it was desirable for the opportunity of Dirksen's farewell visit to be used "to pick up the threads again," after which "perhaps Nadolny can bury the hatchet once and for all by signing a little protocol." "Our friend" reported to Twardowski that Molotov had given up the trip to Ankara, alluded to Litvinov's forthcoming trip to Washington, and "specifically offered his mediation." Litvinov departed Moscow on 28 October, and Dirksen arrived the following day. Gnedin, the first to reconstruct this episode, which he accurately calls an "intrigue," comments that the ground was thereby prepared, deliberately and behind the back of Litvinov, for rapprochement with Hitler's Germany.

What transpired between Molotov and Dirksen in October 1933 is not known. But judging by the royal farewell that Stalin's court gave to Hitler's envoy, the results could not have been displeasing to the general secretary. Dirksen was given a grand farewell dinner that was attended by many dignitaries who normally avoided contact with foreigners. He received a beautiful onyx bowl as a parting gift, and "Voroshilov ordered one of his generals to hand me his gift of a writing-set in lacquer with a modern design but executed in the famous old technique." . . .

On the eve of the congress, storm clouds were gathered in the Far East where Japan, having occupied Manchuria, was threatening Soviet possession of the Chinese Eastern Railway and raising fears of a possible invasion of Soviet territory. In a press interview of 25 December 1933, Stalin suggested that the League of Nations, long a Soviet bugbear, might have peace-preserving uses. About that time the German Embassy in Moscow got wind of a French initiative toward a possible mutual assistance pact with the USSR, and reported that there was a growing inclination in the Soviet Union, under impact of Far Eastern tensions, to respond positively to the French proposal.

Then, on 29 December, Litvinov gave the Central Executive Committee a wide-ranging address on foreign affairs. The postwar "era of bourgeois pacifism" was now giving way, he said, to a new era of diplomacy in which war and peace were again the dominant issue.

He propounded a division of foreign capitalist states into aggressive, unaligned, and those disposed to peace-keeping arrangements. Under the first category he alluded to Germany and Japan. While stating that "With Germany, as with other states, we want to have the best of relations," he pointed to ominous signs of German unfriendliness toward the USSR, including the republication of Hitler's *Mein Kampf* in Germany in a new edition "without any deletions." This referred to the inclusion of chapter 14, with its chilling preview of a future German policy of conquering *Lebensraum* in a Russia whose Bolshevik regime was an agency of international Jewry.

The new German ambassador, a strong *Ostler* Rudolf Nadolny, understandably reacted poorly to the foreign commissar's speech. He said in his first major report to Berlin, sent 9 January 1934, that Litvinov was committed to a decision to switch over to the French group. One of several reasons was that "Litvinov is known to be M. Wallach from Bialystok," that is, Jewish. Policy, however, would be decided by "other important people," among whom, it seemed, "there mostly prevails regret over the falling out with Germany and the desire for reconciliation." Nadolny had been assured — by whom he did not say — that "nothing decisive has yet taken place, that only in case of emergency would the Soviet Union bind itself by treaty to the other side, and that we did not yet have to consider our cause here as lost." Consequently, steps should be taken immediately and energetically, by way of peaceful gestures, to· frustrate the intentions of "the sly M. Wallach" aimed at Russia's inclusion in the French ring.

In a postscript sent the next day, Nadolny reported that Radek had taken the opportunity to express himself to "one of our journalists." Radek had cautioned against undue German alarm at the Litvinov speech. Moscow was following a state policy (*Staatspolitik*), and "Nothing will happen that will permanently block our way to a common policy with Germany." Once the Far Eastern tension subsided, he thought new possibilities would develop with Germany in Europe. Meanwhile, the two must seek common ground. As for the foreign commissar, "You know what Litvinov represents. Over him there is a hard, cautious, and distrustful man endowed with a firm will. Stalin does not know where he stands with Germany. He is uncertain. . . . You must not imagine us to be so foolish that we will fall into the spokes of the wheel of world history. . . . If we carry on a state policy, we must oppose the revision of Versailles at our expense." To underline the latter theme, Radek added misgivings about Nazi machinations in the Baltic and commented that the Baltic states, created by the Entente as a *place d'armes* against the Soviet Union, "are today the most important protective wall for us against the West" (that is, no *place d'armes*). From all this Nadolny drew the conclusion that "Litvinov went too far in his negative attitude," and he argued that "we should utilize this circumstance at once."

Stalin had allowed Litvinov to adumbrate, but without openly espousing, a reorientation of Soviet policy toward collective security in concert with the status-quo powers. At the same time, he was telling the Germans, via Radek, that his real preference was for the German-Soviet collaboration suggested in Hitler's talk with Khinchuk the previous May.

In a suitably circumspect way Stalin repeated this message publicly when he addressed the party congress on 26 January. He echoed Litvinov's theme that the era of "burgeois pacifism" was ending, but omitted the foreign commissar's tripartite division of foreign states. He stated it as a fact that "things are moving toward a new imperialist war." His discussion of the war prospect showed a mind dominated by the idea that history was repeating itself and generating, as in 1914, an imperialist war that would lead to a new round of revolutions. Of the coming war he said, "It will certainly unleash revolution and place the very existence of capitalism in question in a number of countries as happened during the first imperialist war." Further: "Let not Messrs. bourgeois blame us if, on the morrow of such a war, certain governments near and dear to them, now ruling safely 'by the grace of God,' turn up missing." He even hinted at the whereabouts of some of these revolutions by foreseeing the war-caused downfall of "bourgeois-landowner" governments in a number of countries of Europe and Asia. Among the governments seen in Moscow as reflecting a strong land-owner interest where those of Poland and the Baltic states.

Turning to diplomacy, Stalin took special note of a recent change for the better in Soviet relations with France and Poland. But it was not true, he went on, what certain German politicians were saying, that because of German fascism's rise to power the USSR was now orienting itself on France and Poland and had become a supporter of Versailles. Despite all the Soviet lack of rapture for the German fascist regime, fascism had nothing to do with it, as shown by the fact that fascism in Italy did not prevent the USSR from having the best of relations with that country. The difficulty in Soviet-German relations arose from the change in German policy, from the fact that in the contest between difficult foreign-policy tendencies going on in Germany a new line reminiscent of the kaiser's anti-Russian one and represented by people like Alfred Rosenberg was prevailing over the old line embodied in the Soviet-German treaties. As for the USSR's "supposed reorientation," its sole orientation had been and remained on the USSR alone. "And if the USSR's interests demand rapprochement with these or those countries not concerned to violate peace, we embark upon this course without hesitation."

Stalin was thus unambiguously telling Hitler that whenever his government should be disposed to leave Russia in peace and revive the "old line" of German-Russian collaboration, Russia would be ready to reciprocate. Hitler had referred to common interests between the two states, and Stalin was showing his awareness of them. The signal did not go unheeded. In his cable to Berlin, Nadolny noted Stalin-Litvinov differences: Stalin did not mention relations with the League, did not (like Litvinov) treat Germany in conjunction with Japan, did not indicate a commitment to Poland and France, and preserved an un-Litvinov-like "calm tone and strict matter-of-factness." Nadolny thought that a responsive statement should be made on the German side, lest Francophile tendencies in Moscow receive decisive impetus. Up to a point, Hitler obliged. Addressing the Reichstag on 30 January, he gently reproved "M. Stalin" for expressing in his "last great speech" the fear that forces hostile to the Soviet might be active in Germany.

Stalin evidently wanted his own voice to be the sole congress viewpoint on foreign policy. Litvinov attended as a voting delegate but did not speak. . . .

Meanwhile, developments in other countries were making the tactic of waiting for favorable signs from Hitler untenable for Stalin. On the very day of his congress report, 26 January, Germany moved further away from Russia by concluding a nonaggression pact with Poland. Some days later, events in France dictated a new departure in Soviet policy. Antigovernment agitation led by French fascist and right-wing extremist groups culminated in a huge demonstration and fierce street fighting in Paris on 6 February. The Third Republic was in crisis. In this situation the Communists and their Moscow mentors drew back from the course followed in Germany, where the Communists' left-wing extremism had helped the fascists overthrow the democratic order.

On 12 February the French Communists joined the Socialists in a one-day strike against fascism. It was the beginning of the subsequently adopted Communist tactics of the democratic antifascist Popular Front. For Stalin, however, the tactical turnabout did not signify a conversion to an antifascist outlook. . . . Rather, it flowed from his orientation on a European war as the pathway to Russia's emergence into a commanding position on the continent. The existence in Europe of two more or less evenly balanced groups of powers was the prerequisite of that scenario. The rise of fascism in France posed a deadly threat to it. France was the keystone of the anti-German group. The triumph of fascism there would mean the collapse of Stalin's long-term strategy. In these circumstances, his espousal of a united antifascist front in France was of a piece with his earlier resort to fascism-abetting left extremism in Germany. The basic aim was to keep these traditional enemies apart so that they could move onto a collision course.

Even as Stalin gravitated toward the new politics of collective security and the Popular Front, he continued sending signals to Hitler. In early 1934 Voroshilov recalled the German and Soviet armies' past collaboration with nostalgia and urged Ambassador Nadolny to influence his government to follow a less anti-Soviet policy. "Just a few reassuring words from Hitler, he said, would be enough to show the Kremlin that *Mein Kampf* was no longer his basic policy statement." . . .

When popular-front governments arose in France and Spain in 1936, Soviet policy appeared to bear out Stalin's unrevolutionary words. The Spanish elections of February 1936 produced a Communist-supported popular-front government of liberals and Socialists under Manuel Azaña; the French elections of May 1936, a Communist-supported popular-front government of Socialists and Radicals headed by the Socialist Léon Blum. A spontaneous strike movement of unprecedented proportions erupted in France before the Blum government took office. Worker occupation of plants gave it a radical character. This was ominous from the standpoint of Stalin's policy of supporting a strong and stable status-quo France. In Litvinov's words to a correspondent of *Pétit Parisien:* "What is essential is that France should not allow her military strength to be weakened. We hope no internal troubles will favour Germany's designs." When the strikers numbered two million, Thorez, certainly acting on Stalin's instructions, ordered the Communists of Paris to end the strike, and the French Communist Party put out the slogan: "The *Front Populaire* is not the revolution." With Communist help the mass strike was damped down.

Stalin's popular-front politics went along with a realignment of his diplomacy toward collective security against aggression. Soviet entry into the League of Nations in September 1934, whereby Moscow joined forces with the Versailles powers in the previously maligned league, was a turning point in this development, underpinning vigorous efforts to assist the formation of an anti-German grouping of European states.

Fear of further spread of fascism was not the only reason for Stalin's new course in diplomacy; actions on the German side influenced him as well. After consolidating his power in Germany, Hitler's initially cautious and conciliatory moves in foreign policy gave way to greater boldness. By early 1934 his anti-Soviet stance was manifested, among other ways, in German-Polish relations. During 1933 Poland's strongman, Marshal Pilsudski, signaled through informal channels a desire for an understanding with Moscow, and sounded out France and Great Britain about a preventive war against Hilter's Germany while she was still too weak for effective resistance. When it became clear that no positive response was coming, he concluded a nonaggression pact with Hitler on 26 January 1934. Although he thereupon sent his foreign minister to Moscow to convey assurances that Poland had no anti-Soviet intent, Stalin could hardly be in doubt of the new pact's anti-Soviet meaning for Hitler. In March 1934 representatives of the Krupp firm traveled to Moscow to cancel a five-year contract for training Soviet technicians and supplying machinery and steel. . . .

But Stalin did not forsake his earlier orientation on a new and greater Brest — a divisive diplomacy leading to a new European war in which Moscow would remain neutral until a time of its choosing and then carve out his envisaged "socialist borderland." Evidence of this is contained in a letter of 19 July 1934 to his Politburo colleagues rejecting a plan by the editor of *Bol'shevik*, Adoratsky, to reprint Friedrich Engels's essay of 1890, "The Foreign Policy of Russian Tsarism," in the journal's forthcoming special issue for the twentieth anniversary of the outbreak of the World War. Engels had forecast the war on the basis of an acute analysis of the emerging division of European powers into opposed camps. He had also shown an anti-Russian bias, portraying Russian foreign policy since Catherine II's time as a never-ending search for world domination by a talented but unscrupulous cabal of foreign-born adventurers, which he called a "new Jesuit order" and a "secret society."

In his 1934 letter (first made public in *Bol'shevik* in May 1941), Stalin took Engels to task for explaining Russia's policy of aggrandizement more by the presence of the gang of adventurers than by the need for outlet to seas and seaports for enlarged foreign trade and strategic positions. Engels, he wrote, had exaggerated Russia's role by suggesting that war could be averted by the overthrow of tsarism, from which it would follow that a war by bourgeois Germany against tsarist Russia would be a war of liberation. What room did this leave for Lenin's policy? When war broke out in 1914, Lenin refused to support either side, seeking to turn the war between the rival imperialist camps into a series of revolutionary civil wars in the belligerent countries. In making specific reference to that position of Lenin in mid-1934, Stalin was suggesting that Moscow should adopt a position of noninvolvement in the approaching second imperialist war. But he knew that for this war to be advantageous for Moscow, it must be protracted, and for that both sides must be formidably strong.

The Soviet-French talks begun in April 1934 were accompanied by attempts to create an "Eastern Locarno" — an East European security system linking the USSR, Poland, Czechoslovakia, Finland, and the Baltic states, along with France and Germany, in mutual-assistance guarantees. These efforts foundered first on German, and then on Polish opposition. Moscow and Paris proceeded, however, to sign their bilateral pact on 2 May 1935, and a similar mutual-assistance pact was signed two weeks later between the Soviet Union and Czechoslovakia. It bound the USSR to come to the defense of Czechoslovakia in case of invasion after France did. At that time, French Foreign Minister Pierre Laval paid a visit to Moscow. The communiqué on his talks noted that Stalin expressed "full understanding and approval of the policy of state defense that France is pursuing in order to maintain her armed forces at a level appropriate to her security needs." Since it had been Communist policy to withhold parliamentary support for military preparations of bourgeois governments, Stalin's statement caused a sensation. French Communists called off their campaign against the government's plan to extend the period of military service from one to two years. From Litvinov, who had read *Mein Kampf*, Stalin knew about Hitler's long-held notion of conquering France first and then turning on Russia. If Hitler were to open the coming new war, as Stalin hoped he would, by marching against France, Stalin wanted France to be militarily strong enough to keep from being overrun and speedily conquered.

A similar design informed his policy toward Britain at that stage. At the end of March 1935, following a visit to Berlin with British Foreign Secretary Sir John Simon, Sir Anthony Eden, who was then lord privy seal, paid a visit to Moscow and was the first Western statesman of high rank to have a personal interview with Stalin. After reporting to Litvinov on the talks which Simon and he had just conducted with Hitler, Eden was received in the Kremlin by Stalin, Molotov, Litvinov, and the Soviet ambassador in London, Ivan Maisky. He found Stalin well informed, quiet-spoken ("the quietest dictator I have ever known, with the exception of Dr. Salazar"), a good listener prone to doodling, a man of pragmatic temper whose personality made itself felt without effort, whose quality of mind he could not help respecting, and whose courtesy "in no way hid from us an implacable ruthlessness."

Stalin got down to business by asking Eden whether he thought the present European situation "as alarming as, or more alarming than, the situation in 1913." When Eden replied that he would say "anxious" rather than "alarming," Stalin said he considered it basically worse because in 1913 there was one potential aggressor, Germany, and now there were two, Germany and Japan. He spoke of the Germans as a great and capable people with understandable resentment of the Versailles treaty. To Eden he seemed "perhaps more understanding of the German point of view than Litvinov, in the sense that he was less scrupulous and had no prejudice against the Nazis as such, which Litvinov no doubt felt for their treatment of the Jews." Stalin argued for "some scheme of pacts" to deter German aggression. Then he walked to the world map on the wall and "remarked in friendly tones upon the power and influence of so small an island as Britain." He thus made it clear that he could see positive value in the British Empire, and *a fortiori* in its preservation. And as if to warn Eden not to put credence in Hitler's anti-Bolshevism, he remarked on the "duplicity of German policy" as expressed first, in the offer of 200-million-mark credit to the Soviet government and German willingness to include some important contracts for war matériel in the bargain; and, secondly, in the spreading of a story by Germans that Deputy War Commissar Tukhachevsky had made contact with General Goering and pressed some anti-French scheme upon him. . . .

By his collective-security diplomacy, in combination with his popular-front tactics in the Comintern, Stalin was assisting events to take their course toward a European war. An accord with Germany remained a basic aim because it would offer an opportunity to effect a westward advance of Soviet rule while turning Germany against the democracies in what Stalin envisaged as a replay of World War I, a protracted inconclusive struggle that would weaken both sides while neutral Russia increased her power and awaited an advantageous time for decisive intervention. But to make sure that the European war *would* be protracted, he wanted Britain and France to be militarily strong enough to withstand the onslaught that Germany under Hitler was becoming strong enough to launch against them. That explains his moves to encourage ruling elements in both these major states to rearm with dispatch, and his orders to the French Communists to support the French military buildup.

Stalin's collective-security diplomacy was a calculated effort of coalition building in Europe. He earnestly sought to bring about the formation of a strong politico-military anti-German grouping based on France and Britain. But, as we shall see, *it was not a coalition in which he wanted the Soviet Union to participate when war came.*

Stalin's design seems not to have been lost on his tough-minded foreign commissar, Litvinov, who himself was an ideal instrument of the collective-security diplomacy because, as a Moscow *Westler,* he genuinely believed in it and therefore could be a persuasive advocate of it, whether in diplomatic talks or in great public gatherings such as those of the League of Nations in Geneva. In a private conversation after World War II, Jacob Suritz, who was Soviet ambassador in Berlin in the mid-1930s, told his friend Ehrenburg that he had been summoned to Moscow in 1936 for a high-level conference at which Litvinov presented his position and Stalin, after concurring, laid his hand on the other's shoulder and said, "You see, we can reach agreement," to which Litvinov replied: "Not for long." The foreign commissar really meant it when he said, in the phrase that grew world famous at that time, "Peace is indivisible." But for Stalin, who was in charge of Soviet diplomacy, peace was divisible.

Hitler was practicing divisive diplomacy of his own, and doing so at Russia's expense by playing the card of anti-Bolshevism in seeking Western acquiescence in his moves to restore German power. Thus in

March 1935, shortly after letting it be known that Germany had rebuilt a military air force and was reintroducing conscription with the goal of a thirty-six-division army, he received the above-mentioned visit by Simon and Eden for two days of talks during which, while obdurately defending his military moves, he denounced Soviet Russia and offered German support for Britain in exchange for the return of former German colonies. Meanwhile, he publicly declared that he had no claims on France and no aggressive designs on his Western neighbors. If Hitler was thus employing anti-Bolshevism for *his* political purposes, Stalin must have reasoned, why should he not make corresponding use of antifascism for his?

His coalition building was made all the more imperative by a tendency visible in French and especially British diplomacy to seek good relations with Germany. Hitler naturally encouraged this tendency. Desiring to head off an anti-German coalition, he responded to the Franco-Soviet pact with a speech of 21 May 1935 in which he gave assurances of nonaggression to his neighbors (except Lithuania, which allegedly oppressed Germans in Memel), attacked Soviet Russia as a state ruled by a doctrine totally antithetical to Germany's National Socialism, and particularly proffered the hand of peace to France. In the following summer and fall, Laval sought a French rapprochement with Germany. In June 1935, acting on its own, the British government concluded a bilateral naval agreement with Germany, allowing the latter 35 percent of British naval strength in violation of the Versailles treaty. . . .

Influential forces in France and especially in Britain were seeking to tilt official diplomacy toward an accord with Germany. Hitler found a British friend in Lord Lothian, who, after a visit to Germany, wrote in the *London Times* that the new Germany did not want war but only "real equality" and that its very devotion to race would keep it from seeking to annex other nations. In June 1935 the Prince of Wales spoke in support of contact between British and German war veterans' organizations. Lothian and others wanted to turn Hitler eastward. . . .

On 7 March 1936 Hitler took the bold and risky step of marching his forces into the demilitarized Rhineland. At that time his resurgent army was still no match for the army of France. Seeing the potentially decisive change in the power balance that would occur if Hitler's move succeeded, a worried French government considered military action but was dissuaded by London. Britain's orientation on an understanding with Hitler's Germany was showing itself in British promotion of inaction at a critical moment in the drift toward war.

All this went on under watchful Moscow eyes. The Western powers were working both sides of the diplomatic street. So was Hitler. And so was Stalin. In fact, he had resumed his diplomacy of accord with Germany in advance of the developments just mentioned, and he pursued it concurrently with the coalition-building diplomacy of collective security. Aware of Hitler's inclination toward a war against France as a prelude to a *Drang nach Osten*, he could not help knowing that he held a card of great value in the current diplomatic game: the capacity to assure Germany of Soviet neutrality in event of war in the West. Stalin started probing Berlin as soon as Ambassador Schulenburg took up his Moscow post. When the ambassador presented his credentials on 3 October 1934, President Kalinin expressed hope for improved German-Soviet relations. "Too much importance should not be attached to the outcry in the press," he went on. The peoples of the two countries were "in many ways dependent upon each other," and he believed that a way would be found of restoring friendly relations. In the following month the new Soviet ambassador in Berlin, Suritz, told a German foreign-office official that Soviet distrust of Germany "could only be dispelled and the atmosphere calmed on a realistic basis. . . ."

On 8 May 1935, six days after the signing of the Franco-Soviet pact, Litvinov told Schulenburg that he hoped the pact would be followed by a "general pact" involving Germany. That would "lessen the significance of the Franco-Soviet Pact" and "lead to an improvement in relations with Germany, which the Soviet Government desired above all things and which they now considered possible." In the late spring of 1935, Gustav Hilger, Russian-born counselor of the German Embassy in Moscow, took a trip to Kiev where the German consul gave a reception in his honor. Among the several high local functionaries who attended was one Vasilenko, chairman of the Executive Committee of the Kiev Regional Soviet. He said to Hilger that recently some workers had told him they could not understand the current party line toward Germany, which was only trying to free herself from the Versailles shackles. Instead of helping her, the Soviet government was making a pact with Germany's oppressors. "In short," Vasilenko went on, "Litvinov's policy does not convince the masses, and history will soon pass over Litvinov. How absurd of Soviet Russia to ally herself with a 'degenerate' state like France! Peace would be secure only through friendship with Germany. Who cares about the racial concepts of National Socialism?" An experienced Russian hand like Hilger could not but know that such statements by a Soviet official would hardly be coming from the "masses."

The Soviet trade mission in Berlin, offering a channel of communication apart from Litvinov's Narkomindel, played a key role in Stalin's German diplomacy. Between 1935 and 1937 it was headed by a Georgian, David Kandelaki, who let it be known that he was in direct contact with Stalin and enjoyed his confidence. Soon after Kandelaki's arrival at the Berlin post, trade talks that had dragged on since mid-1934 came to favorable fruition in a new agreement signed by him and Reich Minister of Economics Hjalmar Schacht on 9 April 1935. The agreement stipulated that Moscow would pay off half of its outstanding 200-million-mark credit in gold and foreign exchange, the other half in goods, and would place additional orders to the extent of 200 million marks with German industrial firms on the basis of a new five-year credit from a German banking consortium.

Matters took a new turn when Schacht, in June 1935 — the month in which Germany concluded the naval agreement with Britain — raised the possibility of increasing the volume of Soviet-German trade with a 500-million-mark credit extended for a ten-year period. Kandelaki took this news to Moscow, where Stalin put a political interpretation upon it. "Well, now, how can Hitler make war on us when he has granted us such loans? It's impossible," he reportedly said at a Politburo meeting. On returning to Berlin, Kandelaki called on Schacht on 15 July to deliver the reply. Just beforehand his authority was enhanced, and the importance attached to his activity underlined, by a decree awarding him the Order of Lenin for "outstanding merits, energetic efforts, and initiative in the foreign-trade field." Kandelaki told Schacht that he had spoken with Stalin, Molotov, and Foreign Trade Commissar Rosengolts. They had approved the substance of the new conversations, but wanted further arrangements postponed pending completion of the trade program already under way. Then, as Schacht reported it, "after some embarrassment, M. Kandelaki expressed the hope that it might be possible to improve German-Russian political relations." Schacht told him that on such matters the Soviet government must approach the Foreign Ministry through its ambassador.

Undeterred, Stalin persisted in his overtures. It was indicated to the Germans that such known adversaries of theirs as Litvinov and Tukhachevsky would constitute no obstacle to an accord. At the end of October 1935 the departing counselor of the German Embassy, von Twardowski, was surprised when Tukhachevsky (unquestioningly acting on orders emanating from Stalin) appeared among others at a farewell reception for him. He and the German military attaché, General Koestring, had an hour's talk during which the marshal professed great respect for the German army and declared that, although he was a good Communist and a soldier who knew nothing about politics, he hoped that Germany and the Soviet Union would come together again. Twardowski's report on the conversation noted that after Voroshilov, Tukhachevsky was regarded as the most influential man in the Red Army "and is in general reputed to be pro-French." At a dinner on the eve of the 7 November holiday shortly afterward, Litvinov raised his glass to the German ambassador and drank "to the rebirth of our friendship."

Then, as if to follow up on Schacht's suggestion, overtures were made through the Soviet Embassy in Berlin. On 2 December 1935, Embassy Counselor Sergei Bessonov told a German Foreign Ministry official that efforts should be made to achieve a *détente* in Soviet-German relations, and agreed that expanded economic relations could serve as a starter. A week later, he called on von Twardowski and solicited his opinion on how German-Soviet relations could be improved. Ambassador Suritz pursued the same theme when von Twardowski paid a courtesy call on him at that time. He asked: what could be done to improve German-Soviet relations, what effect would a strengthening of economic relations have on the political situation, were more active cultural relations possible, and should he intensify his social activities in Berlin? Suritz also stressed that Litvinov should not be regarded as an opponent of German-Soviet relations. On 20 December Bessonov went to the German Foreign Ministry, expressed optimism about the trade negotiations, and broached to the official with whom he was speaking the idea of a bilateral Soviet-German nonaggression pact, something that he said had already been discussed in a private German-Soviet conversation at the beginning of 1935. Between late November and early December, similar Soviet soundings were made through the German Embassy in Moscow and in Tiflis, where the German consul general was approached by the Narkomindel's man in Georgia, Georgi Astakhov.

Stalin's probes drew no positive response. For Hitler they were premature. Improved German-Soviet relations, not to mention a non-aggression pact, were ruled out by his need to exploit anti-Bolshevism while strengthening Germany's position, as he did with the reoccupation of the Rhineland, which opened the way for his subsequent moves to annex Austria and vanquish Czechoslovakia. Only with those objectives accomplished would he be ready for war in the West, and not until then would he be responsive to overtures from the East. Stalin undoubtedly took this into account. His probes did, however, signal that Moscow would be ready when Berlin was.

Lest there be any doubt of this, Stalin made his position public via Molotov. Interviewed by a French journalist on the Soviet response to the German reoccupation of the Rhineland, the Soviet premier replied as follows to a question whether there were any tendencies in the Soviet Union toward a rapprochement with Germany: "There is a tendency among certain sections of the Soviet public towards an attitude of thoroughgoing irreconcilability to the present rulers of Germany, particularly because of the ever repeated hostile speeches of German leaders against the Soviet Union. But the chief tendency, and the one determining the Soviet Government's policy, thinks an improvement in Soviet-German relations possible."

Jiri Hochman

The Great Purges and Collective Security

In 1934, when the USSR joined the League of Nations the Soviet spokesman in Geneva, Maxim Litvinov, emerged as a proponent of "collective

From Jiri Hochman, *The Soviet Union and the Failure of Collective Security, 1934–39*, pp. 125–142. Copyright © 1984 by Cornell University. Used by permission of the publisher, Cornell University Press.

security." According to this concept, peace-loving nations should unite in opposing aggression by the fascist powers.

Meanwhile, the Soviet government negotiated alliances with France and with Czechoslovakia that appeared as evidence of collective security. But in 1935 the first of the purges began in the Soviet Union. Soon they expanded into a great campaign of terror as Stalin waged war on the Communist Party, the military leadership, the intellectuals, and ultimately the entire nation. Thousands were executed and millions died in slave labor camps. The purges, as Jiri Hochman explains, undermined Soviet foreign policy. How could the Soviet government be trusted in a confrontation with Nazi Germany when the leaders of the armed forces were denounced as German agents and executed?

Between 1934 and 1936, Soviet Russia's international esteem reached its peak. The Soviets were accepted in the respectable world of Western democracies, admitted into the League of Nations, and linked with the Versailles system by alliances with France and Czechoslovakia.

The Soviets were still acclaimed, even idolized, by significant segments of leftist and liberal intellectual circles in Europe as pioneers of socialism. The extent of this support was manifested by the International Writers' Congress in Paris in 1935. Organized behind the scenes by the Comintern, the congress was attended by such world-renowned literary figures as André Gide, Henri Barbusse, André Malraux, J. R. Bloch, Louis Aragon, Bertold Brecht, Heinrich Mann, Lion Feuchtwanger, Johannes R. Becher, Robert Musil, Anna Seghers, Aldous Huxley, Martin Andersen-Nexoe, and many others. The support of leftist and liberal intellectuals significantly eased the admission of the Soviet Union into the democratic club. This process was also facilitated by a parallel relative moderation in the internal development of the USSR and by the gradual relaxation of the political course of the Comintern, which was officially enunciated by the Seventh Congress in the summer of 1935.

In 1935, many friends of the Soviet Union in the West believed that Russia was on her way toward developing a genuine system of democratic socialism. André Gide expressed the opinion that "on the high road of history . . . the Soviet Union has taken the lead in a glorious manner. No doubt a period of mass affirmation was necessary," he added in an effort to explain past violence; but in Gide's view that period was over. "Taking into account the particular idiosyncracies of each individual" was now under way, and eventually Communism would prevail.

When the news became public that a new Soviet constitution was being drafted in the Soviet Union, hopes were widespread in foreign leftist and liberal circles that the hour of democracy in Russia had arrived. Louis Fischer remembers that he "always looked forward to the growth of democracy [in Soviet Russia] at the expense of the dictatorship." . . .

To draft a new constitution was a formal decision taken at the Seventh Congress of Soviets convened in February 1935 — a few weeks after the ominous murder of Kirov, but also halfway between the Soviet entry into the League of Nations and the conclusion of the Franco-Soviet alliance. The constitution, which was promulgated in November 1936, was a farce. Its impressive list of civil rights was supported by no constitutional mechanism to safeguard them. All the high-toned declarations of the new constitution (Bukharin and Radek were among the members of the Drafting Committee of the Supreme Soviet) were rendered virtually meaningless. The fact that the peasantry, which represented a majority of some 70 percent, was given voting rights and thus formally accepted into the Soviet "socialist family" was debased by the complete absence of electoral choice. The existing dictatorship was as strong as ever, merely decorated with a more elaborate system of "transmission handles" in line with the old Leninist prescription, which had of course been designed for a different time and situation. "Under a patina of constitutional and legal procedures lay the dead hand of Nicholas I's official nationalism and some of the macabre touches of Ivan the Terrible."

In other words, Stalin's new foreign policy course was accompanied by no corresponding change in his methods of governing Russia. On the contrary, Soviet Russia's new association with Western democracies was accompanied by the launching of the horror of the Great Purges. And the impact of this internal Soviet development upon foreign public opinion, foreign governments and general staffs — including that of Germany — in a period crucial for the fate of collective security, was catastrophic.

The starting point of this ghastly era appears to have been the murder of Sergei Kirov in December 1934, which was very probably engineered by the GPU [political police] itself. By the second half of 1936 the purges were in full swing, and did not recede before 1939.

Western observers had noticed the atmosphere of fear in Moscow before the real horror broke out. President Beneš remembers his and Massigli's astonishment in Geneva in the summer of 1934, when Maxim Litvinov suddenly exclaimed during an exchange of views on the modalities of the Soviet entry into the League of Nations: "Do you not realize that if I do not return to Russia with an unquestionable success, I'll be put before a firing squad?" During Georges Bonnet's visit to Moscow in August 1934, Ambassador Alphand informed him about the bugging devices in Litvinov's quarter in the Commissariat for Foreign Affairs. When received by the commissar, Bonnet "gladly gave satisfaction to [his] informer. In fact, from the moment when I took a seat by his side, I recognized that his tone changed and Stalin's name appeared more frequently in his speech, always accompanied by the most flattering epithets."

George F. Kennan, who was assigned to the U.S. Embassy in Moscow in the mid-1930s, notes in his memoirs that foreign representatives in Moscow had to deal with two separate governments, of which the formal one, including the Foreign Office, was in fact powerless; the real power lay with the GPU. "Extensive damage has been done to the fabric of Soviet foreign relations over the years by this vicious system." With the outbreak of the purges, "the atmosphere for the conduct of any sort of diplomatic work in Moscow, by anyone, [further] drastically deteriorated."

The fact that Soviet diplomatic personnel became an early target of a prolonged pogrom of the GPU had, of course, special importance for the state of foreign relations of Soviet Russia. Foreign relations of any country are primarily conducted by its officially appointed representatives. In the USSR, only the Commissariat for Foreign Affairs had the license to maintain political contacts with foreign governments and their missions in Moscow. The effect upon foreign diplomats in the Soviet capital and upon the chancelleries abroad of the systematic extermination of their Soviet counterparts, with whom in some cases they had established personal relationships, was an inevitable and significant component in all deliberations concerning international relations whenever Soviet Russia played a part, potential or actual.

Litvinov complained about the GPU's mistreatment of the personnel of the Narkomindel as early as 1931. "Members of our staff have been arrested. . . . In charge is a certain Shkiryatov. . . . Jews are obviously purged first." The assault on the Commissariat was launched in the second half of 1936, and continued with unrelenting intensity through 1937 and even later. The Czechoslovak ambassador to Moscow, Zdeněk Fierlinger, whose sympathies for the Soviet Union are well known, observed: "The atmosphere in Moscow was heavy. Contacts between the diplomatic corps and the Soviet society were interrupted. Every day, the press printed news about acts of sabotage. Officials, with whom the diplomatic corps had been in contact, were disappearing from government offices overnight." . . .

Purges were simultaneously affecting dozens of Soviet missions abroad, such as the important embassy in Paris. "Principal officials of the [Soviet] Embassy were disappearing one after the other, victims of the frequent purges. . . . An atmosphere of distrust and fear descended heavily upon the salons." . . .

Accompanied by a wave of nationalism and xenophobia that even drew an official French protest, the decimation of the Soviet foreign service was followed by a decision to close down as many as twenty-two foreign consulates. This action affected not just unfriendly countries like Germany and Japan, but also Great Britain, Czechoslovakia, Turkey, Scandinavian and Baltic countries, and others. Count Schulenburg called the closing of the Czechoslovak Consulate in Kiev, which had been opened only a year before, "particularly amazing."

An early fallout of the purges was the disenchantment of many liberal fellow travelers. Some of them, like André Gide, decided at once to break with Moscow completely; others postponed their divorce only because of the outbreak of the Spanish Civil War in July 1936, "swallowing their bile and waiting for the day when . . . Russia and the Comintern [would be] ready to become democratic institutions."

Stalin soon extended the purges to the Iberian front line of the anti-Fascist struggle, which even *Pravda* openly reported in December 1936 in its coverage of the Spanish war. One after another, leading Soviet representatives sent to coordinate the aid for the Loyalists were recalled to Moscow and shot. . . . André Gide's *Retour de l'URSS*, which appeared in November 1936 (followed by *Retouches* three months later), expressed the shock and disillusionment of many liberal intellectuals, both those who were already abandoning the ship and those who were still on board, waiting for some miracle that would return their dreams. Gide's verdict, in the most widely read political pamphlet in leftist and liberal intellectual circles in Europe in 1937, sounded like the cry of a betrayed lover:

> *From top to bottom of the reformed social ladder, the most favored are the most servile, the most cowardly, the most cringing, the basest. All those who refuse to stoop are mowed down or deported one after the other. . . . Soon in the heroic and admirable people who deserved so well our love, there will be left only executioners, profiteers and victims.*
>
> *And I doubt whether in any other country in the world, even in Hitler's Germany, thought is less free, more bowed down, more terrorized, more vassalized.*

Contrary to the impression that the falsity of the show trials was immediately obvious, the fact is that diplomatic observers in Moscow took the accusations very seriously — in some cases right up until the last of the trials, in March 1938. With the passing of time, their interpretation of the accusations and verdicts departed from the official Soviet version, and came to differ quite substantially; but it was not based on the assumption that the whole enterprise was a fraud and a witch-hunt. Besides, the purges were followed by far-reaching consequences — disruption of industry, weakening of the armed forces, general political malaise. These stark facts could not be interpreted in any uncertain terms.

Two reports of the French Embassy in Moscow, both filed in January 1937, reflect the seriousness with which the official version presented in the show trials was accepted by the principal Soviet ally in Europe:

> *Opposition in the USSR is a serious matter. This opposition is not counterrevolutionary, as they are trying to tell us here, but it is the expression of — within the framework of the Revolution — various non-conformist and anti-Stalinist tendencies. . . . In any event, there exists an attempt at a collusion between Germany and Japan on one side, and Trotskyism on the other.*
>
> *As far as the Reich is concerned, this trial has revealed, in both countries, the persistence of an undercurrent the importance of which it is impossible to ignore.*

The report concludes that the opposition in the Soviet Union, which had been minimized, had in fact been gaining in strength during the last three years and acquired a terroristic character, which is not unusual in autocratic regimes. "So we see the reappearance of one of the most specific traits of old Russia." . . .

The Tukhachevsky Affair

Of all the arrests, deportations, and executions, the Tukhachevsky affair, in June 1937 — the starting point of the assault of the GPU on the Red Army — was the most shocking, and the most damaging to the Soviet reputation abroad. The previous purge of the GPU itself, following the fall of Yagoda, had produced false expectations abroad that the worst might be over. As Nadezhda Mandelstam noted, the victims, who had meantime "ceased to believe in natural causes of death," did not share that hope. The "new GPU" soon proved that they were right.

Headed by a team recruited in the highest echelons of the party apparatus, with Yezhov as the new boss, the GPU fell upon the armed forces with unrestrained fury, fed by the fact that in the previous purges the Red Army had been left virtually intact. The reaction abroad was immediately vehement, even before it became clear that the affair was not limited to two marshals and a few generals, but was to affect some 50 percent of the entire officer corps of the Soviet armed forces, including three of five marshals, thirteen of fifteen army commanders, fifty-seven of eighty-five corps commanders, and so on — altogether thirty-five thousand officers (90 percent of all generals, 80 percent of all colonels).

The executions of Tukhachevsky and the other leading Red Army commanders had a particularly strong impact in France, "a country with a conscript army which, it was realized, might have found itself taking the field with a power whose high command was conspiring with the common enemy." Ambassador Bullitt reported from Paris that "the executions of Marshal Tukhachevsky and six generals of the Army High Command for the crime of betraying military secrets to Germany caused great consternation" in French military and political circles. Coulondre in Moscow visited Litvinov two days after the announcement of the executions of the military leaders to inform the foreign commissar of "the deplorable impression produced by the massacre show [*jeu du massacre*]" in France and other countries friendly to the USSR, especially now that the Red Army was affected. Two weeks later the French ambassador repeated his demarche, this time informing Potemkin (who was on his way up, over the corpse of Krestinsky, to the position of deputy commissar) that France, as an ally of Soviet Russia, was naturally concerned about the treason affair in the Soviet High Command and demanding information on "how far the executed officers had been involved in the conspiracy with Germany." Potemkin replied that the generals had organized a coup d'etat with the intention of concluding an alliance with Germany. In spite of Potemkin's obvious effort to play down the charges of the generals' direct collusion with Germany, the allegation that a pro-German conspiracy had taken place in the Soviet High Command was confirmed through diplomatic channels, and soon thereafter, the progress of the Red Army purge showed that the conspiracy was also widespread in lower commands.

The case could not fail to affect relations between the French and Soviet general staffs. A secret note of the French Ministry of War in April 1937, summing up the contacts between the two armies, testifies to the French interest in some regularization of the military cooperation. A similar conclusion can be drawn from a note of the General Staff of the Army, compiled for the French government in May 1937. Shortly thereafter another document of the French General Staff, entitled "Note . . . Concerning the Eventuality of Franco-Soviet Military Contacts," dated June 9, 1937, took note of the probable consequences of Tukhachevsky's transfer to a provincial command (shortly before his arrest and execution). This document stated:

> The internal situation of Soviet Russia, and especially the complete lack of stability of the military High Command have substantially reduced the authority of those Russian military men designated to establish contacts with the representative of the French General Staff. . . . It [therefore] seems to be better to wait until the uncertainty of the purges which are raging in the USSR will be over. To act differently would mean to court the risk of seeing the military men with whom negotiations would be conducted and arrangements possibly concluded, disappear shortly afterwards.

That was not an unfounded consideration, as the experience of the Czechoslovak General Staff may illustrate. The two armies reached an agreement, in the summer of 1936, to establish practical cooperation in the field of intelligence work against Germany. (It may be noted, as a less important detail, that the Soviets tried to direct their intelligence operations from Czechoslovakia more against Poland than against Germany.) During the Czechoslovak General Staff delegation's stay in Moscow that summer they were received by Tukhachevsky, and conferred with a group of Soviet officers headed by General M. S. Uritzky. On this level, the agreement on the cooperation in the field of intelligence against Germany was concluded. The Soviets then sent a "courteous and well educated former Tsarist officer" to Prague, who started to work in cooperation with the officers of the Czechoslovak Military Intelligence. A few months later (March 1937), this Soviet officer, code-named "Rudolf" by the Czechs, was suddenly ordered to Moscow, where he was in all probability executed. In June, General Uritzky himself was shot. A Soviet Intelligence delegation arrived in Prague in the fall to resume contacts. None of those who had concluded the agreement of summer 1936 were among them. Clearly, they had all been shot.

The alleged treason case in the Soviet High Command was still affecting the attitudes of the Czechoslovak General Staff in 1938, as can be seen from a German diplomatic report from Prague in March 1938. This report, obviously based on intelligence sources, states:

> *After the shooting of Marshal Tukhachevsky and other very high-ranking officers of the Soviet Army, the Czechoslovak General Staff lost its confidence in the Red Army staff. On this account mutual relations assumed an abnormal form, especially because the Government on their part adhered to their friendly treaty relations with Moscow. On January 28, 1938, the Czechoslovak General Staff . . . turned down the proposal of the Red Army Staff for the appointment of a mixed commission to examine the defense plans of both states. The Czechoslovak General Staff did not reveal secrets regarding the operational plans and armament of Czechoslovakia, as well as the plans for mobilization and their latest aircraft engines. The fears of the Czechoslovak General Staff are shown by the fact that, up to now, it is not yet convinced that, as Moscow maintains, Tukhachevsky was not in contact with the German General Staff, and so might have betrayed to the latter all the Czechoslovak defense secrets, and because it is not sure that some representatives of the Red Army General Staff might not again hand over such secrets to the German General Staff.*

These fears of the Czechoslovak General Staff were far from unsubstantiated, because the Red Army purge was by no means discontinued in spring 1938. At the end of February, quite a short time before the German military attaché compiled his report in Prague, two very high-ranking Red Army commanders were shot — admirals Orlov and Sirkov. The French reaction was similar to that of the Czechoslovak General Staff. Ambassador Bullitt reported from Paris a few weeks after the execution of the Red Army commanders: "Orders were issued to the French ministries and are strictly observed that henceforth no information is to be given to any Soviet representative. . . . An uneasy feeling exists here that information of confidential nature which had been made available to Soviet military leaders may have found its way into German hands." The Abwehr may have had a more direct access to French military secrets at that time, but the impact of the accusation that the executed Soviet military leaders had worked for Germany could not fail to cause great concern. There is little doubt that the GPU's assault on the Red Army High Command in June 1937 hampered the prospects for a broadening of the cooperation between the French and Soviet general staffs, which until then was the trend, however slow and still lacking a properly negotiated framework. It was agreed in April 1937 to open technical conversations between the two general staffs, which certainly constituted an important step toward such mutual cooperation. This agreement followed a round of talks on the subject between Léon Blum and Ambassador Potemkin, and was understood as the beginning of a process in that direction. Then came the announcement of the arrest and the execution of Tukhachevsky and his "accomplices." No technical talks, of course, ever took place.

In the eyes of the French General Staff, the treason case in the Soviet High Command did not appear improbable, in view of the previous close cooperation between the Red Army and the well known Reichswehr, in high French military circles. According to Georges Castellan, the French Deuxième Bureau had informed the French General Staff regularly until 1933 about the numbers of Soviet officers trained in German military institutions — at least 120 senior Soviet officers in early 1930s. Some of these officers (Tukhachevsky, Uborevich) were then accused of collusion with Germany; others, like the chief of the Soviet General Staff, Marshal Yegorov, retained their positions. On the whole, the blow that the affair inflicted upon the confidence of the French military in their Soviet counterparts could not possibly be redressed in the short period then remaining before the Franco-Soviet alliance would be put to practical test.

Diplomatic correspondence from Moscow, including reports filed by the military attachés, shows that foreign observers soon recognized the continuous and systematic nature of the purge, with its inevitable consequences for the commanding structure of the Red Army. All through 1937 and 1938, the progress of the military purge was reported in great detail. Strong emphasis was put on the fact that the extermination of the Soviet officer corps did not slow down in the summer of 1938 or at the time of Munich. In this last development it was the

Soviet Air Force that was particularly affected. Although the previously held radical views about the decisive role of aircraft in modern warfare had to be corrected in the light of the war in Spain, the Soviet Air Force was still considered a formidable factor at the beginning of 1938, believed to be numerically the strongest in the world. In 1938, the Soviet Air Force was purged of its most distinguished commanders (Generals Alksnis and V. V. Khripin and thousands of lower officers; even Tupolev was imprisoned). The reaction of the French air minister in Daladier's government, Guy La Chamber, expressed in May 1938, may be quite characteristic of French and British views:

> *The Russians killed every airplane engineer and constructor they had. They have no new planes and the best they have are their imitations of American models four or five years old. . . . In addition, the officers' corps of the Russian Air Force had been annihilated so completely that the Russian Air Force could not be considered an effective fighting force in spite of the number of planes it contained.*

The British government, on the eve of the final stage of the Czechoslovak crisis at the beginning of September 1938, received from its ambassador in Moscow a report that not only presented a picture of complete administrative disarray, but included a description of the situation of the Soviet armed forces:

> *At the beginning of the year, I reported that during 1937 at least 65 percent of the officers over the rank of Colonel, or the equivalent, in the Red Army, Navy and Air Force, had been liquidated. There is every reason to suppose that this year in the fighting services the successors of those who were liquidated are themselves being liquidated at an equally alarming rate.*

The broadly publicized desertions of Soviet officers fleeing from the purge to the West, across the Pripet River to Poland, and even to the Far East — (a particularly ominous sign, considering the reputation of the Japanese in the Far Eastern Red Army in respect to their treatment of prisoners of war) — further underlined the desperate situation of the Soviet armed forces.

The Soviet Purges and the Military Planning of Other Powers

This whole development could not fail to affect the strategic considerations of all parties involved, directly or indirectly, in the crises of 1938.

"That hecatomb of generals," wrote Coulondre in his memoirs, "caused abroad, and especially in France, a catastrophic impression, which I myself was unable completely to escape." Sir Samuel Hoare noted in his memoirs that in 1938 "the Great Purge seemed to have left the Soviets incapable of any military action." Ambassador Biddle reported in April 1938 that President Beneš had given up his expectations that Soviet Russia could be counted upon as an ally: Beneš "did not regard Soviet Army any longer as an effective force for Western actions." In Biddle's opinion, Moscow "was slipping in her foreign policy line and potentially facing isolation at a moment when [the Soviet] internal structure had registered a new low in terms of stability." In one of his reports in March 1938, Ambassador Coulondre observed: "Emphasizing the thesis of capitalist encirclement, the Kremlin reserves a justification for its abstention in foreign affairs." Litvinov in fact expressed Soviet readiness to be isolated in a conversation with American ambassador Davies as early as November 1937. The French ambassador to London, Charles Corbin, reported from the British capital also in November 1937 that in British opinion, the Soviet Union was not only weakened by the purges, but her reputation in Western Europe was declining and "her diplomatic action is already stricken by sterility." Ambassador Chilston characterized the general Soviet attitude toward the Czechoslovak crises (both in May and September 1938) as "noncommital"; not very surprising at a time when, by conservative estimate, every eighth Soviet citizen was in jail, in a concentration camp, or on his way before a firing squad. Chilston concluded: "It is indeed permissible to doubt whether, in existing conditions, the Soviet government would be capable of maintaining the country's vital industries and administrative machinery on a war footing. . . . The severity of the repressive measures which they have taken cannot have failed to augment the latent hostility of large sections of the population." Alexander Werth, who placed almost the entire responsibility for the failure of the anti-Nazi alliance on France and Great Britain, nevertheless noted "the deplorable effect created in Western Europe by the purges in the Red Army, and the belief that a 'decapitated' army could be of little use." . . . In Ambassador Coulondre's opinion, the French political and military establishment (in 1937–38) judged the Soviet factor of the international situation "primarily in view of the Soviet internal crisis; it made them feel that the USSR was not part of the game anymore." According to Ambassador Davies, "Stalin destroyed the confidence of Western Europe in the strength of his government; that also weakened the confidence of both England and France in the strength of the Russian army and weakened the democratic bloc in Western Europe." Winston Churchill, never inclined to justify the folly of the appeasement policy, confirmed that "to Mr. Chamberlain and the British and French General Staffs, the purge of 1937 presented itself mainly as a tearing to pieces of the Russian Army, and a picture of the Soviet Union as riven asunder by ferocious hatreds and vengeances." The whole problem cannot be objectively assessed without considering the alternative — a peaceful internal development in the USSR in the 1935–38 period, in line with Soviet diplomatic action in Geneva at the same time. The complete inconsistency of one with the other was in itself woeful; after all, in the struggle of the epoch, collective security was essentially the cause of democratic forces, opposed by the totalitarian regimes. By its external, diplomatic action, Moscow had associated with the first. By its internal policies, on the other hand, it surpassed all the horrors that Fascist regimes were themselves practicing at the time. This discrepancy affected the Soviet relationship with friends and allies, actual or potential, in the most detrimental way.

The German diplomacy, which did not fail to recognize this inherent defect in the opposing camp, does not appear to have exploited it with any visible success, at least before 1938. Unable to reconcile German revisionist goals with the decisively antirevisionist attitude of France and, to a lesser degree, England, the Wilhelmstrasse had little to offer to the Versailles powers. As for the Soviet Union, objective lack of meaningful differences with Germany and the growing economic interdependence of the two countries were overshadowed by the ideological dispute; which, however, neither side took too seriously. Hitler himself, according to Hermann Rauschning, viewed Bolshevism in his own special way: in essence, he believed it was a brand of National Socialism that needed to be rid of its Marxist-Jewish coating. Had he applied this view to the purges in Russia, they might appear to him as the kind of "purification" he thought necessary. He obviously did not accept Soviet offers of rapprochement in 1935–37 because he would have had to moderate the traditional Nazi anti-Communism which he still needed vis-à-vis the Western powers.

The fact is that Hitler specified, for the first time, his war aims in November 1937, as they are in their *punktlich* way recorded in Major Hossbach's memorandum. No such specification can be read from

Hitler's instructions for the Four-Year Plan, which simply demanded the accomplishment of readiness for war by both the German industry and German armed forces. In November 1937, Hitler narrowed his goals to the Anschluss of Austria and the elimination of Czechoslovakia. That he viewed these two goals as a necessary prerequisite for a campaign against Poland Hitler disclosed to his generals only two years later, after Munich. This chronology of Hitler's planning shows, first of all, that during the Great Purges in the Soviet Union, and especially the Red Army purge, the Fuehrer was refining his expansionist schemes. It also shows that he gave priority to the southerly direction, against Austria and Czechoslovakia, instead of the more predictable drive against the Polish Corridor and Silesia, the territories that Germany had lost in 1919 (Austria and Bohemia had never been part of Prussia or Germany). In November 1937, the fact that Czechoslovakia was protected by a Soviet guarantee, as embodied in the pacts of May 1935, does not seem to have worried the Fuehrer anymore.

A number of factors were involved in Hitler's decision, but his low assessment of the Soviet capability and readiness to intervene militarily outside their own territory was certainly among them. The contribution that the Sicherheitsdienst is suspected of making to the Tukhachevsky affair is of relatively limited importance in this context; the purge of the Red Army officers' corps seems to have followed inevitably from other purges, anyway, with or without Heydrich's assistance. Besides, as Ambassador François-Poncet reported from Berlin as early as March 1937, "trials against the Trotskyists as well as, undoubtedly, intelligence reports from agents, gave the Hitlerite leaders the idea that the USSR was undergoing a deep crisis and that it would soon become a theater of great upheavals." Rumors then circulating in European capitals may have been of various origins, but two months after the Radek-Pyatakov trial and three months before the Tukhachevsky affair, rumors could not have been wilder. It is not difficult to imagine the impression that the extermination of the Red Army commanders must have made in Berlin, when the earlier purges had already produced the effect described by the French ambassador.

One of the first benefits the Nazis drew from the new wave of executions in Soviet Russia was a not improbable theme for Joseph Goebbels's propaganda machine, which claimed that those in the West who had thought that Soviet Russia would become a normal partner in the system of collective security, suffered a moral catastrophe. More important, however, was the obvious encouragement that this self-inflicted mutilation of France's ally would inevitably produce in Berlin. Those most directly affected recognized the danger immediately; shortly after the execution of Tukhachevsky, the Czechoslovak ambassador in Washington observed to Under Secretary Sumner Welles that "this sudden development might bring a more belligerent attitude on the part of Germany."

Ambassador Schulenburg's correspondence from Moscow testifies that neither the Wilhelmstrasse nor the ruler of the Third Reich missed any important detail in the constant flow of obituaries from Russia. Unlike his French, British, American, or Czech colleagues in the Soviet capital, of course, Schulenburg was not disposed to accept with any degree of confidence the Soviet accusation of Tukhachevsky (or, six months earlier, of Pyatakov and Radek, and then Rykov and Bukharin) as working for Germany. For the German ambassador, it was "not clearly discernible where the wave of terror sweeping over the Soviet Union had its origin and what is its aim." At the same time, he reported to Berlin the course and the results of the purges as effectively as the other foreign envoys. Whereas in Paris or Prague, however, the news from Moscow was unqualifiedly bad, in Berlin it made quite a different impression to learn that, for example, "there is no doubt that the wave of murder and persecution that is still [November 1937] unspent has gravely shaken the organism of the Soviet Union. . . . Today the Soviet Union is politically and economically heading for a depression." Schulenburg advised his government that the purges in the USSR "reduced the specific weight of the Soviet Union in world affairs to such an extent that any of Litvinov's attempts to win over other countries for the Soviet viewpoint would be doomed to failure from the very beginning."

In 1938, Schulenburg's conclusions drawn from the unconcerned Soviet reaction to the Anschluss with Austria and the May crisis concerning Czechoslovakia represented a qualified interpretation of the purges from the point of view of German interests. The German General Staff drew its conclusions, too. A detailed "Strategic Study," drafted by the Supreme Command of the Wehrmacht (OKW) in June 1938, the center of which was *Fall Gruenn* (invasion of Czechoslovakia), did not reckon on any Soviet intervention; it only presumed the intervention of France and, rather surprisingly, of Great Britain. This assessment obviously underwent no changes during the summer months, in spite of the fact that the Soviet diplomacy became more visible than in the previous year and a half. On September 9–10, Hitler held a conference with his principal military advisors, generals H. A. H. W. von Brauchitsch, Wilhelm Keitel, and Franz Halder. In a detailed overview of the preparations, and of the battle plan for *Fall Gruenn*, none of the participants touched upon the possibility of a Soviet intervention, either by land or air forces, even though German diplomatic sources reported from Prague three days before the Nuremberg Conference that Rumania accorded its permission for the overflights of Rumanian territory by Soviet aircraft en route to Czechoslovakia. Hitler and his generals simply did not believe that the Russians would fly, permission granted or not. A few days before that, Ambassador François-Poncet informed Paris from Berlin, as if adding color to the Nuremberg Conference, that "the conviction that Soviet Russia will tumble down has reappeared among the leaders of the Reich. According to them, Stalin is seriously ill; revolt rumbles everywhere; war would serve as a signal."

Amid a continuing flow of reports about "unveiling" of conspiracies and punishment of traitors in July 1938, Litvinov quietly concluded an oral agreement with Schulenburg to tone down mutual recriminations of leaders of both countries. This, according to Hilger and Meyer, was the first step to the pact of August 27, 1939, which "was prepared by the Great Purges and [the removal of] the Bukharins, Krestinskys, Radeks and so forth."

This last assumption represents an interesting point. The Bukharins and the Krestinskys, not to mention the Radeks, had not been known to oppose cooperation with Germany before 1934, and their real stand on the possibility of a return to that policy in the late 1930s is very difficult to ascertain, if one does not want to take seriously Vyshinsky's fairy tales. Leon Trotsky did oppose the Soviet collusion with Nazi Germany, which he in fact predicted in December 1937, but the connection between himself and the defendants in the show trials was a trumped-up charge.

On the other hand, the general background of many of the Old Bolsheviks killed between 1936 and 1939 does substantiate the opinion that they "would have found it very hard to stomach" any alliance between Nazi Germany and Soviet Russia, as finally happened in August and September 1939. Stalin "visualized the coming pact with Hitler as more than merely a way of securing temporary safety from invasion. . . . What he contemplated . . . was a kind of Moscow-Berlin axis, an active collaboration of the two dictatorships of influence in Eastern Europe, the Balkans, and even the Middle East." That would presumably have been too much for the Old Bolsheviks, and naturally for most of the foreign Communists in Moscow as well; hence the active external aspect of the politics of the purges. The case of Bukharin supports this thesis. Bukharin's general profile, analyzed by Cohen, shows a man who could not agree to the policy of the pact of August 1939. Both his speech before the Seventeenth Party Congress in 1934 and his last editorial in *Izvestiya* on July 6, 1936 are clear indications of his principled opposition to Nazism, with which Stalin was then seeking an agreement.

Although all that was not immediately understood at the time of the purges, their overall impact upon the outside world was catastrophic.

Seen in the light of the impression created by the internal events in Soviet Russia, the collapse of collective security does not appear as a series of naive assumptions and diplomatic blunders. The purges destroyed the emerging Soviet reputation as a stable state with growing potential to function effectively in the role of one of the principal sponsors of the international status quo. Paradoxically, the terror launched in 1936 coincided with the time when collective security was passionately defended by the official Soviet foreign policy and its chief spokesman in Geneva, Maxim Litvinov. The fact that internal Soviet life became a scene of mass persecution, deportation, and extermination of millions of innocent people robbed Litvinov's brilliant oratory of most of its credibility. Further, the fact that so many people so highly placed in the civil and military administration of the Soviet Union were routinely accused of treason could not fail to undermine Soviet credibility as an ally. . . . The "treason case" in the Red Army High Command, and the prolonged massacre of the Soviet officer corps, had a particularly damaging effect upon the value the West placed upon the Soviet Union as a possible ally against Germany. From mid-1937 on, conditioned both by the negative and denouncing response abroad and by the objective internal consequences of the purges, Soviet foreign policy gradually moved into semi-isolation. In view of the Soviet offers in Berlin spurned by Hitler, this state also reflected an obvious lack of options.

In Germany, where the purges in Russia met with more complacency than contempt, the gradual apostasy of the Versailles camp by its ally in the East could not fail to result in the encouragement of the Fuehrer to move faster, and more openly after his morbid goals. So, by the totality of their effects abroad and at home, the Great Purges became a critical factor in the fatal processes leading to the Second World War.

Joachim von Ribbentrop and Joseph Stalin celebrate the signing of the Nazi-Soviet pact in Moscow, August 23, 1939. (The National Archives)

VII The Devil's Bargain

German Foreign Ministry

The Nazi-Soviet Pact

In the spring of 1939 when Hitler decided to settle the Danzig question by attacking Poland at the first suitable opportunity, he required an agreement with the Soviet Union. Provided that his price was met, Stalin was eager to oblige. While an Anglo-French delegation vainly negotiated with V.M. Molotov, Soviet foreign minister, Moscow and Berlin agreed on a nonaggression pact. In the early morning hours of August 23, 1939, Molotov and Ribbentrop signed a treaty of nonaggression for their governments. Hitler would now be secure from attack by Soviet armies. Poland was isolated. An escape clause in the pact invalidating it if one party attacked a third party was deliberately omitted. Moreover, the pact became effective the moment it was signed.

A secret protocol to the pact divided eastern Europe up into spheres of interest. It remained secret until the end of the war. For the next forty-five years the Soviet government claimed that it was a forgery.

From *Documents on German Foreign Policy*, series D, vol. VII, published by the United States Government Printing Office, 1956, pp. 245–247.

No one was more pleased than Joseph Stalin, who had attained his long-sought-after deal with Hitler. But the news of the signing of the nonaggression pact shocked the world and caused much soul searching among foreign Communist Party faithful.

Treaty of Non-Aggression between Germany and the Union of Soviet Socialist Republics

The Government of the German Reich and the Government of the Union of Soviet Socialist Republics, desirous of strengthening the cause of peace between Germany and the U.S.S.R., and proceeding from the fundamental provisions of the Treaty of Neutrality, which was concluded between Germany and the U.S.S.R. in April 1926, have reached the following agreement:

Article I

The two Contracting Parties undertake to refrain from any act of violence, any aggressive action and any attack on each other either severally or jointly with other Powers.

Article II

Should one of the Contracting Parties become the object of belligerent action by a third Power, the other Contracting Party shall in no manner lend its support to this third Power.

Article III

The Governments of the two Contracting Parties will in future maintain continual contact with one another for the purpose of consultation in order to exchange information on problems affecting their common interests.

Article IV

Neither of the two Contracting Parties will join any grouping of Powers whatsoever which is aimed directly or indirectly at the other Party.

Article V

Should disputes of conflicts arise between the Contracting Parties over questions of one kind or another, both Parties will settle these disputes or conflicts by means of a friendly exchange of views or if necessary by the appointment of arbitration commissions.

Article VI

The present Treaty shall be concluded for a period of ten years with the proviso that, in so far as one of the Contracting Parties does not denounce it one year before the expiry of this period, the validity of this Treaty shall be deemed to be automatically prolonged for another five years.

Article VII

The present treaty shall be ratified within the shortest possible time. The instruments of ratification will be exchanged in Berlin. The treaty shall enter into force immediately upon signature.

Done in duplicate in the German and Russian languages.
Moscow, August 23, 1939.

For the Government of the German Reich:	With full power of the Government of the U.S.S.R.:
v. Ribbentrop	V. Molotov

Secret Additional Protocol

On the occasion of the signature of the Non-Aggression Treaty between the German Reich and the Union of Soviet Socialist Republics, the undersigned plenipotentiaries of the two Parties discussed in strictly confidential conversations the question of the delimitation of their respective spheres of interest in Eastern Europe. These conversations led to the following result:

1. In the event of a territorial and political transformation in the territories belonging to the Baltic States (Finland, Estonia, Latvia, Lithuania), the northern frontier of Lithuania shall represent the frontier of the spheres of interest both of Germany and the

U.S.S.R. In this connection the interest of Lithuania in the Vilna territory is recognized by both Parties.

2. In the event of a territorial and political transformation of the territories belonging to the Polish State, the spheres of interest of both Germany and the U.S.S.R. shall be bounded approximately by the line of the rivers Narev, Vistula, and San.

The question whether the interests of both Parties make the maintenance of an independent Polish State appear desirable and how the frontiers of this State should be drawn can be definitely determined only in the course of further political developments.

In any case both Governments will resolve this question by means of a friendly understanding.

3. With regard to South-Eastern Europe, the Soviet side emphasizes its interest in Bessarabia. The German side declares complete political *désintéressement* in these territories.

4. This Protocol will be treated by both parties as strictly secret.

Moscow, August 23, 1939.

For the Government of   With full power of the
the German Reich: Government of the U.S.S.R.:
v. RIBBENTROP   V. MOLOTOV

Dmitri A. Volkogonov

A Soviet Version

To date Soviet historians have been permitted only limited access to archival materials. Dmitri A. Volkogonov's account of events in 1939, while critical of Stalin, nevertheless argues that there was no alternative for Stalin other than the Nazi-Soviet Pact. Volkogonov alleges that Stalin agreed to the pact only after he became convinced that Britain and France were secretly negotiating with Hitler.

Robert Tucker insists that Stalin had sought a deal with Hitler long before 1939. Volkogonov implies that Stalin had to make concession to

From "1939, the Drama of Decisions," *Novaia i noveishaia istoriia*, 1989, no. 2.

Hitler's demands. The reverse was true. Stalin held the whip hand. Finally, Volkogonov ignores the secret clause in the Nazi-Soviet pact, which allotted spheres of influence.

Soviet historians have only recently begun to grapple with rethinking Soviet history. Volkogonov's article is a sign of how far Soviet historians have yet to travel.

A retired general, military historian, and biographer of Stalin, Dmitri A. Volkogonov is now a member of the Russian Federation's legislature and a supporter of Boris Yeltsin.

The year 1939 saw the beginning of a world conflagration. Prewar efforts to extinguish its first flames proved futile. Class selfishness was in its heyday. Attentively watching Germany's aggression in Europe, the Soviet leadership understood more clearly that it was facing savage armed conflict with a strong, experienced, and merciless enemy. But down to the last moment, it harbored the illusion that if it did not "provoke" Hitler, war could be avoided.

It was 1940. German troops conquered Denmark, Norway, Belgium, Holland, and Luxembourg. The French army resisted all of 40 days. The British Expeditionary Corps was defeated and its units quickly evacuated to Great Britain. The Wehrmacht overran several Balkan countries.

The capitalist world in fact did not have a force that could stop the aggressor. A great threat arose to mankind and its civilization and culture. In the occupied territories the fascist governments were establishing a savage "new order" with concentration camps, prisons, enslavement, and colonization. Hunger, the gallows, and the whip were the marks of this "order."

The peoples of Europe were paying dearly for the mistakes of their governments. The ruling circles of Britain, France, and the U.S.A. had been shortsighted in appeasing the militarism that was rapidly rising in Germany.

The Soviet leadership also made major military and political mistakes, both in organizing the country's readiness to repulse the fascist aggression and in its efforts to avert the impending war. Many steps taken by the Soviet leadership were evidently politically justified, but their moral aspect — such as the secret agreements with Hitler — deserves censure.

After grabbing Austria, Hitler was getting set to swallow up Czechoslovakia. From March through August 1938, Stalin was ordering his commissar of foreign affairs [Litvinov] to find ways of publicly affirming Soviet readiness to defend Czechoslovakia. Seemingly, Beneš was also inclined to accept this aid. On September 20, 1938, Moscow again sent a positive answer to Prague's query about the U.S.S.R.'s willingness to come to Czechoslovakia's aid in the expected fascist invasion.

The people's commissar of defense, K. E. Voroshilov, signed a directive creating a special grouping of forces in the Kiev Military District; in the Byelorussian Military District troops were to be deployed to form corresponding groupings. The antiaircraft defense system was put on alert. In late September the head of the General Staff, B. M. Shaposhnikov, sent a telegram to the western districts stating that "Red Army soldiers and junior commanders who have completed their term of service in the RKKA [Workers' and Peasants' Red Army] are not to be discharged from the army until further instructions." Some areas saw a partial mobilization. More than 70 divisions were put on alert. Just as the Munich conference was taking place . . . Stalin knew that the fear of "communist plague" would turn out to be stronger than the dictate of reason. And he was not wrong.

In these circumstances the Czechoslovak government was unable to put national concerns above class interests. Under pressure from England and France it capitulated to Hitler. France in fact was taking steps to nullify its treaty [of mutual aid with the U.S.S.R.]. In this situation, thought Stalin, the main thing was not to allow the imperialist countries to form an anti-Soviet coalition. At his behest, first Litvinov and then Molotov began to grope for ways of undermining an imperialist agreement against the U.S.S.R. Stalin was very worried about the dangerous offshoots from the "Munich basket": the Anglo-German nonaggression declaration, signed in September 1938, and the similar Franco-German agreement signed in December of that year. In effect, these agreements gave Hitler a free hand in the East. Worse yet, under certain circumstances the agreements could become the basis for an anti-Soviet coalition. Stalin knew that if this happened, a worse situation for socialism would be hard to imagine.

Beginning in early 1939 Stalin more and more frequently attended to foreign policy. He believed that the bloody purge in the party and the country had stabilized society. It is likely that down to his death

Stalin never fully comprehended the depth of the national tragedy for which he had been chiefly responsible. Despite the many objective indications attesting to the weakening of the party, to the destruction of the best minds in the party, the technological sector, and the military, and to the strengthening of administrative command in society, Stalin continued to believe (as he said at the 18th Party Congress [March 1939]) that his policy was historically justified: a policy of "liquidating Trotskyists and other double dealers" — in fact, all potential nonconformists who, he thought, might threaten his absolute rule.

Now Stalin was focusing on foreign policy problems. Although it is generally believed that World War II began on September 1, 1939, with fascist Germany's attack on Poland, Stalin thought otherwise. Earlier that year, at the March Party Congress, he had announced that "the new imperialist war has become a fact." And this was largely true. Japan was conquering China; Italy had attacked first Ethiopia and then Albania; German and Italian forces had intervened against the Spanish Republic; Germany had seized Austria and annexed Bohemia and (in fact) Slovakia. The world had been set ablaze on many sides. Stalin believed that the crumbs thrown to Hitler at Munich merely "stimulated the aggressor's appetite."

Learning during the Party Congress that Germany had grabbed Klaipeda [Memel] Province in Lithuania and that E. Beneš had signed the Berlin Pact, putting an end to the Czechoslovak state, Stalin ordered a protest sent to Berlin. The note that M. M. Litvinov, people's commissar for foreign affairs, presented to the German ambassador to the U.S.S.R., W. Schulenburg, sharply condemned the German action and informed the Reich's leaders that the Soviet government would never "recognize the inclusion of Bohemia and also Slovakia into the German Reich."

Amid a spreading world conflagration it was necessary to come up with a strategy that would allow the country to carry out its social and economic plans while ensuring a reliable defense against any contingency. The question usually discussed in the inner circle, which Litvinov was occasionally invited to join, was what line to take in the unfolding circumstances. The "honeymoon" of the Popular Front in Europe was over. The revolutionary wave had broken against the militarist and chauvinist barriers of the bourgeoisie. The European continent seemed to have quieted down amid foreboding that it was about to be overwhelmed by Hitler's tank armada. In Spain the drama of the national revolutionary war was almost played out; the Republic was in its death agony. The Marxist parties, many of them either destroyed or forced underground, looked hopefully to the Soviet Union. The Comintern's influence was perceptibly weakening. For this Stalin was also to blame. The general secretary [Stalin] had by his own command discredited the international communist alliance. . . .

[In 1939], in hearing out his associates' opinions on international issues, Stalin was especially attentive to V. M. Molotov, whose arguments, the leader thought, combined the flexibility and firmness that the situation warranted. Together they fomulated the "party's tasks in foreign policy," which Stalin expounded at the 18th Party Congress. The four points of this program, rewritten by the general secretary several times only hours before the Congress met, expressed two closely related ideas.

First: to continue to pursue peaceful means of averting war or, at least, of putting it off as long as possible; to make new efforts to carry out the Soviet plan for collective security in Europe, that is, to prevent the formation of a broad united anti-Soviet front; and to exercise extreme care and not to yield to enemy provocations.

Second: to take all necessary, even emergency, measures to hasten the country's readiness for defense, giving primary attention to strengthening the fighting capacity of the Red Army and Navy.

Many of the Politburo's discussions at this time were devoted to carrying out these dual objectives. Stalin was constantly thinking of ways to increase the efficacy of the country's foreign office and to make maximum use of diplomatic channels. He was not satisfied with the people's commissar of foreign affairs, M. M. Litvinov, who was apt to have his own opinion. Moreover, as a Jew Litvinov was getting hostile treatment in Berlin. Litvinov understood that an alliance between the U.S.S.R. and the western democracies would be the most reliable guarantee in the face of the threat of world war. Such an alliance would protect even the small countries that Hitler's Germany was preparing to swallow. . . .

After his talks with Litvinov, Stalin felt that the commissar did not believe Hitler in the least and was ready to persist in reaching agreements with the western democracies. The commissar's commitment and *a priori* views were suspicious. Stalin ordered [secret police chief] Beria to keep a "closer eye" on Litvinov.

Soon after the May Day celebration Beria was ready to strike at

Litvinov. There were signs of imminent arrest: a "vacuum" was created around the man; he was no longer called to high-level meetings, and NKVD operatives held nightly talks with Litvinov's relatives and associates. Seemingly the worst was about to happen. But Stalin stopped his monster [Beria] at the last moment and limited himself to replacing Litvinov with Molotov as commissar of foreign affairs. In Berlin, Litvinov's removal was perceived as a "good sign." The Soviet chargé d'affaires in Germany, G. A. Astakhov, reported to Moscow that the Germans considered that the chances had opened up for improved German-Soviet relations and that the "prerequisites for this had been strengthened with Litvinov's departure."

Litvinov had been hindering Stalin in his "German policy." By appointing the second highest government figure [Molotov] to the post, Stalin wanted the world to know that the Soviet Union was ascribing great importance to foreign policy questions and the cause of peace. Stalin understood that the mutual aid agreements signed in the mid-1930s with France and Czechoslovakia had "not worked out."

Prior to the 18th Party Congress, Stalin had instructed Molotov to propose to the London and Paris governments trilateral negotiations aimed at working out ways of stopping further fascist aggression. Hoping to put pressure on Hitler, Britain and France agreed to these talks. However, their intentions became clear fairly quickly. The Anglo-French sought to channel Hitler's aggression to the East and would not hear of creating a "defensive wall," as proposed by the Soviet Union. . . .

In early August Stalin confirmed the leadership's instructions for negotiations entitled "Considerations for Negotiations with England and France." The document discussed five scenarios "when our forces may take to the field." The Soviet Union was ready to deploy against "the chief aggressor" (as Germany was called in the document) 120 infantry divisions. But to do this Poland would have to agree to allow [Soviet] troops to cross its territory. To anticipate, we can say that the Soviet delegation saw clearly from the first meetings that the western missions had come to Moscow to listen, to put forward general views, to inform London and Paris about "the Russians' large-scale plans" rather than to try to work out a concrete and feasible agreement. The western powers did not wish to extend guarantees to the Baltic states. Moreover, they furthered their rapprochement with Germany. During the Anglo-French-Soviet negotiations, Hitler imposed his treaties on

Latvia and Estonia. A hostile stance toward the U.S.S.R. was also taken by Horthy's Hungary. At a meeting with Hitler in January 1939 the Polish foreign minister, J. Beck, announced that Poland attached no significance to so-called security systems, which had become bankrupt. The German foreign minister, Ribbentrop, in turn told Beck that he hoped that "Poland would take an even clearer anti-Russian position, otherwise we can hardly have common interests." It became known that during a secret visit to Germany, King Carol of Rumania had told Hitler: "Rumania is opposed to Russia, but cannot show this overtly because of its proximity. But Rumania would never allow Russian troops to cross its soil, although it has often been affirmed that it had supposedly promised Russia to allow its army to pass through. This has no basis in reality."

Stalin, playing this political "solitaire" with Molotov and Voroshilov, became even more convinced: the West had no sincere intentions to reach a mutually acceptable agreement. He resolved once more to propose to Britain and France a 5- or 10-year mutual aid pact with the U.S.S.R. (which would entail military obligations). The alliance would mean that in the event of aggression against any one of the parties to the agreement (including east European ones), the allies would be obligated to come to its aid. The Soviet Union specified which countries between the Baltic and Black seas would be affected. London and Paris gave no reply. Stalin pressed for reminders. The representatives sent to Moscow were low-ranking officials not authorized to make important decisions. At the same time, as Stalin discovered, the negotiating partners had stepped up their secret efforts to reach an acceptable agreement with Hitler. It became clear: England and France were simply stalling while seeking an advantageous agreement for themselves, without taking into account the interests of the U.S.S.R. . . .

In those days Stalin's spacious office was the site of ongoing talks and meetings attended by Politburo members, diplomats, and military men. By the end of the summer it became increasingly clear to the Soviet leaders that, faced with fascist Germany in the West and militarist Japan in the East, the Soviet Union could rely on no one. Stalin's conclusion at the 18th Party Congress turned out to be correct: the anticommunism of Britain and France and their unwillingness to pursue a policy of collective security opened the floodgates of aggression for the members of the Anti-Comintern Pact. Class egocentrism, hatred of socialism, and mercenary motives prevented London and Paris from soberly comprehending the contours of the real danger. The more shortsighted even said: let Hitler launch an anticommunist "crusade" in the East. To them he appeared less dangerous than the U.S.S.R.

All this accounted for our dismal foreign policy situation in the summer of 1939. The U.S.S.R.'s options were very limited. But a choice had to be made. One had to make up one's mind. Stalin understood this sooner than others, although he foresaw that the reaction to such a step would be extremely negative in many countries. But in the course of more than 15 years the autocrat had become used to making decisions that would affect the fate of millions of people. Despite his extreme caution he apparently did not fear responsibility. Usually Stalin resorted to his tried-and-true method: to heap the blame for failure on others — which also meant taking responsibility. Stalin knew that he — the new Caesar — had the last word in party and government decisions. In this case he was acting as the main author of government decisions and steps. Having made his choice, Stalin showed little concern for propagandizing it, relying on his apparatus, particularly on the energetic A. A. Zhdanov.

When Stalin became convinced that the Anglo-French-Soviet negotiations had reached an impasse (and he had had little faith that they would yield a positive outcome), the general secretary resolutely returned to the "German variant." In his opinion there was no other choice: the U.S.S.R. might otherwise have to clash with a broad anti-Soviet front, a situation fraught with the worst perils. We now know, however, that he had not yet exhausted all the means of stepping up the negotiations or his maneuvers to block the military threat. It is likely that the dictator felt himself in the position of a chess player who was exceeding the time permitted for a move. The leader of the party, and in fact also of the state, thought that he had no time to ponder over how this move would be perceived by future generations, historians, and researchers. A war for which he was unprepared stood at the portal. He had to put it off at any price. . . .

In August [1939] a peculiar situation developed. The Germans had been conducting secret talks with London from the end of July. The German ambassador, Dirksen, and a representative of the British prime minister, H. Wilson, sought to find a basis for "multilateral cooperation." But the conflicts turned out to be difficult to resolve.

Simultaneously, Soviet-German relations were evolving swiftly. Here are several milestones.

On August 12, Stalin was reading G. A. Astakhov's report from Berlin: "The conflict with Poland is rapidly coming to a head; decisive events may break out very shortly. . . . The press is conducting itself correctly with respect to us. . . . In contrast mockery of England exceeds the bounds of elementary decency."

On August 13, Astakhov reported that "pursuant to our agreement to hold talks on improving relations, the German government would like to begin them as soon as possible."

On August 15, Schulenburg handed Molotov a memorandum that stated:

> *The German government maintains the point of view that there is not a single question between the Baltic and Black seas that could not be resolved to the full satisfaction of both countries. This includes questions relating to the Baltic Sea, the Baltic states, Poland, the Southeast, and so forth.*

As we see, Berlin's cynicism was not even disguised.

On August 17, Molotov again received Schulenburg. During their talk the latter announced that it was essential to begin German-Soviet negotiations that week. Molotov answered that "Before beginning political talks, we must finish negotiations on a credit and trade agreement."

On August 19, Schulenburg was again meeting with the people's commissar of foreign affairs. "In Berlin [they] are apprehensive of a conflict between Germany and Poland. Subsequent course of events will not depend on Germany." Schulenburg insisted on Ribbentrop's immediate arrival for the conclusion of a nonaggression pact. Molotov agreed to visit on August 26–27. Under pressure from the Germans, the credit agreement was concluded that day. Hitler was in a hurry. He was not satisfied with the 26–27. On those days he was intending to launch his war machine against Poland.

Stalin, behaving unlike his usual self, yielded to Berlin point by point, particularly with regard to the timetable. The Führer had taken the initiative. He not only managed to wreck the Anglo-French-Soviet negotiations (with the British and French lending a hand), but he was also able to persuade Stalin of the greater advantage of a Soviet-German agreement. In his note to the Soviet government Schulenburg wrote: "The capitalist western democracies are the implacable foes of both national-socialist Germany and the Soviet Union. At present they are again trying — through a military alliance — to inveigle the Soviet

Union into a war with Germany. In 1914 such a policy had dire consequences for Russia." In the end, all the declarations, memorandums, and cajolery impelled Stalin to make crucial decisions. All the more since he had learned about the Anglo-German contacts in London.

Stalin lacked sufficient endurance. Usually approaching his goal in small but safe steps, Stalin was acting like a chess player. . . . He finally gave up on the western democracies when Voroshilov put before him Admiral Drax's reply on the morning of August 20. Like his French colleague, Drax had been asked to give quicker replies to Soviet proposals. The note said:

> *Dear Marshal Voroshilov!*
>
> *I regret to inform you that the English and French delegations have not yet received a reply to the political question which you had requested to be sent to our government.*
>
> *In view of the fact that I shall be presiding at the next session — I propose that we meet at 10 A.M. on August 23 or sooner, if we have received a reply by then.*
>
> Sincerely yours,
> *Drax*
> *Admiral — Head of British Delegation*

"Enough of these games," rasped Stalin. He hardly suspected that a meeting of delegations would take place on August 23 — but with a completely different set of people.

On that day, August 20, Hitler sent Stalin a telegram requesting that he receive Ribbentrop in Moscow to conclude the agreement.

> *Mr. Stalin, Moscow*
>
> August 20, 1939
> *1. I sincerely welcome the signing of a new German-Soviet trade agreement as a first step to restructuring German-Soviet relations.*
> *2. The conclusion of a nonaggression pact with the Soviet Union signifies for me a long-range determination of German policy. . . .*
> *3. I accept the draft of the nonaggression pact submitted by your foreign minister, Molotov, but I consider it urgent to clarify questions relating to it as quickly as possible. . . .*
> *4. The tension between Germany and Poland has become unbearable. Poland's conduct toward a great power is such that the crisis may come to a head any day. . . .*
> *6. I believe that if both states intend to enter into new relations with*

each other, it is expedient not to lose time. For this reason I again
propose that you receive my foreign minister on Tuesday, August 22,
or at the latest — Wednesday, August 23.

Adolf Hitler

The German ambassador to the U.S.S.R., Schulenburg, handed
the telegram to Molotov at 3 P.M. on August 21. The telegram's tone
of ultimatum was obvious. Stalin and Molotov sat over the message for
a long time, heard once more Voroshilov's account of the progress of
negotiations with the British and French, and received confirmation of
Berlin's contacts with Paris and London, portending a broad anti-Soviet
alliance. After weighing all the pros and cons, a decision was finally
made. In a big political game one had to take a large crucial step. It
was taken. Stalin got up from his desk and silently paced back and forth
across his office several times. Then, glancing at Molotov, he rapidly
dictated:

A. Hitler, Reichschancellor of Germany

August 21, 1939

I thank you for your letter. I hope that a German-Soviet nonag-
gression pact will bring about a turn to a serious improvement in the
political relations between our countries.

The peoples of our countries need peaceful relations. The German
government's agreement to conclude a nonaggression pact creates a
basis for eliminating political tension and establishing peace and coop-
eration between our countries.

The Soviet government has instructed me to inform you that it
agrees to Mr. Ribbentrop's arrival in Moscow on August 23.

J. Stalin

Hitler, staying in the Obersalzberg with Ribbentrop, was nervous.
He needed a pact. But the Russians were still looking for chances with
the British and French. Even while Stalin was signing his telegram to
Hitler, one last trilateral meeting of the delegations was taking place.
General Doumenc, the head of the French mission, reported to E.
Daladier in Paris: "The meeting scheduled for today was held this
morning. A second meeting was held this afternoon. In the course of
these two meetings we exchanged polite remarks concerning the delay
owing to the political problem of passage [of Soviet troops across Polish
territory — author]. Another meeting — at an unspecified date — will
take place only when we are in a position to answer in the affirmative."

But there was not to be another meeting. The meeting that did take place on August 23 was with a different set of negotiators — Soviet and German.

Two large transport Condors carrying Ribbentrop and his delegation landed in Moscow on August 23. One might add that because of a lack of coordination in the Soviet antiaircraft defenses the planes had been fired on by antiaircraft artillery near Velikie Luki and only by sheer luck were not shot down. Naturally that very day a large group of NKVD [secret police] men arrived there to find out who had organized the "provocation." So the pact might not have been signed on the twenty-third. The evening before, Hitler had met with his military commanders and announced the imminent attack on Poland. Whether or not they intended to, Britain and France had nudged Stalin toward the pact: It won time for the U.S.S.R. — a year and a half — just as Alexander I's meeting with Napoleon at Tilsit had done in 1807. Moscow's unpopular decision was to a large extent forced by circumstances.

Of course today we can say that when Germany attacked the Soviet Union there was neither a Polish nor a French army, and the British Expeditionary Corps had been defeated. By that time almost all of Europe was working for Hitler. We were one-on-one with Germany. We had no choice but to fight, fight, and wait for a second front. The western democracies did not want to establish a "second front" in 1939. Let us repeat, perhaps Stalin did not have enough patience.

Stalin remembered well his long conversation with Ribbentrop on the afternoon of August 23. The tall, thin German had given him to understand that Germany wanted a free hand in the face of a probable clash in the West. Listening to the foreign minister Stalin thought: to gain time at any price. The country and army were not ready for a big war. If he succeeded in concluding the pact, there would be no alliance of the capitalist states against the U.S.S.R. That was the main thing.

During the evening talk that ended with the signing of the pact, Stalin may have thought the country had gained three or four years' postponement. But Stalin must certainly have felt that it would be extremely difficult actually to carry out a policy of neutrality in a stormy sea. This forced neutrality would appear detrimental, possibly even "separatist" [i.e., treasonous], to antifascists and many friends of the Soviet Union. Stalin foresaw this, but believed that there was no other way out. Peace was necessary now so that one might stand one's ground later.

The nature of the mistakes lies not merely in miscalculations, unjustified predictions, or the evil will of an aggressor. The main reason for the mistakes and unforgivable blunders is rooted in autocratic rule. Many decisions with far-reaching consequences were made by him alone (sometimes under Molotov's influence). It is hard to blame the people's commissars and the Main Military Council when the status of "infallible and wise leader" had already evolved. Any disagreement in principle with a particular concept or view might be quickly interpreted as "misunderstanding," "opposition," or "political immaturity" with all its consequences. Many still remembered well the political trials, whose jurisdiction encompassed everything: one's views at the signing of the Brest-Litovsk Treaty; an acquaintance, say, with Peterson, the Kremlin's commandant,* and therefore with plans for the "palace coup"; meetings abroad with an official — naturally giving spy information and so forth. Intimidation, the stereotype of the greatness of just one person, and the need to approve Stalin's decisions immediately — all sharply limited and weakened the possibilities for dialectically analyzing an actual situation, searching for real alternatives, and making genuinely collective decisions.

Although Stalin set positive goals for the country and party, the realization of these goals was not accomplished through collective reasoning or the confrontation of alternatives and different points of view. By his autocratic rule, infallibility, and peremptory conclusions, the general secretary unwittingly closed the channels for obtaining objective information, original proposals, and nonconformist decisions. The absence of a democratic and truly collegial way of working out and making crucial decisions impoverished and limited the "intellectual bunker" of power. . . .

Anything that did not enter into the leader's spectrum of ideas was not accepted. Bursts of creativity or talented thought — if they did not coincide with the autocrat's aspirations — were simply rejected, went unnoticed, or were stifled. The cult of unanimity was one of the main sources of a whole series of errors that influenced the entire course of the war, especially its outbreak. What were the more characteristic errors of the political leadership, above all Stalin, on the eve of the war?

---

* An old Bolshevik of Latvian background who fell victim to Stalin's purges in the 1930s.

In the first place, an especially big mistake was the signing on September 28, 1939, of the German-Soviet Treaty on Friendship and the Boundary Between the U.S.S.R. and Germany. After the signing of the nonaggression pact a month earlier, a step to a considerable extent forced and perhaps historically justified, one should have stopped. The resolutions of the Comintern, the decisions of the 18th Party Congress, and the party's orientation toward the Soviet people all said: fascism is the most dangerous regiment of world imperialism, a regime of terrorist dictatorship and militarism. In the world view of the Soviet people fascism personified the quintessence of the class enemy. And suddenly — "friendship" with fascism?! It is difficult to explain Stalin's and Molotov's slipping into an unintended whitewashing of fascism. One could understand an effort to strengthen the nonaggression pact by trade agreements and economic ties. But to embark on a repudiation of all its former antifascist ideological views — this was too much!

Participating in the negotiations with Ribbentrop, Stalin managed to exclude any expression of our attitude toward Germany's annexation plans. For example, the "Declaration of the Soviet and German Governments," signed that same day, states: the U.S.S.R. and Germany "in free agreement express the opinion that the elimination of the present war between Germany, on one hand, and Britain and France, on the other, would serve the interests of all nations." But the "nations" might ask — how was this to be done? To resign oneself to Germany's conquest of almost all of Europe? Could Poland, lying in ruins, endorse the "mutual agreement" signed by Molotov and Ribbentrop? . . .

The error made by Stalin and Molotov — who took an extremely active part in the Soviet-German Treaty on Friendship and Borders — is an obvious one. The understandable effort to avoid war at all cost went hand in hand with an ideological concession on a matter of principle that confused not only our friends abroad. Propaganda, in seeking to demonstrate the U.S.S.R.'s neutrality, unwittingly disoriented the Soviet people. The propagandists in the country and army were put into an extremely difficult position.

Today it is hard to determine whose initiative "montaged" the concept of "friendship" in the German-Soviet treaty. If this was done by the Soviet side, at best it reflects a political thoughtlessness. If it was done by the German side, it was a subtly calculated sabotage in the sphere of the mind, affecting the social consciousness of an entire nation. In either case Stalin was not on top of the situation. Even though Molotov was later to say that Stalin "had guessed in time Hitlerism's perfidious plans," in this case that is hard to believe. Even today many try to "prove" that World War II started with the Soviet-German nonaggression pact of August 23, 1939. But they forget that by this time the western powers had sacrificed Austria, Czechoslovakia, and Klaipeda and that England and France had done little to save the Spanish Republic. Usually they also fail to mention that Poland, fascist Germany's next victim, also had a nonaggression pact with it. Hitler had planned the attack (Operation White) as early as April 11, 1939, long before Molotov and Ribbentrop had signed the documents. The question of Poland's seizure was discussed at a meeting called by Hitler on January 22, 1939. The demands for the return of Danzig were merely a pretext for large-scale aggression. Hitler's plans with respect to Poland were a secret to no one. The time of attack was known in Washington, London, and Paris, but there it was hoped that Germany's seizure of Poland would hasten Hitler's invasion of the U.S.S.R.

History and an analysis of the situation that emerged at the end of the summer of 1939 confirm that for the Soviet Union the pact was perhaps the only chance to postpone the outbreak of war. And for the U.S.S.R. it threatened to be a war on two fronts. Of course agreement with the western democracies would have been the desired course of action. But the British and French politicians of that time maneuvered too long and essentially ignored this opportunity. Stalin may have been too hasty and shortsighted. A year after the events at Lake Khasan (1938), the Japanese military machine had organized a bloody test of strength along the Khalkhin Gol river.

Stalin could not forget that when the representatives of Britain, France, Germany, and Italy met in Munich in September 1938 no one remembered the Soviet Union. The pragmatic deal with Hitler meant not simply a betrayal of Czechoslovakia. A week after the shameful compact, the French ambassador to Moscow, R. Coulondre, frankly assessed the essence of the agreement: "After the neutralization of Czechoslovakia, Germany had an open road to the East." On the day of the signing of the Munich Pact, September 30, Chamberlain and Hitler signed the Declaration of Nonaggression and Consultations. Stalin was found guilty of inconsistency and of making advances to Hitler, but yet he took the step toward a pact with Berlin a year after the British and French. . . .

The last 1½ to 2 years before the war Stalin focused on two problems: the military buildup and the diplomatic efforts to avert war. These problems resulted from the military and political situation on the European continent, engulfed in the flames of World War II. Although all basic international problems were discussed and decided in the Politburo, they were generally "worked out" in advance in conversations between Stalin and Molotov. Sometimes specialists were invited to discuss specific questions, but the main decisions were made by Stalin alone, taking into account the opinion and suggestions of the people's commissar of foreign affairs. And his opinion did not always coincide with Stalin's.

Marshal G. K. Zhukov later related to the writer K. M. Simonov that he often observed the discussion of questions by Stalin and his closest associates. "I had a chance," said Zhukov, "to see arguments and wrangling, to see the obstinacy shown on some issues, particularly by Molotov; sometimes matters would reach the point where Stalin would raise his voice and even lose his temper, but Molotov, smiling, would get up from the table without changing his mind."

Molotov's stories about his meetings with the Nazi leaders made an impression on Stalin. The leader himself met only with Ribbentrop. Quite often, among his closest associates, he would call Hitler and his entourage "cheats." Even during the negotiations over the nonaggression pact, as attested to by F. Gaus, head of the legal department of the German foreign ministry, Stalin could not resist dropping a malicious phrase synonymous with the word *fraud*. When signing the pact the Soviet leader said, "We do not forget that your ultimate aim is to attack us." Trying to determine whether his calculations for putting off the war were correct, Stalin several times discussed Hitler with Molotov, knowing better than anyone how much in government depended on the dictator.

Stalin scarcely concealed his Machiavellian attitude toward the Nazis. When the ceremony of signing the pact was over, Stalin raised a glass of champagne and said: "I know how much the German people love their Führer. I want to drink to his health!" Ribbentrop rushed to the telephone (the negotiations were held in Molotov's office) and called Hitler in Berlin about the signing of the pact and Stalin's words.

Hitler's answer, joyfully relayed by Ribbentrop, was: "O my great minister of foreign affairs! You don't know how much you have accomplished! Give my congratulations to Mr. Stalin, leader of the Soviet people!" . . .

Gerhard L. Weinberg

The Nazi-Soviet Pact: A Half Century Later

In contrast to Volkogonov, Gerhard L. Weinberg sees the Nazi-Soviet Pact not as the result of the Anglo-French failure to negotiate an alliance with the USSR. Rather it stemmed from Hitler's need to be secure in the east while fighting a war in western Europe. As for Stalin, he had long sought an agreement with Hitler that would enable the German armies to attack the western imperialist nations in a war that would benefit Stalin and Soviet Russia. However, in the end both partners to the nonaggression pact miscalculated.

Early on August 22, 1939, the world was startled to learn from an announcement in the Soviet press that German Foreign Minister Joachim von Ribbentrop would arrive in Moscow on the following day to sign a nonaggression pact. Equipped with instructions from Adolf Hitler authorizing him to sign both a treaty and a secret protocol that would enter into force as soon as signed by the two countries (rather than when ratified later), Ribbentrop left for Moscow that evening. At the airport, the German delegation was met by deputy commissar for foreign affairs, Vladimir P. Potemkin, who earlier that year had declined an invitation to meet with British Foreign Secretary Lord Halifax.

Stalin and Molotov, the commissar for foreign affairs, held several

From "The Nazi-Soviet Pacts: A Half-Century Later" by Gerhard L. Weinberg from *Foreign Affairs*, pp. 175–189. Reprinted by permission of *Foreign Affairs*, Fall 1989. Copyright 1989 by the Council on Foreign Relations, Inc.

conversations in the Kremlin with Ribbentrop and the other German diplomats. During the night of August 23–24 an agreement was reached on all points; the pact and a secret protocol were signed; a celebration party followed in which the participants drank toasts to each other, to German-Soviet friendship and to the absent Hitler.

II

The nonaggression pact, which was published, provided that Germany and the Soviet Union would not attack the other or assist any third power at war with the other, thereby assuring each of the neutrality of the other party should either decide to attack a third country. They promised not to join groups of powers directed against the other and to settle by peaceful means all differences that might arise between them. The pact was to last for ten years and then an additional five years unless a notice of termination were given a year before its expiration.

Immediate effectiveness also applied to a secret protocol attached to the published treaty and governed by a special agreement to ensure its secrecy — an agreement that the Germans maintained until the end of the Third Reich and that the Soviets are only now considering breaking. This protocol provided that Finland, Estonia and Latvia were to be in the Soviet sphere of interest; Lithuania, enlarged by the Vilna area then in Poland, was assigned to Germany. Initially, Germany wanted to divide Latvia between the two powers at the Daugava (Dvina) River; on Soviet insistence, Latvia was quickly turned over entirely to the Soviet Union. As for Poland, with the exception of the Vilna area signed over to Lithuania for inclusion in the German sphere, it was to be partitioned along the line of the Pissa, Narev, Vistula and San rivers. This line divided the core area of Polish settlement within prewar Poland, and the two powers agreed to review at a later time the question of whether or not a rump Polish state would suit their convenience. And during Ribbentrop's second visit to Moscow on September 28, 1939, Germany accepted a Soviet proposal whereby the territory between the Bug and Vistula rivers, together with a small piece of Polish territory in the north, would be traded to Germany in exchange for Soviet control of the bulk of Lithuania. In effect, this agreement left the question of any Polish state in the tender hands of the Germans.

Further south, the original partition scheme of August 23 provided that the Soviet Union could prosecute its interest in Bessarabia —

which Russia had taken from its ally Romania in 1878 only to lose it after World War I — while the Germans declared their complete political disinterest in southeast Europe. It is now known that Ribbentrop was authorized to go even further and agree to Soviet control of Istanbul and the Straits, but Stalin evidently did not ask for this.

The new agreements worked out on September 28 also included a friendship treaty between Germany and the Soviet Union (which was later supplemented by a boundary protocol), a confidential agreement on the exchange of populations across the borders separating the Soviet and German spheres in eastern Europe, a secret protocol to the effect that neither would tolerate Polish agitation concerning territory seized by the other, and several exchanges covering major extensions of the economic agreement that had been signed between the two countries on August 19. These latter agreements were designed to help the Germans break the British wartime blockade by assisting in acquiring raw materials that could then be shipped across the Soviet Union. While these arrangements to support the German war effort were kept secret the two powers publicly called for an end to the war which now that they had divided Poland between them, served no further purpose in the opinions of Berlin and Moscow. It is, of course, essential to recall that between Ribbentrop's two trips to the Soviet capital, the partners of the Nazi-Soviet pact had both attacked Poland; their friendship, in Stalin's phraseology, had been "cemented with blood."

III

As is already clear from the description of the text of the August agreements, they provided the Germans with a green light for an attack on Poland and were so interpreted by all at the time. Unlike prior nonaggression pacts signed by the Soviet Union, this one contained no provision that it would become invalid if either party attacked a third country. Furthermore, the agreements assured the Germans that if England and France honored their promise to go to war on Poland's behalf, the disappearance of the hated Polish state would provide a common border with Russia; this would be a friendly Russia, committed to helping Germany break the British blockade. From the Soviet Union itself, Germany could draw on supplies of oil, grain and nonferrous metals needed for the conduct of war against the western powers; across the Soviet Union, Germany would be able to obtain other important raw materials from the Near East, East Asia and possibly the western hemisphere. Above all, Germany could concentrate all its forces, after the quick defeat of Poland, on the western front.

For the Soviet Union — well informed by its espionage network that the German attack on Poland, when it came, would be a preliminary step to an attack by Germany in the west — the agreement appeared to provide insulation from what was already being referred to as the "Second Imperialist War." The agreement also provided great accretions of territory, the disappearance of the Polish state, which the Soviets hated as much as the Germans did, and an encouragement to Germany, which had drawn back from war in 1938, to launch a war with the western powers that Stalin assumed would weaken both parties equally, satisfying Soviet belief in "the need for a war in Europe." In addition, the pact assured the leaders in Moscow that Japan, whose troops had just been defeated by the Red Army in clashes at Nomonhan on the border between Manchuria and Outer Mongolia, would not dare attempt a new attack on East Asian territories belonging to or controlled by the Soviet Union.

For Poland, the pact clearly meant total isolation in the face of what looked like an imminent German attack. Though not immediately apparent to the Polish government, it also meant that any hope of holding out against German troops in eastern Poland during the winter of 1939–40 could not be realized, because the Soviet Union would invade Poland from the east and seize the territory allocated to it by the secret German-Soviet agreements.

For Great Britain and France, the pact meant that all their hopes of a multifront war against Germany were dashed. In pursuit of those hopes, drawn from a belief that a powerful Germany could most likely be defeated only by a combination of allies, they had made a long series of concessions to the Soviet Union in lengthy negotiations during the summer of 1939; for example, the proposal that a Soviet declaration of war on Germany would be contingent on a *prior* declaration of war by Britain and France. Until August London had postponed signing an alliance with Warsaw in the hope that one with Moscow could be arranged. Now that this possibility was clearly excluded, the treaty with Poland was rushed to signature on August 25. Determined to go to war at the next instance of German aggression if it were resisted, the British government hoped that an obvious and public stand might still deter Germany from war. In a special letter to Hitler, Prime Minister Neville

Chamberlain said that London would go to war with or without allies; he warned both Hitler and Benito Mussolini that once the war started it would not end after any defeat of Poland but would be continued until Allied victory.

For the French, as for the British, the pact dashed any hopes of assistance from the Soviet Union against the German menace. The various French schemes advanced in the winter of 1939–40 for attacking the Caucasus oil fields and for aiding the Finns in their defense against Soviet attack, while occupying the Swedish iron mines along the way, can be seen in part as a reflection of the disappointment and anger in Paris. . . .

IV

How had the agreement between Germany and the Soviet Union come about? Why had the two powers, which for years had made numerous nasty comments about each other in public, worked out secret agreements to partition eastern Europe between them? What led them to call jointly upon the other nations of the world to accept this division, which ended the independence of Poland as well as Czechoslovakia, most of which Germany had swallowed and whose permanent demise the Soviet Union had legally recognized just before invading Poland? The motives of the two partners were different, and we are far better informed on those of the Germans; the motives for each must therefore be examined separately.

With Hitler's rise to power in 1933, Germany began following a policy that called for the establishment of a dictatorship inside the country, the massive rearmament of a racially aware population and, thereafter, a series of wars to secure land on which the German population could feed itself and grow ever larger. It was obvious from a look at the map that most of Europe's agricultural land lay in the east, primarily in the Soviet Union. In the official doctrine of the Nazi state, the peoples living there, most of them of Slavic stock, were racially "inferior." By what Hitler considered an extraordinary stroke of good fortune for the Germans, these people were now ruled by even more inferior and incapable Jews who had come to power as a result of the Bolshevik Revolution — a revolution in which the at least minimally capable old Germanic ruling class of Russia had been replaced by total incompetents.

Hitler believed that the seizure of vast land masses from the Slavic people would be a simple matter and that the inhabitants of the conquered areas could be easily displaced or murdered; before this could be done, Germany's position in Europe had to be strengthened. In particular the French, whose army stood perilously close to Germany's most important industrial area, the Ruhr, had to be crushed, and the British, who could obviously not be separated from them, had to be driven off the continent. The war against the west could, it was believed, be won most easily from a base that included Austria and Czechoslovakia under German control, and these states had accordingly been absorbed into Germany as preliminary steps.

During the years when the Germans were rearming and moving first against Austria and then Czechoslovakia, all soundings from the Soviet Union to improve relations were waved aside. There was, from the perspective of Berlin, nothing that Moscow could do for them under these circumstances. In internal affairs, Germany's Communist Party had once assisted the Nazis in destroying the Weimar Republic by targeting the Social Democratic Party as the main enemy, but now the Communist Party was itself the target of the regime's destructive fury. In the field of rearmament, the Soviet Union had provided the German Republic with the opportunity for secret work in the areas prohibited to Germany by the Versailles Treaty of 1919: armored warfare, poisonous gases and air warfare. The new government in Berlin, however, was carrying out its rearmament program on a vastly greater scale and increasingly in the open so that secret facilities in the Soviet Union were no longer of any special use. As for the building up of a huge blue-water navy, then under way or being planned for war against Britain and the United States, that was a field in which the Soviet Union had never been of assistance to Germany.

In the diplomatic field, there similarly had been nothing in Berlin's eyes that the Russians could have done to help during the years 1933–38. Neither Austria nor Czechoslovakia had a common border with the Soviet Union, and in its preparations for seizing Austria and attacking Czechoslovakia, Germany ignored the Soviet Union entirely. Under these circumstances, the repeated efforts made in Berlin by Stalin's special representatives for the purpose of warming German-Soviet relations were invariably ignored. In the winter of 1938–39 this situation began to change.

Germany had planned to attack Czechoslovakia in 1938, expecting to annex that country as the result of an isolated war. But that project did not work out as Hitler had intended; the very device by which he had hoped to isolate his victim from outside support — the presence of over three million Sudeten Germans in Czechoslovakia — ended up involving Germany in negotiations that ceded to Germany the territory on which the Sudeten Germans lived. To his subsequent regret, Hitler had drawn back from war and had settled for the ostensible rather than the real aims of German policy. Thereafter, he plotted to seize the rest of Czechoslovakia after a "decent interval" while preparing for war with the western powers, which he now intended to launch in the near future. Such a war, in his opinion, would require a quiet eastern border and the subordination of the two eastern neighbors, Hungary and Poland.

In the winter of 1938–39, this aim was attained with regard to Hungary but not with regard to Poland. The litmus test was joining the Anti-Comintern Pact. After much hesitation, Hungary took this symbolic step of obeisance to Germany, but Poland simply would not agree to it. The leaders of Poland were as anticommunist as anyone in Europe, but they were not about to give up the revived independence of their country without a fight. On all other questions they were prepared to make some compromises, but formal obeisance to Berlin was out of the question. It took Hitler a while to recognize that Warsaw meant what it said, but once he realized that the Polish regime would not subordinate itself to the whim of Berlin, he decided that a preliminary war against Poland would be necessary before Germany attacked the west, unless, of course, the western powers joined Poland.

It was in this context that the German picture of relations with the Soviet Union changed. The Soviet Union had a long common border with Poland as well as a long tradition of hostility. A partition of Poland with the Soviet Union appeared to offer a number of advantages to Germany: it would isolate Poland for a quick attack; it might deter Britain and France from aiding Poland and going to war against Germany until the latter picked its own time to attack them; it would open the way for Germany to acquire much needed materials from and across the Soviet Union, thereby invalidating any blockade of Germany even before it was instituted. . . .

Since Hitler believed that the attack on the west was the *difficult but necessary* prelude for the subsequent *simple and fast* attack on the Soviet Union, concessions could easily be made to Moscow. Whatever the Soviets wanted, they could get, including a few things they did not even ask for. These calculations were based on the assumption that once Germany had won its big war in the west, it could take back everything given away in the east — and more. The real question was not, therefore, the terms on which an agreement might be reached but whether the Soviet Union would be prepared to arrive at an agreement in the time frame within which the Germans were working and whether they would provide assurances of economic support as well as the diplomatic aid Germany wanted.

It was from this position that Berlin examined the soundings from Moscow in 1939 and interpreted Stalin's speech of March 10, 1939, and the replacement of Foreign Commissar Maxim Litvinov by Molotov in early May as signs of Soviet seriousness. The vast publicity attendant upon negotiations by the Soviet Union with Britain and France left the Germans in some doubt as to whether their secret talks with the Soviets would really produce an agreement, but the very fact that their own negotiations were being kept secret and that an economic agreement was being worked out combined to make the prospects look good. In order to create a common border, the disappearance of the smaller countries between the two powers was an inviting prospect for Berlin, and ending the independence of these countries by partition with Moscow was acceptable, with the exact terms and demarcations being of no special importance. Here was the chance for Germany to secure its eastern border while fighting a war in the west, and if an agreement with the Soviet Union provided this condition, all the better. But, of course, once the agreement with the Soviets had served its purpose of shielding a German victory over Britain and France, then the campaign in the east against the Soviet Union would follow, hampered neither by the paper barrier of the nonaggression pact nor by the need to keep large forces in the west.

If this was Hitler's perception, it was one that in its essentials was supported enthusiastically by others in the upper levels of Germany. Many of the diplomats had long believed that good relations with Russia, whatever its government, would be good for Germany (though a few were sufficiently alarmed by the prospect of a German-Soviet agreement to warn the United States). The German military leaders could hardly contain their eagerness for war against Poland and welcomed anything that might lead to that happy event. The prospect of a one-front war made the agreement with the Soviet Union all the more desirable. . . .

V

On the Soviet side, a different ideology by a different route led to the same result. Assuming that the capitalist world would remain united against the Soviet state, and incapable for ideological reasons of comprehending the special nature of the Nazi state, Stalin had repeatedly approached the Germans for some agreement that would assist them in turning against what he perceived to be the capitalist imperialist rivals of the Third Reich. A war between Germany and the western powers looked to the Soviet leader like the best prospect for both the safety and the future expansion of Soviet power. Repeated rebuffs by Berlin did not discourage Stalin from making more approaches. In 1938, when it looked as if war might break out over a German attack on Czechoslovakia, a country with which the Soviet Union had a defensive alliance contingent on France honoring its alliance with that country, the Russians took a *public* stance in support of Czechoslovakia while privately declining any opportunity to assist that country. The fact that the Germans funked at war — by contrast with the Japanese who had thrown themselves into war with China without encouragement from anyone — made it look in 1939 as if an agreement with Germany might have the effect of encouraging that country to take the plunge.

In this context, Stalin believed that negotiations with the western powers for an agreement, accompanied by plenty of publicity, might induce the Germans to come to a settlement and to go forward with their plan for war against Poland and the west simultaneously or in sequence. From what evidence we have, it would appear that three factors required clarification in Soviet eyes:

- whether the Germans were serious about an agreement, an issue all the more important to Moscow because in January 1939 the Germans had aborted an economic mission to them under circumstances that left the Soviets both mystified and annoyed;
- whether or not the Germans were prepared to make the concessions that Stalin wanted in terms of territory in Poland;
- whether the Germans saw the need for the disappearance of the independent states of eastern Europe in essentially the same way as Stalin did.

As Stalin subsequently explained to the British ambassador, "the U.S.S.R. had wanted to change the old equilibrium. . . . England and

France had wanted to preserve it. Germany had also wanted to make a change in the equilibrium, and this common desire to get rid of the old equilibrium had created the basis for the rapprochement with Germany."

The negotiations showed the Russians that the Germans were indeed serious about sharing eastern Europe by division with them, contrary to the position of the western powers who hoped to preserve the independence of the countries there. From Stalin's point of view, therefore, it was a matter of stringing along the western powers in public by steadily increasing Soviet demands, a procedure to put pressure on the Germans to raise their offers to the Soviets in private. When Hitler wrote Stalin a personal letter asking him to receive Ribbentrop promptly, the Soviet leader realized that the time had come to take final action. Further stalling would force Germany to postpone an attack on Poland since good campaign weather in eastern Europe was coming to an end. By that time Moscow had already signed a long-term economic agreement with Berlin — a clear sign that the Soviet Union had no intention of joining Britain and France. Now was the moment to receive the German foreign minister and hammer out the details of an agreement. The "old equilibrium" would indeed disappear.

VI

Once the agreement of August 23, 1939, and its secret protocol had been signed, Germany felt free to go to war with Poland. And, after some last-minute efforts to separate that country from its western allies, Germany attacked. Since Hitler intended to strike in the west after beating Poland, it did not appear especially important to him whether the war with France and England came immediately or was postponed. The key point was to obtain a peaceful border in the east for a subsequent campaign in the west, and here was his chance to get it. Once it became certain that the western powers would stand by Poland, he did not even wait out the extra day his own timetable allowed. Acting on the lessons he had drawn from the Munich agreement, Hitler was worried that someone might arrange a compromise at the last minute and cheat him out of war, as had happened in 1938. Now was the time to strike — and the sooner the better. . . .

The bloody fighting that began with the German attack on the Soviet Union on June 22, 1941, pointed up the terrible miscalculations made by both parties to the Nazi-Soviet pact. The Germans would discover that heading east before finishing the war in the west was a dangerous step. They would learn the hard way that their beliefs about the inferiority of Slavs and the weakness of the Soviet Union were delusions derived from the false doctrines of racial determinism. At least a few Germans would also learn that the establishment of a tier of independent states between Germany and the Soviet Union at the end of World War I had been an enormous advantage, not a disadvantage, for Germany. And along with the great blessing in the Versailles Treaty of maintenance of German unity, it had been destroyed by the Germans themselves.

The Soviet leadership was similarly deluded by its own ideology. Just as many Germans had believed in the racial inferiority of the east European peoples, Stalin appeared to have believed in the Marxist-Leninist nonsense about fascism as the tool of monopoly-capitalism struggling for markets, investments and raw materials — a view that left no room for an independent Nazi ideology of racial agrarian expansionism. The shocked surprise with which the Soviet leadership met the German attack — when their own intelligence had warned them, when the British had warned them and when the Americans had provided them with the outlines of the German invasion plan — has to be understood, in my judgment, as the triumph of preconceptions over reality. In 1927, when there had been no signs of an invasion of the Soviet Union, there was a war panic in Moscow. Now that all the signs were in place with innumerable warnings, what should not be could not be.

What made the Soviet miscalculation so horrendous was, of course, that by the time Stalin realized that Chamberlain and Roosevelt were correct in their belief that Germany could be defeated best by an alliance of powers, the Soviets had helped the Germans drive the Allies out of northern, western and southern Europe, leaving the Soviets alone with them on the continent in the east. Millions and millions of Soviet citizens would lose their lives over this disastrous miscalculation; only the incredible endurance of a suffering civilian population, the bravery of the Red Army's officers and soldiers and the diversion of German manpower and resources to an escalating war against the western powers allowed the regime to survive.

VII

During and after the war, the Soviet Union offered a variety of new explanations for signing the pact. Official Soviet statements originally depicted the pact as an instrument of peace, but this line was abandoned after June 1941. It was also asserted that the western powers were about to make a Munich-type agreement with Germany, a somewhat curious line of argument that had to be abandoned in the fall of 1939 when the Soviet Union urged them to make peace with Germany on the assumption that both Poland and Czechoslovakia were to disappear. Other public arguments, then and later, asserted that the western powers would not make sufficient concessions to the Soviet Union, a point that has to be interpreted in terms of Stalin's own belief that ending the independence of the countries of eastern Europe was in the interest of the Soviet Union as well as Germany. The Soviets also claimed afterward that Russia's expansion westward provided an additional buffer against a German invasion, though the events of 1941 would show that the shift from the old defended border to a new one weakened, rather than strengthened, the ability of the Red Army to hold off the Germans.

Until recently Soviet publications have either ignored the existence of the secret protocol of August 23, 1939, or denounced it as a forgery. This question has arisen in face of renewed and ever more open agitation for a greater degree of autonomy in the Baltic states — perhaps real independence — and an entirely new situation in Poland. A new look at the events of August 1939 has major current political relevance.

There cannot be any doubt that the documents that record the partition of eastern Europe between Nazi Germany and the Soviet Union are authentic. The originals were deliberately destroyed by the Germans but only after they had been microfilmed along with many other important documents.

Perhaps a new perception of the past will enable the Soviet Union to see the secret protocol as part of a mistaken and adventurous policy by Stalin — a policy that cost Russia the most horrendous losses, and for which the country had not properly prepared. As Europe moves into a new phase, perhaps the Soviets as well as the Germans may come to see that allowing the peoples living between them to enjoy a real independence can contribute to the security of all countries.

Jewish stores vandalized during Kristallnacht, November 9–10, 1938. (Wide World Photos)

VIII The Holocaust

.
.
.
.
.
.
.
.
.
.
.
.

Lucy S. Dawidowicz

World War II and the Holocaust

During World War II reports filtered out of occupied Europe about the terrible slaughter of the Jewish people. The full horror of the Holocaust was revealed after the fall of Nazi Germany. It has been argued that the Holocaust was a result of the war and that Hitler used the war as a shield to keep the world from learning about the slaughter. But in this selection, the late Lucy S. Dawidowicz, who held the Paul and Leah Lewis Chair in Holocaust Studies at Yeshiva University, shows that the Holocaust was an integral part of Hitler's drive toward war. She traces the Holocaust back to the early push for war. It cannot be separated from the origins of World War II.

As Hitler prepared Germany for war, he took the preliminary steps to institute the Holocaust. The two processes went hand in hand. Neither was an isolated phenomenon. When Germany went to war against Poland

From Lucy S. Dawidowicz, *The War Against the Jews, 1933–1945*, pp. 88–111. Copyright © 1975 by Lucy S. Dawidowicz. Reprinted by permission of Henry Holt and Company, Inc.

in 1939, Hitler also declared war on the Jews. In Hitler's mind it was also a racial war.

The task of German foreign policy, Hitler stated in *Mein Kampf*, was to "preserve, promote, and sustain our people for the future." Because of the Dolchstoss, the sapping of Germany's virility through betrayal, that task had to be executed in two stages; the first, domestic policy, was "to restore," in Hitler's words, "to the nation its strength in the form of a free power state." The second stage entailed war and expansion into foreign territory. In Hitler's view there was no division between domestic and foreign policy. Domestic policy, he wrote, "must furnish the Volkist instrument of strength" for the exercise of foreign policy, and that foreign policy, in turn, would protect and sustain the Volkist instrument.

Hitler had spelled out his foreign-policy ideas and plans in repetitive detail first in *Mein Kampf* and later, in 1928, even more elaborately in a second manuscript, unpublished during his lifetime. These ideological objectives as well as his broad strategical plans remained essentially unchanged in the decade between the writing of *Mein Kampf* and his accession to power. When Hitler became dictator of Germany, his ideology and strategy both became the ends and means of German foreign policy. "In political life there are no principles of foreign policy," Hitler declared early in 1930. "The programmatic principle of our party is its position on the racial problem, on pacifism and internationalism. Foreign policy is only a means to an end. In matters of foreign policy, I shall not permit myself to be bound." This was a cardinal principle in his outlook. In *Mein Kampf* he argued that since the goal of a state's diplomacy was to preserve its people, *"every road that leads to this is then expedient. . . ."* Here were embodied the two integral elements of policies he would pursue — unwavering commitment to National Socialist ideology, and a strategy combining opportunism, expediency, and improvisation.

The first stage of German foreign policy, Germany's internal restoration, was to accomplish two ends. Germany first had to purge itself of its internal enemies, and second, make itself strong. "Whoever wants to act in the name of German honor today must first launch a merciless war against the infernal defilers of German honor," he wrote in his second book. He used the language of war often in speaking of the Jews. The National Socialist movement, he wrote in *Mein Kampf*, "must call eternal wrath upon the head of the foul enemy of mankind," the "inexorable Jew" seeking domination over all nations. Only the sword, he held, could stave off the enemy, in a process that "is and remains a bloody one."

The application of the sword against the Jews would come later, but the first step in this process was purgation, which had been achieved with the promulgation of the laws of 1933 and the Nuremberg Laws.

The second means of restoring German virility was remilitarization. The German people, now racially purified, would have the will to war, but it needed the means to make war, which the hated Versailles Treaty had denied them. In his second book, Hitler declared that "the first task of German domestic policy ought to be that of giving the German people a military organization suitable to its national strength." From his very accession to power, Hitler began to build according to this blueprint. On April 4, 1933, a National Defense Council was set up and began, in secret, the process of military planning and German rearmament. Six months later, Germany withdrew from both the international disarmament conference at Geneva and from the League of Nations. In November the German people enthusiastically affirmed that policy in a plebiscite, while the nations participating in the disarmament negotiations, despite deep misgivings about Germany's course, took no action that would discourage or halt German remilitarization. That passivity continued. Indeed, though the major European powers protested Germany's restoration of universal compulsory military service in 1935, Great Britain — one of the protesters — rewarded Germany with a naval agreement on June 18, establishing naval parity between England and Germany. It was the first of a long series of diplomatic and military acts of appeasement that raised Germany's international prestige and succeeded in strengthening the dictatorship at home.

German rearmament accelerated, though not yet too openly lest France claim violations of the Locarno Pact of 1925, which had reaffirmed the conditions of the Versailles Treaty, stating that the Rhineland was to remain demilitarized. But having prepared his ground diplomatically as well as militarily, Hitler sent German troops into the Rhineland on March 7, 1936, while denouncing the Locarno Pact. Within a week the flurry of crises was over. The British fear of risking war had prevailed over French indecisiveness. Germany had achieved a stunning triumph without cost. . . . In August 1936 Hitler drafted a memorandum, which became known as the Four Year Plan, that was to put Germany on a war footing economically and militarily. Hitler felt that Germany was ready for "the reconquest of freedom for tomorrow."

In his scheme, war was inevitable. "War is life," Hitler said in 1932. "War is the origin of all things." War would be the means to realize his quest for Lebensraum, a word that incorporated Hitler's ideas of racial supremacy into a pretentious geopolitical scheme. War, invasion, expansion, in National Socialist ideology, were not merely the expression of an imperialist drive for natural resources, exploitable markets in underdeveloped countries, or power over vast territories and numerous peoples (though they were that also); primarily they were instruments to serve national/racial survival. In *Mein Kampf* Hitler first expounded his theory of Lebensraum:

> *The foreign policy of the Volkist state must safeguard the existence on this planet of the race embodied in the state, by creating a healthy, viable natural relation between the nation's population and growth on the one hand and the quantity and quality of its soil on the other.*

Hitler's concepts about the basis of a state's physical existence and about population growth in relation to available agricultural land and food supply were derived from geopolitical ideas with which he became familiar in Landsberg. The basic idea was that of population pressure. While population grows, the amount of soil remains constant. Increasing soil productivity is not a satisfactory or long-range solution to relieve the pressure of population growth, Hitler believed. Nor could population control be a solution, for that would contravene the very purpose of the Volkist racial state. . . . The only satisfactory and fundamental way of eliminating the "intolerable" relation between population and territory was war: "The bread of freedom grows from the hardships of war."

Germany was entitled to more land, not only because its people would have "the courage to take possession of it, the strength to preserve it, and the industry to put it to the plough," but because Germany was the "mother of life," not just "some little nigger nation or other." Furthermore, Germany's leaders were justified in shedding even German blood to attain that goal:

. . . we National Socialists must hold unflinchingly to our aim in foreign policy,namely, to secure for the German people the land and soil to which they are entitled on this earth. And this action is the only one which, before God and our German posterity, would make any sacrifice of blood seem justified. . . . The soil on which someday German generations of peasants can beget powerful sons will sanction the investment of the sons of today, and will someday acquit the responsible statesmen of blood-guilt and sacrifice of the people, even if they are persecuted by their contemporaries.

Where would the soil come from? There were, in Hitler's plan, two sources — the "lost territories" and "new soil." The "lost territories" were the lands that would soon become part of Greater Germany — Austria and western Czechoslovakia — and which would have to be won back by war, *"back to the bosom of a common Reich, not by flaming protests, but by a mighty sword."* But these territories would not solve Germany's problems. Only new soil would give Germany "a path to life."

The new soil that would give Germany its Lebensraum could be "only in the East." Hitler spelled it out in *Mein Kampf:* "If we speak of soil in Europe today, we can primarily have in mind only *Russia* and her vassal border states." The rationale for a German conquest of Russia was twofold. Using Rosenberg's ideas, he advanced a historical claim of centuries-old German colonization in Russia. But even more important was the notion, assimilated also from Rosenberg, that the Jews had taken control of Russia by means of revolution and Bolshevism.

War for Lebensraum was thus associated in Hitler's mind with war against the Jews, not alone in an apocalyptic sense of a final struggle between Gog and Magog, between Aryans and Jews, but also in a conventional sense. Back in 1927, Rudolf Hess wrote to a friend that "in Hitler's opinion [world peace would] . . . be realizable only when one power, the racially best one, has attained complete and uncontested supremacy." That such supremacy could be achieved only by war Hess did not spell out, but he clearly articulated Hitler's view that this "great step" toward world understanding was possible only "upon the solution of the Jewish question." War, the Jews, and racial utopia were all interrelated in Hitler's mind. In 1935 he referred to war as a cover for planned murder, when he told Gerhardt Wagner, the NSDAP's [National Socialist German Workers Party, the Nazi party] top medical officer, "that if war came, he would pick up and carry out this question of euthanasia," for then "such a program could be put into effect more smoothly and readily" and in the general upheaval public opposition would be less likely.

Often in discussing foreign-policy matters, Hitler shuttled back and forth between a real world of nations and armies and a phantasmagoric universe ruled by the Jews. For instance, in 1935, shortly after the Nuremberg party congress, Hitler had several occasions to speak to small groups of party and government people. Consul General Fritz Wiedemann, Hitler's adjutant, later recorded Hitler's plans at that time with regard to the Jews: "Out of all the professions, ghetto, imprisoned in a territory where they can disport themselves according to their nature, while the German people looks on as one watches wild beasts." Though Wiedemann mentions no talk of war, Hitler was already fantasizing of a time during or after the war, when some territory, not precious German soil, would be available for the internment of the Jews.

On September 24, 1935, nine days after the Nuremberg congress at which the Law for the Protection of German Blood and German Honor had been promulgated, Hitler called a closed meeting of party leaders, Reich officials, and Gauleiters to share his decisions with regard to racial determinations of the "half-Jews." Hitler spoke with considerable expertness, Bernhard Lösener noted, but then flabbergasted his listeners by breaking off, remarking that he needed to obtain further clarification on some points. He then turned to other subjects, alluding quite unmistakably to his war plans, saying that he still needed about four years to be ready. Lösener thought he was rambling incoherently, but there could be no misunderstanding the associations in Hitler's mind between making fine racial distinctions among different categories of "half-Jews" and his plans for war.

At the end of August 1936, after the Olympic Games, Hitler went to Berchtesgaden, where he prepared his memorandum on the Four Year Plan. The body of the memorandum dealt with practical matters like saving foreign exchange, stepping up fuel production, mass-producing synthetic rubber, and increasing iron ore production so as to make Germany self-sufficient and ready for war within four years, but the ideological preamble on the need for war read like a chapter from *Mein Kampf*. The world, he stated, had been moving toward a new conflict, "the most extreme solution of which is called Bolshevism, whose essence and aim, however, is solely the elimination of those strata of mankind which have hitherto provided the leadership and their replacement by worldwide Jewry." Since the victory of Bolshevism over Germany would lead to the annihilation of the German people, Hitler concluded: "*In face of the necessity of defense against this danger, all other considerations must recede into the background as being completely irrelevant.*" Ideology had clearly superseded rational political and economic calculations. Hitler had decided on war against Bolshevism, which he had long regarded as a contrivance through which the Jews manipulated world power. Thus this holy war against Jewish Bolshevism would defeat the prime and ultimate enemy and win for the German people their Lebensraum.

The Four Year Plan also provided for the expropriation of all Jews when Germany went to war. The Reichstag was to pass a law "making the whole of Jewry liable for all damage inflicted by individual specimens of this community of criminals upon the German economy, and thus upon the German people." With this authority, Göring, as Plenipotentiary for the Four Year Plan, would, after the *Kristallnacht*, levy a billion-mark contribution on the Jews. . . .

Preparations for war proceeded apace. In August 1936, about the time he was working on the Four Year Plan, the term of compulsory military service was extended from one year to two years. In October and November 1936 the Berlin-Rome-Tokyo Axis was forged. . . . The whole Nazi apparatus became engaged in producing enormous quantities of deceitful and deliberately falsified propaganda describing Russia as the center of operations of the Elders of Zion. Goebbels and Rosenberg had major organizations devoted to anti-Communist propaganda and activities.

Yet none achieved Hitler's terrible potency. His speech at the NSDAP congress, on September 13, 1937, dwelled on the worldwide Bolshevik menace, using the themes he had developed in *Mein Kampf*: the preparation for world insurrection "without doubt originates from the authorities of Jewish Bolshevism in Moscow." Having gained a foothold in Russia, the Jews would use it as the bridgehead in their quest for world domination. "I confirm only what is!" Hitler cried out with pathos. National Socialism had already "banished the Bolshevik world peril from the inner heart of Germany." Now it would protect the "community of European-culture nations" from "Jewish world Bolshevism." In a crescendo of hatred, the National Socialists depicted the "Jewish-Bolshevik world conspirators" as the primary enemy of mankind in a campaign that intended not only to justify the launching of the war, but to provide a continuous warrant in defense of both the conduct of the war and the execution of the Final Solution. . . .

Under the all-embracing cover of the Four Year Plan, Hitler planned 1938 as the decisive year to go ahead with the annexation of Austria and the invasion of Czechoslovakia — "Operation Green," whose military planning he ordered early in December 1937. His first spectacular success came on March 12, 1938, when he annexed Austria in an unresisted invasion. A month later, after an unprecedented show of terror and violence, the National Socialists held a plebiscite in which 99.75 percent of the voters supported union with Germany. The war fever then began to be fanned around the manufactured crisis of the Sudeten Germans in Czechoslovakia. The implications for the Jews in Germany grew more sinister, for their total expropriation and ultimate disposition had been awaiting the maturation of Hitler's war plans.

The economic situation of the Jews had been continually deteriorating. By the end of 1937, Jewish professionals and civil servants, actors, musicians, and journalists, numbering tens of thousands, had lost their livelihood. Many Jews, workers and employees, had been dismissed from their jobs under pressure of rabid party and SA members. . . . Innumerable small Jewish businesses were liquidated in the first two years of the regime, after experiencing boycotts and violence. "Voluntary" transfers of Jewish firms to "Aryan" purchasers usually involved smaller businesses; larger ones, especially those that brought large sums of foreign exchange into Germany, managed to continue to operate, partly because of Germany's pressing need for foreign currency and partly because of Schacht's resistance to taking formal action. . . .

Early in January 1938 Göring initiated systematic planning for expropriation, declaring that first of all "it was necessary to have a legal definition of what constitutes a Jewish firm." On March 26, speaking in Vienna (having not Austria, but Germany, in mind), Göring declared that "Aryanization" should not be impaired by wrong or stupid measures, but must be carried out "quite systematically, with full deliberation."

The first decree, issued April 22, 1938, provided that any German engaged in an effort to camouflage the Jewish "character" — that is, ownership — of a business enterprise would be imprisoned or fined. . . . The next decree, issued April 26 over Göring and Frick's signatures, was the fundamental Decree Regarding the Reporting of Jewish Property. It provided that no later than June 30, 1938, every Jew had to report and assess his entire domestic and foreign property, except for personal and household goods, or if the total value of the property did not exceed five thousand Reichsmarks. . . . On July 6 a decree was issued requiring the termination, no later than December 30, 1938, of Jewish businesses that rendered a variety of commercial services. On July 25 a decree forbade Jewish physicians (there were still about 4,000) from practicing as of September 30. (With permission from the Minister of the Interior, Jewish doctors could treat Jewish patients not as doctors, but as orderlies.) On September 27, 1938, Jewish lawyers (still about 1,700) were forbidden to practice law as of November 30. . . .

The war plans were synchronized also with plans to put the Jews under the complete control of the police. On January 5, 1938, a Law Regarding Changes of Family Names and Given Names was promulgated, which authorized the Minister of the Interior to issue regulations about names and to order changes of names that did not conform to those regulations. The ominous character of the law became apparent only on July 23, in a decree requiring all Jews to apply for identification cards, which they would have to carry with them at all times. On August 17, 1938, the Law Regarding Changes of Family Names and Given Names was issued, providing that as of January 1, 1939, all male Jews must assume the given name of Israel and all female Jews the name of Sarah. Furthermore, Jews were forbidden to take as given names any other than specifically designated "Jewish" given names, as listed in an appendix to the decree. . . .

On October 5, 1938, a Law on Passports of Jews, signed by Werner Best, then head of the Sipo administrative office, required Jews to hand in their passports for foreign travel within two weeks; these would be reissued designating the holder as a Jew.

Other disquieting developments occurred. At the very outset of the year Himmler ordered the expulsion within ten days of all Jews in Germany who were Russian nationals, many of whom had been living in Germany since the Bolshevik Revolution. On March 28 a decree was issued, signed by the Führer himself together with the Minister for Church Affairs and the Minister of the Interior, withdrawing from the

Jewish religious communities and their central organizations (*Gemeinden*) their status as public legal bodies and subjecting them to government control. Following the decree a year earlier dissolving the B'nai B'rith, the Law Regarding the Legal Status of the Jewish Religious Communities was to prepare for the eventual centralization of all Jewish affairs in one organization that would be under the total control of the police. . . .

But far worse and more terrifying than the sporadic violence of the mobs and hoodlums was the expanding activity of the Gestapo and SS. On January 25, 1938, the Minister of the Interior issued a new order that extended the definition of "protective custody" to apply to "persons whose behavior endangers the existence and security of the Volk and the State." Under the guidelines of another order the concentration camps were being given new functions, besides detention of political opponents, as state reformatories and labor camps for criminals and antisocials. Mass Jewish arrests began late in May, and most of those arrested were sent to Dachau. On June 1 Heydrich issued instructions that between June 13 and 18 each criminal police district was to take into "preventive police detention at least two hundred male able-bodied persons (antisocials) as well as all male Jews with previous criminal records." They were to be sent to Buchenwald. The action was in implementation of the Four Year Plan and the demands of the war economy to put every able-bodied person to work. This would provide the rationale for turning the concentration camps into forced-labor and then slave-labor camps. The idea had a history going back to the 1923 Putsch. According to the draft constitution prepared then for the eventuality of takeover, concentration camps were to be established for "all persons dangerous to security and useless eaters."

The seizure of some 1,500 Jewish "antisocials" served a different purpose. The police records of many consisted of a parking violation or two. The Gestapo was willing to release them only upon completion of arrangements for their immediate emigration. The Gestapo had begun to coerce emigration along lines that Eichmann had advocated a short while before. After the Anschluss he had the opportunity to carry out his ideas in real life in Vienna.

During the summer of 1938 Buchenwald, Dachau, and Sachsenhausen began to be enlarged and provisions made for the exploitation of their prisoners' labor. Prisoners at Dachau were ordered to sew Stars of David on uniforms in preparation for a mass influx of Jewish prisoners.

The plans for war and for the expropriation of the Jews, the directives providing for their identification, the rash of police arrests, and the explosion of violence all converged that summer of 1938 in a tidal wave of terror. On September 12, at the Nuremberg party congress, Hitler was still sure that Operation Green would come off as planned on October 1, for he continued to promise the Sudeten Germans military assistance. But British Prime Minister Neville Chamberlain, the architect of appeasement, thwarted Hitler's bid for war with the Munich Conference of September 29, 1938. By awarding Hitler the Sudetenland, Chamberlain removed the pretext for Hitler's threatened invasion. Operation Green was called off. Instead, German troops marched only into the Sudetenland on October 1, in accordance with the Munich agreement. But Hitler did not abandon his original plans. Just three weeks later, in violation of that agreement, a new directive was issued to the armed forces for the dismemberment of Czechoslovakia.

The plan for war had, for the time being, misfired and with it the opportunity for taking drastic, but less visible, action against the Jews. But an unexpected opportunity for dealing with the Jews opened up with the assassination on November 7, 1938, of Ernst vom Rath, a third secretary in the German embassy in Paris, by a seventeen-year-old Polish Jewish student, Hershl Grynszpan. Grynszpan's parents, Polish Jews, who had lived in Hanover since 1914, had just been expelled from Germany. In March 1938 the Polish government, fearful that the Germans would soon expel Jews who were Polish nationals and return them to Poland, promulgated a denaturalization decree designed to annul the citizenship of Poles living abroad for more than five years unless they received a special stamp by Polish consular officials by October 31. Lacking that, they would be refused reentry to Poland. About fifty thousand Polish Jews were then resident in Germany. Overnight they became stateless when Polish officials refused to issue the requisite stamp. The German government soon learned that the Polish government was firm in its intention of barring the reentry of Jews. On October 28 the Gestapo, on orders from the Foreign Office, began rounding up Polish Jews to transport them to the Polish border. Prevented from entering Poland, they were kept in appalling conditions in a no-man's-land on the Polish side at Zbaszyn, near Posen. Grynszpan's parents had been among the first rounded up, and the son had become unsettled by their fate.

Hitler himself never uttered a word publicly on vom Rath's assassination or on the events of the Kristallnacht (night of glass). Yet those events could not have occurred without his approval. The incitement against the Jews began on November 8 with the first news report that vom Rath had been seriously wounded (he died two days later of his wounds) and an accompanying incendiary editorial in the *Völkischer Beobachter*. Goebbels called the signals, which were picked up by party and SA leaders all over Germany. In many small towns, meetings were called on November 8 or 9, at which the party leader and the local mayor agitated the assembled mob, which then went into action, setting fire to the local synagogues, destroying Jewish businesses and homes, and manhandling Jews. At that moment in German history, with war fever running high and the Jews already clearly identified as enemies, the rank-and-file National Socialist was eager for a little action on his own. Many times in the past, the NSDAP had bridled these anti-Semitic enthusiasms in the interests of broader goals. Now Goebbels became the advocate of mob violence and the architect of a mob-action program. ·

Early in the evening of November 9, it was learned that vom Rath had died of his wounds. That very evening the NSDAP's leaders were congregating in the Old Town Hall in Munich for the anniversary celebration of the Munich Putsch. Hitler had dinner there with his old comrades and was seen in prolonged conversation with Goebbels. Hitler usually delivered the main speech on this occasion, but this evening he left early. He had been overheard to say that "the SA should be allowed to have a fling." Hitler had presumably decided, at Goebbels' suggestion, that "spontaneous" demonstrations, manifestly not initiated or organized by the party, were not to be discouraged. His absence from the festivities was planned to exculpate him — and the government — from responsibility for the subsequent events. After Hitler left, Goebbels delivered an inflammatory exhortation to the assemblage, calling for "spontaneous" demonstrations. NSDAP members were used to such instructions from the party's earliest days, when it expediently served as the anonymous organizer of violent demonstrations. Now, the party members and SA men took Goebbels' hints as he intended them to be taken: Jewish blood was to flow for the death of vom Rath. . . .

That night fires were ignited all over Germany, and the shattered plate glass that was to give the pogrom its name littered the streets of German towns and cities. (It was later estimated that the amount of plate glass destroyed equaled half the annual production of the plate-glass industry of Belgium, from which it had been imported.) Synagogues and Jewish institutions were burned to the ground. Over seven thousand Jewish businesses were destroyed. Nearly one hundred Jews were killed, and thousands more subjected to wanton violence and sadistic torments. . . . About thirty thousand Jewish men were arrested and incarcerated in Buchenwald, Dachau, and Sachsenhausen.

If the death of vom Rath had triggered Goebbels' pogrom, the pogrom itself provided the National Socialist government with the opportunity, short of actual war, to proceed with the total expropriation of the Jews and the complete removal of their freedom. . . . On November 15, the Ministry of Education issued an ordinance barring all Jewish children from the schools; two weeks later, on November 28, Heydrich issued a decree signed by the Minister of Interior giving various state and district authorities the right to impose curfew restrictions on the Jews. A month later the Führer himself approved Göring's proposal to forbid Jews access to most of the public places specified by Goebbels. . . .

Everything relating to the Jewish question, it seemed, had been disposed of, except the Jews themselves. On January 24, 1939, Göring gave Heydrich the power to take all measures for a stepped-up forced emigration of the German Jews, along the lines that Eichmann had pioneered in Vienna after the Anschluss. SS terror was rampant there, and the Jews were its primary target; thousands were rounded up and incarcerated in Dachau, Buchenwald, and a new camp at Mauthausen; other thousands were forced to clean streets and public latrines. Eichmann then offered "emigration" as an alternative to the terror. He set up the central organization that he had first proposed in 1937, a *Zentralstelle fur jüdische Auswanderung* (Central Office for Jewish Emigration). For its successful operation, he demanded the reestablishment of the *Jüdische Kultusgemeinde* (Jewish Religious Community), which had been dissolved, and the release from detention of some Jewish communal leaders. With their cooperation, procured by terror, Eichmann began to process the forcible exit of Jews from Austria. The application of apposite doses of terror and blackmail, coupled with the centralization of bureaucratic procedures, so successfully speeded up "emigration" that in about six months after the Anschluss, 45,000 Jews had left Austria. Over 100,000 more would leave before war broke out. Eichmann's activities were closely observed in Germany. The most serious drawback, from Göring's point of view, was the depletion of Jewish accounts abroad to finance emigration. All this was discussed at Göring's conference on November 12, 1938, at which Heydrich proposed to set up a similar procedure for the Reich, but without the "mistakes" to which Göring had alluded. To this Göring agreed on the spot. The directive, issued January 24, 1939, provided for the establishment of a *Reichszentrale für die jüdische Auswanderung* (Reich Central Office for Jewish Emigration), operating under Heydrich's direction. Its object was to promote the "emigration" of Jews from Germany "by every possible means." The directive further required that an "appropriate Jewish organization for the uniform preparation of emigration applications" be created. The "appropriate Jewish organization" was to be used in the same way that Eichmann had exploited the Jüdische Kultusgemeinde in Vienna. . . .

On January 21, 1939, Hitler told the Czech Foreign Minister Chvalkovsky: "We are going to destroy the Jews. They are not going to get away with what they did on November 9, 1918. The day of reckoning has come." That was confidential, but on January 30, 1939, Hitler dilated on this theme when he addressed the Reichstag on the anniversary of his accession to power. The most salient passage of that long speech was two paragraphs to which Hitler himself would refer often during the war. They constituted his declaration of war against the Jews:

> *And one more thing I would like now to state on this day memorable perhaps not only for us Germans. I have often been a prophet in my life and was generally laughed at. During my struggle for power, the Jews primarily received with laughter my prophecies that I would someday assume the leadership of the state and thereby of the entire Volk and then, among many other things, achieve a solution of the Jewish problem. I suppose that meanwhile the then resounding laughter of Jewry in Germany is now choking in their throats.*
>
> *Today I will be a prophet again: If international finance Jewry within Europe and abroad should succeed once more in plunging the peoples into a world war, then the consequence will be not the Bolshevi-*

zation of the world and therewith a victory of Jewry, but on the con-
trary, the destruction of the Jewish race in Europe.

Hitler's early invasions had been greeted with flowers, not guns. The entry of the German army into the Rhineland, then into Austria, and thereafter into the Sudetenland were adventures in diplomatic and military brinksmanship that had attained Hitler's goals without war. So, too, Germany's destruction of the Czech republic in mid-March 1939 proceeded without impediment. Hitler annexed Czechoslovakia's western provinces of Bohemia and Moravia as a German protectorate; the eastern province of Slovakia became a puppet state under the rule of Father Jozef Tiso, a right-wing Catholic priest and Slovak nationalist.

On March 15 Prime Minister Chamberlain, addressing the House of Commons, explained that in the light of Slovakia's self-proclaimed independence, Britain did not have to honor its treaty obligations to Czechoslovakia by coming to its assistance in the event of an act of unprovoked aggression. That was the kind of reaction that Hitler had contemptuously expected of the English, and it appeared to vindicate his strategy. But now Hitler miscalculated. Two days later, Chamberlain publicly admitted he had been deceived and disappointed, that the assurances that Hitler had given in Munich in September 1938 had been worthless. (The annexation of the Sudetenland, Hitler had said then, would be "the last territorial claim" he would make in Europe.) Just two weeks later, on March 31, 1939, Chamberlain informed Parliament that the British government would come at once to Poland's aid "in the event of any action which clearly threatened Polish independence and which the Polish Government accordingly considered it vital to resist with their national forces." The French government, too, had authorized him to make it plain that on this question they took the same position as the British.

Hitler's rage at the Anglo-French stand and their agreement with Poland signed on April 6 still did not deter him from the course on which he had already embarked toward Poland's destruction. In March he had begun to make excessive demands of Poland — Danzig became the symbolic issue — and brash diplomatic maneuvers accompanied outrageous propaganda. On April 3 Hitler gave Field Marshal Wilhelm Keitel, Chief of the High Command of the armed forces, instructions to prepare Operation White, the invasion of Poland. In mid-April, addressing top military officers, Hitler argued that since Germany could not count on Poland's neutrality in case of a war with the Western powers, Germany must therefore first eliminate Poland through a lightning campaign (*Blitzkrieg*). He assured the officers that such an undertaking would not lead to another war. . . .

Though the Soviet Union appears to have taken the initiative for a German-Soviet rapprochement, it was Germany that more eagerly pursued the undercover negotiations. On April 28 Hitler denounced his 1934 agreement with Poland. That may have been intended to demonstrate to the Russians the German interest in coming to an understanding. The Russians then signified their interest on May 3 by suddenly dismissing Foreign Minister Maxim Litvinov. Litvinov embodied all that the Germans detested about Bolshevism — he was a Jew, a peace advocate, a supporter of the League of Nations, a friend of the Western democracies, and an opponent of Nazi Germany and its anti-Comintern Axis. Litvinov was replaced by Vyacheslav V. M. Molotov, the complete antithesis to Litvinov: a non-Jew, a close associate of Stalin's, a hard, ruthless man said to favor accommodation with Germany. . . .

At a meeting on May 23, 1939, of his highest-ranking military officers to brief them on "the situation and political objectives," Hitler dilated, as usual, on racial and ideological matters as the basis for Germany's politics and then set forth his military strategy to attain both the racial and the political goals. He said that while "the ideological problems" of the German people had been already solved, the question of German self-sufficiency still awaited solution. That was a question, he told them, not of Danzig but of Lebensraum: "If fate forces us into a showdown with the West it is good to possess a largish area in the East." The decision had to be to attack Poland at the first suitable opportunity. Possible accommodation with Russia was barely hinted at: "Economic relations with Russia are only possible if and when political relations have improved." . . .

Everything was "go" for the Polish invasion. On June 23 Göring, as Plenipotentiary for the Four Year Plan, called a meeting of the Reich Defense Council to discuss manpower problems that war would impose on Germany. Funk was given the responsibility of deciding what kind of work could be assigned to war prisoners and to inmates of penitentiaries and concentration camps. Himmler promised that greater use would be made of the concentration camps during wartime, and Göring talked of employing foreign workers in Germany. The most extensive and inhumane network of forced and slave labor began to be organized.

The summer passed rapidly in the din of German threats against Poland, while official conversations with allies-soon-to-be-enemies concealed the simultaneous pursuit of secret negotiations with the Russians. . . . On August 19 Stalin informed the Politburo that he would sign a pact with Germany, and that same day a trade agreement between both countries was brought off. On August 23 Foreign Minister Ribbentrop arrived in Moscow and in the afternoon conferred with Stalin. In an extraordinary burst of energy, agreement on the text was reached later that day and the pact was signed after midnight. . . .

On August 25 Britain signed a formal treaty with Poland, confirming the guarantees given on April 6. That day Hitler postponed Operation White to September 1, in the hope of eliminating British intervention, but he failed to detach the British from their commitment to Poland. Operation White was nonetheless ordered, and by 6:30 A.M. on September 1, 1939, German troops invaded Poland all along the frontier.

Later that morning Hitler addressed the Reichstag with self-justifying and belligerent rhetoric. Projecting upon the enemy his own intentions, he threatened: "Whoever fights with poison will be fought back with poison gas. Whoever deviates from the rules for the humane conduct of war can expect nothing else from us, but that we will take the same steps." It was one of the few speeches in which he failed to mention Jews. (Was the passage just quoted an esoteric reference?) Yet later Hitler fixedly and repeatedly referred to *this* speech on *this* day as the speech in which he had threatened the Jews with destruction in the event of a war, though he had made *that* speech on January 30, 1939. In his mind he associated his declaration of war on September 1, 1939, with his promise to destroy the Jews.

War and the annihilation of the Jews were interdependent. The disorder of war would provide Hitler with the cover for the unchecked commission of murder. He needed an arena for his operations where the restraints of common codes of morality and accepted rules of warfare would not extend. He had set into motion a twofold war — one that was traditional in its striving for resources and empire and that would be fought in traditional military style, and one that was unconventional inasmuch as its primary political objective was to attain National Socialist ideology and that would be conducted in an innovative style of mass murder.

A German motorcycle unit pauses for a rest in a Polish town destroyed by German shells. (Archiv für Kunst und Geschicte, Berlin)

The Verdict

Donald Cameron Watt

Summing Up

In any examination of the roots and causes of World War II, one must always return to Hitler, according to Donald Cameron Watt, Stevenson Professor of International History at the University of London. The mistakes of the British, French, and Soviet governments all contributed to causing the war. But in the end it all comes back to Adolf Hitler, who willed a war but not the war he wanted. Watt sees Britain as the nation that entered World War II to battle Hitler and his armies over a principle.

What is so extraordinary in the events which led up to the outbreak of the Second World War is that Hitler's will for war was able to overcome the reluctance with which virtually everybody else approached it. Hitler willed, desired, lusted after war; though not war with France and Britain, at least not in 1939. No one else wanted it, though Mussolini

From *How War Came* by Donald Cameron Watt, pp. 610–611, 613–624. Copyright © 1989 by Donald Cameron Watt. Reprinted by permission of Pantheon Books, a division of Random House, Inc.

came perilously close to talking himself into it. In every country the military advisers anticipated defeat, and the economic advisers expected ruin and bankruptcy. Most of their prophecies were realized. There were *bellicistes* in London and Paris. Few were to be found in either Government or Cabinet. The record of the British and French Cabinets, harried and hurried into guarantees that they could not or would not implement, into a system of deterrence they did not understand, and which left them in the last days of August desperately trying to avoid the realization that their policy had failed to deter, is neither a happy nor an edifying spectacle. But it is really open to doubt whether any alternative course would have made any difference. . . .

The biggest British and French failure lay with the Soviet Union. Contrariwise the biggest Soviet failure lay with Britain and France. Soviet secrecy meant that nothing was available to counter the image of Soviet military weakness and military incompetence that made up the professional judgment of those whose job it was to advise Britain and France on Soviet strength. The approach to diplomacy of the Soviet Ambassadors abroad, especially of Maisky in London, made them blind to the changes in opinion and policy taking place in the British Cabinet. Soviet intelligence in the West was used as much, if not more, as a weapon of intrigue, than as a source of political information. Stalin's obsession with the *cauchemar* of a German invasion along the Baltic coast, which Zhdanov may have shared but certainly played upon, added an extra element of distortion to the Soviet viewpoint. Central, however, was the note of almost adolescent sensitivity which saw slights everywhere, in the dispatch of Mr Strang rather than Lord Halifax, and of Admiral Drax rather than the Chiefs of Staff to Moscow, a readiness to take offence which stemmed from the equally questionable assumption that since Hitler had no plans against the Soviet Union in 1939, Britain needed the Soviet Union more than the Soviet Union needed Britain and should behave as if she did. On any calculation the Soviet Union faced a much greater threat from Germany in 1941 than she did in 1939, when the German invasion of Russia had been planned and prepared for over the previous years, when Germany faced no armed resistance anywhere else on the European continent, and when Germany had absorbed and occupied south-eastern Europe.

That being said, the British and French began by feeling the Soviet Union could be marshalled to the service of a policy of deterrence already determined upon. They rejected Litvinov, who believed in collective action. They got instead Molotov, ignorant, short-sighted and dominated by his master's suspicions. They were not well served by their Ambassadors. . . .

General Doumenc and Admiral Drax were sent to Moscow with grossly inadequate briefing and without a single card in their hands. The attitude taken by Marshal Voroshilov — what do you want us to do? We will only commit a percentage of the forces you commit — does not strike one as a serious approach to the problems of war against Nazi Germany either; though it is thoroughly consistent with Stalin's conviction that Britain needed Soviet aid so badly that she should expect to pay whatever price the Soviet Union demanded for Soviet support. It is, incidentally, odd that in one so quick to take offence, the essentially mercenary notion of the relationship with Anglo-French capitalism into which he was contemplating entering, never seems to have struck him.

Roosevelt and the United States ventured less than the Soviet Union, and the United States was to prove the only untrammelled victor in the Second World War. Under the stimulus first of British and French purchases and then of the massive demands of America's own war effort, the American economy, sluggish and barely ticking over at a quarter or less of its capacity in the decade before 1939, took off. Alone of the belligerents America enjoyed a massive rise in its standard of living and consumption in the years of war. In 1939, however, much of American opinion still believed that what happened in Europe, while it might be regrettable, was none of America's business. Roosevelt saw more clearly and truly even if, as with the British Cabinet, much of the evidence on which he acted was misleading or manufactured or both.

He, like Chamberlain, however, faced the same dilemma: whether to try to prevent war coming or to ensure that, when it did, its outcome was the most satisfactory for America's interests as he saw them. He did not share Chamberlain's views as to the desirability of preserving a European comity or harmony, but he did share his views as to the danger of a German victory. Roosevelt's opinion was that any further advance of Hitler's power in Europe endangered his America and his New Deal. Britain and France were the advance guards of America's interest. Their military power and their resolution to resist Hitler were inter-dependent. Both needed strengthening.

His difficulties lay elsewhere. His vision was not matched by his ability in practice to make either his administration or the general machinery of American politics work for him. His own Cabinet, even his most trusted associates such as Bullitt or Sumner Welles, did not share his convictions that an Anglo-German coalition against America was an entirely imaginary danger. The leaders of Congress were more concerned with the threat to American politics they discerned in the growth of Roosevelt's power and the ambitions of his entourage than with Hitler, Mussolini, or Japan. American opinion in general supported Britain and thought Nazism un-American and a threat to American democracy. It believed that if a second world war broke out, America would be drawn in again. Such a prospect was regarded with fear and repulsion. It involved American soldiers fighting in 'foreign wars,' American lives being lost in un-American conflicts. As a spectator sport war was OK. Like all-in wrestling, it involved 'goodies' to be cheered and 'baddies' to be hissed and booed. It most manifestly and certainly did not involve the spectators entering the ring.

Roosevelt had therefore to move in secrecy. It was, anyway, his habitual method of operating. He could not have kept together so ideologically divided, so geographically separated, so mutually incompatible a coalition as the Democratic Party in any other way. This ruled out the kind of overt and direct declaration Chamberlain was to make in 1939. Overtly, Roosevelt could only plead for peace. His aim was not the immediate deterrence of Hitler but the long-term education of American opinion. For him the reality of politics lay in Washington, Chicago, New York, in the valleys of the Ohio, the Mississippi and the Missouri, in the great plains of the Midwest, in the mountain states, in California, Texas and the Pacific states, not in Prague, Warsaw, Rome, Berlin, Paris or London, still less in Bratislava, the Memel or Danzig, Nice, Corsica, Savoy, Albania, Athens, Belgrade or Ankara. Moreover, here as with Britain, Hitler had his own informants, who told him what he wanted to hear. America was divided, ridden by Jews, interested only in making money, incurably isolationist, a view Senator Borah and the majority in the Senate Foreign Relations Committee and the House did their unwitting and ill-considered best to confirm.

In the end the war was Hitler's war. It was not, perhaps, the war he wanted. But it was the war he was prepared to risk, if he had to. Nothing could deter him. He preferred to trust his intuition and his creatures, Ribbentrop, Forster, Abetz, anyone who would tell him what at that moment he wanted or needed to hear. He was no longer prepared to wait on events. He needed to force them, to manipulate them, to manufacture incidents, to create pretexts for action. Thus he could enter the world of ghastly farce, where his minions picked a radio station that could not broadcast, or where his own change of a quarter of an hour in the timing of the attack could distort the timetable on which depended the coup against the bridge at Dirschau, on which he had personally spent so much time.

Placed alongside this obsessive determination, the chapter of misperceptions, misinformations and misunderstandings which propelled the British Government into the decision to commit a major military force to the Continent in January, to come to Romania's aid and to guarantee Poland in March, and to guarantee Romania, Greece and Turkey in April [1939] are historical events of much less consequence. It is of interest that much of this was the result of reports planted by Hitler's enemies in Germany, and much was the product of nerves strained by Hitler's unpredictability and the misunderstandings and misperceptions that two years of Sir Nevile Henderson's Embassy in Berlin had entrenched in British understanding of Hitler. It is ironic that one of Hitler's most perceptive enemies in Britain, Sir Robert Vansittart, should have fathered this disastrous appointment on his political masters.

Sir Nevile Henderson has had so bad a press that it is easy to forget how clearly he perceived the elements of imbalance in Hitler's personal make-up which made setbacks spurs into ever more violent action. But it was the acute form of *déformation professionnelle* from which he suffered (to which few diplomatists are immune), of thinking the maintenance of good relations with the host country the measure of success, which made him such a disaster. He misrepresented Britain to Hitler and Hitler to Britain; and not only to Britain, but to Britain's partners in the Commonwealth, who then fed back his views of German reasonableness as pressure on the British Cabinet to seek accommodation with Germany. It can hardly be a coincidence that a decisive turn in the Cabinet's perception of Hitler occurred during his absence in Britain from November 1938 to February 1939. . . .

In the course of the twelve months, from Munich to the British declaration of war on Germany, the balance of power and influence within the British Cabinet shifted palpably. Chamberlain was the architect of Munich. The attempt to build on the Anglo-German declaration he had sprung on Hitler on the morning of September 30, 1938, the reassurance of the French and the cultivation of Mussolini were his policies, although he shared in their execution with Halifax. But with his return from Rome in January, the balance began to shift subtly towards Halifax. Chamberlain took no real part in handling the war-scare in mid-January. Its outcome, when taken with the evidence of Roosevelt's more active interests in Europe, lulled him into a feeling of satisfaction. He was prepared to play his part even in Halifax's attempt to mend Britain's forces in Europe. But the twin shocks of the German absorption of Czechoslovakia and the Italian attack on Albania destroyed the basis of his policy. If the dictators were not to be trusted, his approach was impossible.

The balance shifted to Halifax and, without the Cabinet, the majority turned in favour of guarantees, containment and an alliance with Russia. Chamberlain sensed and resented this shift, as his querulous comments ('even Halifax') to his sisters amply illustrate. In the end he found the House of Commons and the majority of his own Cabinet in near-mutiny against him. He entered the war reluctantly; to be fair his reluctance was from the heart not the head. He knew that Hitler had left him no alternative and that the hour had come to end the havering on the Friday Hitler's troops attacked Poland. He had known for two months or more that no agreement with Hitler could be relied upon. But it was the direction in which his heart pulled him that suckered him into Bonnet's last-minute efforts to lie his way out of war, and very nearly brought forward to September 2, 1939, the events of May 8, 1940, which were to end his premiership. . . .

Little more needs to be said of France. The Third Republic was in its penultimate stage of decay, led by a politician who was nearly, but not quite, a strong man and a statesman, with a Cabinet whose majority tended towards the *inactiviste* rather than the *belliciste* wing. A Daladier who could tolerate or admire a Bonnet was a man divided in himself, offloading his indecisions upon Bonnet as Bonnet tried to offload France's responsibilities, and depending for his military advice on General Gamelin, a man whose equal aim was to divert responsibility for France's inability even to use the forces she had to back her foreign policy. Passing the buck, like 'Hunt-the-slipper,' was central to the French system of government. . . .

And so the historian has to return to Germany. Here the most difficult area to explore is that of the factions within Hitler's court: Goering, Ribbentrop, backed by Goebbels, Ley and Darré, with the

SS, manipulated by Heydrich, coming up fast on the outside. One has to allow too for mavericks such as Albert Forster, the Gauleiter of Danzig, who dealt with Hitler directly (the SS backed his rival and victim, Arthur Greiser), and Hans Frank, whose occasional appearances on the stage are impossible to tie in with the little we know of Nazi factionalism. Contemporary observers tended to a simple equation, Goering on the side of moderation, Ribbentrop, Himmler, Goebbels, and so on among the extremists. But this picture is wrongly conceived. Goebbels played little or no part in any of the formulation of foreign policy. For much of the time he was in disgrace as a result of the sexual scandals which broke just after Munich (and which Goering's minions boasted their master had engineered). His brief appearance in Danzig may have been orchestrated by Hitler — Goebbels was always Hitler's creation. Himmler was merely the front man for Heydrich; and there was no love lost between Heydrich and Ribbentrop.

The rivalry between Goering and Ribbentrop was more personal than ideological. When Ribbentrop was working for a tripartite German-Japanese-Italian alliance, Goering made himself the advocate of a bilateral alliance with Italy. When Ribbentrop's effort to convert Poland into a German satellite began to break down, Goering began to cultivate the idea of a *rapprochement* with the Soviet Union. When Ribbentrop hijacked that policy, and visibly wrote Britain off, Goering began gently to encourage others to explore the settlement with Britain he knew his Führer still hankered after. When Ribbentrop stopped concerning himself with confusing the British, Goering allowed Dahlerus to invent himself in the role of mediator.

Goering's trouble was that Ribbentrop controlled the Foreign Ministry and the German missions abroad and he did not. He lacked the manpower to conduct anything but the occasional raid into foreign policy, which was after all Ribbentrop's allotted sphere. He was also lazy and, in a very real sense, satiated. As a young man he had been a courageous and daring fighter ace. Defeat, the destruction of his planes on the ground by fire in front of his eyes, had driven him into drug addiction until he hitched his star to Hitler's chariot. Hitler was his anchor and his meal-ticket. His fear of and contempt for Ribbentrop stemmed as much from jealousy and fear of displacement in Hitler's eyes as from any ideological grounds. . . .

Always one returns to Hitler: Hitler exultant, Hitler vehement,

Hitler indolent, Hitler playing the great commander, Hitler bullying the unfortunate President Hácha, raging at Dahlerus, ranting at Count Csáky, lecturing his Generals, hectoring his Army Commanders, threatening, cajoling, and appealing to German destiny. Above all, increasingly in a hurry, always raising the stakes, and losing, as he turned to manipulating events rather than waiting upon them, his uncanny gift for timing, setting himself ever tighter, more impossible timetables, steadily losing touch with reality, but never, as Paul Claudel once prophesied he would, going away. Time's winged chariot urged him on. If there had to be war with Britain, then better in 1939 than ten years later, he said. He had no confidence in his health or his ability to age well. German destiny — world power or downfall — required the strongest, most ruthless, most decisive leadership. Age brought weakness, a loss of faculties, ill health. His doctor Morell lived off Hitler's fears of ageing, ill health and early death, devising ever more potent stimulants to feed his patient's obsession with his health, that same obsession which made him a vegetarian and seems to have kept his relationship with Eva Braun unconsummated.

In much the same way, he more than half-believed his propagandists, with their significant emphasis on castration as the worst of the atrocities they alleged the Poles to be committing against members of the German minority in Poland. The Polish Government had defied him. It had rejected his 'generous offer' (he became more convinced of his generosity every time he spoke of it) with contumely and arrogance. As a righteous punishment, Poland must be destroyed. The Poles, arrogant and proud, though they were of inferior race, would not have dared to defy him if Britain had not encouraged them and backed them. Britain too rejected his offer to guarantee her empire, as she was to reject the offers of peace he was to make in October 1939 and after the fall of France. The SS plans for the treatment of a defeated and occupied Britain were to be as draconian as those applied to a defeated Poland.

The Poles were mere sub-men, Slavs, aping civilization and the ways of the superior race. They were to be 'rotted out.' Bombs, fire, and his loyal Himmler and the SS would cleanse Polish soil and resettle its fertile plains and forests with German peasants. The Poles should have copied the Czechs, the members of whose Government he pensioned off and allowed to retire, or the Slovaks, who did as he wished. Slovakia survived. Slovak forces were to march, in the name of Chris-

5

tianity, alongside the Wehrmacht, against the godless Soviet Union. How could he not be regarded as generous, ever-merciful, slow to wrath, but when aroused as merciless as any divinely appointed judge in the earliest books of the Old Testament? Gods and heroes, agents of the force of history, do not, should not, cannot accept limitations or hindrances which lesser men, unwitting agents of evil, put in their way.

The rank and file of the German armed forces, the urban middle class, the aircraft workers and the German peasants entered the war for a whole variety of reasons, which had only a remote relationship to Hitler's dream of empire. Resignation, fear of identification as a subversive, a renewal of the feelings of isolation from the rest of the world, the habit of civil obedience, a blind confidence in Hitler's previous track record, a feeling of individual helplessness, the lack of any alternative voice, patriotism, loyalty to their fellow Germans as well as a dedicated acceptance of Nazi ideals, and, *vis-à-vis* Britain (as with British reactions towards Germany), a revival of the hatreds, antagonisms and resentments that had been building up before and during the 1914–1918 war; all these motives were at work. . . .

Britain entered the war in 1939, barely equipped for survival and in no position to help her allies; but in certain crucial respects she had the edge. The combination of Spitfire and Hurricane eight-gun fighters, radar and ground-to-air communication, not in place in 1938 and barely in place in 1940, enabled her to survive the onslaught of the Luftwaffe by day. In the electronic war she held her own. Bomber Command and the four-engined heavy bombers of the 1938 programme devastated Germany's industrial cities and much else in the years 1941–1943. Her atomic physicists, with the aid of the French team and the refugees from Hitler's persecution, started Britain towards the atomic bomb, while German scientists lost their way. Poland gave Britain its biggest edge, Polish knowledge of the Enigma cipher machine which, when developed with the mathematical genius of Alan Turing, among others, and the organizational genius that managed to keep Britain's possession of it secret from the Germans throughout the war and for two and a half decades thereafter, was of incalculable value to Britain. In the battle of the Atlantic its possession could well have been all that stood between Britain and German victory at sea of which Raeder wrote so feelingly on September 3, 1939.

In all these important respects, the Polish gift of their work on

Enigma, the transfer in 1940 to Britain of the French atomic scientists and their stock of heavy water, Vichy's co-operation in keeping British knowledge of Enigma secret from the Germans, the work of the refugee scientists, the placing at Britain's disposal of the Czech and Polish intelligence services (which were to bring Britain the first news of the German V1 and V2 guided missile programmes), Europe turned to Britain as the symbol of all in the European tradition that Hitler rejected. . . . If Britain had faltered or compromised; if Hitler had not diverted himself against Russia, in part because he convinced himself that Russia had a hand in keeping Britain's hopes alive in 1940; if Roosevelt had not nailed his hopes of victory over Germany and Japan to Britain's survival under Churchill, Hitler might have succeeded for Europe's despair of any alternative.

By the end of 1941 the Anglo-German war had become the world war, Britain, the Commonwealth and the empire, the Soviet Union and the United States against a Europe forcibly united under Hitler; Britain, the Commonwealth and the empire with the United States and China against Japan. It was the dubious achievement of British diplomacy that in 1939 the war was limited to Britain and France, Germany and Poland, a limited war, constrained and fenced about. Its progressive widening, like its beginning, was Hitler's work. The propensity to resist him was there, as was the desire to avoid involvement. Britain's opposition to Hitler encouraged the propensity to resist him. Hitler brought those who tried to stay out of the war into the ever-widening conflict, some out of greed, most by force or the threat of force.

The Anglo-German conflict did not disappear, however. It was by virtue of the part Britain played that Britain became a founder of the United Nations with a permanent seat on the Security Council. Whatever status Britain has in the world today stems ineluctably from the course of action she followed in 1939, and from the revolt in the House of Commons and Cabinet on September 2, 1939. That revolt, which stemmed in turn from the degree to which British opinion accepted and supported the guarantees for Poland, understood that, whatever the rights and wrongs of Danzig and the Corridor, Poland had become a test case as to whether the 'law of the jungle' or the 'law of nations' was to rule Europe, and accepted that not only British credibility to others, but pride, self-respect, honour and very existence were bound up with the fulfilment of Britain's guarantee. Thus it was that the conclusion of the Nazi-Soviet Pact was dismissed, as the end of reliance on an untrustworthy ally, if not as a betrayal of what British opinion had thought was accepted as a common cause; and that in the end the fall of France itself was seen as a lightening of Britain's sword arm from the restraints of an unhappy and unenthusiastic ally, but in no way as a diminution of Britain's purpose.

In May 1945 Britain was the only power whose people could say that they had entered the war by choice, to fight for a principle, and not because their country was attacked. They entered to fight Hitler and those who supported him; that they made increasingly little distinction between Hitler and Nazism and Germany and its traditions is evidence of the degree to which in Europe the Second World War was both a war between nations and a pan-European civil war. But it is odd that the greatest reproach so often made against the Government which commanded a majority in the House of Commons and in the country is that it did not go to war against Hitler a year earlier. A Churchill, a Duff Cooper, an Eden, as a citizen of that country, has the right to lay such a charge; but not the citizens of countries whose Governments waited until their countries were attacked, still less citizens of countries whose Governments gave aid and encouragement to the power that was to attack them. . . .

Hitler willed, wanted, craved war and the destruction wrought by war. He did not want the war he got. Its origins lay through his own miscalculations and misperceptions, as much as through those of his eventual opponents, not least in their belief that he was bluffing, that he would recoil, that in Paul Claudel's words, '*Croque-mitaine se dégonflera*' (the bogeyman will go away). Be firm and it will not happen. If Hitler spoke on the Obersalzberg as Raeder recorded it on September 3, 1939, then he proved himself a liar. When it became clear that settling with Poland would, despite all his hopes, involve war with Britain, he did not postpone that settlement for more than a week.

Neither firmness nor appeasement, the piling up of more armaments nor the demonstration of more determination would stop him — or, if it did, it stopped him only from 7 p.m. on August 25 until 4 p.m. on August 31, 1939. The only people who could have stopped him permanently were those least conditioned to do so, his Generals, and their soldiers, if they had been ready to obey, by a *coup d'état*, or an assassin capable of penetrating into the Reichs Chancellery from which, in the last days of peace, Hitler never emerged. History knows this did not happen.

Adolf Hitler

A Confession

Poland had fallen, but Britain and France remained at war with Germany. Hitler summoned his generals to the Reich Chancellery for a conference on November 23, 1939.

Many of the officers in the audience were distrustful of Hitler. Some had opposed his plans to invade the West earlier in the month. (Poor weather forced cancellation of the invasion.) Some generals feared that instead of another glorious victory, Germany would once again endure a repetition of the 1914–1918 stalemate and final defeat. Consequently, Hitler had to strengthen the faith of those who doubted his military genius.

In his long harangue, Hitler tried to give the impression of inspired leadership. He proudly acknowledged his responsibility for Germany's past successes in foreign affairs. He even confessed to a series of aggressions and mentioned future aggressions.

Hitler's confession contradicted the argument that he had somehow stumbled into war as the result of his errors and those of British and French politicians. Instead he admitted with pride that he alone had involved Germany in war, and he looked forward with anticipation to conquests in western Europe and in Russia. He took all the credit for the war.

Nov. 23, 1939, 1200 hours. Conference with the Fuehrer, to which all Supreme Commanders are ordered. The Fuehrer gives the following speech:

The purpose of this conference is to give you an idea of the world of my thoughts, which governs me in the face of future events, and to

From *Nazi Conspiracy and Aggression*, vol. III, printed by the United States Government Printing Office, 1946, pp. 572–578.

tell you my decisions. The building up of our armed forces was only possible in connection with the ideological education of the German people by the Party. When I started my political task in 1919, my strong belief in final success was based on a thorough observation of the events of the day and the study of the reasons for their occurrence. Therefore, I never lost my belief in the midst of setbacks which were not spared me during my period of struggle. Providence has had the last word and brought me success. On top of that, I had a clear recognition of the probable course of historical events, and the firm will to make brutal decisions. The first decision was in 1919 when I after long internal conflict became a politician and took up the struggle against my enemies. That was the hardest of all decisions. I had, however, the firm belief that I would arrive at my goal. First of all, I desired a new system of selection. I wanted to educate a minority which would take over the leadership. After 15 years, I arrived at my goal, after strenuous struggles and many setbacks. When I came to power in 1933, a period of the most difficult struggle lay behind me. Everything existing before that had collapsed. I had to reorganize everything beginning with the mass of the people and extending it to the armed forces. First reorganization of the interior, abolishment of appearances of decay and defeatist ideas, education to heroism. While reorganizing the interior, I undertook the second task: to release Germany from its international ties. Two particular characteristics are to be pointed out: secession from the League of Nations and denunciation of the disarmament conference. It was a hard decision. The number of prophets who predicted that it would lead to the occupation of the Rhineland was large, the number of believers was very small. I was supported by the nation, which stood firmly behind me, when I carried out my intentions. After that the order for rearmament. Here again there were numerous prophets who predicted misfortunes, and only a few believers. In 1935 the introduction of compulsory armed service. After that militarization of the Rhineland, again a process believed to be impossible at that time. The number of people who put trust in me, was very small. Then the beginning of the fortification of the whole country especially in the west.

One year later, Austria came, this step also was considered doubtful. It brought about a considerable reinforcement of the Reich. The next step was Bohemia, Moravia and Poland. This step also was not possible to accomplish in one campaign. First of all, the western fortification had to be finished. It was not possible to reach the goal in one effort. It was clear to me from the first moment that I could not be satisfied with the Sudeten-German territory. That was only a partial solution. The decision to march into Bohemia was made. Then followed the erection of the Protectorate and with that the basis for the action against Poland was laid, but I wasn't quite clear at that time whether I should start first against the east and then in the west or vice-versa. Moltke [Prussian chief of staff in 1870] often made the same calculations in his time. Under pressure the decision came to fight with Poland first. One might accuse me of wanting to fight and fight again. In struggle I see the fate of all beings. Nobody can avoid a struggle if he does not want to lose out. The increasing number of people requires a larger living space. My goal was to create a logical relation between the number of people and the space for them to live in. The struggle must start here. No people can get away from the solution of this task or else it must yield and gradually die out. That is taught by history. . . .

Struggles are different than those of 100 years ago. Today we can speak of a racial fight. Today we fight for oilfields, rubber, treasures of the earth, etc. After the peace of Westphalia Germany disintegrated. Disintegration, impotence of the German Reich was determined by decree. This German impotence was removed by the creation of the Reich when Prussia realized her task. Then the opposition between France and England began. Since 1870 England has been against us. Bismarck and Moltke were certain that there would have to be one more action. The danger at that time was of a two-front war. Moltke was at times in favor of a preventive war. To take advantage of the slow progress of the Russian mobilization. German armed might was not fully employed. Insufficient sternness of the leading personalities. The basic thought of Moltke was the offensive. He never thought of the defense. Many opportunities were missed after Moltke's death. The solution was only possible by attacking a country at a favorable moment. Political and military leadership always declared that it was not yet ready. In 1914 there came the war on several fronts. It did not bring the solution of these problems. Today the second act of this drama is being written. For the first time in 67 years it must be made clear that we do not have a two-front war to wage. That which has been desired since 1870 and considered as impossible of achievement has come to pass. For the first time in history we have to fight on only one front, the other front is at present free. But no one can know how long that will remain so. I have doubted for a long time whether I should strike in the east and then in the west. Basically I did not organize the armed forces in order not to strike. The decision to strike was always in me. Earlier or later I wanted to solve the problem. Under pressure it was decided that the east was to be attacked first. If the Polish war was won so quickly, it was due to the superiority of our armed forces. The most glorious appearance in history. Unexpectedly small expenditures of men and material. Now the eastern front is held by only a few divisions. It is a situation which we viewed previously as unachievable. Now the situation is as follows: The opponent in the west lies behind his fortifications. There is no possibility of coming to grips with him. The decisive question is: how long can we endure this situation? Russia is at present not dangerous. It is weakened by many incidents today. Moreover, we have a pact with Russia. Pacts, however, are only held as long as they serve the purpose. Russia will hold herself to it only so long as Russia considers it to be to her benefit. Even Bismarck thought so. Let one think of the pact to assure our back. Now Russia has far-reaching goals, above all the strengthening of her position in the Baltic. We can oppose Russia only when we are free in the West. Further Russia is striving to increase her influence on the Balkans and is striving toward the Persian Gulf. That is also the goal of our foreign policy. Russia will do that which she considers to benefit her. At the present moment it has retired from internationalism. In case she renounces this, she will proceed to Pan-Slavism. It is difficult to see into the future. It is a fact that at the present time the Russian army is of little worth. For the next one or two years the present situation will remain. . . .

Five million Germans have been called to the colors. Of what importance if a few of them collapse. Daring in the army, navy and Luftwaffe. I cannot bear it when one says the army is not in good shape. Everything lies in the hands of the military leader. I can do anything with the German soldier if he is well led. We have succeeded with our small navy in clearing the North Sea of the British. Recognition of the small navy, especially the High Command of the Navy.

We have a Luftwaffe which has succeeded in safeguarding the entire living space of the Germans.

The land army achieved outstanding things in Poland. Even in the West it was not shown that the German soldier is inferior to the French.

Revolution from within is impossible. We are superior to the enemy numerically in the West. Behind the Army stands the strongest armament industry of the world.

I am disturbed by the stronger and stronger appearance of the English. The English are a tough enemy. Above all on defence. . . . There is no doubt that England will be very much represented in France at the latest in six to eight months.

We have an Achilles heel: The Ruhr. The progress of the war depends on the possession of the Ruhr. If England and France push through Belgium and Holland into the Ruhr, we shall be in the greatest danger. That could lead to the paralyzing of the German power of resistance. Every hope of compromise is childish: Victory or defeat! The question is not the fate of a national-socialistic Germany, but who is to dominate Europe in the future. The question is worthy of the greatest efforts. Certainly England and France will assume the offensive against Germany when they are armed. England and France have means of pressure to bring Belgium and Holland to request English and French help. In Belgium and Holland the sympathies are all for France and England. . . .

If the French army marches into Belgium in order to attack us, it will be too late for us. We must anticipate them. One more thing. U-boats, mines, and Luftwaffe (also for mines) can strike England effectively, if we have a better starting point. Now a flight to England demands so much fuel that sufficient bomb loads cannot be carried. The invention of a new type mine is of greatest importance for the Navy. Aircraft will be the chief mine layers now. We shall sow the English coast with mines which cannot be cleared. This mine warfare with the Luftwaffe demands a different starting point. England cannot live without its imports. We can feed ourselves. The permanent sowing of mines on the English coasts will bring England to her knees. However, this can only occur if we have occupied Belgium and Holland. It is a difficult decision for me. None has ever achieved what I have achieved. My life is of no importance in all this. I have led the German people to a great height, even if the world does hate us now. I am setting this work on a gamble. I have to choose between victory or destruction. I choose victory. Greatest historical choice, to be compared with the decision of Frederick the Great before the first Silesian war. Prussia owes its rise to the heroism of one man. Even there the closest advisers were disposed to capitulation. Everything depended on Frederick the Great. Even the decisions of Bismarck in 1866 and 1870 were no less great. My decision is unchangeable. I shall attack France and England at the most favorable and quickest moment. Breach of the neutrality of Belgium and Holland is meaningless. No one will question that when we have won. We shall not bring about the breach of neutrality as idiotically as it was in 1914. If we do not break the neutrality, then England and France will. Without attack the war is not to be ended victoriously. I consider it as possible to end the war only by means of an attack. The question as to whether the attack will be successful no one can answer. Everything depends upon the favorable instant. The military conditions are favorable. A prerequisite, however, is that the leadership must give an example of fanatical unity from above. There would not be any failures if the leaders always had the courage a rifleman must have. . . .

The spirit of the great men of our history must hearten us all. Fate demands from us no more than from the great men of German history. As long as I live I shall think only of the victory of my people. I shall shrink from nothing and shall destroy everyone who is opposed to me. I have decided to live my life so that I can stand unshamed if I have to die. I want to destroy the enemy. Behind me stands the German people, whose morale can only grow worse. Only he who struggles with destiny can have a good intuition. In the last years I have experienced many examples of intuition. Even in the present development I see the prophecy.

If we come through this struggle victoriously — and we shall come through victoriously — our time will enter into the history of our people. I shall stand or fall in this struggle. I shall never survive the defeat of my people. No capitulation to the outside forces, no revolution from the interior forces.

Suggestions for Additional Reading

No attempt is made here to list all of the numerous books that deal with the origins of World War II. Only the more important works, which students should find useful, are noted.

A satisfactory full-scale study of interwar diplomacy has yet to be written. There are brief surveys of pre–World War II diplomacy. Students can begin with two books from which selections were excerpted for this book: P. M. H. Bell, *The Origins of the Second World War in Europe* (London, 1986); and Keith Eubank, *The Origins of World War II*, 2d ed. (Arlington Heights, IL, 1989); in addition to A. J. P. Taylor's *The Origins of the Second World War* (London, 1961, and subsequent American editions). For an excellent analysis of Taylor's book, consult *The Origins of the Second World War Reconsidered: The A. J. P. Taylor Debate After Twenty-five Years*, edited by Gordon Martel (Boston, 1986). Other studies of the origins of World War II include Anthony Adamthwaite, *The Making of the Second World War*, 2d ed. (London, 1979); Lawrence Lafore, *The End of Glory: An Interpretation of the Origins of World War II* (Philadelphia, 1970); Joachim Remak, *The Origins of the Second World War* (Englewood Cliffs, N.J., 1976); Maurice Baumont, *The Origins of the Second World War* (New Haven, 1978); Esmonde M. Robertson, ed., *The Origins of the Second World War: Historical Interpretations* (London, 1971); Hans Gatzke, *European Diplomacy Between Two Wars, 1919–1939* (Chicago, 1972). The best book on international affairs before 1933 is Sally Marks, *The Illusion of Power: International Relations in Europe 1918–1933* (London, 1976). There is also Martin Kichen, *Europe Between the Wars: A Political History* (New York, 1988). On the outbreak of war, the best work is Donald Cameron Watt, *How the War Came: The Immediate Origins of the Second World War, 1938–1939* (New York, 1989), from which a selection was taken for this anthology.

The best study of the origins of appeasement is Martin Gilbert, *The Roots of Appeasement* (London, 1960). Martin Gilbert and Richard Gott, *The Appeasers*, rev. ed. (Boston, 1963), is a more critical study of appeasement. Neville Thompson, *The Anti-Appeasers: Conservative Opposition to Appeasement in the 1930s* (Oxford, 1971), is a scholarly work on the story of those who tried to halt appeasement. William R. Rock, *British Appeasement in the 1930s* (London, 1977), is a competent analysis. For the most recent work on appeasement, see *The*

Fascist Challenge and the Policy of Appeasement, edited by Wolfgang J. Mommsen and Lothar Kettenacker (London, 1983). Most of the books on the 1920s are dated. Jon Jacobson, *Locarno Diplomacy: Germany and the West, 1925–1929* (Princeton, 1972), is excellent. The standard work on the League of Nations is still F. P. Walters, *A History of the League of Nations*, 2 vols. (New York, 1952). No recent study examines the entire question of the Treaty of Versailles and its influence on European history. Paul Birdsall, *Versailles Twenty Years After* (New York, 1941), is still useful. Ferdinand Czernin, *Versailles 1919* (New York, 1961), contains a helpful collection of documents on the Peace Conference. One of the best studies of the Paris Peace Conference is Seth P. Tillman, *Anglo-American Relations at the Paris Peace Conference of 1919* (Princeton, 1961).

A greater wealth of works deals with the period 1933–1939. The best book on the Rhineland occupation is James T. Emmerson, *The Rhineland Crisis: March 6, 1936* (London, 1977), from which a selection was used in this anthology. The Franco-Soviet Pact can be studied in William R. Scott, *Alliance Against Hitler: The Origins of the Franco-Soviet Pact* (Durham, 1962). On the history of Austria and the Anschluss, there are Gordon Brook-Shepherd, *The Anschluss* (Philadelphia, 1963); Radomir Luza, *Austro-German Relations in the Anschluss Era* (Princeton, 1975); Jurgen Gehl, *Austria, Germany and the Anschluss, 1931–1938* (London, 1963). On the Austrian Nazis there is an important book, Bruce F. Pauley, *Hitler and the Forgotten Nazis: A History of Austrian National Socialism* (Chapel Hill, 1981). For France, there is Robert J. Young, *In Command of France: French Foreign Policy and Military Planning 1933–1940* (Cambridge, 1978); and Anthony Adamthwaite, *France and the Coming of the Second World War, 1936–1939* (London, 1977), an important work. On European armed forces, see Donald Cameron Watt, *Too Serious a Business: European Armed Forces and the Approach to the Second World War* (London, 1975). For the role of the general staffs there is *General Staffs and Diplomacy Before the Second World War* (London, 1978), Adrian Preston, editor. The best study of British rearmament is N. H. Gibbs, *Rearmament Policy* (London, 1976), vol. I in J. M. B. Butler, ed., *Grand Strategy* in the *British Official History of the Second World War*. For British military policy, consult Brian Bond, *British Military Policy Between the Two World Wars* (Oxford, 1980).

On military intelligence, there is Christopher Andrew, *Her Maj-*

esty's Secret Service: The Making of the British Intelligence Community (New York, 1986); Breach of Security: The German Secret Intelligence File on Events Leading to the Second World War (London, 1968), David Irving, editor; Knowing One's Enemies: Intelligence Assessment Before the Two World Wars (Princeton, 1984), Ernest May, ed.; and a book from which a selection was taken for this anthology, Wesley K. Wark, The Ultimate Enemy: British Intelligence and Nazi Germany, 1933–1939 (Ithaca, 1985).

The crisis over the Sudeten Germans and the fate of Czechoslovakia produced a number of important studies. Czechoslovak history can be studied in A History of the Czechoslovak Republic, 1918–1948 (Princeton, 1973), Victor Mamatey and Radomir Luza, eds. The most recent work on the Munich crisis is Telford Taylor, Munich: The Price of Peace (New York, 1979). Older studies include Keith Eubank, Munich (Norman, 1963); Keith Robbins, Munich, 1938 (London, 1968). John W. Wheeler Bennett, Munich: Prologue to Tragedy (New York, 1948), is a brilliantly written work. Keith Middlemas, Diplomacy of Illusion: The British Government and Germany, 1937–1939 (London, 1972), is concerned chiefly with the Czechoslovak crisis. Williamson Murray, The Change in the European Balance of Power, 1938–1939, The Path to Ruin (Princeton, 1984), is a major revisionist study based on wide research. For the Sudeten German problem there is Radomir Luza, The Transfer of the Sudeten Germans: A Study of Czech-German Relations; 1933–1962 (New York, 1964, and Ronald M. Smelser, The Sudeten Problem, 1933–1939: Volkstumspolitik and the Foundation of Nazi Foreign Policy (Middletown, CT, 1975). Sidney Aster, 1939: The Making of the Second World War (London, 1973), is a significant study that is based on extensive research in British archives and private papers.

Still one of the best studies of the Polish crisis is Anna M. Cienciala, Poland and the Western Powers, 1938–1939: A Study in the Interdependence of Eastern and Western Europe (London, 1968). An important revisionist interpretation of Anglo-Polish relations is Anita Prazmokska, Britain, Poland and the Eastern Front, 1939 (Cambridge, 1987).

John W. Wheeler Bennett, The Nemesis of Power: The German Army in Politics, 1918–1945 (New York, 1964), and Telford Taylor, Sword and Swastika: Generals and Nazis in the Third Reich (New

York, 1962), are still worth reading for the role of the German armed forces in bringing on the war. More recent studies include Wilhelm Diest, *The Wehrmacht and German Rearmament* (London, 1981); William Carr, *Arms, Autarchy and Aggression: German Foreign Policy, 1933–1939* (London, 1979); Matthew Cooper, *The German Army, 1933–1945* (London, 1978), and *The German Air Force* (London, 1981); and Williamson Murray, *Luftwaffe: A History, 1933–44* (London, 1985).

On the role of economics as a cause of the war, David E. Kaiser, *Economic Diplomacy and the Origins of the Second World War* (Princeton, 1980) is important. For the Great Depression consult Charles P. Kindleberger, *The World in Depression, 1929–1939* (Berkeley, 1973).

Many memoirs provide personal views of the causes of this conflict. Many are nothing more than apologia; nevertheless, they ought not to be overlooked. Among the more important are Winston S. Churchill, *The Gathering Storm* (Boston, 1948), which is useful but not infallible. The official biography, Martin Gilbert, *Winston S. Churchill, 1922–1939; The Prophet of Truth*, vol. 5 (Boston, 1977), contains useful information. William Manchester, *The Last Lion, Winston Spencer Churchill: Alone, 1932–1940* (Boston, 1988), is well worth reading. An illuminating memoir, based on his letters and diary, is Anthony Eden, *Facing the Dictators* (Boston, 1962). For a more critical biography read David Carlton, *Anthony Eden* (London, 1981). Samuel Hoare, Viscount Templewood, defends appeasement in *Nine Troubled Years* (London, 1954); Thomas Jones, *A Diary with Letters* (London, 1954), discusses a great deal about appeasers and appeasement. *The Diaries of Sir Alexander Cadogan* (London, 1971), edited by David Dilks, reveal much about the implementation of British foreign policy. The condition of British defenses that affected British foreign policy can be studied in *Time Unguarded: The Ironside Diaries, 1937–1940* (New York, 1962); *The Liddell Hart Memoirs*, 2 vols. (New York, 1965–1966); *Chief of Staff: The Diaries of Lieutenant-General Sir Henry Pownell*, Brian Bond, ed., vol. I, 1933–1940 (Hamden, CT, 1973); and Sir John Slessor, *The Central Blue: Recollections and Reflections* (London, 1956). The British view from Berlin can be found in Nevile Henderson, *Failure of a Mission* (London, 1940), and Ivone Kirkpatrick, *The Inner Circle* (London, 1959). For Stanley Baldwin there is Keith Middlemas and John Barnes, *Baldwin* (London, 1969). At this writing, there is no biography of Neville Chamberlain based on British government archives.

Probably no official from any government has been as revealing in the record he left behind as Count Galeazzo Ciano, Mussolini's son-in-law and foreign minister. *The Ciano Diaries, 1939–1943* (New York, 1946), *Ciano's Hidden Diary, 1937–1938* (New York, 1953), and *Ciano's Diplomatic Papers* (London, 1948) indict the fascist leaders for their irresponsibility. For a good survey of Italy under Mussolini, read Alan Cassels, *Fascist Italy*, 2d ed., (Arlington Heights, IL, 1984).

Prominent among German memoirs is of course Adolf Hitler's *Mein Kampf* (Boston, 1943), from which a selection was taken. *Hitler's Secret Book* (New York, 1961) is another important source for Hitler's ideas and program. Other sources for Hitler's ideas are H. R. Trevor-Roper, ed., *Hitler's Secret Conversations, 1941–1944* (New York, 1963), chiefly after-dinner conversations; H. R. Trevor-Roper, ed., *Adolf Hitler: The Hitler-Bormann Documents* (London, 1961). Hermann Rauschning, *The Voice of Destruction* (New York, 1940), is an important source for Hitler's ideas on foreign policy. Hitler's speeches are in Norman Baynes, ed., *The Speeches of Adolf Hitler, April 1922–August 1939*, 2 vols. (Oxford, 1942). A fascinating source of information on the personality and life-style of Hitler can be found in Albert Speer, *Inside the Third Reich* (New York, 1970). Among the biographies of Hitler, Alan Bullock, *Hitler: A Study in Tyranny*, rev. ed. (New York, 1962), has become a classic. Joachim Fest, *Hitler* (New York, 1973), is the best recent biography. William Carr, *Hitler: A Study in Personality and Politics* (London, 1978), is an important work. On interpreting the Hitler era, Ian Kershaw, *The Nazi Dictatorship: Problems and Perspectives of Interpretation* (Baltimore, 1985), is very useful. For a history of Nazi Germany there is the brilliant synthesis of Karl Dietrich Bracher, *The German Dictatorship: The Origins, Structure and Effects of National Socialism* (New York, 1970). The most authoritative account of Hitler's foreign policy is Gerhard L. Weinberg, *The Foreign Policy of Hitler's Germany: Diplomatic Revolution in Europe 1933–1939* (Chicago, 1973), and *The Foreign Policy of Hitler's Germany, Starting World War II, 1937–1939* (Chicago, 1980), from which a selection was used in this book.

On Hitler's ideas, plans, and goals, consult Eberhard Jackel, *Hitler's World View: A Blueprint for Power* (Cambridge, 1981); Klaus Hildebrand, *The Foreign Policy of the Third Reich* (Berkeley, 1973); Norman Rich, *Hitler's War Aims: Ideology, the Nazi State, and the Course of Expansion,* 2 vols. (New York, 1973); and Andreas Hillgruber, *Germany and Two World Wars* (Cambridge, 1981). Selections from the last two books were used in this anthology.

There is much of value in books by the Polish ambassador: *Papers and Memoirs of Jozef Lipskii; Ambassador of Poland: Diplomat in Berlin, 1933–1939* (New York, 1968); and *Diplomat in Paris, 1936–1939: Papers and Memoirs of Juliusz Lukasiewicz, Ambassador of Poland* (New York, 1970).

Documentary source materials from government archives have been published in multivolume series. The German Foreign Ministry archives were captured almost intact by the Allied armies at the close of World War II. The documents relating to the Nazi period have been published in *Documents on German Foreign Policy, 1918–1945,* series C and D (Washington, 1949–). The years prior to 1933 are covered in *Akten zur deutschen auswartigen Politik, 1918–1945* (Göttingen, 1966–). These documents from the German Foreign Ministry archives do not tell the entire story because official dispatches were supplemented by telephone conversations, unofficial contacts, and private correspondence that did not get into the files. Some of the missing material can be found in the collections dealing with the trials of German war criminals at Nuremberg, 1945–1946. Among these collections are *Trials of the Major War Criminals Before the International Military Tribunal, Proceedings and Documents* (42 vols., Nuremberg, 1947–48); *Nazi Conspiracy and Aggression,* 10 vols. (Washington, 1946–1948), which were documents presented in evidence by the prosecution.

British documentary materials can be found in *Documents on British Foreign Policy, 1919–1939* (London, 1947–). The collection is still in the process of being published. The records of the British government in the Public Record Office are now open to 30 years from the current year with certain exceptions. On the other side of the English Channel, the French government is publishing documents from the files of the Foreign Ministry for the years 1932–1939 in *Documents diplomatiques français, 1932–1939* (Paris, 1964–). The Italian documents will ultimately cover the period 1869–1943 in the collection *I Documenti Diplomatici Italiani* (Rome, 1952). Belgian documents are available in *Documents diplomatiques belges, 1920–1940,* vols. 4

and 5, *La politique de sécurité extérieure 1936–1940* (Brussels, 1965–1966). Czechoslovak documents can be found in *Germany and Czechoslovakia, 1918–1945*; Documents on German Policies, edited by Koloman Gajan and Robert Kvacek (Prague, 1965); *Das Abkommen von München 1938: Tschechoslowakische diplomatische Dokumente 1937–1939*, edited by Vaclav Kral (Prague, 1968); *Die Deutschen in der Tschechoslowakei, 1933–1947*, edited by Vaclav Kral (Prague, 1964); and *New Documents on the History of Munich* (Prague, 1958). *Soviet Peace Efforts on the Eve of World War II* (September, 1938–1939, 2 vols. (Moscow, 1973), contains some revealing documents on Soviet negotiations.

The only published collection of official documents available for the period 1919–1939 is *Foreign Relations of the United States: Diplomatic Papers*, published annually. Reports of American diplomats are an important source of information regarding prewar negotiations and events.